UFOs in the 1980s

**The UFO Encyclopedia
Volume 1**

**The UFO Encyclopedia
Volume 1**

UFOs
in the
1980s

By
Jerome Clark

Omnigraphics, Inc.

Penobscot Building
Detroit, MI 48226

Library of Congress Cataloging-in-Publication Data

Clark, Jerome.
  UFOs in the 1980s / by Jerome Clark.
       p.   cm. – (The UFO encyclopedia ; v. 1)
  Includes bibliographical references and index.
  ISBN 1-55888-301-0 (lib. bdg. : alk. paper)
  1. Unidentified flying objects–History.   I. Title.   II. Series.
TL789.U13 vol. 1
001.9'42 s–dc20
[001.9'42'09048]   90-40291
                                                    CIP

Copyright © 1990 by Apogee Books, an imprint of Omnigraphics, Inc.
Penobscot Building, Detroit, Michigan 48226

ISBN 1-55888-301-0

Printed in the United States of America

Contents

Introduction

The UFO Encyclopedia is the first attempt in over a decade to provide a comprehensive encyclopedic survey of the phenomenon of unidentified flying objects, the nature of research on UFOs, the persons who study them, and the related social, scientific, and religious manifestations of interest in anomalous aerial phenomena. In this volume and the two that will follow it, we look at the phenomenon, and the controversy surrounding it, in all their dimensions. We shall examine the cases, the theories, the organizations, the personalities, the responses of governments, scientists and media, the effects on popular culture, the hoaxes, the flying-saucer religious movements, the debunkers, and all else that is relevant. My hope is to produce a full overview of an astonishingly complex issue which is all too often misunderstood or misrepresented. The UFO phenomenon is not something that reduces to easy answers, whatever some may claim, but the answers, we can be sure, are out there somewhere. Some, yet unrecognized, are almost certainly in the pages that follow.

While two such surveys have previously appeared, Ronald D. Story's *The Encyclopedia of UFOs* (1980) and Margaret Sachs' *The UFO Encyclopedia* (1980), both the extraordinary developments in the field and the number of new resources that have become available more than justify a new reference tool. The new *Encyclopedia* will cover numerous topics not touched upon in the prior works. Since the major areas not previously covered in an encyclopedic reference book concern the events and evolution of ufology over the decade of the 1980s, it was decided to concentrate this first volume on the major personalities, UFO sightings, and research organizations that have dominated its most recent history. That period is covered below in 84 entries, including lengthy entries on the major foci of recent ufology: the UFO abduction phenomenon; crashes of UFOs; government cover-up of UFO data; new theoretical approaches to solving the mystery of unidentified flying objects; and surveys of ufology in Australia, Canada, France, and Great Britain.

Features of this Edition

This first volume of *The UFO Encyclopedia* provides a number of helpful features for the reader. An introductory essay provides a brief orientation to the person approaching the topic of ufology for the first time. It highlights some major events and trends prior to the 1980s. It also includes a note on UFO terminology and jargon, some mastery of which is necessary in order to maneuver freely through the complex and at times bizarre realms of UFO phenomena.

As a prime feature, this volume has separate lengthy entries on seven topics of continuing interest to the ufology of the 1980s as it moves into the 1990s. These entries are:

Abduction Phenomenon (p. 1), which examines the controversy surrounding claims of kidnappings by UFO entities;

Contactees (p. 51), which surveys the claims of persons who report continuing contact with benevolent extraterrestrial entities and the relationship of individuals and groups built around such claims to ufology;

Crashes of UFOs (p. 56), which discusses allegations that the wreckage of extraterrestrial spacecraft and the bodies of alien beings have been retrieved by government agencies;

Earthlights and Tectonic Strain Theory (p. 77), two related hypotheses which hold that UFOs are a product of natural effects caused by stresses along geologic faults;

Extraterrestrial Biological Entities (p. 85), which reviews claims that the United States government has established communications and an ongoing relationship with beings from outer space;

Fantasy-prone Personality Hypothesis (p. 111), which reviews claims that UFO abductions have their origin in the imagination of certain kinds of individuals;

Psychosocial Hypothesis (p. 172), which argues that UFO phenomena are entirely the product of cultural processes and unusual mental states.

Twenty-six entries cover the most prominent individuals in ufology from A (**Walter H. Andrus, Jr.**) to Z (**Jennie Zeidman**). Each biographical entry offers basic biographical data while concentrating upon each person's individual contribution to or significance within the UFO community.

Twenty-two entries are devoted to UFO research and extraterrestrial-contact organizations. These vary from major scientific research facilities such as the **J. Allen Hynek Center for UFO Studies** (CUFOS) to religious groups such as the **Universe Society Church** which have made UFOs and claims of contact with extraterrestrial and extradimensional entities integral to their religious beliefs and practices. The organizations cited in this volume have been chosen because they have been dominant organizations in ufology. Some, for example the **Fund for UFO Research**, are relatively new and hence have not appeared in previous works.

Appended to each entry is a list of source material which includes both the sources cited in the entry and related material for further reading. Biographical entries, for example, will list all of the UFO books authored or co-authored by the individual.

Cross-References

The volume is extensively cross-referenced. Whenever the title of an entry is first mentioned in another entry, it has been highlighted in boldface.

Index

The reader is referred to the extensive index covering persons, organizations and subjects for a number of topics that are discussed in the body of this text.

Acknowledgements

Since my teenage years, I have followed the phenomena of flying saucers and UFOs with what at times seemed like a youthful all-consuming infatuation while at other times suspecting that the time spent on UFOs had been all but wasted. Over the years, however, I have had the benefit of being so positioned as a writer and editor that I had to keep up with all developments in ufology while listening to the arguments of colleagues on every side. They never allowed me to rest complacently in half-thought-out opinions and always forced me to probe more deeply into the subject. Out of what has now become three decades of reflection on the UFO phenomenon, I have not entirely lost the enthusiasm of my earlier years, but have arrived at a mature confidence that whatever the solution(s) to the UFO phenomenon is (are), I have been participating in a field on the frontiers of science.

In the mid-1970s I co-authored my first book concerning UFOs, *The Unidentified* (1975, with Loren Coleman). In 1976, I joined the editorial staff of *Fate*, the original UFO magazine. While there, I helped plan the First International UFO Congress which met in 1977 on the occasion of the 30th anniversary of the original sighting of the flying saucers by Kenneth Arnold in 1947. I eventually became editor of *Fate*, then published in suburban Chicago. Living in the Chicago area, I was able to work closely with J. Allen Hynek and the Center for UFO Studies, an association which claimed even more of my time through the 1980s, until my resignation from *Fate* and return to my native Minnesota in 1989. I remain active with CUFOS, having served as its vice-president since 1986 and the editor of its *International UFO Reporter* since 1985. Consequently, in 1989 when the Santa Barbara Centre for Humanistic Studies suggested that we produce a comprehensive encyclopedia of ufology, I was both delighted and well-positioned.

I would like to thank the following individuals for their generous help in seeing to it that *The UFO Encyclopedia* project first got off the ground and then stayed in flight:

First, while I have written the great majority of entries for this volume, I have called upon and received generous assistance with entries that required specialized knowledge, especially in the surveys of ufology in foreign lands. Thanks especially to Bill Chalker (Australia), Claude Mauge (France), Jenny Randles (Great Britain), and Chris Rutkowski (Canada). Also thanks to J. Gordon Melton who wrote the entries on Ann Druffel and the Invisible College.

Second, I wish to thank J. Gordon Melton, director of the Institute for the Study of American Religion, and Aidan A. Kelly, president of the Santa Barbara Centre for Humanistic Studies, both in Santa Barbara, California, for initially promoting the project and seeing to it that this book flew and landed safely, and to my wife, Nancy, my constant source of encouragement when the project seems too immense to be accomplished by a single mortal.

Thanks also to my colleagues at the J. Allen Hynek Center for UFO Studies: scientific director Mark Rodeghier, Don Schmitt, Michael D. Swords, George M. Eberhart (whose two-volume bibliography *UFOs and the Extraterrestrial Contact Movement* [1986] made my job immeasurably easier), John P. Timmerman, Jennie Zeidman, and Sherman J. Larsen, and to Michael Corbin, William L. Moore, Stanton T. Friedman, Budd Hopkins, David M. Jacobs, Marcello Truzzi, Thomas E. Bullard, D. Scott Rogo, Lucius Farish, Grant R. Cameron, Barry Greenwood, Larry Fawcett, Edward Walters, Richard Heiden, Hilary Evans, Bruce Maccabee, and Richard Hall, and to all those organizational heads and magazine/newsletter editors who responded to my inquiries.

Jerome Clark
January 1990

The UFO Phenomenon before 1980

Even in 1947 Kenneth Arnold was not the first. It only seemed that way. On that memorable June 24 Arnold was still in the air, halfway between Yakima, Washington, and Pendleton, Oregon, when the word went out that the Boise, Idaho, private pilot had seen some "tailless jets." When he landed, a crowd was waiting to hear his story of the nine silvery crescent-shaped objects he had seen flying in formation over the Cascade Mountain range at 1200 mph.

It was not enough of a sensation to make the papers, however. In fact, by the next day most of those persons who knew about it—not a great many, to start with—had forgotten about it. Pendleton had other things to get excited about, such as the arrival of a 60-plane air fleet promoting the use of private aviation by business. Late in the morning Arnold, his moment of glory apparently over, was walking the streets alone when a man from nearby Ukiah stopped him and said he, too, had seen a formation of "mystery missiles" the day before. At least, Arnold reflected, someone besides himself had not forgotten and was still puzzled.

Even more troubled than before, he made his way to the office of Pendleton's *East Oregonian* and told his story. Two reporters listened carefully and concluded Arnold was sincere and sane. One of them, Bill Bequette, started typing up a story for the Associated Press wires. He hesitated momentarily when it came time for him to give a name to what Arnold had seen. Well, Bequette thought, Arnold had described their motion as similar to that of saucers skipping across water—so why not "flying saucers"?

Why not, indeed? And so a legend was born.

Never mind the mystery "airships" reported in the late nineteenth and early twentieth centuries, or even the "saucer"—his word—that John Martin saw over Denison, Texas, on January 24, 1878. And forget about the "foo fighters," weird amorphous lights which plagued both Allied and Axis pilots during World War II, or the "ghost rockets" whose appearances over northern Europe in 1946 sparked unfounded rumors about Soviet military intentions. Never mind, for that matter, the mysterious object government meteorologists at Richmond, Virginia, observed through a theodolite two months before Arnold made his sighting, or the equally enigmatic phenomena seen in Oklahoma, Colorado, South Carolina, Tennessee and New Jersey the following month, not to mention the "strange meteor" Chilean astronomers watched as it "moved slowly through the ionosphere, producing at intervals discharges of whitish smoke," then suddenly hovered for a while before shooting across the horizon at incredible speed.

But circumstances, not strict adherence to historical reality, would make June 24, 1947, the day on which the Age of Unidentified Flying Objects began, and in the days and weeks ahead sightings of silvery discs and huge cigars would enthrall and perplex witnesses (who included scientists, airline pilots, soldiers and others who presumably knew what they were seeing and who could be trusted to report it honestly and accurately) and everybody else who was willing to listen to them. For a brief period of time, less than a day, newspaper readers in North America and Europe would even be led to believe that Army Air Force personnel had recovered the remains of a flying saucer which crashed in remote Lincoln County, New Mexico. Within 24 hours the authorities had put out a correction. What really happened, they said, was that an excitable rancher had found a downed weather balloon and a comedy of errors ensued, leading local reporters, law-enforcement officers, and representatives of Roswell Field to believe they had found the remains of a flying disc from another world. It would take three decades (and interviews with over 150 direct or indirect participants in the incident) for the truth to emerge: that the object was *not* a weather balloon, that it was something so extraordinary that military and government officials went to considerable length to ensure that all aspects of the recovery operation (during which, some informants were to claim, bodies were found) remained a well-guarded secret. If civilian investigators had known that in 1947, if journalists had been more skeptical of the cover story, it is certain UFO (and perhaps other) history that followed would have been vastly different. As it is, we now know there is a voluminously-recorded public history of the UFO phenomenon and there is a sparsely-documented hidden one. We know much about the former; the latter is something which ufologists came to recognize only in the 1980s. That story, what is known of it, is related elsewhere in this book.

The public history, briefly told, is this:

Investigators for Project Sign, the Air Force's first known UFO project, were to conclude that UFOs were probably extraterrestrial visitors and in 1948 they stated as much in a classified "Estimate of the Situation" which went to Air Force Chief of Staff Hoyt S. Vandenberg, who rejected it and ordered all copies to be burned. To this day no copy has surfaced and for years the Air Force would deny that such a document had ever existed. The Air Force wanted the UFO reports explained and so it rid itself of the extraterrestrial hypothesizers in Project Sign and replaced them with the UFOphobes who comprised Project Grudge, an appropriate moniker if ever there was one. During what a later Air Force UFO investigator would characterize as the "Dark Ages," Project Grudge personnel energetically debunked UFO reports, which they declared (often without investigation, as those who witnessed its operations up close have testified) to be the product of astronomical phenomena, sundogs, mirages, weather balloons, conventional aircraft, hallucinations, spots in front of the eyes, hoaxes—anything, in short, but something genuinely anomalous. In time internal grumbling within the Air Force led to a shake-up. Grudge was out and in late 1951 Blue Book was in, under the direction of the late Capt. Edward J. Ruppelt, who considered UFO reports worthy of serious investigation and who would go on to write one of the classic works in the literature, *The Report on Unidentified Flying Objects* (1956). When Ruppelt left in 1953, Blue Book became Grudge in all but name and spent the next 16 years (ending when it closed in 1969) debunking much and investigating little, to the consternation of the one scientist who was part of Blue Book, astronomer J. Allen Hynek, who one day would write a scathing account of the incompetence he had observed.

In 1966, responding to growing public dissatisfaction with its UFO efforts, the Air Force dropped the problem in the lap of the University of Colorado and physicist Edward U. Condon. Condon was supposed to conduct an objective investigation, but according to Hynek, the Air Force understood all along that at the end of its inquiries the Condon Committee (as it was called) would declare UFO reports to be unworthy of further attention. The committee was barely four months old before Condon was publicly scoffing at the subject, and soon staff members who had taken too literally the mandate to conduct an objective investigation were fired. (With journalist R. Roger Harkins, one of the fired investigators, psychologist David Saunders, was to write an expose, *UFOs? Yes!: Where the Condon Committee Went Wrong* [1968].) In 1969 the Condon Committee issued its report. Those who read only Condon's introduction were informed that "further extensive study of UFOs probably cannot be justified in the expectation that science will be advanced thereby." Those who went on to read the rest of the book found that committee investigators, their skepticism notwithstanding, had been unable to explain a third of their cases. These were not fleeting "insufficient-data" types of cases but well-documented radar/visual, photographic and similarly extraordinary reports. One individual who read the entire report, French aerospace engineer Claude Poher, became convinced from it that UFOs may be real after all. Poher went on to become the founding director of the French government's UFO project. In November 1970 the UFO subcommittee of the American Institute of Aeronautics and Astronautics released its own report, which rejected Condon's conclusions and urged further scientific research.

Nonetheless in the wake of the Condon report, public interest in UFO matters declined, to be revived in the fall of 1973, when a UFO wave erupted across America. Many of the reports described encounters with UFO occupants. On October 11 the reported abduction of two Pascagoula, Mississippi, fishermen, Charles Hickson and Calvin Parker, by robotlike beings attracted particular attention. Between August and December 1973 well over 70 such close encounters of the third kind came to the attention of investigators, leading ufologist David Webb to call 1973 the *Year of the Humanoids* in a monograph published by the Center for UFO Studies. More evidential was an extraordinary encounter in the air on October 18 between four occupants of an Army helicopter and a UFO. At one point during the encounter the helicopter inexplicably ascended 1800 feet, even when the instruments were directing it to descend. The incident was independently witnessed by observers on the ground.

From the beginning the UFO phenomenon was worldwide in occurrence, and the patterns were everywhere the same. Most sightings were explainable, but the best—those that Hynek would characterize as having a "high-strangeness" quotient—consistently resisted accounting, as would be repeatedly demonstrated. One of the earliest demonstrations of this fact was *Project Blue Book Special Report 14*, one of the major documents of the UFO controversy. The report was the result of a massive statistical analysis of approximately 4000 sightings the Air Force collected between June 1, 1947, and December 31, 1952. The study was conducted by the Battelle Memorial Institute, a Columbus-based think-tank which often performs classified work for government agencies. The scientists involved were directed to find out if UFO reports "represented technological developments not known to this country" and to build a model "flying saucer" from the data.

Of the 4000 reports, according to the Blue Book document, "the majority were received through military channels or in the form of observer-completed questionnaires; a few were accepted in the form of direct letters from unquestionably reliable sources." The investigators proceeded carefully to weed out 800 reports so inadequately documented as to be worthless. That left 3201 sightings. These were broken down into nine categories of evaluation: balloon, astronomical, light phenomena, birds, clouds and dust, insufficient information, psychological, unknown and other.

The first step in the evaluation was to ascertain the essential facts from the reports. The second involved determination of the observer's credibility and the report's self-consistency as well as its general quality. The third step was the categorization or identification of the object.

The initial "identification" was done by the individual who transcribed the report onto a worksheet. Afterwards a member of the identification panel judged the report without knowing what the other person's conclusions were. If the two arrived at the same identification, it was accepted as the final conclusion— but only if one or the other or both did not call the object an unknown. If they disagreed on a conventional explanation, other panel members analyzed the case. If either or both suggested the object was an unknown, the whole panel studied the case.

As physicist Bruce Maccabee observes in a detailed review of the Blue Book study (*Journal of UFO Studies*, vol. 1, no. 1, 1979), "It should be clear . . . that the individual report evaluation done by the BB#14 investigators was quite orderly and 'scientific.' Moreover, it should be clear that they took special precautions to assure that UNKNOWNS really were unknown."

This was no group of dewy-eyed believers. Yet *Special Report 14* statistics reveal that the more fully-documented a report and the more qualified the observer, the more likely the sighting was to be of an unknown. One would expect precisely the opposite, of course, if the unknowns were really identifiable flying objects. Furthermore, the unknowns were most likely to be seen for long-enough periods of time—between 30 seconds and 30 minutes—so that there would have been a better chance for the observers to identify them. Maccabee remarks, "This finding contradicts the generally held feeling that most UNKNOWNS result from short term observations (i.e., a few seconds)."

The investigators addressed the question of whether or not the knowns and the unknowns were identical. To do so they took six characteristics and subjected them to the chi-square test (used in statistical practice to determine the probability that one thing is truly different from another). The results:

Probability That "Unidentifieds" Are the Same as Identifieds:

COLOR: Probably less than 1%.
DURATION OF OBSERVATION: Probability very much less than 1%.
NUMBER: Probability very much less than 1%.
LIGHT BRIGHTNESS: Probability greater than 5%.
SHAPE: Probability less than 1%.
SPEED: Probability much less than 1%.

As the late Dr. Hynek would write (in *The Hynek UFO Report* [1977]), "Now any statistician will tell you that statistical tests are not infallible. He will also likely tell you that examining any one characteristic, such as color, might involve subtle subjective differences, or purely unknown causes that would negate the results. But he will definitely tell you that it is most unlikely that all six of the characteristics examined by the Battelle study could be subject to the same sorts of errors, leading to an erroneous result. A quick calculation shows that the probability of all six UFO-characteristic chi-square tests giving the same results by chance (and thus making the conclusion drawn from the tests wrong) is much less than one chance in a billion."

The best evidence for the anomalous nature of the UFO phenomenon comes from interesting reports made by reliable observers. Yet early on the UFO phenomenon would develop a fringe reputation which it has never been able to shake, although by 1990 the number of scientists and other professionals privately monitoring developments in ufology would never be higher. But elite scientists would scoff, even when their pronouncements on the subject did not exactly evince overwhelming knowledge of the subject. Astronomer Carl Sagan, for example, has said repeatedly that there are no UFO cases that are both interesting and reliable. Besides an obvious ignorance of the Battelle study and other basic matters, he seems unaware that UFO witnesses have included astronomers (most prominently the late Clyde Tombaugh, discoverer of the planet Pluto) and that a 1977 poll of members of the American Astronomical Society revealed a surprising degree of open-mindedness about UFOs. Twenty-three percent of the respondents felt the phenomenon "certainly" deserves scientific attention, 30 percent "probably" and 27 percent "possibly." Sixty-two had seen UFOs themselves. Only three percent felt "certainly not." Although the poll was conducted by the eminently respectable Institute for Plasma Research at Stanford University, little note would be taken of it (in October 1989, for example, University of Minnesota astronomer Ed Ney would assert that no "good observing astronomer . . . has observed" a UFO), and journalists and professional debunkers would continue to declare that "science" had determined the UFO phenomenon to be bogus. In fact, to the degree that science has paid attention to the problem, it has tended to validate the intuitive feeling of UFO witnesses and lay citizens that the phenomenon is indeed a puzzling one.

But those scientists who are interested prefer mostly to stay anonymous, lest professional harm befall them if they come forward to declare what they fear their colleagues will deem an outrageously unacceptable conclusion. But if an objective view of the phenomenon suggests UFO reports should be taken seriously, regardless of whether we believe in extraterrestrial visitors or not, an "objective" view is by this time more a theoretical concept than a practical possibility. After all, from the beginning the phenomenon has sparked a remarkably emotional response which has rendered clear thinking a rare commodity. One problem for a scientist who wishes to keep his reputation intact, free of attacks in the public organs of professional skeptical inquirers, is that ufology has always attracted fringe personalities, individuals who have sought support for occult beliefs through UFO reports and who have produced a vast literature of eccentric publications and dubious speculations.

UFO research in this and other countries has been left mostly in the hands of nonscientists, "ufologists," whose intelligence, education and critical ability have spanned the spectrum. The field's most serious, thoughtful figures have sought, with varying degrees of success, to bring some discipline to UFO study. In the 1950s such organizations as Civilian Saucer Intelligence (New York), the Aerial Phenomena Research Organization, and the National Investigations Committee on Aerial Phenomena rejected extreme claims and speculations while embracing a conservative version of the extraterrestrial hypothesis. In the 1970s the Mutual UFO Network brought the term "scientific ufology" into the vocabulary and in its best moments—and there have been many of them—has actually practiced it. In 1973 Hynek helped bring the Center for UFO Studies into being. CUFOS (renamed the J. Allen Hynek Center for UFO Studies in 1986, following its cofounder's death) was the first major organization to take an agnostic position on the ultimate nature of the phenomenon; it argued only that UFO reports can be investigated scientifically—and ought to be, because scientists are likely to learn something interesting from them.

Still, within ufology's ranks it is not hard to find the cracked and the credulous as well as the sane and the sensible. Ufology has no system of formal training, education and certification, and so anyone can call him- or herself a "ufologist." Like any stereotype, the stereotype of the ufologist as dingbat is not *entirely* unfounded. But the fascination of these sorts of individuals with the UFO phenomenon is more a social fact, a reflection of elite science and society's marginalization of the subject rather than a comment on its true nature, which—so over four decades of evidence attest—is neither occult, as the most fervent believers think, nor mundane, as the most committed debunkers would have it. The debate must be, as it often is not, about the best evidence, not the worst, and be argued by the smartest students, not the silliest.

A NOTE ON UFO TERMINOLOGY

In this book I have used terms that are in the vocabulary of all ufologists and, with the exception of (thanks to Steven Spielberg) "close encounters of the third kind," not very many other people. One of these words is "ufologists." Ufologists are persons who study the UFO phenomenon, and ufology (yoo-FAHL-uh-gee) is the study of the UFO phenomenon. Many ufologists prefer to speak of the "UFO phenomenon," which undeniably exists (as *reports* of UFOs) rather than "UFOs," which may or may not exist as a class of anomalous phenomena presumably of unearthly origin. When referring to the concept of UFOs in its broadest sense, I have tried as much as possible to use the phrase *UFO phenomenon*. (Incidentally, those who think UFOs exist and are otherworldly spacecraft are called proponents of the "extraterrestrial hypothesis," often shortened to ETH.)

Other terms are self-explanatory. Daylight discs, another expression from ufological jargon, are objects, apparently metallic, apparently structured, and obviously disc-shaped, which are observed between dawn and dusk. Nocturnal lights are what people report at other times of the day. Nocturnal lights are the kinds of ostensible UFOs that investigation is most likely to turn into IFOs—identified flying objects, the sorts of mundane stimuli (airplanes, planets, stars, meteors, weather balloons, satellite debris, and the like) that people mistake for something more interesting. Nonetheless genuinely anomalous nocturnal lights, often performing fantastic aerial gymnastics, have been reported on numerous occasions. Radar/visual cases are those, of course, in which UFOs are picked up on radar and seen by the eye.

In his book *The UFO Experience* (1972) the late Dr. Hynek devised a classification scheme for close encounters. Despite occasional efforts to change or modify it, the categories have been accepted by virtually all ufologists and UFO writers, including this one:

Close encounters of the first kind (CE1s): the appearance of a UFO within 500 feet or less of the witness.

Close encounters of the second kind (CE2s): incidents in which a UFO affects the environment in some way, for example by scorching vegetation, leaving landing traces, or burning or otherwise injuring witnesses. In a CE2, in Hynek's words, a UFO has a "measurable physical effect on either animate or inanimate matter."

Close encounters of the third kind (CE3s): reports of beings, usually humanoid, in connection with UFO sightings. One subset of CE3s is the abduction experience, in which persons allegedly are taken against their will into UFOs and subjected by their humanoid occupants to physical tests or experiments before they are released, in two cases out of three with some sort of memory impairment; memory may return later through hypnotic regression or spontaneous recall. A few writers have sought to put these latter cases into a close-encounter category of their own, "close encounters of the fourth kind," but this idea has failed to catch on, probably because it is neither helpful nor necessary. In fact (or, more specifically, in allegation), the dividing line between CE3s and "CE4s" is vague at best, since many cases once thought to be traditional CE3s, in which witnesses reported occupants but no abduction, later turned out to be abduction cases. The famous story of Barney and Betty Hill, the New Hampshire couple whose supposed kidnapping by extra-terrestrials became the subject of a best-selling book and a popular television movie, was known to ufologists as a typical CE3 for the first four years of its existence. Only when the Hills underwent hypnotic regression with Boston psychiatrist Benjamin Simon did the abduction aspect emerge. Moreover, the beings who figure in abduction stories and nonabduction CE3s are basically alike. There is, in short, no radical discontinuity between the CE3 and the abduction; the latter seems but one kind of the former.

A radical discontinuity does exist, however, between CE3s and contactee experiences. Contactees are individuals who claim to be in frequent communication with wise, beautiful, godlike beings from other worlds here to save earthlings from destroying themselves. These contacts may take place physically or (far more frequently) psychically. Contactees tend to be individuals with a long history of involvement in occultism and metaphysics. Unlike the overwhelming majority of UFO witnesses, including CE3 percipients, who have no prior interest in UFOs, anomalies or the paranormal, contactees have in some sense waited all their lives for word from the Space Brothers, as such beings are usually called in the contactee literature. The occupants who figure in CE3s do not look or act like this; they are almost always small, grotesque-looking and minimally communicative. Contact claims represent a visionary religious response to the UFO phenomenon; in them older occult doctrines are wrapped in Space Age garb. Although fraudulent contactees do exist, the typical contactee is sincerely convinced of the reality of his interactions with otherworlders. But such interactions are nearly always ones that cannot be shared. Although there are many multiple-witness CE3s, multiple-witness cases among contactees not engaged in outright hoaxing are virtually nonexistent, suggesting subjective rather than objective causes.

A

ABDUCTION PHENOMENON

In the 1980s the abduction phenomenon, a body of testimony by apparently sincere individuals who claimed (frequently under hypnosis) to have been briefly kidnapped by extraterrestrials, emerged as one of the two principal concerns of American ufology (the other was the alleged official cover-up of UFO evidence). Ufologists had known of the phenomenon since 1965, when a Boston newspaper reported on Barney and Betty Hill's soon-to-be-famous September 1961 experience. A year later a book-length account, John G. Fuller's *The Interrupted Journey*, attracted much attention, in part because it was serialized in the mass-circulation *Look* magazine.

UFO Abductions in the 1960s and 1970s: When first reported to investigators shortly after its occurrence, the Hills' story of a UFO sighting on a lonely New Hampshire road seemed to be a more-or-less-typical close encounter of the third kind (a UFO sighting in which occupants are reported); Barney claimed to have seen a being inside the object as it hovered over their car. What made the incident unique was the Hills' conviction that two hours had passed unaccountably following the sighting. Two and a half years later, when the couple, suffering from stress which they linked to the sighting, underwent hypnosis in the office of Boston psychiatrist Benjamin Simon, they related that gray-skinned humanoids with large heads and small mouths had taken them aboard the UFO and given them a medical examination.

Dr. Simon later expressed the view that the "incident" was a shared dream, an explanation with which all skeptics and even many ufologists were happy. Probably the story would have been remembered as little more than a curiosity if other, similar accounts had not begun to appear, notably a case involving a Nebraska policeman, Herbert Schirmer, whose December 1967 sighting and missing-time experience were investigated by no less than the Air Force-sponsored University of Colorado UFO project (usually known as the Condon Committee, after director Edward U. Condon). Under hypnosis Schirmer told of encountering five-foot humanoids with gray-white skin and long, thin faces. The two entity types described in the Hill and Schirmer cases—the big-headed, gray-skinned humanoids and the slightly taller, thin-faced, smaller- though also slant-eyed ones—would be noted in many subsequent reports. (The latter would figure in the majority of British reports, as **Jenny Randles** would document in her 1988 book *Abduction*.)

In the mid-1960s a Brazilian case, publication of which an American UFO group had suppressed because of its outlandish character, was recounted in a series of articles in England's *Flying Saucer Review* (*FSR*). The October 1957 incident, investigated by physician-ufologist Olavo T. Fontes and journalist Joao Martins, involved a young farmer named Antonio Villas-Boas, who said he had been grabbed by humanoids, dragged into a UFO and seduced by a short, mostly-human-looking female. Fontes and Martins, considered responsible investigators, took the story

ABDUCTION PHENOMENON (*continued*)

seriously, despite its apparent absurdity. Other sexual-abduction cases from Brazil would be reported in the 1970s and early 1980s but received little attention outside the pages of *FSR*, which published translations from Portuguese- and Spanish-language accounts. English-speaking ufologists paid practically no heed to them and they are not rehashed in the UFO books of the period. Only later—in 1987, to be precise—would their significance become clear.

During the 1970s abduction reports were featured regularly in both popular and specialist UFO magazines. A handful—especially one at Pascagoula, Mississippi (October 1973), another in North Dakota (August 1975), and a third in Arizona (November 1975)—got nationwide press coverage. In the Arizona episode seven loggers reportedly saw a UFO. One of them, Travis Walton, ran toward the object and was struck by a beam of light emitted from it. His terrified companions fled. When they returned a few minutes later, Walton and the UFO were nowhere to be seen. Search parties failed to locate the missing man, who did not reappear until five days later. Walton claimed to remember only about two hours of his experience on board the craft. He said he had awakened on a table and seen big-headed, large-eyed, hairless beings (of the sort ufologists would come to call, with wry humor, "standard-issue humanoids"), then later met uncommunicative apparent humans with peculiar-looking eyes (Walton, 1978).

The Walton case generated by far the most controversy of the '70s reports. The reason was simple: if true, it meant that Walton's abduction (as well as by implication other such accounts) was a literal, consensus-reality, physical event, presumably involving extraterrestrial kidnappers. In other instances skeptics could grant claimants' sincerity while rejecting a face-value interpretation of their stories, which in doubters' minds could be laid to hypnotic confabulation, dreams or hallucinations. If this reading was to stand, those unwilling to concede the possibility of alien kidnappings knew they would have to demonstrate

that Walton and his coworkers had fabricated the story. Professional UFO debunker **Philip J. Klass** went after Walton with a vengeance and tried with no great success, though with an enormous amount of verbiage, to prove that he and the alleged eyewitnesses were lying. The case remains controversial, not because there is compelling negative evidence (if it exists, it has yet to surface) but because its implications were unacceptable even to many in the UFO community. Yet Walton's description of the UFO's interior and of the craft's occupants (including its not-quite humans) would be echoed in numerous subsequent accounts.

The 1970s saw the publication of a small number of books on abductions, among them *Encounters With UFO Occupants* (1976) and *Abducted!* (1977), both by **Coral and Jim Lorenzen**, directors of the Aerial Phenomena Research Organization (APRO), David Haisell's *The Missing Seven Hours* (1978) and Raymond E. Fowler's *The Andreasson Affair* (1979). In 1980 writer D. Scott Rogo produced a paperback anthology, *UFO Abductions*, and cowrote (with **Ann Druffel**) *The Tujunga Canyon Contacts*, based on an investigation of a web of interrelated abduction experiences in California.

By this time the abduction phenomenon was a part of the ufological scenery, but it was not universally welcomed there. Not a few ufologists suspected abduction tales were the product of hypnotic confabulation, in which an individual replaces a gap in his or her memory with a created story that is then accepted as true. Hypnotic confabulation is a common explanation of past-life "memories." In an attempt to test this possibility, three California investigators devised an experiment in which student volunteers were hypnotized and directed to imagine abductions. In 1977, one of the investigators, Alvin H. Lawson, declared that there no longer could be any question: imaginary and "real" abductions are described identically. That being the case, the latter must be imaginary, too, in other words, subjective mental experiences which draw on images from popular culture.

Critics charged that these conclusions were not supported by a careful reading of the data and that the experiments were flawed, owing to amateurish methodological errors on the experimenters' part. Also, they suggested that the imaginary and "real" accounts are distinctly different. Among other significant differences, the imaginary abductees "encountered" humanoids only 10 to 20 percent of the time, whereas humanoids figure in over 70 percent of the "real" encounters.

For a time, however (the first major critique was not published until 1981), Lawson's claims were received mostly uncritically—by debunkers, of course, but also by ufologists, including so sophisticated a one as Allan Hendry, whose otherwise-insightful *UFO Handbook* (1979) unqualifiedly endorses Lawson's dubious interpretation. Nonetheless, whatever the shortcomings of the California experiments, ufologists' caution in the face of hypnotically-elicited abduction testimony was warranted. True, consciously-recalled stories did exist, but these could be hoaxes, as debunkers believed, or hallucinations and visions, as proponents of the emerging **"psychosocial hypothesis"** theorized. True, nearly all those who underwent hypnosis had conscious recollections of UFO sightings, missing time and other suggestive anomalies. Still, in the middle of this were holes that could be filled only with hypnosis. And hypnosis, all authorities on it agree, is no royal road to the truth. People can lie under hypnosis; sincere people can fantasize under it without realizing they are doing so. The latter is particularly likely to happen if the hypnotist is incompetent and asks leading questions or otherwise directs his subject to give the desired answers.

These unresolved concerns led to an agnosticism about the abduction phenomenon even among many ufologists sympathetic to the extraterrestrial hypothesis. If abduction research was going to be anything more than the collecting of scary stories, serious problems and major questions had to be addressed. Researchers needed to address, for example, the questions related to the efficacy of hypnosis as a method for retrieving true memory as opposed to confabulated fantasy. They needed to do formal psychology inventories of abductees to determine, to start with, whether there is a link between pathological states and the belief that one has been abducted by extraterrestrials. (Ufologists had informally observed little evidence of mental illness among abductees whose claims they had investigated, but critics could always claim, and did so claim, that ufologists lacked the professional training to make diagnostic judgments in this area.) They also had to determine, via standard objective analytical procedures, whether the patterns they sensed in the data stood up to searching inquiry over a large number of cases.

The Work of Budd Hopkins: All of this would be accomplished in the 1980s, owing in considerable part to the reinvigoration of abduction investigation that would follow the appearance of **Budd Hopkins** on the UFO scene. Hopkins, a New York City-based artist and sculptor, had developed an interest in the UFO phenomenon after a sighting of a daylight disc moving in and out of clouds over Truro, Massachusetts, in August 1964. By the mid-1970s Hopkins was privately collecting sighting reports, though he had no ties to the UFO community. But an investigation of a remarkable CE3, with independent witnesses confirming parts of the story, in North Hudson Park, New Jersey, in November 1975 led to Hopkins' meeting Ted Bloecher, a veteran ufologist who specialized in reports involving occupants. Through Bloecher, Hopkins met a young man known to the UFO literature as "Steven Kilburn." Kilburn had no recollection of a UFO sighting but, he said, "something has bothered me about a certain stretch of road I used to pass through whenever I left my girlfriend's house in Maryland."

Subsequently Hopkins and a psychiatrist who uses hypnosis in his practice, Dr. Robert Naiman, worked with Kilburn and others to explore periods of "missing time" which in most cases (unlike Kilburn's) were associated with UFO sightings. Later psychologist Girard Franklin became involved for a time. Active for a longer period was Aphrodite Clamar, a psychologist affiliated with New York University. For the first

ABDUCTION PHENOMENON (*continued*)

time mental-health professionals were participating in the study of what by now was beginning to look like a phenomenon, not just a one-time fantasy experience a New Hampshire couple had just happened to share some years earlier. The apparent patterns were striking. The UFO beings the abductees described were virtually identical from case to case: little gray humanoids with large heads, big, slanting eyes, thin bodies. The beings subjected the abductees to apparent medical examinations and usually said little about themselves. In some cases abductees reported that small, ball-like implants had been placed inside them, usually through the nose or ear. Some abductees bore scars for which they could not account, resulting from wounds whose origin they could not explain even at the time of their occurrence. Under hypnosis they would relate these wounds to cuts inflicted on them by UFO occupants. Typically these events happened when the abductees were children and often the wounds were *under* clothing which was not ripped or torn. The resulting scars fell into two categories: a straight line (resembling, Hopkins suggests, a "scalpel cut") and a small depression in the flesh ("like a little scoop mark").

To the UFO community, and also to the small number of psychologists, psychiatrists and physicians who read the book and were intrigued by it, Hopkins' *Missing Time* (1981) was the most important work on abductions since Fuller's *Interrupted Journey*. It was the beginning not only of ufologists' decade-long obsession with the phenomenon but also of the professionalization of the investigation. Perhaps even more impressive than Hopkins' discovery of such aspects as implants and scars were the pronouncements of Clamar, who contributed an afterword in which she specifically rejected the idea that abductees exhibited pathological systems; rather she found them neither psychotic nor psychic, but very normal. She went on to conclude, "If there is anything that links these people to one another, it is that all of them are deeply perplexed and troubled by their experience. . . . [T]he events recounted by a variety of people from scattered

places are strikingly similar, suggesting that there might be more to the whole business than mere coincidence. . . . The content of these accounts is markedly different from most of the fantasies reported in psychological literature." Clamar confessed that she was puzzled, calling the abduction phenomenon a "mystery" and urging further investigation of what seemed to her a "real problem."

Clamar noted that abductees had "not been subjected to the kind of psychological testing that might provide a deeper understanding of their personalities." By the time her words had appeared in print, an effort was being made to arrange for such testing. In 1981 Hopkins, Bloecher and Clamar, having secured a grant from the **Fund for UFO Research** for the purpose, hired a psychologist, Elizabeth Slater, to administer five standard tests. Slater was told only that she was to "determine similarities and differences in personality structure as well as psychological strengths and weaknesses." She did not know that the nine individuals whose tests she was evaluating believed they had been taken aboard UFOs.

Slater found that while the subjects were otherwise quite different, they had in common a "relative weakness in the sense of identity" and consequently a "certain orientation towards alertness . . . interpersonal hypervigilance and caution. . . . Anxiety was prominent in all nine subjects, some of whom were simply flooded by it. . . . In addition to the relative propensity for emotionally disorganizing experience, another factor common to the nine subjects . . . is a modicum . . . of narcissistic disturbance. It is manifest along at least three dimensions: identity disturbance. . . . One spoke of 'somebody being crushed by something,' pointing to a sense of smallness and victimization in the face of overwhelming outer forces."

After turning in her report, Slater learned that the nine were UFO abductees. "She was, it is safe to say, flabbergasted," Bloecher, Clamar and Hopkins would write. When she had recovered from her astonishment, Slater was given a copy of

Missing Time to read. (Some of the abductees she tested were among those whose stories were related in that book.) Afterwards she met with the three investigators. Reflecting on about the abduction phenomenon, she prepared an addendum to her original report. It says in part:

"The first and most critical question is whether our subjects' reported experiences could be accounted for strictly on the basis of psychopathology, i.e., mental disorder. The answer is a firm no. In broad terms, if the reported abductions were confabulated fantasy productions, based on what we know about psychological disorders, they could only have come from pathological liars, paranoid schizophrenics, and severely disturbed and extraordinarily rare hysteroid characters subject to fugue states and/or multiple personality shifts. . . . It is important to note that not one of these subjects, based on test data, falls into any of these categories. Therefore, while the testing can do nothing to prove the veracity of the UFO abduction reports, one can conclude that the test findings are not inconsistent with the possibility that reported UFO abductions have, in fact, occurred. In other words, there is no apparent psychological explanation for their reports. . . .

"From another, more speculative point of view, one can consider how UFO abduction . . . might affect the victim. . . . Certainly such an unexpected, random and literally otherworldly experience . . . during which the individual has absolutely no control over the outcome, constitutes a trauma of major proportions. Hypothetically, its psychological impact might be analogous to what one sees in crime victims or victims of natural disasters, as it would constitute an event during which the individual is overwhelmed by external circumstances in an extreme manner. . . . Psychological traits which arose consistently in the subjects first included a surprising degree of inner turmoil as well as a great degree of wariness and distrust. Logically, such emotional upheaval and accompanying caution about the world might certainly follow in the wake of an [abduction] experience."

Another explanation for the inner turmoil and suspicion abductees experience, Slater suggested, had to do with societal skepticism of such experiences, making them "something that cannot be readily shared with others as a means of obtaining emotional support. Consequently, one would likely find a deep sense of shame, secretiveness and social alienation among the victims. . . . The closest analogy might be the interpersonal alienation of the rape victim, who has been violated most brutally but somehow becomes tainted by virtue of the crime against her" (Bloecher, Clamar and Hopkins, 1985).

Slater's remarks anticipate a psychological model that would come into prominence late in the decade. The abductee would be seen as a victim of post-traumatic stress disorder, a category of diagnosis originally applied to the suffering of Vietnam-war combat veterans. This interpretation assumes that a real event, perhaps even of the kind the abductee reports, occurred. It does not seek to "explain" the precipitating event, only to treat its consequences. But because Slater also remarked that the subjects had a "richness of inner life that can operate favorably in terms of creativity or disadvantageously to the extent that it can be overwhelming," two ufologists in Australia would link abductees to another newly-proposed psychological type: the **"fantasy-prone personality."**

Alternative Interpretations: In the early 1980s two other psychological interpretations, both intended to explain abduction accounts as internally rather than externally generated, briefly attracted attention. The more modest of them was the "imagery hypothesis" of Keith Basterfield of UFO Research Australia (UFORA), who speculated that what percipients experience as close encounters are hallucinations which occur during false awakenings and other dreamy mental states. "The imagery content is visual, or auditory, in the main," he wrote, "but also include[s] sensation[s] of heat/cold, smell, or touch. They [sic] may be reproductions of the events of the day or strange, bizarre images of pleasing or frightening proportions. There seems to be little control over their appearance, and thus a person could

ABDUCTION PHENOMENON (*continued*)

certainly be frightened by their sudden onset. Reality and images of this kind can be readily confused" (Basterfield, 1981). Ideas borrowed from folklore and popular culture cause modern persons to "see" aliens and spaceships instead of fairies and witches, he suggested.

If Basterfield's speculations were based on mental phenomena whose reality few psychologists would dispute (even if many would disagree that healthy persons are likely to sustain such images for a long period of time and continue to mistake them for external physical objects), the "birth-trauma hypothesis" of Alvin Lawson, an English teacher at a California state university, would go far beyond conventional psychological wisdom. To Lawson, convinced that he had already proven abductions to be fantasies, the only remaining question for researchers to address was the source of the images on which imaginary abductees, "real" abductees, and **contactees** (individuals claiming nonabduction encounters, physical and psychic, with angelic Space Brothers)—Lawson made no distinction among these groups—drew as they conjured up visions of extraterrestrials and spacecraft. In a paper delivered at a 1981 conference sponsored by the Center for UFO Studies (now the **J. Allen Hynek Center for UFO Studies**), Lawson declared, "The many imagery parallels among abduction analogs suggest that they have a common source. One of the most likely is the birth experience and its associated trauma . . . " (Lawson, 1981). In other words, abductees are reliving life in the womb and the terror allegedly associated with emergence therefrom.

Although the notion of birth trauma was not original with Lawson (it was suggested originally by Otto Rank, a contemporary of Freud, and picked up on by such modern figures as Scientology founder L. Ron Hubbard and radical psychiatrist Stanislav Grof), its application to UFO experiences was Lawson's own inspiration. In arguing his case, he claimed not only that gray-skinned, large-headed humanoids look like fetuses but that "every human being who ever lived was—

for a few hours at least—literally shaped like a UFO. With that in mind one can speculate: perhaps the embryonic disc does manifest itself as a Jungian mandala or saucer archetype in everyone's sensibility during the embryonic stage; later it could emerge as part of a percipient's UFO-related imagery. Thus UFO witnesses might have been predisposed to perceive saucer-shaped 'somethings' in the presence of whatever psycho-physical stimulus constitutes the UFO phenomenon—though what witnesses perceive may be an archetypal echo of experiential imagery from their own prenatal development." Later, as the embryo develops, it becomes oval- and then pear-shaped (Lawson notes that witnesses have described UFOs with those shapes, too), "and about day 22 the beginnings of the brain and spinal cord have formed a comparatively huge neural tube down the length of the tiny embryo." Abductees, Lawson said, have reported tunnels in UFOs.

"Many abduction/BT [birth-trauma] parallels are obvious," he said. "The fetus, taken from warmth and comfort and subjected to prolonged distress in the birth 'tunnel,' emerges into a strange world with bright lights, unconfined space, 'entities,' an 'examination,' and various sensory stimuli. Similarly, 'abductees' are levitated through a tunnel of light into a UFO's vast, brilliant interior where alien creatures examine and probe their bodies, often painfully. Additional parallels include such staples of CE-III reports as a loss of time, absurd events, womblike rooms, umbilical pain, sexual seduction, and a sense of ineffability about the experience. There are many, many others." So many, in fact, that when a questioner asked Lawson to describe an abduction story *without* "birth-trauma" elements, he could not answer. Lawson had presented his idea as "testable," but at least as he outlined it, it appeared unfalsifiable. He also failed to explain how a fetus, much less a single cell, would know what it looks like.

Even debunkers who had hailed Lawson's original claims about the supposed imaginary components of abduction stories would not endorse these sweeping speculations, which seemed at least as extraordinary as the theory that extraterrestrials are abducting people. Yet the birth-trauma hypothesis attracted a small, committed following at the fringes of ufology. Dennis Stillings, a New Age-oriented parapsychological theorist, would elaborate on Lawson's concept and add yet another extraordinary element to it: superpsychokinesis. He believes that images from birth memories may be projected into the world as "materialized psychisms"—what occultists call "thought forms."

Among the critics of Lawson's hypothesis was D. Scott Rogo, who emphatically dismissed it (along with the imaginary-abductions experiment which preceded it) as "utterly unconvincing." He wrote that the theory is "inconsistent with basic embryology. . . . The baby in no sense glides down a tunnel-like canal into the hands of welcoming figures. The infant would experience an unpleasant crushing, suffocating sensation while exiting from a totally dark environment out through the womb into a lighted area. The head of the child rests close to the opening of the cervix (i.e., a few inches), so the infant would not experience anything like a tunnel. . . . It could not even see very much." Besides these and other problems, Rogo complained that Lawson's methodology was flawed; "he never formally mapped out what should and should not be considered valid birth imagery before he undertook his survey of the literature. He seems merely to have read through several abduction accounts looking for such imagery, then reported—out of context—anything that struck him as suspicious. This procedure allows just about anything to be considered a birth image according to Lawson's very loose and unstructured criteria" (Rogo, 1985).

Another critic, folklorist **Thomas E. Bullard**, whose exhaustive survey of the abduction phenomenon is discussed below, found a "pretty poor" match between "birth imagery" and "actual descriptions in abduction reports. . . . A firm course of happenings in abduction reports has no parallel in birth events, since the witness enters into the ship before leaving from it, and the examination occurs inside rather than on

departure. . . . [T]unnel-like passageways appear in only 20 out of 125 ships, and these tunnels usually conform to the design of the craft rather than the patterns of anatomy. The multiplicity of the beings, their purposeful activities, interactions with the witness and role as examiner ill accord with an assumption that the witness remembers himself still unborn. And by what scale does a fetus understand its shortness while alone in the womb?" (Bullard, 1987a).

Nonetheless, one prominent proponent of a psychosocial approach to UFO phenomena, British ufologist **Hilary Evans**, developed a series of theories about what he called "entity encounters"—entities defined as everything from religious deities, discarnates, fairies, monsters and UFO beings—using Lawson's "persuasively demonstrated" claims as virtually his sole empirical support for the operating assumption that imaginary encounters and "real" ones are identical and that birth traumas are in part responsible for them. He writes that the encounter experience is "something like a self-administered rite of passage," including a "return-to-the-womb element." We have these experiences because inside our minds "there exists a creative, intelligent, sympathetic and understanding capability, whose function is to fabricate non-real scenes and scenarios. . . . This capability, which for the sake of convenience we may call the *producer*, may plausibly be conceived as a parallel personality to our conscious personality" (Evans, 1984).

As attempts to explain abductions by various real or hypothetical subjective mechanisms were outlined in UFO books and magazine articles, critics noted that the psychological theorizers were not themselves psychologists. The psychologists who were investigating the reports firsthand were perplexed by them and acknowledged that they could not account for them. As Hopkins continued his investigations, he consulted regularly with a number of mental-health professionals, some with international reputations. In 1985 he wrote, "I think it is fair to say that I have spent more time exploring the possibility of a psychological explanation for abduction accounts,

ABDUCTION PHENOMENON (*continued*)

have consulted more psychiatrists and psychologists on the subject, and involved a wider array of these professionals in actual investigations than most researchers. And no psychological explanation, even tentatively, has resulted." Hopkins said that any attempt to explain abductions had also to deal with the physical evidence, such as scars and landing traces, as well as the extraordinary congruities in descriptions of the "'perpetrators' and their basic *modus operandi*" (Hopkins, 1985).

The Work of Thomas E. Bullard: The most comprehensive study of the phenomenon—and the only rigorously objective one ever published—was undertaken by Thomas (Eddie) Bullard, a folklorist who had written his doctorate on UFO beliefs for Indiana University. After securing a grant from the Fund for UFO Research, Bullard collected every case he could find in the literature through 1985, some 300 cases, which he then compared and analyzed looking for common and dissimilar elements. As he remarks in the introduction to the 650-page, two-volume work that resulted from his inquiry, *UFO Abductions: The Measure of a Mystery* (1987), "If the beings look alike from case to case, if they do similar things in approximately the same order, if different witnesses report the same mental and physical effects over and over again, then abductions take on the appearance of a coherent phenomenon. The more unanimous the descriptions, the stronger our reason to believe that diverse witnesses experienced the same kind of event. . . . If differences predominate then chances are good that these narratives stem from purely personal fantasy rather than from a similar experience shared by many people." Yet even if alike, the stories may "originate in a subjective experience duplicated among independent witnesses" or perhaps "their narrators draw on other abduction stories for ideas." Bullard, who sees all these as testable hypotheses, devotes the next several hundred pages to an intensive scrutiny of the phenomenon, from its most obvious components to its most subtle.

Bullard found that abductions are a modern phenomenon, with no very specific precedent in history or folklore, that abductees comprise a wide variety of human beings, and that if "you once pass 30 without ever being abducted, you have little to worry about." The stories break down into a maximum of eight chronologically-consistent elements, beginning with "capture" and "examination" and ending with "return" and "aftermath." Bullard confirmed Hopkins' assertion that little gray men are the principal (though by no means the only) abductors. He said, "The standard being in an abduction has a bulging, hairless head often tapering to a pointed chin, large unblinking eyes, a hole or slit for a mouth, a tiny nose or holes only, and vestigial ears. With great consistency the skin is gray or pale and sunless. . . . The beings usually wear tight, featureless one-piece uniforms and expose at most only their hands and head region. . . . A leader seems in charge of the crew or at least of the witness when abductors number more than two or three, and a difference in height may single him out as distinct from the rest. The beings usually treat the witness with politeness and courtesy, but these manners are studied rather than spontaneous and hide an underlying insensitivity not altogether accountable as a result of ignorance, since these beings display some emotions of their own. Highly efficient and mission-oriented, the beings seem to sacrifice ethics for work and resort to any means at their command to manipulate the witnesses into cooperation."

Bullard uncovered other striking patterns, some never noted even by experienced UFO investigators, including "doorway amnesia"—the curious inability of abductees to remember passing through or out of the door of the UFO into which they were taken. This in itself put into question a favorite skeptical argument, one that figures prominently in Philip J. Klass' *UFO-Abductions: A Dangerous Game* (1988), which Bullard would review scathingly (*International UFO Reporter*, November/December 1987): that the similarities in abduction stories are more apparent than real, because ufologists ask hypnotized subjects leading questions, based on the investigators' knowledge of other accounts, and the subjects oblige them with the answers they are seeking. Bullard examines the issue further and determines that consciously-recalled abductions (one-third of the total) and hypnotically-recalled ones are identical in all important regards. Moreover (again contradicting a claim Klass would make), the similarities held up regardless of who the investigator or hypnotist was. Hypnotism, long said to be the "cause" of abduction "fantasies," turns out, Bullard says, to be irrelevant to it.

In the end Bullard comes to no firm conclusions, but he makes it clear that the abduction phenomenon is no trivial issue. He concludes, "At least something goes on, a marvelous phenomenon rich enough to interest a host of scholars, humanists, psychologists and sociologists alike as well as perhaps physical scientists, and to hold that interest irrespective of the actual nature of the phenomenon. If abductions are literally true, they are the greatest story of all time. If they are subjective, they offer a seldom-equalled opportunity to gain insight into human mental functions, the interaction of belief with experience, and the social transmission of ideas. . . . A darker side of human suffering lends urgency to the abduction problem, so no further arguments are necessary to justify continued and serious research."

By the late 1980s the aspect of "human suffering" to which Bullard alludes would more than anything else bring the phenomenon to the attention of mental-health professionals, many of whom were encountering abductees in their practice. Reasonable persons could disagree on the cause of abductions; no one could dispute that many who claimed to be abductees showed symptoms of acute anxiety, insecurity, even terror, which they believed had their origin in an all-too-close encounter with alien kidnappers. These were individuals who gave no evidence otherwise of suffering from delusions. Through them psychiatrists and psychologists started to realize a strange new phenomenon was making an appearance.

The Continuing Debate: In 1987 two major but

very different books, Hopkins' *Intruders* and **Whitley Strieber's** *Communion: A True Story*, brought the abduction phenomenon to the best-seller lists. *Communion*, from an investigator's point of view the less interesting of the two, nonetheless was the greater commercial success, a hugely popular work which sold voluminously in both hardcover and paperback and which went on, in 1989, to become a widely-panned and financially-disappointing movie.

Strieber, a fairly prominent author of Gothic and futuristic fiction, declared, in a book that read much like a novel, that he had been abducted repeatedly over the course of his life, though he had not realized this until a spectacular December 26, 1985, event which took place at his family's cabin in a remote wooded area in upstate New York. A few weeks later Strieber phoned Hopkins, who he learned lived only a few minutes' walk from Strieber's Manhattan residence, and the two met. Hopkins referred Strieber to Dr. Donald Klein of the New York State Psychiatric Institute, and with Klein conducting the hypnosis, Strieber would recount a series of traumatic encounters with little gray humanoids (whom he would call "the visitors"). These "memories" would form the basis of *Communion* and Strieber would conclude that these hidden encounters explained much of the seemingly rootless anxiety, as well as the spiritual searches, that had characterized his life.

By the time the sequel, *Transformation: The Breakthrough* (1988), was published, the humanoids, for all the fear and disruption they had caused in Strieber's life, had become benevolent entities keenly interested in Strieber's spiritual development. "I do not now find the small, gray beings terrible," he writes. "I find them useful, as work with them is an efficient way to assault the dark battlements of fear and acquire the wisdom beyond." The visitors, he contends, "must be counted the allies of our growth." This was a message few abductees, who believed their kidnappers to be coldly indifferent to their well-being, would endorse, but it was one the contactee movement, to which Strieber rapidly became a hero, enthusiastically embraced, even though it

ABDUCTION PHENOMENON (*continued*)

was different from the traditional view of kindly, loquacious Space Brothers. Strieber is the first, though probably not the last, to wed the abductee experience to the contactee message, in what might be called a shotgun marriage.

Even before *Communion* had appeared in print, Strieber and Hopkins had become bitter enemies, quarreling over this and other, more personal matters. Soon Strieber was criticizing not just Hopkins but virtually the whole UFO-research community, which had not exactly rushed to praise his optimistic reading of the abduction experience. Strieber, now a fixture on the New Age lecture circuit, warned abductees to stay away from ufologists who, being more in love with their theories than with the realities of the visitor experience, could only mislead them and, worse, even harm them.

On its most basic level Hopkins' *Intruders* is a journalistic investigation of a number of related abduction experiences, with attendant physical and physiological evidence, reported by one family and its friends and acquaintances in suburban Indianapolis. But it was more than that; it was a radical new view of the phenomenon, one that purported to answer the *why* of the experience. According to *Intruders*, abductions occur—or so testimony by a variety of independent persons suggests—because aliens, presumably extraterrestrials, are creating a hybrid race of human-humanoids, perhaps to replenish their own exhausted genetic stock. Female abductees like "Kathie Davis" (Debra Tomey), the book's central character, may experience pregnancies (following "dreams" or other shadowy events in which they experienced paralysis and then sexual penetration either by a needlelike mechanical device or by a humanoid being) which abruptly end after a missing-time experience. Under hypnosis memories of vaginal penetration by a suctionlike mechanism emerge and the woman immediately senses that her "baby" has been taken from her. A few years later the abductee may be taken inside a UFO and presented with a child, with both human and alien features, who she is led to

believe is hers and whom she is asked to hold, as if in a bonding ritual. The child is often described as delicate or sickly and it says nothing.

Male abductees also report bizarre sexual experiences involving either intercourse, a la Villas-Boas, with what usually seem to be more-or-less-human-looking females or a kind of mechanical rape, in which a sperm sample is taken after a device has been placed over the genitals. Neither of these experiences is in any way erotic. To the contrary, both male and female abductees compare it to rape.

After listening to abductee testimony, gynecologist John Burger said the procedure being described is called laparoscopy, in which ova are removed from women for, among other purposes, the production of test-tube babies. The procedure (along with the physiological responses) was described so precisely, according to Hopkins, that Burger suspected the women had undergone such operations in normal life and incorporated them into vivid dreams. But when asked, the women denied having such experiences in their medical histories. Burger confessed to bafflement and fascination. The only explanation that made sense to him, he said, was that the events occurred as reported.

From his research Hopkins uncovered a pattern in the reports: "An individual, male or female, is first abducted as a child, at a time possibly as early as the third year. During that experience a small incision is often made in the child's body, apparently for sample-taking purposes, and then the child is given some kind of physical examination. There will often follow a series of contacts or abductions extending through the years of puberty. In some cases sperm samples will be taken from young males . . . and ova samples taken from young females. . . . In the cases in which artificial insemination is attempted, the women are apparently re-abducted after two or three months of pregnancy, and the fetus is removed from the uterus. However, it seems that some of these same women have been taken at later times during ovulation for the removal of ova from the Fallopian tubes. Why these two very different reproductive procedures have been used on some of the same women is unclear. But in a parallel way some of the male abductees who have had sperm samples taken have also been subjected at later times to a kind of involuntary sexual intercourse. There seems to be no logical reason why two different reproductive methods have been employed with both male and female abductees, but this is what the data suggests."

Hopkins' findings would be replicated by other investigators both within the UFO community (David M. Jacobs, for example) and outside (Jo Kopeland Stone). Psychological studies of abductees undertaken by the growing number of mental-health professionals involving themselves in abduction research confirmed that such perceived experiences did not grow out of pathological states. Probably the most famous psychiatrist to acknowledge publically the seriousness of the issue was Yale University's Robert Jay Lifton, who said on an April 10, 1987, *Today Show* appearance that accounts such as those outlined in *Intruders* defied explanation and deserved serious investigation. Outlandish as the stories Hopkins told seemed to be, his book received largely respectful notices, most prominently in the *New York Times Book Review* and *Kirkus Reviews* (which said that Hopkins' subjects' "uniform similarities of description of their UFO abductions and of the aliens bear a sense of faithful fact that could sway many an ironclad skeptic").

Nonetheless, these new reports were not accepted uncritically by ufologists. No one disputed the evident sincerity of abductees, but scientist **Michael D. Swords** spoke for a number of cautious ufologists when he wrote that for a number of reasons (which he outlined in a *MUFON UFO Journal* article) the idea of human-extraterrestrial hybridization is biologically implausible, perhaps even impossible, even given an advanced alien technology. Other critics declared that an advanced extraterrestrial race would not need to abduct great numbers of human beings even if it could accomplish human-ET hybridization, that once the basic reproductive materials had been gathered, they could be

duplicated in cosmic laboratories.

Responding to Swords, Jacobs, whose own so-far-unpublished work had uncovered patterns identical to those recounted by Hopkins, wrote that it is the "*abductees* who say that the babies look like a cross between the two [humans and aliens] and they continually refer to the babies as 'hybrids' or 'cross-breeds.'" In any case, he argues, who can say that an extraordinarily advanced technology could *not* find a way to effect such hybridization? "Moreover," he said, "to suggest that aliens can or cannot do something is to pass judgment on their scientific capabilities and to display a rather thorough knowledge of alien biotechnology and psychology that is not found in the evidence" (Jacobs, 1989).

As for the argument made by others that the cumbersome duplication of abductions makes no sense, Hopkins responded with an analogy: "When we on earth make a scientific breakthrough, let's say we discover an antitoxin, it's manufactured in a laboratory, it is turned out in vast quantities, it is taught in medical schools, and so forth. But when we want to learn how to ride a bicycle, each one of us has to get on a bicycle and have Daddy give us a push and teach us how to ride. That can't be bottled in a laboratory or taught in classrooms. The weird thing about the UFO phenomenon is that we seem to be in a situation where the occupants of UFOs are behaving more like people trying to learn how to ride a bicycle, one by one, than they are like someone teaching in a university, bottling the material in a laboratory and handing out samples around the universe. We're dealing with a very peculiar one-on-one situation. It really makes no sense in terms of earthly science but it may in some other way" (Clark, 1988).

The debate about the likelihood or otherwise of human-ET hybridization was clearly not to be resolved any more quickly than the debate about the general cause and reality status of abductions. By the end of the decade, however, two psychological explanations for abduction narratives were cast into doubt. The first, proposed by Philip J. Klass in a debunking book on abductions

ABDUCTION PHENOMENON (*continued*)

as well as by many other critics from *The Interrupted Journey* onward, held that such stories were the product of hypnotic confabulation; Klass elaborated on the theory to suggest that abductees patterned their stories to reflect the particular personalities of the hypnotist-investigators. But Thomas E. Bullard found that abduction reports told both by those with full conscious memory (some 30 percent of the total of reports, as critics seemed not to know or acknowledge) and by those under hypnosis are identical.

"Weighed and found wanting time and again," Bullard wrote in a long study published in the *Journal of UFO Studies*, "hypnosis cannot shoulder nearly as much responsibility for abductions as the skeptics have proposed. None of their appeals to confabulation, influence by the hypnotist, and experiments with non-abductees stand up under a comparative examination. In light of these findings, the burden of proof now drops on the skeptics. They can no longer repeat their old claims as meaningful answers. For any future rebuttals the skeptics must look deeper into the phenomenon itself rather than simply deduce the hazards of hypnotic testimony from scientific studies of hypnosis, or read theoretical interpretations into abduction reports from a safe distance. The skeptical argument needs rebuilding from the ground up."

A 1989 testing of the fantasy-prone-personality hypothesis by Kenneth Ring, a University of Connecticut psychologist who is skeptical of the extraterrestrial interpretation of abduction claims, found that abductees are no more fantasy-prone than nonabductees. Another psychiatrist investigating the abduction phenomenon, Rima E. Laibow, also rejected fantasy explanations, writing that the "abductee does not seem to be involved in the reworking of personal mythologies against the canvas of the [human] race's mythology. The details and contents of the scenarios seem, upon extensive investigation, to bear little thematic relevance to the issues inherent in the life of the abductee. Intensive follow-up investigation frequently yields no thematic, archetypal, primary

process symbolic meaning to the shape or activities of the abductors and the scenario of the abduction itself. Instead, therapeutic work in these cases centers around the issues inherent in the powerlessness and vulnerability of the individual even if this were not a prominent theme in his life before the putative abduction. In other words, the customary richness of association and creativity found in the examination of dreams and other fantasy material is lacking. . . ."

By the end of the decade all that could be said for certain about the abduction phenomenon was that it had resisted conventional accounting. If no one had yet suggested a persuasive psychological explanation, at the same time even those inclined to take seriously a literalist (extraterrestrial) interpretation were having a hard time believing that alien kidnappings could be taking place on so grand a scale as the volume of reports indicated. The evidence, in the form of multiple witnesses, scars, wounds, missing time (a genuine symptom not reducible, as early critics contended, to mere "absent-mindedness"), and the extraordinary similarity of reports over time and space, was certainly suggestive though, in the absence of physical artifacts such as recovered implants, hardly conclusive. (In 1989, however, an alleged implant would be uncovered and handed over for analysis, under conditions of great secrecy, to a physicist at a prominent eastern university. Presumably his findings will be reported in 1990.) No one could be blamed for suspecting that some extraordinary new phenomenon having nothing to do with alien body-snatchers is afoot, even if no one can explain what it is. In terms of the status of the debate, at the moment the proponents seem to have the better of the argument, but the controversy is far from over and the scientific investigation of the abduction phenomenon in its broadest aspects has barely begun.

The one thing all serious inquirers could agree on was that many abductees are hurting. David M. Jacobs has coined the phrase "post-abduction syndrome" to denote the "devastating" effects of the abduction experience. Going farther than most other investigators are willing to go, he says that the "vast majority of abductees wish that their experiences had never happened and most of them live in fear that it will occur again. They suffer a variety of physical and psychological sequelae that can be so harmful it often robs them of conscious, rational control of the course of their lives" (Jacobs, 1988). This is certainly true of *some* abductees. Working with a group of 18 abductees to whom she gave psychological tests, Jo Kopeland Stone determined that three-quarters of them "appear to have no conscious fear or phobic reactions concerning their direct UFO experiences." But those who did have such reactions "appeared traumatized. . . . [T]hey evidence many of the symptoms associated with post-traumatic stress syndrome: hypervigilance, denial and repression in the face of flashbacks which are traumatizing to them, and bouts of depression" (Stone, 1988). Their obsession with the experience sometimes negatively affected their family and professional lives.

In May 1989 a small, invited group of mental-health professionals and ufologists met at Fairfield University in Connecticut to spend a weekend discussing methodological and clinical issues related to the abduction experience. The meeting, organized by Rima Laibow, led to the creation of **Treatment and Research on Experienced Anomalous Trauma** (TREAT). In the months that followed, TREAT was plagued by internal conflict and many of the original participants, including a European aristocrat who was the major financial backer, left the group amid plans to form a similar one more to their liking. Meanwhile Laibow announced a second meeting of TREAT to be held at the Virginia Polytechnic Institute in February 1990.

Despite the problems, the prospects for meaningful study of the abduction phenomenon in the 1990s appeared excellent, as ufologists, physicians, psychiatrists, psychologists, social workers, scientists, and others came together to address a bizarre human experience which so far remains one of ufology's deepest mysteries.

Sources:

Basterfield, Keith. *Close Encounters of an Australian Kind-UFOs: The Image Hypothesis.* Sydney: Reed, 1981.

Bloecher, Ted, Aphrodite Clamar, and Budd Hopkins. *Final Report on the Psychological Testing of UFO "Abductees."* Mount Rainier, MD: Fund for UFO Research, 1985.

Bullard, Thomas E. "Hypnosis and UFO Abductions: A Troubled Relationship." *Journal of UFO Studies* 1 (new series, 1989): 3-40.

Bullard, Thomas E. *On Stolen Time: A Summary of a Comparative Study of the UFO Abduction Mystery.* Bloomington, IN: The Author, 1987a.

Bullard, Thomas E. *UFO Abductions: The Measure of a Mystery. Volume 1: Comparative Study of Abduction Reports. Volume 2: Catalogue of Cases.* Mount Rainier, MD: Fund for UFO Research, 1987b.

Clark, Jerome. "A Conversation with Budd Hopkins." *International UFO Reporter* 13, 6 (November/December 1988): 4-12.

Evans, Hilary. *Visions, Apparitions, Alien Visitors.* Wellingborough, Northamptonshire, England: The Aquarian Press, 1984.

Hopkins, Budd. *Intruders: The Incredible Visitations at Copley Woods.* New York: Random House, 1987.

Hopkins, Budd. *Missing Time: A Documented Study of UFO Abductions.* New York: Richard Marek Publishers, 1981.

Jacobs, David M. "Hybrid Thoughts." *MUFON UFO Journal* 250 (February 1989): 10-11.

Jacobs, David M. "Post-Abduction Syndrome." In Walter H. Andrus, Jr., and Richard H. Hall, eds. *MUFON 1988 International UFO Symposium Proceedings,* 86-102. Seguin, TX: Mutual UFO Network, Inc., 1988.

ABDUCTION PHENOMENON (*continued*)

Klass, Philip J. *UFO-Abductions, A Dangerous Game*. Buffalo, NY: Prometheus Books, 1988.

Laibow, Rima E. *Clinical Discrepancies Between Expected and Observed Data in Patients Reporting UFO Abductions: Implications for Treatment*. Dobbs' Ferry, NY: The Author, 1989.

Lawson, Alvin. "A Testable Hypothesis for Fallacious Abductions: Birth Trauma Imagery in CEIII Narratives." In Mimi Hynek, ed. *The Spectrum of UFO Research: The Proceedings of the Second CUFOS Conference, Held September 25-27, 1981, in Chicago, Illinois*, 71-98. Chicago: J. Allen Hynek Center for UFO Studies, 1988.

Lorenzen, Coral, and Jim Lorenzen. *Abducted! Confrontations with Beings from Outer Space*. New York: Berkley Publishing Company, 1977.

Randles, Jenny. *Abduction: Over 200 Documented UFO Kidnappings Investigated*. London: Robert Hale, 1988.

Ring, Kenneth. "Toward an Imaginal Interpretation of 'UFO Abductions'." *ReVision* 11, 4 (Spring 1989): 17-24.

Rogo, D. Scott. "Birth Traumas from Outer Space." *International UFO Reporter* 10, 3 (May/June 1985): 4-5, 16.

Stone, Jo Kopeland. *Preliminary Data on Eighteen of Thirty Subjects Reporting UFO Abduction*. Sherman Oaks, CA: The Author, 1989.

Strieber, Whitley. *Communion: A True Story*. New York: Beach Tree/William Morrow, 1987.

Strieber, Whitley. *Transformation: The Breakthrough*. New York: William Morrow and Company, Inc. 1988.

Swords, Michael D. "Extraterrestrial Hybridization Unlikely." *MUFON UFO Journal* 247 (November 1988): 6-10.

Walton, Travis. *The Walton Experience*. New York: Berkley Publishing Company, 1978.

AERIAL ANOMALIES INTERNATIONAL
Box 66404
Mobile, Alabama 36606

Aerial Anomalies International, founded on June 26, 1989, by Robert D. Boyd, former head of the investigative network of the **J. Allen Hynek Center for UFO Studies**, and announced the following October, may be the most conservative UFO organization currently in existence. Although the term "UFO" has been in circulation since the early 1950s, AAI rejects it as too liberal an interpretation of what people report.

Boyd writes, "Observations by witnesses of truly enigmatic occurrences in the sky fall into two broad categories: (1) Natural aerial phenomena and/or (2) Unknown aerial phenomena (having an apparent intelligent source). Both categories deserve serious disciplined study. It is essential that we differentiate between the two categories and classify, when possible.

"Because of this crucial need, we do not go beyond the point of referring to anomalous aerial phenomena by other names such as spaceships, flying saucers and UFOs. To do so would be equivalent to stating that we study spaceships, flying saucers and unidentified flying objects, none of which would be accurate. We use such terms only as historical and reported references, not as verified identifiable nomenclatures."

AAI has not yet announced a publication (though Boyd has authored a biographical volume about UFO researchers) or opened itself to general membership, asking only that "investigators, researchers and serious students of aerial phenomena . . . share their work and findings with us. We endeavor to make as much factual information available as possible to both our associates and . . . the public at large."

14

Sources:

"Aerial Anomalies International: Introduction."
Orbiter 19 (July/August 1989): 6.

Boyd, Robert D. *International Who's Who in Ufology Directory*. Mobile, AL: The Author, 1988.

ANCIENT ASTRONAUT SOCIETY
1821 St. Johns Avenue
Highland Park, Illinois 60035

The Ancient Astronaut Society was incorporated in Illinois on September 14, 1973, as a tax-exempt, nonprofit organization operated exclusively for scientific, literary and educational purposes. Its founder and president, corporate attorney Gene M. Phillips, runs the organization to this day from his home in a North Shore suburb of Chicago. The organization has held conferences in the United States, Switzerland, Yugoslavia, Brazil, West Germany, New Zealand and Austria. The most recent conference, held in Chicago between August 25 and 27, 1989, drew over 500 members from 15 nations. The society issues a bimonthly bulletin, *Ancient Skies*, reporting on new developments and theories. It is published in an English edition edited by Phillips and a German one edited by Erich von Däniken. Von Däniken operates the society's office in Switzerland.

Although von Däniken was not the inventor of the concept of "ancient astronauts"—the idea figures in 1950s books by George Hunt Williamson, M. K. Jessup, Desmond Leslie and others—his *Chariots of the Gods?*, published in English in 1969 and later, in 1970, in a mass-market Bantam paperback edition, was the first international best-seller on the subject of supposed extraterrestrial visitations in mankind's far past. Von Däniken's speculations about alleged archaeological evidence of space people and their superscience struck a responsive chord among many, including Phillips. He says, "Von Däniken presented challenges to the scientific community which appeared to me to be based on logic, and his explanations offered much more satisfying

answers to the questions of the origin of life and the foundation of religions than did the speculations of some scientists. It became obvious to me that a new organization was needed to investigate such matters from a completely different point of view and with an open mind, not controlled by scientists and not affiliated with any established doctrine or dogma. I wanted to afford the opportunity to interested people around the world to become actively involved in the quest for the truth about mankind's past" (Phillips, 1988).

The society hopes to establish a library and museum, publish a journal and inaugurate a professorship—a chair for ancient astronauts—at an American university. Meanwhile it sponsors regular expeditions to archaeological sites on six continents, where, Phillips says, "members may have an opportunity to examine the evidence firsthand." The "evidence," according to a statement prepared for the society by von Däniken, is everywhere, in the origins of earthly life, the emergence of intelligence, global mythology, the "vanishing of religious and mythological apparitions into 'Heaven,'" the "time-shift effects mentioned in old writings," and the "origins of the giant figures carved or drawn on the Earth's surface as if to be seen only from the air" (Phillips, 1988).

There is little overlap between the ancient-astronaut movement and ufology, even though the latter first saw print in the early UFO and **contactee** literature. As the ancient-astronaut movement came into its own, however, it drew few ufologists, who found von Däniken's speculations unconvincing. The first English-language, book-length debunking of ancient astronauts, Ronald Story's *The Space-Gods Revealed* (1976), prominently credited such ufologists as **J. Allen Hynek** and J. Richard Greenwell for their help, and Story went on to write two sympathetic books on the UFO phenomenon. The Ancient Astronaut Society's lists of speakers at conferences reveals few names likely to be familiar even to veteran ufologists. Yet society publications occasionally mention UFOs. To the extent that ufologists and ancient-

ANCIENT ASTRONAUT SOCIETY (*continued*)

astronaut theorists have anything in common, it is a mutual interest in alien visitation, though the two disagree on what the evidence for such visitation is. Moreover, while many ufologists doubt the reality of such visitations from outer space, past or present, the ancient-astronaut seekers are inclined not only to accept that reality, but to reorient their view of the world, especially of history and cultural development, on that assumption.

Phillips writes, "The evidence which has been accumulated to support our objectives is truly overwhelming. There is no doubt that technologically-advanced civilizations flourished on Earth in eons past. From the surviving remnants of their accomplishments, we can only imagine the stupendous heights of culture and technology which they achieved. The written accounts which have survived of these past great civilizations describe technological wonders which we, even with our level of achievement, have not duplicated to this day. Consequently, most of these accounts are labeled as *myth*.

"But we must still seek to determine whether extraterrestrial beings influenced, directly or indirectly, the development of intelligence and technology on Earth. To date there is a very large amount of evidence of extraterrestrial intervention, but it is circumstantial or conjectural. However, logic dictates that intelligence in human beings could not have simply *erupted* overnight, in one giant evolutionary step forward.

"If human intelligence on Earth *did* occur all of a sudden as we are taught, then surely it did not *evolve*, but was brought here, in one form or another. *Mankind* is, of course, the best evidence of the intervention of intelligent beings from outer space. Either we are their *product*, or we are their *descendants*."

Thus Phillips concludes, "We shall continue our search for the evidence which will *prove* that civilization, technology and intelligence *originated* in outer space."

Sources:

Krassa, Peter. *Disciple of the Gods: A Biography of Erich von Däniken*. London: W. H. Allen, 1978.

Phillips, Gene M., ed. *"Come Search With Us!"* Highland Park, IL: Ancient Astronaut Society, 1988.

Story, Ronald. *The Space-Gods Revealed: A Close Look at the Theories of Erich von Däniken*. New York: Harper and Row, 1976.

Von Däniken, Erich. *Chariots of the Gods?* New York: G. P. Putnam's Sons, 1969.

Von Däniken, Erich. *The Gold of the Gods*. London: Souvenir, 1973.

Von Däniken, Erich. *In Search of Ancient Gods: My Pictorial Evidence for the Impossible*. London: Souvenir, 1974.

Von Däniken, Erich. *Miracles of the Gods: A Hard Look at the Supernatural*. London: Souvenir, 1975.

ANDRUS, WALTER HARRISON, JR.

Since 1970 Walter Harrison Andrus, Jr., has been international director of the **Mutual UFO Network** (MUFON), which he had helped found the previous year.

Andrus was born in Des Moines, Iowa in 1920, graduated from the Central Technical Institute in Kansas City, and was a teacher in the U.S. Navy's technician program during World War II. Between 1949 and 1982 he worked in a managerial capacity at Motorola factories in Quincy, Illinois, and Seguin, Texas. Since his retirement he has worked full time for MUFON.

Andrus' interest in the UFO phenomenon stems from a daylight sighting of four UFOs in formation over Phoenix on August 15, 1948. His wife Jeanne and son Donald also witnessed the objects. In 1964 he became a field investigator for the Aerial Phenomena Research Organization, but left it in 1969 to found MUFON. In Andrus' view, UFOs represent "extraterrestrial visitation."

Sources:

Andrus, Walt. "Director's Message." *MUFON UFO Journal* 259 (November 1989): 30, 39.

ARCTURUS BOOK SERVICE
Box 831383
Stone Mountain, Georgia 30083

Arcturus Book Service deals exclusively with new, old, in- and out-of-print books and other materials on UFOs and unexplained phenomena. It issues a monthly catalog of currently-available printed matter, with commentary by proprietors Robert Girard and Monica Williams-Girard. Arcturus purchases "single books, lots, collections and entire UFO-related libraries." It does not want "very common titles, ex-library discards, or damaged/defective material," a note in the December 1989 issue of the catalog warns. Still, "we're buying 99.9% of all titles ever published!"

In addition to the valuable service as a distributor of UFO materials, Acturus has also published or reprinted a number of items which have filled gaps in the literature and made some hard-to-retrieve documents available.

Sources:

Bethurum, Truman. *Truman Bethurum's Scrapbook.* Ed. Robert C. Girard. [Scotia, NY]: Arcturus Book Service, 1970.

Girard, Robert C. *The Cosmic Sheepdog.* Scotia, NY: Arcturus Book Service, 1985.

Girard, Robert C. *1981 UFO Literature Reference Guide & Catalog.* Scotia, NY: Arcturus Book Service, 1981.

Girard, Robert C. "The Ultimate Cover-up." *Pursuit* 16 (1983): 67-69.

Pobst, Jim. *Swedenborg: A Manual.* Scotia, NY: Arcturus Book Service, 1984.

Rigberg, James S., comp. *The International Flying Saucer Directory.* New York: Flying Saucer News, 1956; [Scotia, NY]: Arcturus Book Service, 1982.

AUSTRALIAN UFOLOGY

UFO phenomena in Australia are fully as various as those reported elsewhere in the world. Nocturnal lights, daylight discs, radar-visual events, close encounters of all three kinds, and abductions and contacts all are said to have occurred in a nation regarded as the world's largest island; the large land mass and thinly-spread population create unique and daunting problems for investigators. Yet Australia has a rich UFO tradition and a potent attendant controversy about its significance.

UFO Organizations: In the 1980s Australian ufology has taken a multifaceted approach to the UFO problem. Investigations are carried out by civilians, either as individuals or as members of groups, and by military officers, usually associated with the Royal Australian Air Force (RAAF). The decade has also seen the growth of a more critical-minded style of research. This trend is related to the establishment, in 1974, of the Australian Coordination Section (ACOS) of the late **J. Allen Hynek's Center for UFO Studies** (CUFOS). Intended originally to act as a clearinghouse for quality UFO reports to be channeled through to CUFOS, ACOS quickly evolved into a vital and innovative organization. A reflection of this growth was marked in 1980, when ACOS changed its name to the Australian Centre for UFO Studies (ACUFOS), which sought, with some considerable success, to coordinate serious research.

The 1960s had seen a similar attempt with the formation of the Commonwealth Aerial

AUSTRALIAN UFOLOGY (*continued*)

Phenomena Investigation Organization (CAPIO). It began well but internal conflicts killed it before it could enter the 1970s. The UFO Network tried to fill the void in the early 1970s but it, too, succumbed to the problems of securing cooperation among differing personalities and groups. ACUFOS, though less active than it once was, has weathered the storms and still provides a focal research point. It has accumulated a large database and provides a specialized research-document service. In 1985 ACUFOS published the excellent *UFOs Over Australia*, a collection of articles drawn from the *ACOS Bulletin* and the *Journal of ACUFOS*. It focused on research, historical and physical aspects, psychological issues, and theories.

Many of the individuals and groups associated with ACUFOS are also working with UFO Research Australia (UFORA). UFORA was formed in 1984 by two former ACUFOS coordinators, Vladimir Godic and Keith Basterfield, who saw their group as more informal than (and noncompetitive with) ACUFOS. Their interest was in attracting a loose network of persons dedicated to coherent, scientific research into the UFO phenomenon. *UFO Research Australia Newsletter*, established in 1980, acts as UFORA's major publication outlet. UFORA also puts out a research digest and other occasional information-resource documents.

Other groups continue to thrive. The well-known Victorian UFO Research Society (VUFORS), formed in 1957, was particularly prominent in uncovering alleged official cover-ups. It continues to publish its newsletter, *Australian UFO Bulletin*, and occasionally a magazine, *Australian UFO Review*. In 1978 VUFORS produced a valuable study of the 1954 UFO wave, one of the most significant of the early sighting flurries in Australia.

UFO Research (Queensland) (UFOR[Q]), formerly known as the Queensland UFO Research Bureau, has been active, like VUFORS, since 1957. It publishes a newsletter entitled *UFO Encounter*.

UFO Research (New South Wales) (UFOR[NSW]), based in Sydney, was formed from the UFO Investigation Centre in 1977. UFOIC in turn developed from the Australian Flying Saucer Bureau (AFSB), the country's first UFO group, organized by Edgar Jarrold in July 1952. In 1980 UFOR(NSW) ceased publication of its *Australian UFO Researcher* (previously *UFOIC Newsletter*) to join the cooperative *UFO Research Australia Newsletter*. Among the cases UFOR(NSW) has investigated are a UFO landing with associated physical trace at Orange, New South Wales, in 1977, the earliest retrospective inquiry into a UFO "contact vision" (an 1868 episode), and one of Australia's first known abduction reports (1978).

The island state of Tasmania hosts the Tasmanian UFO Investigation Centre (TUFOIC). Formed in 1965 and based in Hobart, it regularly publishes a UFO annual and a small newsletter. One of the best civilian groups in Australia, TUFOIC for years has kept statistics on the Tasmanian cases it receives. From before 1965 to 1986 TUFOIC investigated 2131 reports, finding 21.1 percent to be of "unknowns" and laying the rest to conventional causes. By way of contrast, between 1950 and 1984 the RAAF investigated no more than 1612 reports *for the entire nation*. This sort of comparison suggests that the civilian groups have a greater claim than the official examiner, the RAAF, to having thoroughly "investigated" the UFO phenomenon.

UFO Research (South Australia) (UFOR[SA]), Inc., formed in 1968, pioneered a more business-like approach to research and investigation, inspiring other Australian groups to do the same. Until the initiation of *UFO Research Australia Newsletter*, UFORSA, Inc., produced a newsletter featuring local events. A multiply-witnessed CE3 event near Kimba in 1973 was one of many significant cases the group investigated. Somewhat less critical-minded and more controversial is the other main South Australia group, Australian International UFO Research, Inc. (AIUFOR), also known as the Australian Flying Saucer Research Society (AFSRS), originally formed in 1955. The group periodically puts out a magazine.

Other groups include UFO Research (Far North, Queensland) (UFOR[FNQ]), based in Cairns, and the Perth UFO Research Group (PUFORG). UFOR(FNQ) is interested in local UFO activity, understandably so, since the far north of Queensland has long been seen as a hotbed of UFO sightings, especially since the classic UFO landing and "nest" reports in the Tully area in 1966. PUFORG was put together in 1957 and published a regular newsletter until recently. It has investigated trace events at Mount Barker (1977) and Northhampton (1980) and a dramatic series of close-encounter events centered on the Perth suburbs of Midland and Middle Swan (January 1984).

Other groups have appeared from time to time but they have not had the longevity of the ones, such as ACUFOS, UFORA, and VUFORS, recounted above.

In many ways 1980 was a turning point in the evolution of coherent, critical, scientific research into UFOs in Australia. It was also a significant year for the Australian study of CE2 and CE3 cases.

In June of that year the Australian Centre for UFO Studies published Keith Basterfield's *An Indepth Review of Australasian UFO Related Entity Reports*—a 110-page study of CE3 reports. Sixty-seven reports formed the main focus of the study, which spanned the period 1868 to 1978. Supplementary lists of possibly relevant "entity" reports covered a further 37 events. Basterfield's analysis suggested that of the 67 central CE3 accounts, only 27 "appear to have sufficient documentation/investigation." Of these he concludes that only five are "high strangeness cases with reliable reporters." From his study, he concludes, "There do in fact exist a few reliable reported observations of 'saucer' style flying objects with associated beings which demand further study. . . . [T]o me it appears that the very randomness of cases, the descriptions of the entity, etc., more fit a human-based cause than [one] involving alien stimuli."

Basterfield's 1980 study evolved from his longterm research into such events. As early as 1977 he had formed the Australian Entity Study Group to encourage investigation and research into these sorts of cases. The initial stimulus for a more detailed study of the Australian CE3 experience came with the publication, in September 1976, of an *Australian Catalogue of Close Encounter Type Three Reports* coauthored by Basterfield and Bill Chalker. That document represented the first attempt to bring together details of Australian CE3s. It examined 36 such cases.

Physical Traces: Nineteen eighty also saw a series of incidents ostensibly related to the physical dimension of the UFO phenomenon. The Gippsland region of Victoria took center stage during the latter half of the year with a puzzling array of events which featured the disappearance of substantial bodies of water. By far the most interesting of these, and certainly one of the most interesting physical-trace cases to have occurred in Australia, was the UFO landing that took place on September 30 near Rosedale.

The incident began when the caretaker of a property was awakened by stock disturbances. He observed the passage of an extraordinary object: a domed disc with a white top, moving at about eight feet above the ground. Orange and blue lights shone on its surface. The object, apparently some 28 feet in diameter and 15 feet high, hovered for a short time over an open 10,000-gallon water tank. It then descended to the ground, 50 feet from the tank.

The witness got on a motorbike and approached to within 30 to 50 feet of the UFO. A whistling noise was emanating from the object. Then suddenly an "awful scream" replaced it and a black tube appeared around the object's base. There was a tremendous bang and the object lifted up and off the ground. Meanwhile a blast of hot air nearly knocked the witness off his vehicle. At about 30 feet out from the landing site and eight to 10 feet in the air, the object fell silent. At this point debris (largely stones, cape-weed and cow dung) dropped from the base of the object. The UFO flew away and was eventually lost to view in the eastern sky.

AUSTRALIAN UFOLOGY (*continued*)

The caretaker rode onto the landing site and observed a ring of "black" flattened grass 30 feet across. Feeling disoriented, he found his way back to the house.

With daylight he returned to the site and found the ring stood out clearly in the blanket of yellow flowers then in the paddock. The ring was near-black or brown in color, consisting of grass flattened in an anticlockwise manner to a width of 18 inches. Inside the ring there was only green grass; the yellow flowers had been removed. The total diameter of the site was 28 feet. Evenly spaced within the ring were six "spokes" of relatively undamaged grass. Debris around the site was consistent with the material seen falling from the UFO during the night.

Other extraordinary effects were reported. Ten thousand gallons of water which had been in the water tank had vanished. Muddy residue in the middle of the base of the tank was built up in a cone shape to a height of two feet. If the tank had been emptied by prosaic means, it would have shown signs of being emptied from the side of the tank. The witness experienced an unusual recurring headache for seven to eight days. Vomiting and diarrhea also persisted for the same period of time. For three days after the incident, the witness' watch would not work when he wore it. Before and after this period it functioned with no problem.

Chalker, who investigated the case, took samples and had them subjected to analysis. Of particular interest was the discovery, in December 1980, of another series of traces (10 in number, all "rings" as in the Rosedale case) at Bundalaguah, near Montgomery Park, not far from Rosedale. The traces were again associated with losses of water in a nearby reservoir. Because the annulus widths of the Montgomery Park rings were identical to those of Rosedale, they were seen as a possible area of comparison. The variety of ring diameters reported at Montgomery Park also heightened the likelihood of prosaic causes (e.g., "fairy rings"). Although similarities and differences were found

in the analyses, it proved impossible to establish any mundane explanation for the incident or the physical traces.

Like so many high-strangeness physical-trace episodes, the Rosedale case could have benefited from a thorough, professional study. Chalker tried without success to interest laboratories in the material. Still, though many questions remain unanswered, the Rosedale case seems a remarkable one.

Even before its occurrence, Chalker had been interested in trace and other cases suggestive of physical UFOs. In 1979 he presented a paper, "Physical Evidence for UFOs in Australia," at UFOCON4, the fourth conference organized by ACOS. In July 1983 he circulated an 85-page paper, *A Study of Physical Trace Events*, concluding that of 237 such accounts, only 33 (or 13.9 percent) appeared to have probative UFO correlations.

This cross-section of Australian physical-trace data provides a microcosm of the world-wide experience. The physical dimension of the UFO phenomenon seems certain. The vexing question for researchers, Chalker wrote, is to resolve unambiguously the nature of these events and to determine whether or not this evidence is consistent with an "alien" reality. Chalker's study emphasized the need for a well-supported study of UFO-related physical-trace events. To date sophisticated, professional and funded investigations of such cases have been rare (the **Trans-en-Provence CE2** being a notable exception) and until such investigations become commonplace, the evidence will remain inconclusive.

One happy development, occurring in Australia as it has elsewhere, is the growing instance of collaboration between ufologists and scientists. In Australia Dr. Herbison Evans developed a UFO-identification kit (which included a diffraction grating and polaroid slide set) and another scientist, Dr. G. Stevens, has performed thermoluminiscent analyses of a number of physical traces.

Two notable cases from the late 1980s, only five weeks apart, involved physical evidence—and, unfortunately, some frustrating ambiguities.

The first of these began at 9:30 p.m. on December 14, 1987. A motorist was traveling in a 14-month-old Mercedes car, 31 km southeast of Launceston, Northern Tasmania. Earlier he had noticed some lights which seemed to be following him, but he thought little of the matter until about a kilometer from the junction with the Evandale main road the lights apparently passed over his car. A mass of light landed on the road in front of him, his car lights failed and the motor stopped. The driver clutched the emergency brake and brought the car to a halt. In front of him was an egg- to cigar-shaped object blocking the road. It was so bright that it hurt his eyes to look at it. The light seemed to be coming from brilliant white lights beneath the object; the rest of the object was gray in color. The object was some five to six meters wide and not much more than two meters high.

Badly frightened, the witness fled the car and threw himself behind some nearby bushes. He felt sick and would feel so again the next morning.

The man then noticed, to his considerable astonishment, that the car was moving toward the UFO, even though the handbrake was on. The car was dragged 10 meters, leaving rubber marks on the road and scuffing the tires. As this was happening, the witness had the impression that some considerable time had passed, but later decided that the incident occurred over no more than three minutes.

Another vehicle approached, a Landcruiser. Its lights failed but the motor kept running. The driver, a man, thought there had been an accident. The Mercedes driver emerged from the bushes and walked toward him. At this point the object on the road lifted off with a high-pitched whine, and at an angle, then curved away to the south and disappeared. The Landcruiser driver suggested the two of them not tell anyone else what they had seen. The Mercedes driver returned to his car, which started immediately. The road bitumen, where the object had rested, appeared to have been melted. Subsequently he found some bitumen splattered on the front of his car. He thought this may have occurred through splashing as he drove away from the site.

The witness was obliged to make a phone call as soon as he got home. He was surprised when the person he called complained about the lateness of the hour—around midnight. The witness was puzzled because the drive from the encounter site to his house should have taken only 20 minutes.

In the days after the incident, the Mercedes began to suffer from electrical problems and the driver was required to purchase some new parts. Because of the problems, the vehicle was subsequently sold.

The driver returned to the site on the next weekend. It looked to him as if the road had been repaired. He decided to report the incident to the Victorian UFO Research Society, which in turn directed the witness to the TUFOIC. He contacted the group on December 21. By that time it was difficult to find independent confirmation of the story. The car could not be examined and the Landcruiser driver could not be located. The witness claimed he had had strange dreams. In March 1988, he would subsequently report, three men approached him in Launceston and told him not to talk about the incident. Afterwards he broke off contact with the Tasmanian group for a period of time.

The Mundrabilla Incident: The other incident is better known because it received worldwide publicity. It is now known as the Mundrabilla incident. It involved the Knowleses (Faye [43], Patrick [24], Sean [21], and Wayne [18]), who were in transit across the Nullarbor Plain, on their way to Melbourne, during the early hours of January 20, 1988. At about 4 a.m. the family was between Madura and Mundrabilla. All were wide awake. Sean was driving with Patrick beside him in the front seat. Wayne sat behind Patrick and their mother, Faye, behind Sean. Sunrise was some time away.

AUSTRALIAN UFOLOGY (continued)

At first a bright light was seen ahead. Mrs. Knowles initially thought it was a truck. It was apparently an extremely bright white. Sean, who thought it was something decidedly out of the ordinary, asked Patrick if it was a "spaceship." Patrick rejected the idea but Sean sped up to get a closer look and satisfy his own curiosity.

The Knowleses claim they were then confronted with an extremely bright white light, apparently 50 to 60 feet in front of them, seemingly traveling along in front of their moving car. They described it as being three feet wide. They could make no estimate of its height, beyond noting that at times it seemed to block their view of the road ahead. They said the object looked something like a slightly angular egg in an egg cup; there was a yellow light at its center.

According to the Knowleses, the object, at first either on the ground or slightly above it, began to move back and forth. Sean swerved on to the opposite side of the road to avoid the object, only to have a near-collision with a vehicle towing a caravan coming the other way. This car was thought to be a white Holden HQ station wagon. Its occupants have never come forward, despite (or maybe because of) the massive publicity the incident would receive.

The object appeared to circle around the right-hand side of their car, then gave chase to the second car. For a time, apparently, the UFO was lost to the Knowleses' view. They would make two U-turns during this phase of the experience, first to pursue the object and later, as their concern mounted, to escape it. The Knowleses by then had gained the impression that it was after them.

Although they did not actually see the object in the immediately ensuing phase, the family nonetheless felt the UFO not only had returned but had landed on top of their car. They claimed there was a clunking noise at this point, that the car may have been pulled backward for a moment and that the car seemed to be being pushed down by some heavy weight from above. By now the Knowleses were badly frightened. The sequence of events that followed, consequently, is complicated and difficult to recount in proper order.

At this point the family thought the car had been lifted off the road but none was able to say for how long or how high. Mrs. Knowles wound down her window, reached for the roof and then felt something soft, spongy and rubbery. It was hot but did not burn her hand. When she brought her hand in front of her face, she found it was covered with a dark gray dust. This apparent confirmation of an unknown presence on the roof threw the already shaken Knowleses into a state of terror. Patrick rolled down his window, only to see large amounts of black, powdery dust come into the car. Accompanying it was a foul odor, comparable, the witnesses thought, to what might be caused by "dead bodies or something."

A high-pitched whirring noise sounded and the two dogs in the car went crazy. The Knowleses felt disoriented and noticed that their voices had become slow and deep. They thought they had lost their minds and were going to die. Patrick felt as if the UFO were taking over his body and that he was—literally—going out of his head, as if his brain "was being sucked out." Mrs. Knowles said it was like "something was going into our heads."

At some point the family felt the car was either dropped or forced down onto the road. As the tires hit the road, the one on the right-hand side burst. Sean slammed on the brakes and brought the car to a halt just before he blacked out.

According to their account, the Knowleses fled the car and hid in the bushes. The UFO remained in the vicinity of their car for a while. After it seemed to have left some 15 minutes later, the family returned to the car, quickly changed the tire and drove away.

Before doing so, however, they had attempted to wave down a truck which was heading toward Mundrabilla, some 40 km to the west. The truck carried a woman named Anne, who was driving, and John De Jong, who was sleeping. Anne roused John to see if she should stop but John said no, deeming it unwise to stop for strangers in a remote location at a late hour. Neither saw any unusual lights.

But unknown to them or the Knowleses, De Jong's friend Graham Henley, who was driving ahead of them in another truck, closer to Mundrabilla, saw a strange light behind him, in his rearview mirror, at about 4 a.m. He described it variously as like a "very high-powered spotlight . . . like a [big] fried egg hung upside down." It was in view for five minutes. He felt it was too high in the air to be the light from a motor vehicle. Henley continued on to Mundrabilla and arrived there at about 4:30 a.m.

Further back along the road De Jong's vehicle was overtaken by a speeding vehicle. After it had passed De Jong and was some distance ahead of him, it switched off its lights. Inside the car were the Knowleses, terrified and racing toward Mundrabilla.

Shortly after Henley had arrived at a truck stop in Mundrabilla, he saw the Knowleses' blue 1984 Ford AR Telstar GL sedan pull up. He was confronted by four nearly hysterical individuals all trying to talk at once. One said they had been burned, another that they had been grabbed by a flying saucer, and yet another that they had been picked up and dropped. One of the boys would open and close his mouth but only garbled sounds would come out. Out of concern for them Henley offered to put the car in his empty refrigerator van and drive them to where they wanted to go, but they declined.

Henley confirmed the presence of black ash all over the car, both inside and outside. He likened it to "silicon type sand . . . very, very fine, almost like ground glass . . . fine and dry. And it was black and had this horrible bakelite [burned] smell about it." Henley told Chalker he had been on the road since 1957 and in addition to that had a lot of experience with race cars. He was sure he could tell the difference between brake dust and

the siliconlike dust he saw and handled at Mundrabilla on the Knowles car. He said it was like the "bull dust" that built up on vehicles in the old days of crossing the Nullarbor on a dirt surface; in other words, it was akin to heavy road-dust film. He also confirmed the presence of four indentations on top of the car. Of the car's damaged tire he reflected, "It was the most unusual burst tire I had seen in my life."

De Jong and Anne arrived just before the Knowleses left. They, too, saw how badly frightened they were. De Jong gave the car only a cursory glance and noticed no unusual dust.

The Knowleses, who were desperate to leave the area, drove off at 4:50, just as the first pink of daylight started to appear.

Henley, De Jong and Anne spent some time at Mundrabilla after the Knowleses' departure. Indeed they were probably the first people who went to the site of the encounter, where they observed physical evidence (skid marks, footprints, tread tracks and so on) which they felt confirmed the Knowleses' account of their movements. Henley and his friends told the Eucla police of what had happened.

By the time the Knowleses, still on the road, got to Ceduna, the story had preceded them and the police were waiting for them. They were interviewed by Sgt. Jim Furnell of the Ceduna police and by a forensic police officer visiting the station. They found the family in a state of great anxiety, "visibly shaken by the ordeal." The police found "superficial dents to the four corners of the hood although the remainder of the hood appeared undamaged. The exterior of the vehicle was covered by a fine black/gray dust similar to a road film left on a vehicle in need of washing. That same dust was obvious on the upholstery within the vehicle."

Sgt. Furnell contacted Ray Brooke of UFO Research (South Australia), at about 2:30 p.m., January 20, while the Knowleses were still present at the police station. Arrangements were made for the witnesses to proceed to Adelaide for

AUSTRALIAN UFOLOGY (*continued*)

further investigation by UFO Research (SA). Forensic samples of the dust were taken, along with other statements. Brooke brought Keith Basterfield of UFO Research Australia, also of Adelaide, into the investigation. It appeared that an extraordinary close encounter with possible physical evidence might be available for a careful scientific investigation, although the investigators felt the well-being of the distraught family had to be the first priority. Unfortunately things did not work out that way.

Channel 7, an Adelaide television station, got wind of the story from Adelaide police. Its chief of staff, Frank Pangallo, contacted a former journalist colleague, Paul "Porpoise" Jackson, who ran the Eyre Highway Motel at Wudinna. When the Knowles family reached Wudinna late on the afternoon of the 20th, Jackson was sitting outside the motel waiting. He persuaded the Knowleses that it was important they tell their story. They were frightened, however, and had no interest in doing so, even for money; they just wanted to get away. But by some fast talking Jackson got them to wait for Pangallo and the Channel 7 team. Mrs. Knowles said she was concerned about other people who might run into the light on the Nullarbar.

By morning the story was national news and was breaking internationally. Channel 7 paid the Knowleses a relatively paltry $5000 for exclusive coverage of their story. But if the Knowleses had known what they were going to encounter as they entered the media arena, it is doubtful they would ever have gone public.

In this way a promising scientific investigation was undone by checkbook journalism. Brooke and Basterfield had to negotiate with Channel 7 to be able to talk with the Knowleses on the 21st, all the while competing with the media circus that played around them. Channel 7 commissioned the Amdel laboratories to examine the car. They concluded that dust samples they took, significantly from around the front wheels of the car, were indeed consistent with brake dust and

that "no significant dust was observed on the vehicle as presented for inspection." For some days Channel 7 would not permit UFO investigators to examine the car. Finally Paul Norman of VUFORS, Brooke and Basterfield were separately allowed to examine it on February 1 and 2. Norman vacuumed the vehicle in search of samples. Brooke and Basterfield observed nothing that did not strike them as ordinary road dust. Norman passed his samples on to the United States and **Richard F. Haines**. Haines arranged to have the samples scanned with an electron microscope. After doing so, Haines concluded that the dust from inside the car was different from that around the wheels. He observed that the interior dust was not road dust, but neither, he also noted, was there anything anomalous about it. Attempts are underway to secure samples from the spot where the incident occurred to see if this dust is consistent with what one would expect from normal accumulation on a trip across the wilds of the Nullarbor.

There were also a number of separate UFO reports in the area of the Knowles experience. They lend some weight to the possibility that something out of the ordinary may have taken place. In the end, however, we have a situation in which the Knowleses witnessed a so-far-unexplained light, experienced severe fright and reported some extraordinary effects. So far there is no compelling physical evidence that supports an exotic event. We are left with a fascinating story and puzzled witnesses.

During the 1980s Bill Chalker undertook extensive research into official UFO investigations in Australia, eventually being granted (in 1982) direct access to Royal Australian Air Force UFO files. His several visits led him into direct liaison with the Air Force intelligence officers responsible for UFO investigation, namely from the Directorate of the Air Force Intelligence, and also into contact with a number of more clandestine sources in other official departments.

Mark Moravec has carried out excellent research into the psychological and paranormal dimensions of UFO experiences, and Basterfield and Robert

E. Bartholomew, two proponents of the **psychosocial hypothesis**, have written on possible psychological causes of UFO-abduction stories. In 1981 Basterfield wrote *Close Encounters of an Australian Kind–UFOs: The Image Hypothesis*, which sought to explain many UFO experiences as waking dreams.

As in the United States, the **abduction phenomenon** has become a central focus of UFO research in Australia. But Australia has been slow in active investigation, due largely to the apparent paucity of available data. In the 1980s such accounts began to increase. In 1989 Basterfield and Vladimir and Pony Godic summarized the accounts in an article in *International UFO Reporter*, noting that "abduction accounts have never made front-page headlines or featured heavily in the electronic media within Australia. . . . [T]he reports documented here have come to attention either through UFO research organizations or through low-key press articles. This has meant that to date researchers have been able to pursue cases out of the media spotlight. On the other hand, with little mass publicity abduction cases may lie undiscovered, with potential abductees being unaware that there are responsible organizations to which they could take their stories. . . .

"What, then, have we learned about the abduction experience in Australia? We have learned that there are cases that parallel those in other countries. Researchers have not been able to pursue and fully document many of these cases. Reasons for this include the sheer vastness of the Australian land mass and distances to percipients; the small number of serious researchers; the attitudes of some UFO investigators; and the unwillingness of percipients to be involved with full investigations."

Since 1988 Chalker has worked with a clinical psychologist who specializes in hypnotherapy in examining persons who reported missing-time or abduction experiences. The most interesting case, now being investigated, involves a complex of abduction-related events from Gisborne, New Zealand, in 1978. Other cases are being pursued across the country.

Bill Chalker

Sources:

Basterfield, Keith. *Close Encounters of an Australian Kind–UFOs: The Image Hypothesis*. Sydney: Reed, 1981.

Basterfield, Keith, Vladimir Godic, and Pony Godic. "The Abduction Phenomenon in Australia." *International UFO Reporter* 14, 4 (July/August 1989): 11-13, 24.

Chalker, Bill. *The Australian UFO Experience*. Sydney: Australian Centre for UFO Studies, 1988.

Chalker, Bill. "Working with the Government." In John Spencer, and Hilary Evans, eds. *Phenomenon: Forty Years of Flying Saucers*, 248-259. New York: Avon Books, 1989.

Good, Timothy. *Above Top Secret: The Worldwide UFO Cover-up*. New York: William Morrow and Company, 1988.

Moravec, Mark. *Psiufo Phenomena: A Study of UFOs and the Paranormal*. Gosford, N.S.W.: Australian Centre for UFO Studies, 1982.

Moravec, Mark, and John Prytz, eds. *UFOs Over Australia: A Selection of ACUFOS Research Findings and Debate*. Sydney: Australian Centre for UFO Studies, 1985.

Prytz, John. *Who's Who in Australasian Ufology*. ACUFOS Report d-13. Gosford, N.S.W.: Australian Centre for UFO Studies; Scotia, NY: Arcturus Book Service, 1982.

Randles, Jenny. *The UFO Conspiracy: The First Forty Years*. New York: Blandford Press, 1987.

B

BORDERLAND SCIENCES RESEARCH FOUNDATION
Box 429
Garberville, California 95440

Borderland Sciences Research Foundation was founded by N. Meade Layne in February 1945, almost 2½ years before the term "flying saucers" and general awareness of unidentified flying objects entered public consciousness. The organization, then known as Borderland Sciences Research Associates, published a periodical, *Round Robin*, which reported on Layne's theories about the etheric world. These in turn were based in large part on the mediumship of Mark Probert, who channeled the teachings of four spiritual masters. One of them, the Yada Di'Shi'ite, lived 500,000 years ago in an advanced civilization in the Himalayas. The etheric world, which exists in another dimension where matter is denser, is the source of paranormal and anomalous manifestations such as UFOs.

The organization was incorporated on May 21, 1951. Riley Hansard Crabb succeeded Layne as director in 1959. In 1985 Thomas Joseph Brown became president. Peter A. Lindemann is vice-president and Alison Davidson serves as secretary-treasurer. BSRF's periodical *Journal of Borderland Research* appears bimonthly. Its coverage includes, a formal statement says, "Archetypal Forms and Forces of Nature and the Use of the Imagination and intuition to Perceive Them, Ether Physics, Light and Color, Radionics and Radiesthesia, Orgone Energy, Nikola Tesla & The True Wireless, Viktor Schauberger's Water Technology, Electricity & The Evolving Soul, Initiation Science, Dowsing, Hollow Earth Mysteries, Anomalies and Fortean Phenomenon [sic]. Hypnosis, Photography of the Invisible, and Unidentified Flying Objects" (*Journal of Borderland Research*, 1989).

Despite its long existence BSRF's ideas have been mostly ignored by mainstream ufologists, although they have made an impact on those interested in flying saucers with an occult or **contactee** perspective. Contactee chroniclers Bryant and Helen Reeve complained, "Not too many saucer enthusiasts we have met are familiar with these researches. What a pity—or maybe it is not a pity—because possibly they are just a little too advanced for the average 'fan'" (Reeve, 1957). One of the few major ufologists to comment on Layne's theories was **Richard Hall**, who once wrote, "Mr. Layne refers to UFO's as 'etheric ships.' That would be a perfectly acceptable nametag, if it were not soon apparent that 'etheric' is supposed to actually refer to a real place from which the UFO's come. A name, however, does not endow a concept with physical reality by virtue of being spoken or written" (Hall, 1958).

Sources:

Hall, Richard. "Rationalism in Ufology." *Saucer News* 5, 4 (June/July 1958): 7-8.

BORDERLAND SCIENCES RESEARCH FOUNDATION (*continued*)

"The Journal of Borderland Research." The Journal of Borderland Research 45, 3 (May/June 1989): ii.

Reeve, Bryant, and Helen Reeve. *Flying Saucer Pilgrimage*. Amherst, WI: Amherst Press, 1957.

BRITISH UFOLOGY

British society is deeply conservative. No new idea is easily accepted, and tradition, bureaucracy and a stiff-upper-lip mentality act as brakes on the pace of social change. Consequently the British were unusually slow to accept the idea of UFOs. Among many who have in the UFO-research community, there is a stubborn but thoroughly British tendency to reject what is perceived elsewhere to be the fashion of the moment.

The First UFOs: In the early days, in the late 1940s, newspapers reported on the UFO subject only occasionally, as if it were an American craziness—a manifestation of either peace euphoria or Cold War jitters. The British, in fact, had much else to think about: a country that had been devastated by German bombers and in which food and other rationing continued well into the 1950s. Austerity ruled amid a new social upheaval which brought the socialists into power with a promise of a "fair deal" for all society.

Even so, a British author nearly produced the first UFO book. Gerald Heard's *The Riddle of the Flying Saucers* (published in the United States as *Is Another World Watching?*) appeared in 1950 only weeks after Donald E. Keyhoe's groundbreaking *The Flying Saucers Are Real*. Heard's little-remembered book anticipated much of what was to follow: it rehashed much-publicized cases and subjected them to the author's outside evaluation. In other words, Heard was more observer than investigator, making him a pioneer of what would become known as "armchair

ufology"—a practice that still dominates much of British ufology.

Heard's book was mostly ignored and the turning point in British attitudes was reached only in the fall of 1952, in the aftermath of the spectacular Washington, D.C., radar/visual sightings. During a British NATO exercise, Operation Mainbrace, in mid-September, witnesses on the ground, in the air and at sea saw wobbling silvery objects maneuvering in the daylight. A Royal Air Force Meteor jet was sent after one target seen above Topcliffe Air Base in Yorkshire, but the UFO outmaneuvered the state-of-the-art aircraft.

These dramatic events were followed by other cases in which RAF aircraft came into close proximity with UFOs. Within a few months of the Mainbrace sightings a top-secret experimental Canberra, stripped bare and equipped with electronic monitoring gear, had a close encounter with a daylight disc above RAF Boscombe Down in Sussex.

Reports of the caliber of this one (which was made by Flight Lt. Cyril George Townsend-Withers, who was later to become a wing commander and a leading scientific specialist with the Ministry of Defense [MoD]) had a substantial impact. MoD sent advisers to the Pentagon to find out what the Americans were doing. Ralph Noyes, now active as a ufologist and retired from the government (where he had some involvement in UFO studies), says he was on the staff of Air Chief Marshall Cochran at the time and sat in on Cabinet-level debates about the issue.

The British government had apparently believed Gen. Hoyt Vandenberg's rejection of the U.S. Air Force Project Sign report which argued for the extraterrestrial origin of the flying discs. Now, suddenly faced with UFO sightings so worrying they were impossible to ignore, British officials wanted to know how these squared with such a rejection. We know from documents obtained in recent years through the Public Records Office (where they became available only after the passage of 30 years) that even Prime Minister

Winston Churchill was asking provocative questions about UFOs during 1952 and 1953.

The consequence of all this was twofold. Some of the stories appeared in the press and the British people were awakened to the subject. Several small local groups began a quest to learn more, usually following the pattern already set in the United States. The British Flying Saucer Bureau (BFSB) was set up as an offshoot of the American group founded by Albert K. Bender; it survives today as the oldest UFO body in Britain, although now reduced to a small local team in the Bristol area under the auspices of a rather subdued elder statesman of ufology, Graham Knewstub. The BFSB is also now associated with the main national group, the British UFO Research Association (BUFORA).

The other consequence was that the covert investigation of UFOs began at the level of the Air Ministry (later to become part of MoD).

During 1954 and 1955 **contactees** appeared and promptly flourished in Britain as they had already done in the United States. George Adamski's book *Flying Saucers Have Landed* (1953) was coauthored by an Irish ufologist, Desmond Leslie.

Leslie also had a part in the launching of one of the world's most famous UFO publications, *Flying Saucer Review* (*FSR*). After 35 years it survives under the editorship of linguistics expert and longtime ufologist Gordon Creighton, although its sometimes wild speculations and uncritical acceptance of questionable reports have caused its reputation to decline. *FSR* was at its peak under the 20-year stewardship of editor Charles Bowen, who preceded Creighton.

The mid-1950s also saw the arrival of alien-contact encounters (which in time would be called close encounters of the third kind) with the great October 1954 European wave spilling over into Britain. Best known is the Ranton, Staffordshire, case of Jessie Roestenberg and her children who observed what were later to become the classic British entities: blond-haired, blue-eyed and fair-skinned.

On the contactee front, a London chauffeur, George King, claimed a visit from aliens. Soon he was taking trips into space and receiving telepathic messages from Jesus on Venus. Soon an occult religious group, the Aetherius Society (Aetherius being one of the invisible alien spirits), was spreading King's teachings. The society is now a leading element of the contactee movement. Today a global organization with a strong base in Britain, it continues to generate extraordinary levels of publicity. Although the group's members conduct no investigations of UFO reports and are not ufologists at all, the mainstream media still present them as typical of people who believe in the existence of UFOs.

Another significant event was the publication, in 1954, of *Flying Saucer from Mars* by the pseudonymous Cedric Allingham, a book purporting to describe a 1954 conversation with a Martian who landed in a UFO. The book was enthusiastically embraced by contactee-oriented persons, although "Allingham" remained curiously elusive. Subsequent research, undertaken in the early 1980s, has shown that the book was a hoax—still unadmitted—by a prominent television personality and popular-science writer known today for his emotional debunking of UFOs.

UFOs in the 1960s: During the next decade, which has been termed the "dark ages of ufology," good cases occurred but many were subject to government secrecy or not widely reported in the increasingly skeptical British media. The encounters at several RAF bases in East Anglia, especially Lakenheath, on the night of August 13-14, 1956, were especially important because they included both radar and visual observations. Their influence on the decision of the British government to continue UFO monitoring was substantial.

In 1962 BUFORA became incorporated by the agreement of a number of older local groups, including the London UFO Research Organization (LUFORO) and Direct Investigation Group Into Aerial Phenomena (DIGAP) in Lancashire. BUFORA commenced a slow process of trying to coordinate effective investigation throughout Britain. The country, though geographically small,

BRITISH UFOLOGY (*continued*)

has a high population density, and in a subject where there are so many differing motivations for involvement, grand personality clashes were inevitable, and quarrels between local groups for the few reported cases all ensued. The groups had widely divergent methods and attitudes about ufology and so heated clashes became a common occurrence.

October 1967 brought the biggest wave of UFO activity Britain had ever seen. Police officers chased a cross-shaped light across the skies in Devon and Cornwall. (In later years UFO investigators would conclude this incident was precipitated by a misidentification of the planet Venus.) Warminster in Wiltshire was the home of UFO spotters from all over the world as readers flocked there to see "the thing" made famous in the somewhat gullible books of local journalist Arthur Shuttlewood.

Meanwhile debate raged in the Houses of Parliament. It was revealed that the MoD, insistent that UFO sightings were no defense threat, carried out routine destruction of all files at five-year intervals. Because of the public concern the 1967 wave had generated, this practice was ordered to cease immediately and reports (coming in at the rate of a few hundred a year) were to remain indefinitely stored. The order remains in effect. So 1962 is the earliest year for which records are retained. These will not be made public until 1992.

From the public's point of view, relatively little was to change over the next several years. Every now and then the media rediscovered UFOs, but generally speaking, the responsible press accepted MoD's assurances of the subject's lack of importance and it hardly ever mentioned sightings. Few books on UFOs (beyond the occasional American import) were published in Britain. When domestically-produced books did appear, they were usually the eccentric writings of aristocrat Brinsley le Poer Trench (Lord Clancarty) whose speculations led him to theorize that God was an astronaut and that an advanced

civilization exists inside a hollow earth.

New Trends for the 1970s: Within ufology, however, new trends were developing, albeit slowly. Out of the rebellious university counterculture that permeated British society in the 1960s and early 1970s (spawning, among other things, the Monty Python comedy team) came a neoufology magazine first called the *Merseyside UFO Bulletin* and later **Magonia**. *Magonia* originally championed the "new ufology" of **John A. Keel** and **Jacques Vallee**, then went beyond it to argue that the UFO phenomenon might well be the product of psychology, sociology and gullibility. (Subsequently this view, which a number of other ufologists in other countries would endorse, would be called the **psychosocial hypothesis**.) By criticizing groups, investigation methods, and theoretical writings, and by churning out complex (often largely incomprehensible) articles from its small team of erudite writers, it achieved one important thing. It made a new generation of British ufologists reexamine basic conceptions and recognize the fundamental importance of investigatory skills. If the raw data of ufology are unreliable and contaminated with ufologists' biases, then ufology rests on a shaky foundation indeed.

In 1973, when **Jenny Randles** became an active ufologist and a BUFORA investigator, she conferred with others who lived in the north of England and attempted to bring some order to the chaos.

BUFORA was heavily focused on London and the southeast and had few members north of Birmingham. So Randles and her associates created something unique in world ufology: a sort of union. As many of the small local groups as they could persuade were encouraged to join the Northern UFO Network (NUFON) and yet retain their total autonomy. NUFON operated (and still does operate) without any governing body or rules. It serves merely as a community, rather like the United Nations, which offers a common database for sighting reports, a communal publication outlet (*Northern UFO News*), now published as a news resource in a monthly sequence with a more issues-and-debate-oriented journal titled, after the ancient British name for the northern kingdom, *UFO Brigantia*.

In due course the NUFON alliance and BUFORA coordinated their efforts and worked to improve investigative standards. NUFON and BUFORA choose cases worthy of in-depth evaluation, putting aside the earlier practice of simply logging every report that came in. They also took a new look at the largely-neglected problem of IFOs—identified flying objects. This new breed of ufologists might even seem like debunkers to those from a past era, but their view is that the case for UFOs can be made only if investigators are properly skeptical and cautious.

Britain has also begun to publish UFO literature at an impressive rate. Peter Warrington and Randles were contracted to write *UFOs: A British Viewpoint* after they challenged the publisher (Robert Hale) about the dreadful quality of its previous imported UFO books and suggested a rebellious approach which was termed an "honest look at what the UFO subject really is, not what people wish it to be." They caught the mood of the nation and the book was successful enough to lead to a new dawn of hard-hitting UFO writings from British authors (although most of this considerable output has never been published outside the home market).

The skeptical approach to UFO investigation has been applied as a matter of course by most newcomers, weaned on these books. The first British abductions, for instance—those at Aveley, Essex (1974, although reported first in 1978), and Todmorden, Yorkshire (1980)—have received endless incisive discussion. In Britain there are still those who favor the extraterrestrial hypothesis (ETH) of UFO origin, but they are in a minority. In Britain even those who declare that *all* sightings can be explained get a sympathetic hearing even from those who disagree with them. In fact, these naysayers are closer to the British ufological mainstream than the ETH proponents, who tend to form their own subculture. The champion of this group is Timothy Good, whose *Above Top Secret* (1987) was the best-selling UFO

title of the decade. There is also the Yorkshire UFO Society (YUFOS), which is never afraid to rebuke anything or anyone it does not agree with.

Recent Developments: The rise in public support for ufology has less to do with sober UFO study than with the rise of the tabloid newspapers. The equivalents of these in the United States are the likes of the *National Enquirer* and *Weekly World News*. The difference is that in Britain such publications are the national dailies read around the breakfast tables by over half the population. They regularly cover the most outlandish UFO stories and ceaselessly pursue new angles to better rivals in the circulation war.

Officially the Ministry of Defense continues to receive reports from all Coast Guard units, police stations and airports and now has over 20,000 cases on file. The alleged incidents at RAF Woodbridge and Bentwaters in December 1980, when U.S. Air Force officers encountered UFOs and where physical traces were left behind, were seminal. Through persistent inquiry and use of the Freedom of Information Act, American ufologists were able to secure documentation, proving both the occurrence and its puzzling nature. But the story died for most serious people in Britain when the tabloid press made huge capital out of it. Since any UFO tale the tabloids promote is treated as highly suspect by the more restrained media, the revelations did not inspire massive public demands for the truth or crusading journalists' probes. Instead a few stray facts were strung together in a wholly unconvincing way and the case was dismissed as a joke. Sadly, this trend shows little sign of disappearing and the arrival of the *Sunday Sport* in 1988 has only made matters worse.

The *Sport* was in desperate trouble in its attempt to be an outrageously sensationalistic newspaper until it discovered that it could sell copies by publishing ridiculous UFO tales under the pretext that they were true and were endorsed by British ufologists. Circulation soared.

Typical of the yarns is one about a boy turned into an olive by alien ray guns and promptly eaten

BRITISH UFOLOGY *(continued)*

with a martini by the investigating police officer. Thanks to such material and the counter-reaction of the more "serious" tabloids, British press coverage of ufology has risen dramatically. Between 1982 and 1986 there was a total of 1464 stories on the subject (roughly 300 a year). In the three years since, over 2100 have appeared, more than twice the previous level of attention. Yet little of this has reflected favorably on the subject and serious ufologists continue mostly to be ignored.

Despite all this some progress has been made. Britain has been at the forefront of research into "natural" UFOs, or earthlights. In 1982 Paul Devereux published his book *Earth Lights* which contended that geophysical processes in the rocks at a location could give rise to all manner of strange reports. Various research projects followed and a more persuasive treatment, *Earth Lights Revelation*, also written by Devereux, appeared in 1989 with input from other ufologists and scientists.

At the same time extensive research has been carried out into mysterious circular marks which have turned up in cereal fields throughout Britain since 1980. The media and the ETH supporters (notably *FSR*) have proposed that alien spacecraft are to blame. BUFORA has been working closely with professional physicists and meteorologists, mostly Terence Meaden, editor of the *Journal of Meteorology*. A unique jointly-funded research institute was one of the fruits of this liaison. The outcome is a novel theory to explain the circles, involving a rotating column of air generating an intense local ionized plasma. This hypothesis, if valid, has major implications for many other aspects of ufology.

There is a danger, however, that such work will be spoiled by those who want it to explain too much, namely every facet of the UFO phenomenon. In fact, the very existence of these two independent research streams suggests that the phenomenon is not a single field of endeavor. If anything, this is the one major contribution that

modern-day British ufology has made. Perhaps the term "UFO" encapsulates an assortment of different phenomena. Some may have a great deal to do with human perception or abnormal psychological states. Others are clearly physical and may be the product of one or more novel natural phenomena currently on the fringes of accepted science. Indeed the phrase "UAP" (for unidentified atmospheric phenomenon) is now in regular use within British ufology to illustrate this recognition that some UFOs are not considered even remote contenders for extraterrestrial origin.

The **abduction phenomenon** is present in the United Kingdom, but it could by no means be said that abduction fever had gripped Britain in the 1980s. Twelve fully-studied abduction cases exist but there is no deluge of new cases in the wake of *Communion* or *Intruders*. Both of these books were published in Britain but predictably received a limited and more skeptical response than in their native United States. Clearly they have not had the impact on the psyche of the nation that they have had in the United States.

The best ufologists in Britain are still undecided as to whether any cases (even abductions) are the results of a truly alien phenomenon. Ideas about altered states of consciousness (as suggested by **Hilary Evans**) and hallucinations triggered by energy emitted from unusual natural phenomena (Devereux) receive at least as much attention as do theories of alien motivation. But the economy of the extraterrestrial solution for some of the data is still recognized. For the future it is easy to predict how British ufology will develop.

There will be no sudden changes in approach. Skepticism will still dominate but the nagging suspicion that alien intelligences may be responsible for at least some UFO reports will continue to bedevil all brave efforts to wish the UFOs out of popular mythology.

Jenny Randles

Sources:

Evans, Hilary. *Visions, Apparitions, Alien*

Visitors. Wellingborough, Northamptonshire, England: The Aquarian Press, 1984.

Good, Timothy. *Above Top Secret: The Worldwide UFO Cover-up*. New York: William Morrow and Company, Inc., 1988.

Randles, Jenny, and Peter Warrington. *UFOs: A British Viewpoint*. London: Robert Hale, 1979.

Spencer, John, and Hilary Evans. *Phenomenon: Forty Years of Flying Saucers*. New York: Avon Books, 1989.

Trench, Brinsley le Poer. *The Sky People*. London: Neville Spearman, 1960.

BRYANT, LARRY W. (1938-)

Larry W. Bryant has been interested in UFOs since he was 19 years old. His special interest has been in what he calls the "politics of ufology": the policies the U.S. government pursues concerning UFO matters. In the late 1970s he helped found **Citizens Against UFO Secrecy** (CAUS) and now directs its Washington, D.C., office from his home in Alexandria, Virginia. Bryant has sued agencies of the U.S. government on several occasions in an unsuccessful effort to get them to own up to classified UFO information, including that related to crashed discs and recovered alien bodies.

In 1987 one of Bryant's cases went all the way to the Supreme Court. Two years earlier, his employer, the U.S. Army (Bryant works professionally as an associate editor of the Army News Service), gave him a low job-performance rating, in sharp contrast to previous high ratings. Bryant believed he was being punished for his placing of ads in military newspapers seeking to encourage UFO whistle-blowers. When Bryant placed one such ad in the Fort Dix, New Jersey, newspaper about a 1978 incident in which a humanoid being allegedly had been shot and killed at the base, the publisher complained to Bryant's superiors. Not long afterwards a Pentagon official, Col. Douglas H. Rogers, urged Bryant to be more discreet. Bryant went ahead and tried to place an ad in the Fort Rucker, Alabama, post newspaper soliciting information about the **Cash-Landrum CE2**, offering $1000 to anyone who could provide "verifiable evidence/testimony leading to the identity and testimony of the organization(s) and aviators associated with the score or so tandem-rotor helicopters seen maneuvering around the huge, radiant UFO on the night of December 19, 1980, near Dayton, Texas" (*CAUS Washington Report*, 1985). The testimony would help, the ad said, in a "UFO-related-injury damage suit" against the government. The base refused the ad and when Bryant protested, one of his superiors called him in for a performance-counseling session and then produced a letter threatening an end-of-the-year "unsatisfactory" job rating. "They said I was an embarrassment," Bryant related (McClain, 1989).

Lower courts ruled that Bryant had no constitutional right to sue his employer, but in an October 1987 decision the Supreme Court disagreed, saying that Bryant had a right to a new trial. At a new trial in Alexandria Bryant lost, this time on the grounds that he had failed to prove his case. But by 1989 Bryant's job rating was back to excellent.

Bryant was born on February 26, 1938, in Shenandoah, Virginia, and grew up in Newport News. He attended the College of William and Mary in Williamsburg, Virginia. He became a federal employee in May 1958 and now works as a writer-editor in the Pentagon. He sees himself as "something on the order of the Ralph Nader of ufology or, perhaps, the I. F. Stone of ufology. . . . But not, mind you, the Paul Revere of ufology" (Bryant, 1989).

Sources:

Bryant, Larry W. Personal communication (October 1, 1989).

McClain, Buzz. "Alexandria Man Gets UFOric About His CAUS." *Alexandria Journal* (August 25, 1989).

BRYANT, LARRY W. (*continued*)

"Pentagon Retaliates Against Army Employee's Pursuit of Crashed-Saucer Records." *CAUS Washington Report* (December 1985): 1-4.

BULLARD, THOMAS EDDIE (1949-)

Thomas E. Bullard, a folklorist and one of the most widely respected figures in ufology, is best known as the author of a massive comparative analysis of abduction reports, the two-volume *UFO Abductions: The Measure of a Mystery* (1987), based on a study financed by the **Fund for UFO Research**. *UFO Abductions* is the only rigorously objective book-length examination of this contro-versial phenomenon ever published. Bullard's Ph.D. dissertation was titled *Mysteries in the Eyes of the Beholder* (1982) and examined UFO pheno-mena from a folkloric point of view. He also compiled *The Airship File* (1982), a comprehensive collection of late-nineteenth-century and early-twentieth-century newspaper articles reporting apparent UFO sightings. His articles on the **abduction phenomenon** and other UFO questions have appeared in *Flying Saucer Review, MUFON UFO Journal, Magonia, International UFO Reporter*, and *Journal of American Folklore*.

Born in North Carolina in 1949, Bullard received his undergraduate degree from the University of North Carolina at Chapel Hill and his masters and Ph.D. (1982) in folklore studies from Indiana University.

Over his years of research, Bullard developed an opinion frequently encountered among ufologists—an underlying "faith" that UFO reports can be explained in a conventional manner juxtaposed beside a well-considered conclusion that some cannot. Reflecting on his research, he says, "One conclusion I feel certain about is the absence of anything unknown during the airship waves. Here is a cautionary tale to show that people can believe they saw something out of the ordinary, when in fact they saw only Venus or fire balloons. The power of social and cultural expectation to influence reports is beyond doubt, and I suspect that most UFO reports can be explained this way. Yet like **J. Allen Hynek**, I cannot dismiss that residuum of detailed, well-observed, well-investigated reports that continue to stand despite all efforts to explain them.

"Abductions belong to this category, but they combine a bedeviling mixture of implausible, surrealistic elements with seemingly physical events. As a folklorist, I am impressed by the many parallels between abductions and fairylore, shamanic initiations, near-death experiences and the like. I could easily conclude that these parallels 'prove' a common and probably psychological origin. But as a folklorist, I am also impressed by the consistency of the accounts, even when variation is the hallmark of folklore. If parts of a story can vary, they probably will. The parts in an abduction story do not, so I have little confidence that these narratives belong to oral tradition.

"My personal faith is that abductions are probably psychological in origin, but the evidence I have seen—the consistencies, physical evidence, multiple-witness cases—leave me with no choice but an objective event for the answer. The explanation of extraterrestrial activity serves the evidence well enough in most cases, so I have to give this explanation serious consideration. Questions of the ultimate nature and purpose of these visitations hold only secondary interest to me, as long as the answers rely on speculation rather than evidence for their substance. Piling one mystery on top of another just doesn't appeal to me, and I prefer the less imaginative course of following the evidence where it leads, with only short excursions beyond it."

Sources:

Boyd, Robert D. *International Who's Who in Ufology Directory*. Mobile, AL: The Author, 1988.

Bullard, Thomas E. "The American Way: Truth, Justice and Abduction." *Magonia* 34 (October 1989): 3-7.

Bullard, Thomas E. "How to Make an Alien." *International UFO Reporter* 14, 6 (November/December 1989): 10-16.

Bullard, Thomas E. "The Mechanization of UFOs." *International UFO Reporter* 13, 1 (January/February 1988): 8-12.

Bullard, Thomas E. *Mysteries in the Eyes of the Beholder: UFOs and Their Correlates as a Folkloric Theme Past and Present.* Bloomington: Indiana University, Ph.D. dissertation, 1982.

Bullard, Thomas E. *On Stolen Time: A Summary of a Comparative Study of the UFO Abduction Mystery*, Bloomington, IN: The Author, 1987.

Bullard, Thomas E. "UFO Abduction Reports: The Supernatural Kidnap Narrative Returns in Technological Guise." *Journal of American Folklore* 102 (1989): 147-70.

Bullard, Thomas E. *UFO Abductions: The Measure of a Mystery. Vol. 1: Comparative Study of Abduction Reports. Vol. 2: Catalogue of Cases.* Mount Rainier, MD: Fund for UFO Research, 1987.

Bullard, Thomas E. "Waves." *International UFO Reporter* 13, 6 (November/December 1988): 15-23.

Bullard, Thomas E., ed. *The Airship File: A Collection of Texts Concerning Phantom Airships and Other UFOs Gathered from Newspapers and Periodicals Mostly During the Hundred Years Prior to Kenneth Arnold's Sighting.* Bloomington, IN: The Author, 1982.

C

CANADIAN UFOLOGY

Throughout the history of ufology, Canada has played a significant role. One of the largest countries in the world, it shares a border with the United States and therefore, in most fields, the two nations are thought of as one. Even in ufology, however, the struggle for a distinct Canadian identity is apparent.

Because of the nature of the land, most of Canada's population live within a few hundred kilometers of the United States. The rest of Canada is sparsely populated. For this reason, despite its size, Canada has far fewer UFO reports than one might expect.

Like its neighboring government to the south, the Canadian government denies having any official interest in UFO reports. But as has happened in the United States, various individuals have successfully tracked down many documents which testify to the collecting of information about UFOs, witnesses and investigators. The primary security agency in Canada is the Royal Canadian Mounted Police (RCMP). Because Canada is not broken into counties or small districts, the RCMP are involved both locally and nationally in criminal investigations. Recently another security service, the Canadian Security Information Service (CSIS), was created. The role of CSIS is not entirely clear and there have been numerous reports of jurisdictional battles between CSIS and the RCMP. The RCMP and CSIS are roughly the equivalent of the FBI and the CIA. Canada also has the equivalent of the supersecret National Security Agency, called the Communications Security Establishment (CSE).

We do not know exactly what role the RCMP, CSIS and CSE play in official UFO investigations. It is known that the RCMP do cooperate with the National Research Council (NRC) of Canada in the investigation of "nonmeteoric" objects seen in the sky. The NRC has had a long interest in meteors and the recovery of meteorites, and this policy has allowed for the collection of data about certain kinds of nocturnal lights. Both "meteoric" and "nonmeteoric" sightings are telexed to NRC headquarters in Ottawa and filed there. Any report that is clearly not of a meteor is filed and officially ignored. No further investigations are normally made.

A typical breakdown of Canadian UFO reports received by the NRC during any one year is as follows: 50 percent from Ontario and Quebec; 25 percent from British Columbia and Alberta; 15 percent from Manitoba and Saskatchewan; and 10 percent from all other provinces. Between 50 and 100 "nonmeteoric sighting" reports are filed each year.

The First UFO Sightings: Historically, Canada had one of the first official projects about UFOs. In December 1950 the Department of Transport formally introduced Project Magnet, under the direction of radio engineer Wilbert B. Smith. One of the most controversial claims has Smith detecting UFOs with the use of specialized equipment at a UFO-detection station near Shirley Bay, Ontario, in 1954. Soon after, Project Magnet

CANADIAN UFOLOGY (*continued*)

was shut down, and government spokesmen asserted that Smith did his UFO research only in his spare time and without the full sanction of the Department of Transport. But a parallel project was underway as well.

Project Second Storey was set up in April 1952, under the direction of Omand Solandt of the Defense Research Board. Its stated purpose was to study investigation procedures related to UFO study, but after only five official meetings Second Storey seemed to cease to exist, although some classified documents which were later released show that Second Storey was to continue in some form indefinitely. In 1989 Dr. Solandt would state, "We never found anything that even suggested the existence of a UFO." To date, however, the existence of any official Canadian project beyond about 1954 has not been verified.

A number of important UFO cases have taken place in Canada. One of the most prominent occurred on September 1, 1974, near Langenburg, Saskatchewan. While swathing rapeseed one morning, farmer Edwin Fuhr saw a dome-shaped object sitting in his field. Initially he thought it was some kind of duck blind or someone's idea of a practical joke. He dismounted from his tractor and walked to within a few feet of the object. It was shiny, metallic, revolving and hovering a few inches above the ground. He went back to his tractor and from his perch saw four more objects nearby. After several minutes the objects rose up one at a time and were soon lost in the clouds. The circular landing traces which remained were investigated in great detail, but no full explanations were forthcoming.

On November 11, 1975, the Canadian Forces Radar Station at Falconbridge, near Sudbury, Ontario, was buzzed by several unidentified objects. Four officers observed the objects and took photographs. Some hours later jets were scrambled from the U.S. Air Force base at nearby Selfridge, Michigan. Reporters were later told that the photographs were never taken and that the sightings were attributable to Venus and reflections off high cirrus clouds.

One of the few Canadian cases investigated by the University of Colorado UFO project, usually called the Condon Committee after its head, physicist Edward U. Condon, was the Falcon Lake incident. On May 20, 1967, Stefan Michalak was engaged in some amateur prospecting in eastern Manitoba when he observed two disc-shaped objects. One landed on a rock outcropping about 150 feet from him. After watching it for a few minutes, he walked up to the craft, which shortly took off with a blast of hot gas which set his clothes on fire. The resulting pattern of burns on his body was studied by physicians and other investigators. The site was found to have some radioactive contamination; samples subsequently taken from the site remain radioactive today. The Condon Committee declared the case "unexplained."

The Decade of the 1980s: The 1980s have been a dramatic decade in Canadian UFO history. Some remarkable reports from this period have been investigated and entered into the literature.

Near Kamloops, British Columbia, on May 16, 1981, a fisherman heard a noise "like water being poured into a frying pan." About 100 yards away the river's surface roiled and a saucer-shaped object rose out of the water and flew away. As it soared overhead, pelletlike material rained down from the sky. Some of the material was collected and analyzed, with inconclusive results.

In October of the same year, Hannah McRoberts, near Eve River on Vancouver Island, decided to take a picture of a distant mountain. When the photograph was developed, a shiny metallic object was clearly visible.

But certainly the strangest story from British Columbia is the tale of Granger Taylor. Taylor, a resident of Vancouver Island, was considered something of an eccentric. In October 1980 he confided to a friend that he was in mental contact with an alien force from another galaxy; he had recurring dreams in which the aliens were inviting him to board their spacecraft. The dreams inspired him to build his own flying saucer in his backyard (it was made out of two satellite dishes). He furnished the "saucer" and often slept inside it. In November a storm struck the island and when it ended, Taylor was gone. He left a note to his parents telling them that he was going on board the spaceship and would not be back. They have not heard from him, and he has not been seen since. A decade later his fate remains unknown.

The early 1980s saw a rash of alleged cattle mutilations in Alberta. Investigators claimed that some of these incidents were linked to UFOs, but the RCMP were convinced that satanic cults were responsible. In the same province "spooklights" have been reported, among them the Tabor light near Nanton. As recently as January 1988 the RCMP were asked to investigate reports of the bobbing phenomenon. A photograph of an unusual light was taken by a witness in Edmonton on August 16, 1980. Investigators were unable to explain the light, which at first was thought to be Venus. That planet, however, was not visible at the time of the sighting.

Near Stony Plain, Alberta, on June 25, 1987, a number of pilgrims at a religious shrine reported a "miracle." Dozens of persons claimed to have watched the sun spin and dance during a ceremony.

That same year a nocturnal light buzzed Stony Rapids, Saskatchewan, and a "missile-shaped" object flew over the town of Ardil. But the most significant Saskatchewan sighting of the 1980s took place on March 15, 1988. At the Port of Entry on the U.S./Canada border near Estevan, seven persons, including two customs officers and a policeman, observed a silver, cylindrical object come within 200 yards of the customs building. It hovered at an altitude of about 150 feet for a few minutes, then headed into the northeast. Investigations determined that no balloon launches had occurred that evening.

In Manitoba spooklights were seen at Woodridge and Sperling. A number of photographs were taken. In 1985 the RCMP at Dauphin responded to a UFO report by sending out several cruisers. Officers observed several objects and gave chase at speeds over 100 mph. Subsequently investigators concluded that the "UFOs" were Venus and a bright star. In 1982 a Springfield woman awoke early one morning to see an object resembling an "upside-down washtub" resting in her yard. Bright lights were shining from the object and it made an eerie noise. It left no traces in the yard.

In 1987 two major sightings were reported in the province. Early one morning in January a man driving toward Lorette found that a cross-shaped object was keeping pace with his car. When they approached the town, the object veered up and away from the houses. But when the man got near his house, he saw the object approaching him once again. After moving toward him whenever he tried to enter the house, the object, apparently tiring of the game, finally departed. In July a priest driving near Carberry saw an "emergency vehicle" move onto the road ahead of him. The "van" was totally black but with three parallel stripes of small red lights running over the top of its body at the front, middle and rear. It was only when the priest tried to pass the strange vehicle that he realized it had no wheels, windows, chrome or lights upon its surface. When his car got within a few feet of the "van," the object vanished into thin air.

During the week before the San Jose, California, earthquake in October 1989, nocturnal lights were reported near Winnipeg. Michael Persinger, whose tectonic strain theory (TST) has caused much controversy in ufology, has claimed that the Winnipeg UFOs were related to the West Coast earthquake, despite the 1500 miles separating the two locations.

With the largest population of any Canadian province, Ontario has the most UFO sightings reported. Southern Ontario boasts many reports and these are noted by the several UFO organizations there. Mystery lights are often seen near Niagara-on-the-Lake, and nocturnal lights are frequently observed over the Great Lakes. In June 1980 a silver saucer was observed over

CANADIAN UFOLOGY (*continued*)

Milton. It appeared to hover in a stationary position in the sky and was seen by a number of persons.

Probably the most important Ontario sighting took place far from populated areas. On May 16, 1987, a Canadian Airlines 737 was en route from Toronto to Winnipeg north of Thunder Bay when a large object appeared on its radar scopes. The object was calculated to be about 80 kilometers away from the plane, with a relative speed of over 5200 kilometers an hour. It remained on the radar for over four minutes; the radar return was noted by all crew members, who had never seen anything like it before. Nothing was seen visually due to bad weather conditions in the area, but the flight crew was convinced that some physical object had been tracked. The size of the object was thought to have been "several times the size of a DC-10." This was reminiscent of the **JAL sighting** only a few months earlier on the Yukon/Alaska border.

Because of language difficulties, little communication exists between Anglophone and Quebecois ufologists. Consequently only a limited amount of news about Quebec UFO sightings makes its way into English Canada, and no spectacular sightings are known to have been reported in the 1980s. Similarly, though English is the principal language of the Maritimes, no sightings of note were made in this past decade.

After a long quiet period western Canada experienced a major wave during the fall of 1989. Localized flaps occurred in British Columbia, Saskatchewan and Manitoba in mid-October. On the 10th UFOs were reported at Dawson Creek, British Columbia; Langenburg, Saskatchewan; and Winnipeg, Manitoba. Around this time a daylight close encounter with a disc-shaped object reportedly occurred in Langenburg. That same week saw over a dozen reports from southern Manitoba. The sightings coincided with the Draconid meteor shower, though many of the reports were not of meteors, if witnesses' descriptions are to be taken seriously.

The last significant claimed UFO event of the 1980s occurred in Kenora, Ontario, at 11:30 p.m. on November 19. A number of persons living on the east side of town reported unusual electrical activity. Telephones would ring and when answered emit only a buzzing sound. Burglar and fire alarms sounded and lights flashed on and off. These occurrences reportedly occurred at the same time that an orange-reddish glow was observed in some trees. Police switchboards were flooded with calls, and the fire department confirmed that there were many electrical problems that night. According to at least one report, the glow "pulsated," causing house lights to flash to fade and brighten in time with the pulsation.

On the 24th Ufology Research of Manitoba (UFOROM) contacted Ontario Hydro, which stated there had been a power break east of Kenora in the Jaffray-Melick area. It was suspected that high winds blew a branch into a transmission line and created the break. The surges occurred during the time the system was trying to correct itself before going offline. Ontario Hydro theorized that these surges were responsible for the behavior of the phones and alarm systems, though it acknowledged that only local service would have been affected. Linemen were sent out in the early morning hours of the 20th and they found and closed the problem circuit by approximately 2 a.m.

It is likely that the glows and flashing in the trees were due to the electrical shorting of the circuits. A sighting made by a motorist heading east toward Kenora at 9:30 on the evening of the 19th was probably of a star, most likely Sirius.

Canadian Ufologists: For its size Canada has few investigators and researchers. Usually a province has only one ufologist, if any. Frequently sightings are made hundreds of miles away from the nearest investigator. (The exception to this rule is southern Ontario, which is densely populated compared to the rest of the country.) This makes investigation a challenge and unfortunately disallows proper study of some cases when travel is prohibitive. Nevertheless a number of researchers have made important contributions.

John Magor of British Columbia remains active, although he no longer publishes his magazine *Canadian UFO Report*. His second book, *Aliens Above, Always*, was published in 1983. Recently an abductee support group was formed in British Columbia. Graham Conway is also working in the area. Newcomers Michael Strainic, Rob Bennett and Lorne Goldfeather have all received a fair amount of attention in the province as UFO investigators.

In the 1970s John Brent Musgrave received a grant from the Canadian government to study UFO cases, and his report makes fascinating reading. An astronomer by profession, Musgrave has continued to be active in the 1980s and late in the decade he moved to Slave Lake, Alberta.

Photojournalist Douglas Curran's widely-reviewed *In Advance of the Landing: Folk Concepts of Outer Space* was published in 1985. Curran left his home in Edmonton to travel through North America in search of those who dreamed of extraterrestrial life, and flying-saucer **contactees** and their groups figure prominently in this highly readable narrative.

Until 1988 Saskatchewan had an excellent investigator in Tim Tokaryk, an archaeologist living in Regina. Tokaryk left ufology to devote more time to his main field of interest, and the province is now without an investigator. But recently Laurie Vassos, a medical practitioner in Saskatoon, has been examining subjects who are abductees and treating them with hypnotic regression.

Manitoba, which borders Saskatchewan, boasts several notable ufologists. Grant R. Cameron is best known for his recent work on claimed **crashes of UFOs** and for his investigation of the life of Wilbert Smith. In fact, Cameron has been investigating UFOs since the 1970s and has been instrumental in studies of Manitoba UFO incidents. He is currently working with American ufologist T. Scott Crain on a book tentatively titled *UFOs, MJ-12 and the Government*.

Chris Rutkowski, active in Manitoba ufology

since 1974, is known for, besides his case investigations, his critical writing on Persinger's tectonic strain theory. He has written numerous articles for various UFO magazines and is a contributing editor to **International UFO Reporter**, a bimonthly periodical published by the **J. Allen Hynek Center for UFO Studies**. In 1989 he published *Visitations?*, a book dealing with Manitoba UFO experiences, including abductions.

Brian James is a Winnipeg graphic designer, and his illustrations can be found in many UFO books from around the world. Although active as an Aerial Phenomena Research Organization (APRO) investigator in the 1970s, he has since preferred to exercise only his drawing skills. Kenneth McCulloch is a retired meteorologist and astronomer living in northern Manitoba. He has had a number of personal sightings and is a familiar face at UFO conferences. His writings include the book *Mankind: Citizen of the Galaxy*, published in 1985. Roy Bauer, Guy Westcott and Walter Nilsson have also investigated UFO reports in the 1980s.

Bauer, Cameron, Nilsson, Rutkowski and Westcott are part of an informal organization known as Ufology Research of Manitoba (UFOROM), which began as a cooperative venture in the 1970s. Also involved in Manitoba ufology is Edward Barker, an artist and producer at the Manitoba Planetarium. He and Ernst Spielman constitute the Manitoba Centre for UFO Studies, which at the time of its inception in the 1970s included Rutkowski and others.

Ontario is rife with ufologists and related researchers. Some of the more active are Joe Muskat, Larry Fenwick and Harry Tokarz, co-directors of the Canadian UFO Research Network (CUFORN), based in Toronto. Founded in 1977, the group is busy with investigations and public programs in the southern part of the province. CUFORN is probably the best-known Canadian UFO group.

An important new figure on the Toronto scene is psychiatrist David A. Gotlib. Professionally Dr. Gotlib specializes in the treatment of depression

CANADIAN UFOLOGY (*continued*)

and anxiety disorders and uses hypnosis in his work. In this capacity he encountered the **abduction phenomenon**. The abductees, he says, "had tried to get help from a number of physicians before coming to me. Those physicians had refused to see them because they were too 'weird' or 'crazy.' At that time I was less interested in their particular experience than the fact that they were obviously in need yet denied medical care in an arbitrary manner." Gotlib eventually met other mental-health professionals with similar experiences and concerns. He was among the 40 to 50 professionals and investigators who helped create **Treatment and Research on Experienced Anomalous Trauma** (TREAT) at a May 1989 conference at Fairfield University in Connecticut. For a few months Gotlib served on the organization's ethics committee but was among those who left the group amid internal conflicts concerning policy and direction. In December 1989 he released the first issue of *Ratchet Patrol: A Monthly Networking Newsletter About Experienced Anomalous Trauma for Interested Scientists*.

Bonnie Wheeler heads the Cambridge UFO Research Group (CUFORG), not far from Toronto. The group publishes a large newsletter and holds regular meetings with guest speakers on a variety of topics. Tom Mickus is a relative newcomer to Canadian ufology but has already placed himself at the forefront of topical research and discussion. He runs a UFO-related computerized bulletin-board service, called UFONET BBS, from his home in Toronto. Arthur Bray, who has been involved in ufology for years, has written two books on the subject. His specialty is document retrievals. He has extensive files. Gene Duplantier, another veteran figure on the UFO scene, operates a mail-order company selling UFO literature out of Toronto.

John Robert Colombo is one of Canada's most prolific writers. Several of his books have dealt with UFOs in some fashion, though he has not been involved in any investigations himself. His most interesting book is *Mysterious Canada* (1988).

Mr. X is the legal name of a Kingston resident once known as Scott Foster. Although more active in the 1970s than he is now, X catalogs anomalous events, including UFO sightings.

Finally, Michael Persinger has probably written more scientific articles about UFOs than anyone else in Canada. Though not well-versed in ufology itself, Persinger advocates the tectonic stress theory which suggests relationships between UFOs and seismic energy. He is the head of the department of physiological psychology at Laurentian University in Sudbury.

Although itself a large province, Quebec has few active ufologists. Two are Claude Macduff and the contactee-oriented Ronald W. J. Anstee. Jean-Claude Dupont is a folklorist who has studied the traditional beliefs of French Canada, including those involving UFOs. He works in the area of Sainte-Foy, Quebec.

Only one active ufologist resides in eastern Canada and the Maritimes. Although an American citizen, **Stanton T. Friedman** now lives in Fredericton, New Brunswick. One of the most popular figures in today's ufology, Friedman, trained as a nuclear physicist and still tied professionally to the discipline, has lectured in every state and province at least once and has appeared on numerous television programs, radio shows and films about UFOs. In 1984 he took the *Globe and Mail*, Canada's national newspaper, before the Ontario Press Council on charges that it published biased and inaccurate information about UFOs in a story that appeared on January 21, 1984. The story, which alleged that UFO sightings have all but disappeared since the 1960s, was, Friedman charged, deliberately "misleading." Moreover, the *Globe*, citing "space limitations," did not print a letter Friedman wrote to correct the error. The *Globe* admitted that "editorially, we take a skeptical view" on UFOs. Friedman's complaint was eventually dismissed by the council. Currently he is involved in research on the MJ-12 briefing document and the Roswell UFO crash.

UFO magazines continue to be published in Canada, though there are fewer titles than there used to be. Currently-existing periodicals include the *CUFORN Bulletin* (Toronto), the *Cambridge UFO Research Group Newsletter* (Cambridge), and *Swamp Gas Journal* (Winnipeg). John Musgrave also sends his own version of a clipping service to interested parties on exchange.

Because of its proximity to the United States, Canada is often put into the category of "American." This can be true in ufology, since Canadians are heavily influenced by media originating from the United States. The reverse is not true, however, and for that reason Canada is largely unknown to its southern neighbors.

When Jim Brandon defined his "Mystery Meridian" in *Weird America* (1978), it was only suspected that it extended northward across the border. The Meridian, between 97 and 98 degrees west longitude, passes through Canada in Manitoba. It traverses Winnipeg, Sperling, Gimli, Thompson and Norway House, all locations that have hosted anomalous events including UFO sightings. This illustrates that in the context of American ufology, care should be taken to include Canada for geographical if not for social reasons.

George M. Eberhart has many listings for Canada in his massive *Geo-Bibliography of Anomalies* published in 1980. Furthermore, it can be pointed out that Canadian cases can be found in most official American UFO projects, including Blue Book and the Condon Report. And it is no secret that Canadian cases are included in the files of Aerial Phenomena Research Organization (APRO), the National Investigations Committee on Aerial Phenomena (NICAP) and the **Mutual UFO Network** (MUFON). This is certainly testimony that Canada and its ufologists play a significant role not only in American ufology but in global UFO study.

Chris Rutkowski

Sources:

Bondarchuk, Yurko. *UFO Sightings, Landings and Abductions: The Documented Evidence.* Toronto: Metheun, 1979.

Colombo, John Robert. *Mysterious Canada: Strange Sights, Extraordinary Events, and Peculiar Places.* Toronto: Doubleday Canada Limited, 1988.

Curran, Douglas. *In Advance of the Landing: Folk Concepts of Outer Space.* New York: Abbeville Press, 1985.

McCulloch, Kenneth C. *Mankind: Citizen of the Galaxy.* The Pas, MB: Rings of Saturn Publishing, 1985.

Magor, John. *Aliens Above, Always: A UFO Report.* Surrey, BC: Hancock House, 1983.

Musgrave, John Brent. *UFO Occupants and Critters: The Patterns in Canada.* New York: Global Communications, 1979.

Rutkowski, Chris A. *Visitations?: Manitoba UFO Experiences.* Winnipeg, MB: Winter Press, 1989.

CASH-LANDRUM CE2

On the evening of December 29, 1980, near Huffman, Texas, three occupants of a 1980 Oldsmobile Cutlass observed a remarkable sight. The witnesses, Betty Cash, Vickie Landrum and Vickie's seven-year-old grandson Colby, were on their way home to Dayton from a meal at a truck stop in nearby New Caney and were driving through the southern tip of the east Texas piney woods when they noticed a large light above the trees some distance ahead. Thinking it was an airplane on its way to Houston International Airport, they paid little attention to it. The light was briefly lost to view, but they saw it again when after rounding a curve they found themselves on a straight stretch of two-lane road on Highway FM 1485. This time it was approaching them, floating above the road at less than treetop height, and in short order it was belching flames from its bottom. Cash and the Landrums were only about 130 feet from the object.

Vickie Landrum, who feared they would be

CASH-LANDRUM CE2 (*continued*)

burned alive, screamed for Betty, who was driving, to stop. As the car slowed, however, Vickie decided they were seeing the Second Coming of Christ. She consoled Colby by assuring him, "That's Jesus. He will not hurt us" (Schuessler, 1988). But Colby was still terrified.

Escape was out of the question because the road was narrow and rain early in the evening had made the shoulders soggy. If Cash tried to turn around, she knew, the car would get stuck. There was no other traffic on the desolate highway, so she stepped outside, as did the elder Landrum. But Colby's frantic screams brought her back into the car. She held him even as she continued to stare at the object ahead of them. Meanwhile Cash stepped to the front of the vehicle, mesmerized by the bizarre sight.

The object, intensely bright and a dull metallic silver in color, was shaped like a huge, upright diamond, about the size of the Dayton water tower, with its top and the bottom cut off so that they were flat rather than pointed. Small blue lights ringed the center and periodically over the next few minutes flames shot out of the bottom, flaring outward to create the effect of a large cone. Every time the flame dissipated, the UFO floated a few feet downward toward the road. But when the flame blasted out again, the object rose about the same distance.

All the while the witnesses felt heat which cut through the chilly evening. The heat was such, in fact, that the women could feel their faces burning. The car was too hot to touch. At one point Vickie Landrum, leaning out the front window, steadied herself by putting her hands on the dashboard, only to find it molded to the shape of her fingers. (The imprints were still there when John Schuessler of the **Mutual UFO Network** [MUFON] examined the car sometime later.) A few minutes later, when Cash tried to get back into the car, the doorhandle burned her fingers and she had to use her leather coat as a hot pad.

With a final blast of fire and heat, the UFO ascended slowly into the sky. But then, just as it cleared the tree tops, helicopters flew in from all directions. The helicopters and the UFO were lost to view and once Cash's eyes got used to the dark again, she started her car and the three resumed their journey. They passed along another long curve in the road and in five minutes arrived at the intersection of FM 1485 and FM 2100, where they saw the UFO and the helicopters again. This time Cash was able to pull off the side of the road and count 23 helicopters, all clearly visible because the light from the diamond-shaped object was reflecting off them. The closest helicopter was not far from them and made a great racket. Many of the aircraft were subsequently identified as large, double-rotor Boeing CH-47 Chinooks, a kind used by the Army and the Marines.

Cash drove on, the diamond and the helicopters still in front of her, until she came to a road that would take them to Dayton. Even then she could see the object in the rearview mirror for the next few minutes. The whole incident—or at least this part of it—lasted a total of 20 minutes.

She dropped the Landrums off at their house and proceeded on to her own, where four friends were waiting. But by this time Cash was feeling sick. She sat in a chair and waited for the feeling to pass, but in the next hours the headache and nausea remained and large knots formed on her neck and scalp. Soon they became blisters. Meanwhile her skin was reddening and her eyes swelled. She threw up repeatedly and experienced severe diarrhea. By morning her friends feared she was about to die.

The Landrums were suffering similar distress, though not quite so intensely. Their skin looked and felt as if it had been badly sunburned, and their stomachs were upset. Over the next days Vickie repeatedly applied baby oil to herself and Colby to alleviate the pain associated with their reddened skin.

Meantime Cash had lapsed into near-unconsciousness. Her friends frantically sought

44

medical help, but the groggy Cash, who had had heart problems in the past, could not identify her cardiologist; so they were forced to call strange physicians. Those they could reach during this holiday period had no interest in taking on an unfamiliar patient with a history of cardiac disorder and, moreover, with a crazy story about having been injured by a UFO.

Knowing of nothing else to do, the friends brought Cash to Vickie Landrum's. Landrum tried to feed Cash, but she rejected food and water and continued to grow weaker. Finally Landrum called a local druggist and persuaded him to look through his prescription records for the name of Cash's cardiologist. As soon as she found out who he was, Landrum phoned and was instructed to take Cash to the Parkway Hospital emergency room right away.

The Betty Cash who was taken into the hospital on January 3, 1981, had lost large patches of skin and large clumps of hair. She could not walk. She was released after 12 days, though her condition was not much better, and she later returned to the hospital for another 15 days. The Landrums improved slightly, though the sores on their skin and the damage to their eyes persisted. Vickie suffered periodic sickness for the next few years and her eyesight never entirely recovered. Colby had problems with chronic illness, sores and hair loss.

A radiologist who reviewed the victims' medical records for MUFON concluded, "We have strong evidence that these patients have suffered damage secondary to ionizing radiation. It is also possible that there was an infrared or ultraviolet component as well" (Schuessler, 1988).

Ufologists learned of the case when the witnesses reported it to a NASA representative in Houston. He suggested they talk with John Schuessler, an aerospace engineer and NASA supervisor with a longstanding interest in UFOs. Schuessler and some MUFON colleagues then interviewed other witnesses, some of whom had seen the UFO and the helicopters for as long as an hour and a half. They also sought the source

of the helicopters. The **Fund for UFO Research** commissioned Allan Hendry, one of ufology's most skilled investigators, to find out where the aircraft had come from. No airport, civilian or military, would own up to knowledge of the helicopters.

Cash and Landrum began a long, frustrating campaign to get answers from government agencies. After getting nowhere with local officials and military installations, they contacted their senators, John Tower and Lloyd Bentsen, who talked with representatives of the Department of Defense. The senators urged Cash and Landrum to take their complaints to the Judge Advocate Claims Officer at Bergstrom AFB in Austin. In August 1981 they met with Air Force lawyers at Bergstrom. They were given blank forms and told that if they could find a lawyer willing to represent them, they should file a claim with the U.S. government for compensation for their injuries. New York attorney Peter Gersten volunteered to help them. The case worked its way through military and federal courts over the next years but got nowhere because the witnesses and Gersten were unable to prove that either the diamond-shaped object or the helicopters were U.S. government property. On August 21, 1986, the U.S. District Court judge dismissed the case, citing expert testimony that no such craft as the UFO the witnesses described existed in the U.S. military arsenal. Nothing was said about the helicopters.

The only known official investigation of any significance was conducted by Lt. Col. George Sarran, whom the Department of the Army Inspector General (DAIG) directed to look into the case in 1982. Sarran interviewed the witnesses and the ufologists who had studied the case, and he tried to determine where the helicopters had come from. No one would admit to knowing anything about them. At the end of his inquiries Sarran concluded, "Ms. Landrum and Ms. Cash were credible. The DAIG investigator felt [four lines censored] . . . the policeman and his wife [who had reported seeing 12 Chinook helicopters in the Huffman area on the night of the incident] were also credible witnesses. There was no perception that anyone was trying to exaggerate the truth.

45

CASH-LANDRUM CE2 (*continued*)

All interviewees were extremely cooperative and eager to be helpful in any manner. Through the course of inquiry the DAIG investigator tried to concentrate on any reason or anyone or organization which might have been flying helicopters that particular evening in that general area. There was no evidence presented that would indicate that Army, National Guard, or Army Reserve helicopters were involved" (Schuessler, 1988).

Meanwhile, according to Schuessler, "Betty Cash has been hospitalized at least 25 times, [and] has had two operations for cancer (after having shown no previous signs of it). She has had blood problems [and] trouble with her eyesight. Her hair has regrown, though in a different texture, but she is still very weak and has to spend a good deal of time in bed" (Schuessler, 1988).

Sources:

Schuessler, John. "Cash-Landrum Case Closed?" *MUFON UFO Journal* 222 (October 1986): 12, 17.

Schuessler, John. "Cash-Landrum UFO Case File: The Issue of Government Responsibility." In Walter H. Andrus, Jr., and Richard H. Hall, eds. *MUFON 1986 Symposium Proceedings*, 175-182. Seguin, TX: Mutual UFO Network, Inc., 1986.

Schuessler, John. "Medical Injuries Resulting from a UFO Encounter." In Mimi Hynek, ed. *The Spectrum of UFO Research: The Proceedings of the Second CUFOS Conference, Held September 25-27, 1981, in Chicago, Illinois*. Chicago: J. Allen Hynek Center for UFO Studies, 1988.

CAVEAT EMPTOR
8 Gate House Lane
Edison, New Jersey 08820

Caveat Emptor folded after publishing 15 issues in the early 1970s. More like a freewheeling science-fiction fan magazine than a UFO periodical, it strayed frequently from its ostensible subject matter to feature often highly-personal ruminations by editor Gene Steinberg and ex-wife-to-be Geneva on occult, political and autobiographical matters. In 1988 Gene Steinberg revived the magazine as a 36-page quarterly in essentially the same format, with his former wife (now Geneva Hagen) as assistant editor and columnist. Now subtitled "A New Age Journal," the magazine covers ufological topics of interest to the editor, but is somewhat removed from current developments in the UFO field, of which Steinberg seems unaware or uninformed. Its focus, now broadly New Age, covers ufology along with a widely divergent literary menu which seems to appeal to editors and loyal readers. Many of these relate to controversies that were raging when the old *Caveat Emptor* was new.

Sources:

Steinberg, Gene. "Editorial: Birth, Death & Resurrection." *Caveat Emptor* 16 (Winter 1988-89): 2-6.

CERGY-PONTOISE (FRANCE) HOAX

At 5 a.m. on November 26, 1979, when a police officer in Pontoise, a Paris suburb, picked up a ringing phone and heard someone exclaim, "A friend of mine's just been carried off by a UFO!" he would be the first victim of France's most notable—and certainly most widely-publicized—UFO hoax. The call brought officers to the apartment of Jean-Pierre Prevost, a 26-year-old who made a none-too-prosperous living selling clothes in street markets.

As the story went, the previous evening Franck Fontaine, an 18-year-old business associate who lived two miles away, had stayed overnight at Prevost's apartment, because the two planned to wake up early in the morning and travel to Gisors, 37 miles away, to secure a good place at the street market there. Another reason to arise early was that they were having trouble with the starter on their car. They woke up at 3:30 and the two, together with Salomon N'Diaye, another business partner who lived in a neighboring apartment, went downstairs to push the car to get its engine going. Once this had been accomplished, Fontaine sat behind the steering wheel and made sure the engine kept running while his two companions brought down the clothing they would be selling and set it inside the car. As this was going on, Fontaine spotted a bright cylindrical light in the sky and Prevost and N'Diaye ran inside to fetch a camera.

Meanwhile Fontaine decided to drive out of the parking lot in hopes of getting another view of the UFO, which had disappeared behind a building. As he entered the street, the engine stopped and a ball of light enveloped the vehicle. The two other men, who had observed this from upstairs, rushed outside, leaving the camera behind, and ran toward the car, now partly swallowed up by the glowing cloud, around which smaller balls of light were moving. All but one of the smaller balls were absorbed into the cloud, which now assumed a cylindrical shape, like that of the UFO observed a few minutes earlier, and shot away, vanishing in the sky. As the two recovered from their shock, they discovered that the door on the driver's side was open and Fontaine had vanished.

While N'Diaye went to call the police, Prevost witnessed the final act of the drama: the remaining ball of light nudged the car door shut. Then it, too, shot away.

After a police interview lasting several hours the two young men phoned Radio-Tele-Luxembourg, which gave their story considerable play and brought it to the attention of the press. Soon accounts of the alleged UFO kidnapping were being reported all over the world.

On December 3, precisely a week after his disappearance, Fontaine returned. First word of his reappearance was from a caller, later identified as N'Diaye, who told Radio Luxembourg that he had seen Fontaine emerge from a ball of light

landed in a cabbage patch along the road on which he had vanished. Fontaine would subsequently claim to have been in a dazed state, thinking he had fallen asleep among the cabbages and not realizing a week had passed. At first he could remember only vague details of the events of the past days, but later memory returned sufficiently to enable him to recall meeting extraterrestrials and spending time in a laboratory.

Because no crime had been committed, the authorities dropped out of the case. Ufologists, journalists and cultists quickly took their place. French ufologists were skeptical, noting numerous discrepancies among "witnesses'" various accounts. For example, the three men, while claiming to know nothing about UFOs, had plenty of immediate exposure to relevant material. The night of the incident French television had run a discussion of the UFO phenomenon, and the magazine *Tele-Poche*, a copy of which was in Prevost's apartment at the same time, was running a picture serial about a man who disappeared after being abducted by aliens. In fact, some of the story the "witnesses" told seemed lifted from this science-fiction tale. Prevost's brother was a local representative of the Aerial Phenomena Research Organization (APRO), based in Tucson, Arizona. Fontaine had seen the film *Close Encounters of the Third Kind* and was interested in occultism.

The UFO group CONTROL monitored the stories the three men told over the next weeks and months, finding numerous contradictions, even in the descriptions of the UFO that supposedly abducted Fontaine. Moreover, a neighbor saw nothing out of the ordinary at the time of the "abduction," just two men who got into a car and drove away. Where Fontaine's return was concerned, two different stories were related, one in which Prevost saw Fontaine emerge from the UFO, the other (which Prevost told to reporter Iris Billon-Duplan) stating that Prevost learned of Fontaine's reappearance when the latter knocked at his door early in the morning.

Although by now it was obvious to any but the most credulous observers that the story was

CERGY-PONTOISE (FRANCE) HOAX
(*continued*)

suspect, in 1980 science-fiction writer Jimmy Guieu rushed into print with a book on the subject. "I hold *a priori* their story to be true," he said. The book, titled (in English translation) *Cergy-Pontoise UFO Contacts*, reported that the true target of the extraterrestrials was not Fontaine (who refused to undergo hypnosis to restore the missing "memories") but Prevost. Accordingly Prevost began to channel messages from the abductors, who identified themselves as *Intelligences du Dehors* (IDDs; in English, "Intelligences from Beyond"). **Hilary Evans** describes Guieu's book as "written in a particularly irritating French manner, rich in rhetorical questions, excited exclamations and sentences ending with a suggestive. . . . And the incidents he relates, even if they start on a just-credible level, soon slide into the utterly bizarre. Jean-Pierre, while his companions are fast asleep, is confronted by three sinister figures, two of them zombies. Jean-Pierre is teleported to a mysterious assignation in Marseilles. Jean-Pierre is taken to a secret rendezvous in a unused railway tunnel in the mountains. Jean-Pierre, not Franck, now occupies center stage" (Evans, 1982).

Later that same year Prevost had his own book out, *The Truth About the Cergy-Pontoise Affair*, which, though barely mentioning Fontaine's abduction, is filled with new stories of extraterrestrial contacts and messages about the sad state of the earth. At one point Prevost writes, revealingly, that "no testimony, no proof, is necessary to diffuse the Truth. . . . What does it matter to know, at the factual level, where real life ends and imagination takes over? Isn't it more important to take into consideration the content of the messages?"

On July 7, 1983, Prevost confessed. He told the newspaper *Le Parisien*, "I confirm that the Cergy affair was a hoax from the beginning to the end. I am the only one to be held responsible. I organized and put together the whole story. . . . Franck Fontaine had spent the eight days of his 'disappearance' in the apartment of a friend in Pontoise. I took him there and brought him back." His motive, Prevost said, was to get "people together and to pass on to them my message. . . . Knowing that people are not interested anymore in traditional religions and that they need some support, I thought of extraterrestrial beings" (Bonabot, 1983). Since the incident Prevost said he had tried without success to create a mystical-religious sect.

In the summer of 1982 Fontaine, the hero of the episode, was sentenced to prison for robbery.

Sources:

Bonabot, Jacques. "1979 Fontaine Case in France Now Admitted to be a Hoax." *MUFON UFO Journal* 190 (December 1983): 10.

Evans, Hilary, with Michel Piccin. "Who Took Who for a Ride?" *Fate* 35, 10 (October 1982): 51-58.

Guieu, Jimmy, Franck Fontaine, Jean-Pierre Prevost, and Salomon N'Diaye. *Contacts OVNI Cergy-Pontoise.* Monaco: Editions du Rocher, 1980.

CITIZENS AGAINST UFO SECRECY
Box 218
Coventry, Connecticut 06238

Citizens Against UFO Secrecy (CAUS) was formed in 1977 by W. Todd Zechel, Brad Sparks and Peter Gersten. The organization's purpose was to uncover government UFO data through the Freedom of Information Act, lawsuits against government agencies, and investigation of reports, especially highly-evidential ones (such as radar sightings, close encounters, and physical-evidence cases), made by military, intelligence and other official personnel. Zechel, the first head of the group, edited a newsletter, *Just Cause*, which detailed new developments. He left the organization in 1980. In June of that year CAUS was reorganized, with Peter Gersten as director and Lawrence Fawcett as assistant director. A short-lived newsletter, *UFORMANT*, prepared by **Larry W. Bryant,** replaced the old *Just Cause.* In 1984 Barry Greenwood revived *Just Cause*, which has continued as a quarterly ever since. Since 1980 CAUS has added seven lawyers to its staff and continues its effort, by legal means and direct investigation, to dislodge government UFO secrets.

Sources:

Bryant, Larry W. *From Within the Blackout: An Analysis of Secrecy on the Local UFO Scene.* Newport News, VA: The Author, 1960.

Bryant, Larry W. *Harry Truman's UFO Americana. CAUS Special Report.* Alexandria, VA: Citizens Against UFO Secrecy, 1985.

Fawcett, Lawrence, and Barry J. Greenwood. *Clear Intent: The Government Coverup of the UFO Experience.* Englewood Cliffs, NJ: Prentice-Hall, Inc., 1984.

COMMITTEE FOR THE SCIENTIFIC INVESTIGATION OF CLAIMS OF THE PARANORMAL
Box 229
Buffalo, New York 14215

The Committee for the Scientific Investigation of Claims of the Paranormal (CSICOP) was formed at an April 30, 1976, meeting of the American Humanist Association, as an effort by intellectuals and academics to combat unorthodox beliefs about extraordinary phenomena including, among many others, UFOs. A year and a half after its formation, co-founder Marcello Truzzi left, complaining that the organization had taken a dogmatic hard-line position, exemplified in the view, repeatedly expressed by chairman Paul Kurtz, that belief in anomalies and the paranormal not only is misplaced but actively threatens civilization. "The list of people and things we challenge is endless," Kurtz told Copley News Service in May 1978. "It includes astrology, Uri Geller, the so-called Bermuda Triangle, thinking ivy plants, yetis

and Loch Ness monsters, biorhythms, Jeane Dixon, ESP and flying saucers. . . . What we have getting started with this new kind of nonsense is the emergence of a new religion of the paranormal," representing a "retreat from the ideals of logic and rationality and a primitive reversion for our technical society. It is leading to the delusion of millions who will be out of touch with the external world. We think that is insidious." CSICOP figures such as James Oberg have compared groups interested in UFOs to the "bizarre irrational . . . cults which preceded the fall of democratic Germany in the 1920s" (Oberg, 1981). Robert Sheaffer, a CSICOP Fellow and a columnist for its magazine, claims that ufology is a "reaction against science and reason" (Sheaffer, 1981).

Among the original members of CSICOP, and now the head of its UFO Subcommittee, is veteran debunker **Philip J. Klass.** The subcommittee's members include Sheaffer and Oberg, both authors of books condemning UFOs and ufologists. Their articles and commentary appear in CSICOP's quarterly *Skeptical Inquirer,* a magazine devoted to often fierce criticism of pro-UFO claims and opinions. Kurtz is president of Prometheus Books, the major publishing outlet for anti-UFO books, including Sheaffer's and Klass'.

Sources:

Clark, Jerome. "Phil Klass vs. the 'UFO Promoters.'" *Fate* 34, 2 (February 1981): 56-67.

Klass, Philip J. *UFO-Abductions, A Dangerous Game.* Buffalo, NY: Prometheus Books, 1988.

Klass, Philip J. *UFOs Explained.* New York: Random House, 1974.

Klass, Philip J. *UFOs–Identified.* New York: Random House, 1968.

Kurtz, Paul. *The Transcendental Temptation: A Critique of Religion and the Paranormal.* Buffalo, NY: Prometheus Books, 1986.

COMMITTEE FOR THE SCIENTIFIC INVESTIGATION OF CLAIMS OF THE PARANORMAL (*continued*)

Oberg, James E. *UFOs and Outer Space Mysteries: A Sympathetic Skeptic's Report.* Norfolk, VA: Donning Company/Publishers, 1981.

Sheaffer, Robert. *The UFO Verdict: Examining the Evidence.* Buffalo, NY: Prometheus Books, 1981.

COMMUNION FOUNDATION
Box 1975
Boulder, Colorado 80306

The Communion Foundation was formed in 1989 by **Whitley Strieber**, author of *Communion: A True Story* (1987) and *Transformation: The Breakthrough* (1988), as a way of dealing with the many letters he received from readers of his books on the **abduction phenomenon** in general and his abduction experiences in particular. "Its main purpose," Strieber says, "is to provide grants for genuine research into the nature of the visitor experience and how best to help people who have had the experience" (Strieber, 1989). Hoping to find the "kind of hard physical evidence that will attract the interest of the best thinkers and scientists to our situation," it has arranged for magnetic resonance imaging scans of persons who believe they have alien implants inside them. It also publishes the quarterly eight-page *Communion Letter*, edited by Dora Ruffner.

The foundation, essentially a New Age group in which the **contactee** message has been grafted onto the abductee experience, takes a positive view of the abduction phenomenon, which UFO investigators and most percipients usually have seen as negative, even traumatic. But in Strieber's view this is the fault of "abduction researchers" who, being out of sympathy with the "visitors'" benevolent mission and out of a desire to "control others," have unnecessarily frightened abductees. He encourages his followers to stay away from ufologists and to form groups in which they can compare experiences and even seek out contact with UFO beings.

Sources:

Klass, Philip J. *UFO-Abductions, A Dangerous Game.* Buffalo, NY: Prometheus Books, 1988.

Strieber, Whitley. *Communion: A True Story.* New York: Beach Tree/William Morrow, 1987.

Strieber, Whitley. "The Communion Foundation Is Formed." *The Communion Letter* 1 (Spring 1989), 6.

Strieber, Whitley. *Transformation: The Breakthrough.* New York: William Morrow and Company, 1988.

CONTACTEE
Box 12
New Milford, New Jersey 07646

Contactee is, in director Ellen Crystall's words, a "loose organization," as much a publication (the quarterly bulletin *Contactee*) as formal group. It calls itself "The First Organization for Research of UFOs by Direct Observation." Crystall's interest in UFO-observing came about in part because of a 1971 close encounter of the third kind she experienced one night in California. Since 1980 she has made regular trips to the Pine Bush, New York, area, often in the company of friends and associates, and there seen many hundreds of what she regards as UFOs: the "full range of sightings," of everything from distant lights to close-up discs. She has taken over 1000 pictures. *Contactee* (which, its title notwithstanding, is not devoted to channeling or contacts with Space Brothers) reports on Crystall's latest adventures and offers tips to UFO hunters.

Sources:

Crystall, Ellen. Interview with Jerome Clark (November 12, 1989).

CONTACTEES

Contactees are individuals who believe, or claim to believe, they are in regular communication with benevolent extraterrestrial intelligences, often referred to as the Space Brothers. The Space Brothers are essentially angels in spacesuits: strikingly handsome or beautiful (there are also ET women, but for some reason the phrase "Space Sisters" has never caught on), usually with longish blond hair and a wise, patient manner. They are here because the earth is something of an outlaw planet whose warlike ways alarm members of the Galactic Federation, an alliance of good ETs who are doing battle against evil forces in the universe, usually represented as unlovely beings such as the big-eyed humanoids who figure in UFO-occupant reports made by noncontactees. The earth is about to undergo vast changes resulting from geological upheaval in which much of the population will be destroyed. Those who survive will enter a golden age under the tutelage of the Space Brothers and their earthly agents, the contactees.

The words "contactee" and "abductee," though sometimes used interchangeably, in fact describe two categories of claimed experience whose only common element is an encounter with extraterrestrials. Contactees are often individuals with a history of involvement with occultism and New Age doctrines. The kinds of UFOs they observe (and sometimes photograph), as well as the UFO occupants they meet, are unlike those reported in noncontactee sightings and encounters. Abductees, in common with other UFO sighters, tend to be more ordinary persons, with little or no previous interest in unorthodox subjects. Unlike many contactees, abductees have not sought out the experience, and again unlike the majority of contactees they are likely to experience fear and trauma because of it. Abductees usually report humanoids who say little about themselves or their purpose and who treat their human captives as something akin to laboratory animals. Contactees encounter kind, and long-winded, Space Brothers who discourse at length on cosmic science, philosophy and ethics. Abductions, whatever their cause, seem clearly to be a part of the UFO phenomenon, whatever its cause.

Contacts seem clearly to be a social and religious response to the UFO phenomenon, not a part of the phenomenon as such. In fact, the core of the contactee message is simply a continuation of the teaching of the occult-metaphysical religious tradition, a slight flying-saucer-age elaboration on the teachings of Emanuel Swedenborg, an eighteenth-century Swedish seer, Helena P. Blavatsky, a nineteenth-century figure who founded Theosophy, and their more contemporary successors.

Another difference between abductees and contactees concerns the issue of fraud. Conscious fraud (as opposed to unconscious confabulation) has not been a significant issue in the controversy over abductions, but the contactee movement was tainted quite early by the well publicized antics of certain flamboyant figures in the 1950s. Even now many ufologists tend to regard contactees as deliberate hoaxers, although in reality the great majority of contactees are sincere. Nonetheless ufologists' memories of George Adamski and his associates are long and contactees have been victimized by guilt by association.

Adamski: Prior to his alleged first contact, with a Venusian named Orthon in the California desert on November 20, 1952, Adamski was circulating dubious photographs he had taken of "spaceships"—pictures that photoanalysts have determined to be of cardboard cutouts and small models. Since the 1920s Adamski had made his living as a teacher in the California occult scene and in the 1940s wrote a self-published science-fiction novel, *Pioneers of Space*, whose content bore a curious resemblance to his later "true" stories of meetings with Venusians, Martians and Saturnians recounted in his books *Inside the Space Ships* (1955) and *Flying Saucers Farewell* (1961). Adamski all but admitted to close associates that his claims were fraudulent, and on one or two occasions he was caught red-handed. Yet he had a worldwide following which even now, 2½ decades after his death (he died in April 1965), has not entirely faded away.

Most contactees from Adamski on would describe benevolent visitors from a densely-

CONTACTEES (*continued*)

populated universe, but not all contactees would be like Adamski (and in fact most were not). Two kinds of contact claimants would come into prominence. The first, those who like Adamski alleged physical encounters and who produced "evidence" to prove it, dominated the scene in the 1950s and were nearly universally despised by ufologists, who felt that their actions were making the whole UFO question look ridiculous. "Sincere" was an adjective seldom used to characterize the testimony of these individuals, who were essentially con artists. (One even peddled packets of hair from a "Venusian dog"; another sold shares in quartz mines he had seen from a spaceship while in the company of the Space Brothers.) Though dominating the attention of both UFO and non-UFO media in the 1950s, these more questionable contactees were less representative of the movement than the other type, around whom the movement has traditionally been built.

The Contactee Mainstream: The second kind of contactee reported being the recipients of psychic messages from extraterrestrials. These messages came in various fashions: through automatic writing, voices in the head, dreams, visions and channeling. One of the first notable psychic contactees was Dorothy Martin (now known as Sister Thedra and headquartered in Mount Shasta, California), a Chicago woman who received communications via automatic writing from Sananda, an extraterrestrial who said he had been Jesus in an earlier incarnation. Martin was told that cataclysmic earth changes would take place on December 20, 1954, and that she and her faithful followers would be rescued by a flying saucer just before a massive tidal wave destroyed the city. As the date approached, she and the group were instructed to inform the press of the imminent end of the world. When none of the prophesied events occurred, Martin and company were subjected not only to massive public ridicule (their story had been widely publicized) but, in some cases, to sanity hearings. Martin's principal follower, Charles Laughead, was forced to resign his position on the staff of Michigan State College

Hospital. Others had quit their jobs, given away their money or dropped out of school in anticipation of apocalyptic things to come. A classic study in the sociology of religion, *When Prophecy Fails* (1956), by Leon Festinger, Henry W. Riecken and Stanley Schachter, has assured lasting notoriety for this episode.

Psychic contactee Gloria Lee first began hearing a voice inside her head one day in 1953. The voice belonged to a resident of Jupiter, J.W. Over the next several years Lee wrote down J.W.'s messages and published them in *Why We Are Here* (1959), a popular book in contactee circles. Lee became most famous, however, as a martyr of the movement. In the fall of 1962 J.W. instructed her to go on a fast for peace. The fast would end when a "light elevator" arrived to take her to Jupiter. Some weeks into the fast he told her she was to travel to Washington, D.C., and present spaceship blueprints to government officials. On November 28, as she waited for word in a Washington hotel room, she slipped into a coma and on December 2 she died. Her fast had lasted 66 days.

To ufologists as well as to observers in the cultural mainstream, contactees seemed little more than bizarre examples of fraud and social pathology. It was implicitly assumed that their numbers were few. In the 1960s, however, writer/investigator **John A. Keel** remarked on the surprising number of "silent contactees," as he called them to differentiate them from the public ones, he was finding out in the field. Keel concluded that these people were having real experiences but not with, as they thought, benevolent Space Brothers. The beings were amoral paranormal "ultraterrestrials" bent on doing contactees harm. This interpretation would be embraced by conservative Christian UFO chroniclers who think that the Space Brothers are demons in disguise. In 1973 **Brad Steiger's** *Revelation: The Divine Fire* took note, a decade before mainstream media became aware of it, of the growing channeling movement. Many of the channelers were getting messages, warnings and admonitions from Space Brothers. In a sequel, *Gods of Aquarius* (1976), Steiger dealt exclusively with the new generation of flying-saucer contactees. The book contains Steiger's first mention of "Star People" who are "becoming active at this time in an effort to aid mankind survive a coming Great Purification of the planet." In a later chapter he relates his discovery of "Star Maidens," beautiful, intelligent, compassionate earthwomen who in an earlier life were extraterrestrials.

Subsequently Steiger would be married for a time to one Star Maiden, Francie Paschal, and they would further develop the concept of Star People. Star People got their widest exposure in the May 1, 1979, issue of the *National Enquirer*, which reported on the Steigers' theories and brought them a flood of mail and telephone calls from persons claiming to be Star People. Some said that just before the story appeared, ETs had appeared in dreams to tell them, "Now is the time." Beginning in 1981 Berkley would publish five paperbacks by the Steigers in the "Star People Series," spreading the message further. The Steigers reported they were finding two groups of space-linked people: the Starseeds (the true Star People, who have both alien and human genes) and the Star Helpers ("Old Souls," descendants of the disciples of the ETs). At one point the couple was receiving as many as 70 letters a day from "activated Star People," some of whom were prophesying a catastrophic pole shift between 1982 and 1984, a world famine in 1982, World War III before 1985, and planetwide space contacts in 1986. The collapse of the Steigers' marriage and metaphysical partnership in the mid-1980s only momentarily slowed the Star People movement.

Throughout the 1970s and 1980s, religious studies scholar J. Gordon Melton, director of the Institute for the Study of American Religion, in Santa Barbara, California, tracked the growth of the contactee movement as a new expression of metaphysical religion. In the several editions of *The Encyclopedia of American Religions* (1979, 1989), he traced the development of the organized contactee groups, some of which (for example, the Aetherius Society, Mark-Age, and Unarius) developed national and even international followings.

The Rocky Mountain Conferences: Another important figure, probably even more influential than Brad Steiger, in the contactee movement of the 1980s is **R. Leo Sprinkle**, who until his retirement into private practice in 1989 was a psychologist in the counseling department of the University of Wyoming. Sprinkle was unusual in having a foot in both the ufology and contactee camps, though the latter, the focus of his deeper sympathies, would claim his greater attention as the decade passed. Sprinkle entered ufology as a consultant to the Aerial Phenomena Research Organization (APRO) and as a participant in the 1968 Symposium on Unidentified Flying Objects, at the U.S. House Committee on Science and Astronautics. As a hypnotist he worked with a number of abductees, including Nebraska police officer Herbert Schirmer, Carl Higdon, Sandy Larson and others whose stories would be widely reported in the UFO literature. In the 1970s Sprinkle entered into correspondence with contactees who had written him about their psychic communications with beings whom Sprinkle would good-naturedly call "UFOlk." Sprinkle helped the contactees get in touch with each other by mail. By decade's end he had established a small network of like-minded persons who were able to share ideas and experiences.

The next step, Sprinkle thought, was to have these people meet in person. So in May 1980 the first Rocky Mountain Conference on UFO Investigation was held in Laramie, on the university campus. Attendance was small; barely 20 persons showed up, but from those attendees, Sprinkle was able to develop some initial impressions. They seemed to be average, normal people in their social and psychological functioning, though highly susceptible to hypnotic suggestion. Most seemed to experience many psychic phenomena and possess some psychic abilities. He was impressed with their loving concern for all humanity. A great many of them reported a feeling of being monitored or experiencing continued contact with UFO entities and, on occasion, a feeling of having been chosen or selected as a UFO contactee. As a result, they often expressed a sense they had an important mission or task in life. They sometimes expressed

CONTACTEES (*continued*)

anxiety about the state of humankind, and they warned others of the possibility of future catastrophes. They often possessed a deep conviction that they were not only Planetary Persons but also Cosmic Citizens and sometimes acted as if their real "home" is beyond earth (Sprinkle, 1980).

In the next years, despite an unpromising start, the Rocky Mountain conferences soon became as popular a pilgrimage site for contactees as the Giant Rock, California, conventions had been in the 1950s. The 1989 conference attracted a record attendance of 185. It should be noted that there is relatively little overlap among attendees from year to year; each year brings a largely new, not repeat, crowd. This is not a situation, in other words, of a small number of persons who get together continually to regale each other with the same stories. It is, however, an indication that the contactee underground is larger than is generally recognized.

The Rocky Mountain conferences serve to validate contactees' experiences. Left to themselves, individual contactees may come to disbelieve the messages they are hearing. Some even conclude that their source is within their psyches, not on another planet. But when contactees gather at Laramie, they are able to see themselves not as isolated individuals undergoing fantastic visions which cause them to question their own sanity but as members of a larger community with a cosmic mission.

Many contactee stories recount instances of personal transformation, demonstrating in unambiguous fashion the classically religious nature of the experience. The tale Merry Lynn Noble, a Colorado housewife and Rocky Mountain conference attendee, tells is a particularly dramatic example:

At one time in her life, she says, she was an "expensive hooker, one of the leading call girls in the western United States." Deeply unhappy, she suffered from both drug addiction and alcoholism.

In an effort to change her life, she turned to spiritual studies. Then in February 1982, depressed and exhausted, she went to Montana to visit her parents. One evening they went rabbit-hunting together. They drove through back roads on a clear, dark night until, having found no rabbits, they decided to stop the car and talk. Their conversation turned to religion and Noble declared, "I believe in some Power that unites the universe. And I believe God is connected with UFOs." Her father laughed and said, "You've been in the city too long."

Suddenly, Noble says, "there was a *whoosh* sound and the car was covered with white light. I tried to look out the window but the light was too bright. I did get a glimpse, no more than a few seconds, of a saucer-shaped outline, a dark gray disc. It was about 100 feet over the car. I looked at my parents. They were just frozen there. It was like a movie that's suddenly stopped. Then I felt my astral body rising through the roof of the car. I felt a sense of freedom that I'd never felt before. The light was no longer blinding. I began communicating telepathically with a source inside the UFO—a Presence. I was saying things and answers were being given.

"It's hard to describe in words. It was absolute ecstasy, total peace, womblike warmth. I felt a sense of relief. 'I'm so glad to leave that body,' I thought. 'No way I can go on, no way I can handle this life.' I put my hands up and said, 'Thy will be done.' The Voice said, 'That's all I wanted to hear—that you would give up and do my will. Now go back to your body and do My will.'

"I said, 'I need help, strength, support. I can't go back to my old life.' Then I received a sense that I would have help. My old soul went on. It had a big ego and it was worn out with emotional problems. A new soul came into my body, with new energy, new humility. At that moment I was dropped with a jolt into my body. The first thing I thought was, 'This body is so heavy.'

"My parents had no awareness that anything had happened. It was like their memories were blanked out" (Clark, 1986).

Soon afterwards Noble returned to Denver where through, she says, a "series of 'coincidences'" her life took an abrupt turn for the better. She got a good job and joined Alcoholics Anonymous. There she met Dan McLerren. "The Voice told me he was the one," she says. Before long they were married, and both have remained sober ever since. Noble's space contacts continue and she has written an unpublished autobiography, *Sex, God and UFOs*.

There is no reason to believe such experiences are generated by mental illness. Another University of Wyoming psychologist, June O. Parnell, wrote her Ph.D. dissertation on a psychological study of over 200 contactees who had attended the conference at various times. She found no detectable psychological differences between contactees and "normal" persons. Religious historian J. Gordon Melton, the leading academic authority on the contactee movement, says that attempts to characterize contactees as "kooks" are "reminiscent of the way Pentecostals were dismissed as psychopathological by psychologists who had never studied Pentecostalism. Recent studies have indicated that as a whole Pentecostals have a higher mental-health rate than the general population. When people claim that contactees have a pathological bent, it would be a very good idea to ask, 'Where are your data?' since unorthodox behavior and beliefs are no sign in themselves of psychopathology" (Fuller, 1980).

Meier's Pleiades Contacts: The one remaining contactee in the Adamski tradition is a Swiss farmer named Eduard ("Billy") Meier, who in the 1970s came forward with clear photographs of "beamships" carrying "cosmonauts" from the Pleiades star system. Meier's farm drew occult pilgrims from all over Europe. In 1979 some American entrepreneurs brought Meier's tales to the United States with the publication of a coffee-table collection of beamship pictures, followed over the next 10 years by several fat, amateurishly-written volumes recounting "investigations" of Meier's claims. In 1987 an independent journalist, Gary Kinder, and Atlantic Monthly Press brought out *Light Years*, a sympathetic but naive inquiry

into the affair. Meier and his followers had a hard time explaining away such gaffes as the picture of a beautiful Pleiades woman later found to be of a model in a magazine advertisement. Scathing critiques of Meier's stories and photographs were published in the *MUFON UFO Journal* and *International UFO Reporter* and in Kal Korff's self-published expose *The Meier Incident: The Most Infamous Hoax in Ufology* (1981). Outside contactee circles, where Meier is regarded as something of a hero, he has few defenders. One of this small group is James W. Deardorff, a retired Oregon State University atmospheric physicist, who has presented pro-Meier papers at scientific conferences.

In 1987 **Whitley Strieber's** *Communion: A True Story*, an account of the author's abduction experiences, rode high on the best-seller lists for many weeks. A sequel, *Transformation: The Breakthrough*, was published the next year. In 1989 Strieber organized the **Communion Foundation** whose newsletter quickly became a forum in which Strieber could express his unhappiness with the UFO community, which refused to recognize that the "visitors," i.e., the abducting aliens, have a benevolent mission. Ufologists, Strieber complained, "are not helping us to understand our fears and build our relationship with the visitors. The visitor experience is rich, complex and fruitful. It is often terrifying, I won't deny that. . . . But it can be used by the individual as a source of strength and self-knowledge. As such it is something to be treasured, not thrown away to satisfy the curiosity of researchers, or altered to fit their theories" (Strieber, 1989b). In his novel *Majestic* (1989a), based on the Roswell UFO-crash story, Strieber calls the aliens "angels," who offer "freedom: the soul in the open sky. . . ."

Heretofore extraterrestrials who did not look like earthly movie stars—in other words, such beings as the little gray men of abduction lore—were considered agents of the dark forces of the universe. Now Strieber was saying they are good guys, too, though their means of displaying their good intentions are far from straightforward. They teach not by directing cosmic philosophy

CONTACTEES (*continued*)

into the throat of a channeler or by whispering into the ear of an automatic writer but by subjecting their students to near-traumatic ordeals, a Space Age version of traditional rites of passage at the end of which the seeker emerges mature and wise. How appealing this model of the contact experience will be remains to be seen, but it is one of the few new ideas to enter contactee theology since Adamski.

Sources:

Beckley, Timothy Green. *Psychic and UFO Revelations in the Last Days*. New Brunswick, NJ: Inner Light Publications, 1989.

Clark, Jerome. "Waiting for the Space Brothers." *Fate* Pt. I. 39, 3 (March 1986): 47-54; Pt II. 39, 4 (April 1986): 81-87; Pt. III. 39, 5 (May 1986): 68-76.

Curran, Douglas. *In Advance of the Landing: Folk Concepts of Outer Space*. New York: Abbeville Press, 1985.

Eberhart, George M. *UFOs and the Extraterrestrial Contact Movement: A Bibliography. Volume Two: The Extraterrestrial Contact Movement*. Metuchen, NJ: The Scarecrow Press, Inc., 1986.

Fuller, Curtis G., ed. *Proceedings of the First International UFO Congress*. New York: Warner Books, 1980.

Kinder, Gary. *Light Years: An Investigation Into the Extraterrestrial Experiences of Eduard Meier*. New York: Atlantic Monthly Press, 1987.

Korff, Kal K., with William L. Moore. *The Meier Incident: The Most Infamous Hoax in Ufology*. Fremont, CA: The Author, 1981.

Melton, J. Gordon. "The Contactees: A Survey." In Mimi Hynek, ed. *The Spectrum of UFO Research: The Proceedings of the Second CUFOS Conference, Held September 25-27, 1981, in Chicago, Illinois*, 99-108. Chicago: J. Allen Hynek Center for UFO Studies, 1988.

Melton, J. Gordon. *The Encyclopedia of American Religions*. 2 vols. Wilmington, NC: Consortium, 1979. Third edition: Detroit: Gale Research Company, 1989.

Sprinkle, R. Leo, ed. *Proceedings of the Rocky Mountain Conference on UFO Investigation*. Laramie, WY: School of Extended Studies, 1980.

Steiger, Brad. *The Fellowship*. Garden City, NY: Dolphin/Doubleday, 1988.

Steiger, Brad, and Francie Steiger. *The Star People*. New York: Berkley Books, 1981.

Strieber, Whitley. *Majestic*. New York: G. P. Putnam's Sons, 1989a.

Strieber, Whitley. "A Message from Whitley Strieber." *The Communion Letter* 1 (Spring 1989b): 1-2.

Zinsstag, Lou, and Timothy Good. *George Adamski: The Untold Story*. Beckenham, Kent, England: Ceti, 1983.

CRASHES OF UFOs

Spaceships from other worlds have been crash-landing on American soil since 1884, when the *Nebraska Nugget*, a weekly newspaper published in Holdrege, reported on June 6 that cowboys at work in remote Dundy County had seen a blazing object plunge to earth, spraying "fragments of cog-wheels and other pieces of machinery . . . and glowing with heat so intense as to scorch the grass for a long distance around each fragment and make it impossible for one to approach it." The brilliant light cast by the object blinded one of the cowboys, the *Nugget* said. On the 10th a Dundy County correspondent reported in Lincoln's *Daily State Journal* that the vehicle's remains vanished in a rainstorm, "dissolved by the water like a spoonful of salt" (Clark, 1986).

The story, of course, was a hoax, more specifically a practical joke, as were tales of "airship" crashes related in 1897 papers during what some would regard as the first great modern UFO wave. The most famous of these tales had it, as the *Dallas Morning Post* claimed on its front page two days later, that on April 17 a spaceship collided with Judge Proctor's windmill in Aurora, Texas, and left in the wreckage the body of a Martian. The *Post* reported on the same page the same day that a Farmersville "eye witness" had seen a passing airship in which three men were singing "Nearer My God to Thee" and distributing temperance tracts. If the *Post*'s intention was to poke fun at public credulity, it failed. In 1973 a UFO enthusiast showed up in Aurora, newspaper reporters in tow, to demand that the community exhume the grave in which the enthusiast claimed the Martian lay. Among other fictions in the *Post* story, Judge Proctor had no windmill.

Crash claims had a dubious pedigree from the beginning and were central to the second great hoax of the UFO age. (The first was a complex episode known as the Maury Island affair, perpetrated in the wake of Kenneth Arnold's and other sightings in the summer of 1947.) In 1950 *Variety* columnist Frank Scully produced the best-selling *Behind the Flying Saucers*, passing on, apparently innocently, what proved to be fraudulent claims about crashes of Venusian spacecraft in New Mexico and Arizona. In a devastating expose published in 1952, *True* magazine showed that Scully's principal informants were veteran con artists.

The *True* article discredited not only the Scully stories but all stories of crashed discs, and the major ufological organizations of the 1950s, such as Civilian Saucer Intelligence (New York), the Aerial Phenomena Research Organization (APRO), and the National Investigations Committee on Aerial Phenomena (NICAP), would have nothing to do with them, even though most ufologists of the period thought the government was probably being much less than forthcoming about its knowledge of extraterrestrial visitation. In the late 1950s and into the 1960s NICAP, under director Donald E. Keyhoe (author of

widely-read books such as *The Flying Saucer Conspiracy* [1955] and *Flying Saucers: Top Secret* [1960]), lobbied vigorously for Congressional hearings to end the "cover-up," but the cover-up was thought to be of gun-camera films of discs and of other impressive instrumented evidence. Crash claims were never mentioned and when NICAP received them, it filed them away and forgot about them.

Rumors of Crashes: Even as they were being ignored, the stories continued. In their usual form they went like this:

In the late 1940s and maybe even later, several flying saucers crashed in the Southwest. The remains, including the bodies of gray-skinned humanoid beings, were retrieved by government and military agencies. The material was taken for study to Wright-Patterson Air Force Base in Dayton, Ohio, and subsequently some of it was sent elsewhere. The entire matter is highly classified and only a small number of individuals within the government know the whole story. The secrecy has been maintained both to prevent panic and to keep the Russians from knowing that we have access to extraterrestrial technology. At the appropriate time the government will release the information.

Most of the stories containing these allegations came from second-, third- and fourth-hand sources and were easy to dismiss as folklore. In some cases, however, the sources were individuals who claimed to have this information from their own knowledge or from the testimony of their own sources. For example, one informant was a woman who worked at Wright-Patterson for a number of years. Possessing a high security clearance, she was given access to much classified material. In due course she retired and subsequently learned that she was dying of cancer. Before her death she confided to a ufologist (remarking, "Uncle Sam can't do anything to me once I'm in my grave") that her work had included the cataloging of all incoming UFO material. She processed about 1000 items, she claimed, seeing to it that they were photographed and tagged. Some of the items were from the interior of a

CRASHES OF UFOS (*continued*)

crashed UFO which had been brought to the base. She also saw two bodies carried on a cart from one room to the next. The bodies, preserved in chemicals, were of generally human appearance, although they were only four or five feet tall and had larger-than-normal heads and slanted eyes.

Other persons making such claims seemed sincere, but their stories about glimpsing something at Wright-Patterson or being present at crash-retrievals were unverifiable. Apparent sincerity was hardly enough to make believable so fantastic a claim. Ufologists took to referring to these, and not favorably, as the "little-men-in-a-pickle-jar" story and their persistence was noted even by folklorists, who began reporting them in papers and books about "urban legends."

At one point in the mid-1960s Sen. Barry Goldwater, a brigadier-general in the Air Force reserve, tried to check out the rumor that at Wright-Patterson there was a secret "Blue Room" where UFO remains were kept. When he asked his friend Gen. Curtis LeMay about the story, LeMay gave him "holy hell," Goldwater would tell the *New Yorker* (April 25, 1988), informed him that he did not have the necessary clearance, and warned him never to bring up the subject again.

The first prominent UFO investigator to urge ufologists to reconsider their long dismissal of crash claims was Leonard H. Stringfield. A respected figure in the field since the 1950s, he had edited an excellent newsletter, *C.R.I.F.O. Orbit*, between 1954 and 1957. In September 1955 the Air Defense Command (ADC) approached him and asked if he would screen the UFO reports he received and send on the best ones. He was also told that the Ground Observer Corps in the Cincinnati area, where he lived, had been instructed to forward reports to him for his evaluation. The ADC gave Stringfield a telephone code number which would connect him with the command filter center. Stringfield was also told that he was not to "ask any questions." His experiences with the ADC convinced him that a high-level UFO cover-up existed.

With the passing of time Stringfield began to suspect that maybe what was being covered up involved matters even more dramatic than the radar/visual cases he had learned of as an ADC associate but that the Air Force denied to the press. He found himself rethinking the crashed-disc story, recalling accounts told by persons who it was hard to believe were liars, such as, in one case, a Presbyterian minister. In his 1977 book *Situation Red, The UFO Siege!* he devoted 10 pages to the subject.

Before long Stringfield was inundated with crashed-saucer tales, and they quickly became the major focus of his interest. In 1978 he related some of them to the annual conference (held that year, ironically, in Dayton, home of the notorious Wright-Patterson) of the **Mutual UFO Network** (MUFON). None of the stories had any independent confirmation, and Stringfield concealed the identities of nearly all of his informants, to the frustration of those who wanted to investigate further. He played a tape in which one man related his alleged experience as a guard at a UFO crash site. Later, when the man's name became known, other investigators determined that the story was fictitious. Over the next few years, as he presented periodic updates of the crash stories and reports that had come his way, Stringfield would be criticized by a number of ufologists, who complained that the evidence being presented was feeble for so extraordinary a claim. Some (most prominently historian **David M. Jacobs**) argued that such a thing as a crashed saucer was impossible on *a priori* grounds. Such a secret could not be kept (to which proponents rejoined that the secret had *not* been kept; it just had not been believed). The most ingenious argument came from longtime ufologist George W. Earley, who wrote in *Fate* that heavy, bulky objects such as flying discs could not have been transported from the Southwest to Ohio on the relatively primitive, pre-interstate highway system of late '40s/early '50s America.

The *a priori* arguments aside, from the critics' point of view the basic problems with the crash/retrieval claim were two: first, there were a significant percentage of anonymous informants and second, there were simply too many crash stories, none of the same event, thus no mutual confirmation. All that would be changed with the Roswell incident, which has emerged as the single most significant crashed saucer account.

In January 1978 **William L. Moore,** a schoolteacher and aspiring writer from Herman, Minnesota, and **Stanton T. Friedman,** a physicist and UFO lecturer, met to discuss rumors they had been hearing about an obscure incident from three decades ago, something that existed as little more than a footnote in the early history of the UFO phenomenon. As the story went, in early July 1947 a weather balloon had dropped on the property of a rancher near Corona, New Mexico, and through a comedy of errors a story had gone out through the Army Air Base at nearby Roswell that the remains of a flying disc had been recovered. Soon a correction went out and there the matter ended, no more than a silly misunderstanding.

But was it? In the mid-1970s a California forest ranger had told the late Bobbi Ann Gironda, a writer interested in UFOs, that his mother had had an interesting UFO experience in New Mexico. When Gironda and Friedman interviewed her, the woman, Lydia Sleppy, told a strange story.

She said that at four o'clock in the afternoon of July 7, 1947, as she was operating the teletype at radio station KOAT in Albuquerque, she got a phone call from Johnny McBoyle, reporter and part owner of sister station KSWS in Roswell. KSWS had no teletype of its own but used KOAT's when it had something to go out.

McBoyle excitedly reported that one of those flying saucers everyone had been talking about had crashed near Roswell. He had seen it himself. It looked like a "big crumpled dishpan." The Army was there and was going to pick it up. Even more amazing, Army personnel were saying something about having recovered "little men" from the craft. McBoyle told her to start putting the story on the teletype immediately.

Sleppy typed as McBoyle dictated the story.

But no more than a few sentences later the teletype stopped. Assuming there was a mechanical problem, Sleppy told McBoyle what had happened. McBoyle suddenly seemed distracted. From what she could overhear, it sounded as if he were talking with someone else. Then he said to her in a strained voice, "Wait a minute. I'll get back to you." At that moment the teletype resumed working. Now it was spelling out a message apparently directed to Sleppy: "ATTENTION ALBUQUERQUE: DO NOT TRANSMIT. REPEAT DO NOT TRANSMIT THIS MESSAGE. STOP COMMUNICATION IMMEDIATELY."

Astonished, Sleppy informed McBoyle of what she was seeing. McBoyle replied tersely that she could forget what he had said, that she was not supposed to know about it.

When Friedman located McBoyle and asked him about the incident, McBoyle said, "Forget about it. . . . It never happened."

On January 20, 1978, Friedman was in New Orleans to lecture at Louisiana State University. While promoting the lecture at one of the local television stations, he was introduced to the manager who casually suggested he should talk to Maj. Jesse A. Marcel. Marcel, he said, had actually handled a UFO "way back." He had known Marcel a long time because of their mutual interest in ham radio. Friedman called Marcel, who claimed that while in the Army Air Force in New Mexico, he picked up a great quantity of material from a crashed UFO near Roswell. Friedman thought he sounded sincere and sensible, but he understood that without a great deal of confirmation from other sources this was just another anecdote about the "Ultimate Secret," as ufologists would come to call it.

He and Moore discussed the two stories and decided that since they had some names, they had something to go on, as was usually not the case with crash tales, and therefore further investigation was not only warranted but doable.

The Roswell Incident: In the next few years they

CRASHES OF UFOS (*continued*)

found about 100 informants, one-third of them firsthand ones, another third family members, friends or neighbors of the direct witnesses, the last third individuals who provided useful background information. In 1980, with Charles Berlitz, Moore published a premature and much-criticized book, *The Roswell Incident*, which mixed documented material with rumor and speculation. (One critic characterized it as "about as bad a book as could be written on a subject of such potential importance" [Clark, 1981]). But Moore and Friedman continued to track down witnesses and other informants and to issue occasional reports to the UFO community. The evidence that something extraordinary had taken place, followed by an equally extraordinary cover-up, seemed all but undeniable. Within ufology the number of scoffers dwindled, and even newspaper and television reporters who looked into the story were puzzled and intrigued.

In broad outline, the story Moore and Friedman pieced together went like this:

On the evening of July 2, 1947, a Roswell couple, Mr. and Mrs. Dan Wilmot, saw a glowing object "like two inverted saucers faced mouth to mouth" passing from southeast to northwest—in the direction of Corona, 75 miles away, in Lincoln County. That same evening, as an electrical storm raged over Lincoln County, W. W. (Mac) Brazel, the manager of a sheep ranch, and two of his children (the rest of the family lived elsewhere) heard a strange explosion, unlike thunder. The next morning, when he went out to check on the sheep, Brazel found wreckage of some kind of aircraft scattered over a band a quarter-mile long and several hundred feet wide. He showed it to his brother-in-law and a few friends and heard from them for the first time about the then-new phenomenon of "flying saucers."

Brazel took the material along on a subsequent business trip to Roswell, where he brought it to the sheriff's office. The sheriff's office immediately notified Roswell Field, home of the 509th Bomb Group, the only atomic-bomb unit in the world at the time, and Maj. Jesse Marcel, the ranking staff officer in charge of intelligence, interviewed Brazel. The base commanding officer, Col. William H. Blanchard, ordered Marcel and Sheridan "Cav" Cavitt, a Counter-Intelligence Corps agent, to the site. They found, Marcel recalled in 1979, "all kinds of stuff—small beams about 3/8ths or a half-inch square with some sort of hieroglyphics on them that nobody could decipher. These looked something like balsa wood and were of about the same weight, although flexible, and would not burn. There was a great deal of an unusual parchmentlike substance which was brown in color and extremely strong, and a great number of small pieces of a metal like tinfoil, except that it wasn't tinfoil. I was interested in electronics and kept looking for something that resembled instruments or electronic equipment, but I didn't find anything. One of the other fellows, Cavitt, I think, found a black, metallic-looking box several inches square. . . ."

The parchment symbol, Marcel said, "had little numbers and symbols that we had to call hieroglyphics because I could not understand them. They could not be read, they were just like symbols, something that meant something, and they were not all the same, but the same general pattern, I would say. They were pink and purple. They looked like they were painted on. These little numbers could not be broken, could not be burned. I even took my cigarette lighter and tried to burn the material we found that resembled parchment and balsa, but it would not burn—wouldn't even smoke."

According to Marcel, the metal was as thin as the foil in a pack of cigarettes and weighed practically nothing. But it could not be bent, or even dented, with a 16-pound sledgehammer. Nor could it be torn and cut. "It was possible to flex this stuff back and forth, even to wrinkle it, but you could not put a crease in it that would stay. . . . I would almost have to describe it as a metal with plastic properties," he said.

Others who saw the material, including Brazel's children, CIC agent Bill Rickett, and Walt Whitmore, Jr. (son of the owner of the Roswell radio station), all described it the same way. In 1981 Jesse Marcel, Jr., whose father had shown it to him upon his return from the site (the junior Marcel was then 12 years old), remarked that the "crash and remnants of the device left an impression on my memory that can never be forgotten. I am currently undergoing training as a Flight Surgeon in the Army Air National Guard, and have examined the remnants of many conventional aircraft that have undergone unfortunate maneuvers, and what I saw in 1947 is unlike any of the current aircraft ruinage I have studied. This craft was not conventional in any sense of the word. . . . [M]any of the remnants, including the eye-beam pieces . . . , had strange hieroglyphic type writing symbols across the inner surfaces. It appeared to me at that time that the symbols were not derived from the Greek or the Roman alphabet, nor of Egyptian origin with their animal symbols."

Meanwhile Lt. Walter Haut, public-information officer at Roswell, had alerted Associated Press, announcing, "The many rumors regarding the flying disc became a reality yesterday [July 7] when the intelligence office of the 509th Bomb Group of the Eighth Air Force, Roswell Army Air Field, was fortunate enough to gain possession of a disc . . ." Within hours the story was in the headlines of newspapers worldwide.

Soon afterwards, however, Col. Blanchard found himself at the receiving end of what the *Washington Post* called a "blistering rebuke" from his superiors, Eighth Air Force Commander Brig. Gen. Roger M. Ramey and Deputy Air Force Chief Lt. Gen. Hoyt S. Vandenberg, who were furious about the press release. They told him they wanted the material shipped immediately to Eighth Air Force Headquarters (now Carswell AFB) in Fort Worth, Texas. So Blanchard ordered Marcel to load the material aboard a B-29 and deliver it to Ramey. From there it was to be flown, with Marcel again watching over it, to Wright Field (now Wright-Patterson AFB) where it would be analyzed.

When Marcel got to Fort Worth, Ramey ordered him not to talk with reporters. Then Ramey called in the press and said the "disc" was really just a weather balloon. As proof he displayed a weather balloon and brought in the base weather officer, Irving Newton, to identify it as such. Newton would recall that the balloon material was "very flimsy—you would have to be careful *not* to tear it"—unlike the material at Roswell. Nonetheless reporters were led to believe that the balloon and the "flying saucer" were one and the same.

In fact, the real material was secretly flown to Wright Field. Marcel was not aboard the plane. Instead, he was sent back to Roswell and warned to say nothing more. As he would tell Moore, "The cover story about the balloon [was] just to get the press off [Ramey's] back. The press was told it was just a balloon and that the flight to Wright was canceled; but all that really happened was that I was removed from the flight and someone else took it to Wright."

According to retired Air Force Brig. Gen. Thomas J. DuBose, who in July 1947 served as adjutant to Gen. Ramey's staff in Fort Worth, the order to effect a cover-up using a phony balloon identification came directly from the Pentagon, specifically from Gen. Clements McMullen. There were, DuBose said, "orders from on high to ship the material . . . directly to Wright Field by plane."

CIC officer Rickett stated, "The Air Force's explanation that it was a balloon was totally untrue. It was not a balloon. I never did know for sure exactly what its purpose was but it wasn't ours." The late Col. Blanchard's former wife Emily Simms recalled, "At first he thought it might be Russian because of the strange symbols on it. Later on, he realized it wasn't Russian either."

Brazel was held incommunicado for a week and surfaced only twice when, accompanied by agent Cavitt, he appeared at the office of the *Roswell Daily Record* and at the KGFL studio. In each case he told (under what the members of his family, Cavitt's assistant Rickett and two local reporters all have described as duress) the story

61

CRASHES OF UFOs (*continued*)

that the Army Air Force was now circulating: that the object was only a weather balloon.

Members of the Brazel family long remembered their father's bitterness (he died in 1965) about how he had been treated. The entire family was warned not to discuss the incident. "Back in those days," Bessie Brazel recalled, "when the military told you not to talk about something, it wasn't discussed." The family says Mac Brazel died without ever telling all he knew.

During his detention the Air Force sent soldiers to the site to collect every scrap of material they could find. Aerial reconnaissance was conducted and both air and surface photographs were taken. (It was during this reconnaissance, according to several informants, most of them interviewed years later in an independent investigation by Kevin D. Randle and Don Schmitt of the **J. Allen Hynek Center for UFO Studies**, that four bodies of humanoid beings, who apparently had ejected from the craft, were located. One of these bodies was badly mangled, but the rest were intact.) The only evidence that remained was in the hands of Brazel's son Bill, who tells this story:

"The Air Force had a whole platoon of men out there picking up every piece and shred they could find. Still, every time I rode through that particular pasture I would make a point to look. Seems like every time after a good rain I would manage to find a piece or two that they had overlooked. After about a year and a half or two years I had managed to accumulate quite a small collection—about enough that if you were to lay it out on this tabletop it would take up about as much area as [a] briefcase."

Then one night in 1949 Bill Brazel visited a bar in Corona. After a few drinks he was talking about his collection of flying-saucer artifacts. The next morning a staff car from Roswell Field showed up and four soldiers, a captain and three enlisted men, came to his door. They wanted to see his collection. As Brazel showed it to them, he was told that he would have to surrender it.

"I didn't know what else to do," Brazel later related, "so I agreed. Next he wanted me to take them out to the pasture where I had found this stuff. . . . After they had poked around a bit and satisfied themselves that there didn't appear to be any more of the material out there . . . the captain . . . said that if I ever found any more of it, it was most important that I call him at Roswell right away. Naturally I said I would but I never did it because after that I never found any more."

So far non-UFO explanations of the Roswell incident have not withstood investigation. Some theorists have proposed that the object was a Skyhook balloon, part of the secret U.S. Navy Skyhook project to conduct tests in the upper atmosphere. Investigators determined that the first Skyhook balloon was launched from Camp Ripley, Minnesota, five months after the Roswell event. A number of balloon experiments *were* conducted in the Southwest in 1947, but such balloons were familiar to local people, both military and civilian, and were unlikely to be mistaken for something like the Roswell craft. When Gen. Ramey showed Irving Newton a balloon and identified it as the object recovered at Roswell, Newton was surprised that the Roswell people hadn't recognized it. "It was a regular Rawin sonde," he recalled. "They must have seen hundreds of them." Two weather-balloon crashes occurred around the same time, in Ohio, but the military quickly identified the devices and they were not sent on to higher authority as happened at Roswell. Classified rocket experiments (using V-2s) took place at Fort Bliss in El Paso, Texas, on June 12 and July 3 but in both cases the missiles were recovered.

Ten of the 30 firsthand witnesses Moore and Friedman interviewed identified the Roswell object as a spacecraft. The rest said simply that they had no idea what it was. The material that the officers from Roswell Field recovered was reported to be unlike anything used, then or now, in the construction of aircraft, balloons or guided missiles. Later investigators both from the mainstream media and from the UFO community found other informants and other evidence, but no suggestion that the Roswell material, and the bodies that some claim were associated with it, were anything less than extraordinary.

Revised History: Despite what seemed solid evidence for the Roswell incident, ufologists were puzzled by the absence of any indication in the public history of official UFO projects (Sign, Grudge and Blue Book) that anything like a UFO crash had ever occurred. To the contrary, that history painted a picture of an Air Force strangely unconcerned (except for brief periods, specifically 1947-48 and 1952) with what to others looked like extraordinarily evidential reports—among them eyewitness and instrumented sightings of structured craftlike objects whose appearance and maneuvers clearly implied, if they did not prove, the operations of an advanced technology—which presumably would have all kinds of national-security significance.

Over the years civilian investigators would regularly hear reports of UFO encounters by military personnel who were ordered not to discuss what they had seen and whose evidence (film, for example) was confiscated. As early as 1949 Donald Keyhoe, a retired Marine Corps major and aviation journalist, became convinced that a cover-up of a very big secret was in force. He wrote magazine articles and books citing government and military sources who confirmed his suspicions. Keyhoe went on to direct NICAP, which sought to enlist influential citizens and members of Congress in the struggle against UFO secrecy. Keyhoe, who died in 1988, came to believe a highly classified group of top scientists and government officials were directing the cover-up, but he could not prove it.

In the 1970s a remarkable Air Force document came to light through the Freedom of Information Act, an internal memo dated October 20, 1969, written by Brig. Gen. C. H. Bolender. In the memo, Bolender said that reports of UFOs which could affect national security were not part of the Blue Book system but were handled through the standard Air Force procedures designed for that purpose. (The full text appeared in Fawcett and

Greenwood's *Clear Intent* [1984].) To ufologists this was an astonishing admission, confirmation of a long suspicion that Blue Book was little more than a public-relations exercise and the sensitive cases were going elsewhere. But what were the "standard Air Force procedures" for handling these sensitive reports?

If the Roswell object was a UFO, ufologists concluded, the true history of the U.S. government's investigation of UFOs was hidden from public view from the very beginning. In 1983, reflecting on the Roswell evidence, **Bruce Maccabee**, director of the **Fund for UFO Research** and a U.S. Navy physicist familiar with classification procedures, considered what this hidden history may have been. In a monograph titled *Revised UFO History* he wrote:

"The Revised History proceeds from the assumption . . . that the Air Force knew by the middle of July 1947 that saucers were real and not man-made. Furthermore, it is not unreasonable to add the corollary that the Air Force knew that the technology represented by the [recovered] disc . . . was so far beyond our own that it could not be understood immediately. Instead, it could take years of research in advanced physics to understand how a disc worked. Moreover, clearly whoever has discs 'wins' in a military sense. Therefore it would become necessary to treat the disc as a military secret. This would mean containing all information about it within some small group. The military agencies best equipped for *containing* information are the intelligence agencies. Therefore the disc would be placed in the custody of an intelligence arm of the Air Force."

Further, in Maccabee's view the public Air Force projects received "civilian/military verbal reports while the top Air Force generals maintain[ed] absolute secrecy about the real thing. That way they got to collect data which might have been useful without having to reveal what they knew. To the outside world it looked as if the Air Force was fulfilling its duty to investigate unknowns in the sky but with little hope of finding anything."

CRASHES OF UFOS (*continued*)

The cover-up was directed by a small secret group of intelligence specialists who reported directly to the President, the Secretary of Defense and the Joint Chiefs of Staff. Just below the group was another, larger one whose function was research, analysis and field investigation. The Air Materiel Command, the Air Technical Intelligence Center and the various public UFO projects at the bottom of this chain of command knew little or nothing of the secret work being done elsewhere, although each of these branches had at least one "mole" in its ranks. The mole's function was to be sure that the secret group learned immediately if—accidentally or otherwise—the public project got a sensitive case (such as a crash report) which was none of its business.

Maccabee believes that a principal purpose of the Air Force's relentless debunking of the subject was to discourage scientists from examining UFO data. A concerted effort by the scientific community to explain the UFO phenomenon, the engineers of the cover-up feared, might uncover the truth about extraterrestrial visitation and so reveal to the general public what was seen as the Ultimate Secret.

If Maccabee is right, it worked. Nonofficial UFO research was left in the hands of civilian ufologists lacking the technical expertise, funding or institutional support to do what needed to be done. And scientists fell victim to a sophisticated hoax.

Majestic-12: In 1982, in a lecture to the annual MUFON conference, Canadian ufologist Arthur Bray reported that a memo in his possession confirmed that authorities in Washington were covering up crashed UFOs. The memo, prepared by the late Wilbert B. Smith, a Canadian government engineer, recounted a September 15, 1950, interview, in an office of the Defense Department, with physicist **Robert Sarbacher**, who in answer to questions confirmed that UFOs "exist. . . . [W]e didn't make them, and it's pretty certain they didn't originate on the earth." Sarbacher refused to say more about the recovered

craft, a subject, he said, "classified two points higher even than the H-bomb. In fact it is the most highly classified subject in the U.S. Government at the present time." A small group under the direction of Vannevar Bush, President Truman's chief science advisor, was in charge of studying the wreckage.

In the 1980s other investigators, such as Stanton Friedman and Bruce Maccabee, located Sarbacher in semiretirement in Palm Beach, Florida. Sarbacher told them he had not been directly involved in the UFO project and knew only what he had been told, and he had forgotten much of that. He did recall, he told one inquirer, that "certain materials reported to have come from flying saucer crashes were extremely light and very tough" (shades of the Roswell residue). "I remember in talking with some of the people at the office," he said, "that I got the impression these 'aliens' were constructed like certain insects we have observed on earth . . . " (Good, 1988).

In December 1984 a curious item arrived in the mail at the North Hollywood, California, home of television producer Jaime Shandera. Since 1982 Shandera had been working with William Moore on the cover-up story, though on a level no investigators before them had operated, at least over an extended period of time. In September 1980 Moore had come into contact with military-intelligence personnel who were telling him that the U.S. government not only had retrieved crashed UFOs and humanoid bodies but also was in contact with the extraterrestrial intelligences responsible. Although these sources had promised massive documentary evidence to back up these extraordinary claims, little had been forthcoming. One of the few documents to be produced came to Moore from Sgt. Richard Doty, an Air Force Office of Special Investigations agent at Kirtland AFB in Albuquerque. Doty presented the document as basically authentic but indicated certain small changes had been made so that its authenticity could be denied if someone were to make a public issue of it. The document, a purported AFOSI teletype stamped SECRET and dated November 17, 1980, discusses several alleged UFO films, then concludes with a brief discussion (claimed by Doty and Moore to be part of the "authentic" message) of how government agencies deal with UFO data. It notes, "RESULTS OF PROJECT AQUARIUS IS [sic] STILL CLASSIFIED TOP SECRET WITH NO DISSEMINATION OUTSIDE OFFICIAL INTELLIGENCE CHANNELS AND WITH RESTRICTED ACCESS TO 'MJ TWELVE.'" "MJ TWELVE" is not defined or explained.

The item came in a manila envelope with no return address. Shandera and Moore have never revealed what the postmark indicated about the package's origin, except to say that it came from somewhere within 500 miles of Los Angeles. This has led some to speculate that the source was Albuquerque, home to both Kirtland AFB and Doty. In any case, the envelope contained a roll of 35mm film which, when developed, depicted nine pages of a document stamped TOP SECRET/MAJIC/EYES ONLY and titled BRIEFING DOCUMENT: OPERATION MAJESTIC 12/ PREPARED FOR PRESIDENT-ELECT DWIGHT D. EISENHOWER: (EYES ONLY)/ 18 NOVEMBER, 1952. The briefing officer was identified as "Adm. Roscoe H. Hillenkoetter (MJ-1)." (Hillenkoetter was the first director of the CIA, a post he held between 1947 and 1950. Later he would serve for a time on the NICAP board. In 1960, in that capacity, he said publicly that "behind the scenes, high-ranking Air Force officers are soberly concerned about UFOs. But, through official secrecy and ridicule, many citizens are led to believe the unknown flying objects are nonsense. . . . [T]o hide the facts, the Air Force has silenced its personnel" [*New York Times*, February 28, 1960].)

Page two of the document stated, "OPERATION MAJESTIC-12 is a TOP SECRET Research and Development/Intelligence operation responsible directly and only to the President of the United States. Operations of the project are carried out under control of the Majestic-12 (Majic-12) Group which was established by special classified executive order of President Truman on 24 September, 1947, upon recommendation by Dr. Vannevar Bush and Secretary [of Defense] James Forrestal." The members were identified as Hillenkoetter; Bush; Forrestal; Gen. Nathan F. Twining, Air Force Vice Chief of Staff (he had also headed the Air Materiel Command at Wright Field in 1947, when the Roswell material was shipped there); Gen. Hoyt S. Vandenberg, Air Force Chief of Staff; Detlev Bronk, a prominent scientist and a specialist in aviation physiology; Jerome Hunsaker, head of the MIT aeronautics department and chairman of the National Advisory Committee on Aeronautics; Sidney W. Souers, a confidant of Truman's, first Director of Central Intelligence (predecessor to the CIA), then first Executive Secretary of the National Security Council (1947); Gordon Gray, a prominent, well-connected attorney who served in many capacities in government, including Secretary of the Army, head of the CIA's Psychology Strategy Board, and others; **Donald H. Menzel,** the famous Harvard University astronomer who between 1953 and 1976 would write or co-write three books debunking UFOs; Gen. Robert M. Montague, in 1947 the commander of Fort Bliss and the White Sands Proving Ground, then head of a classified (and never-revealed) special project at Sandia Base near Kirtland AFB; and Lloyd V. Berkner, first Executive Secretary of the Defense Department's Joint Research and Development Board (on which Sarbacher also served), later to serve on the CIA's January 1953 Robertson Panel (which recommend the debunking of UFO reports) and in 1957-58 as head of the International Geophysical Year. The document noted that between Forrestal's death on May 22, 1949, and August 1, 1950, his place on MJ-12 was unfilled; then "Gen. Walter B. Smith was designated as permanent replacement." Smith, who during World War II had been Eisenhower's chief of staff, had replaced Hillenkoetter as CIA director.

The document mentions the hundreds of sightings made in late June and early July 1947, when "flying saucers" first entered public consciousness, and notes how at times the public responded with "near hysteria." Then one of the objects crashed 75 miles northwest of Roswell Field. "On 07 July, 1947, a secret operation was begun to assure recovery of the wreckage. . . . During the course of this operation, aerial reconnaissance discovered that four small human-

CRASHES OF UFOS (*continued*)

like beings had apparently ejected from the craft at some point before it exploded. These had fallen to earth about two miles east of the wreckage site. All four were dead and badly decomposed due to action by predators and exposure to the elements during the approximately one week time period which had elapsed before their discovery."

A "covert analytical effort" under the direction of Dr. Bush and Gen. Twining, "acting on the direct orders of the President," concluded that the crashed disc was probably a "short range reconnaissance craft." Dr. Bronk, who arranged autopsies of the bodies, deduced that despite their humanlike appearance "the biological and evolutionary processes responsible for their development has [sic] apparently been quite different from those observed or postulated in homo-sapiens. Dr. Bronk's team has suggested the term '**Extraterrestrial Biological Entities**', or 'EBEs', be adopted as the standard term of reference for these creatures...." Although there was some speculation that the craft had come from Mars, the document says, "some scientists, most notably Dr. Menzel, consider it more likely that we are dealing with beings from another solar system entirely."

The document goes on, "Numerous examples of what appear to be a form of writing were found in the wreckage. Efforts to decipher these have remained largely unsuccessful. . . . Equally unsuccessful have been efforts to determine the method of propulsion or the nature or method of transmission of the power source involved. . . .

"A need for as much additional information as possible about these craft, their performance characteristics and their purpose led to the undertaking known as U.S. Air Force Project SIGN in December, 1947. In order to preserve security, liason [sic] between SIGN and Majestic-12 was limited to two individuals within the Intelligence Division of Air Materiel Command whose role was to pass along certain types of information through channels. SIGN evolved into Project GRUDGE in December, 1948. The operation is currently being conducted under the code name BLUE BOOK, with liason [sic] maintained through the Air Force officer who is head of the project." (That officer would have been Capt. Edward J. Ruppelt, who would write one of the classic works in the UFO literature, *The Report on Unidentified Flying Objects* [1956]. Although cautiously sympathetic to the idea of extraterrestrial visitation, Ruppelt ridicules cover-up proponents such as Donald Keyhoe. Just before the author's death in 1960, a new edition of the book came out, with three new chapters denouncing UFOs as a "Space Age myth.")

The next paragraph reads: "On 06 December, 1950, a second object, probably of similar origin, impacted the earth at high speed in the El Indio-Guerrero area of the Texas-Mexican boder [sic] after following a long trajectory through the atmosphere. By the time a search team arrived, what remained of the object had been almost totally incinerated. Such material as could be recovered was transported to the A.E.C. facility at Sandia, New Mexico, for study." (Allegations about a crash along the border circulated through the UFO community in the 1970s, owing to the enthusiasms of W. Todd Zechel. Zechel, a founder of **Citizens Against UFO Secrecy** (CAUS), said he had heard about the crash as an Army enlisted man in Korea from a co-worker who claimed his uncle had participated in the recovery. No sooner had Zechel appeared on the UFO scene than he was enlisting financial support from film companies, television producers and book publishers so that he could conduct a proper investigation. In later years Zechel would claim to have found over 70 witnesses and informants to the event, but the names of few have ever surfaced and Zechel has never published whatever information he may have uncovered. But when the MJ-12 document became known, he asserted its account of the crash was all wrong, that the craft had come to earth relatively intact, and that the body of one of its occupants had been recovered. He charged that Moore had forged the document to discredit "his"—Zechel's—crash case even as the importance of the Roswell case was being underscored.)

Page six of the document is an "ENUMERATION OF ATTACHMENTS." B through H are listed as Operation Majestic-12 reports. Shandera received only attachment A, a TOP SECRET EYES ONLY document on White House letterhead. Supposedly written and signed by Harry Truman, it is dated September 24, 1947, and addressed to Forrestal:

"As per our recent conversation on this matter, you are hereby authorized to proceed with all due speed and caution upon your undertaking. Hereafter this matter shall be referred to only as Operation Majestic Twelve.

"It continues to be my feeling that any future considerations relative to the ultimate disposition of this matter should rest solely with the Office of the President following appropriate discussions with yourself, Dr. Bush and the Director of Central Intelligence."

Shandera and Moore did not rush to release the document but made an effort to confirm or disconfirm it. In this they were aided, they say, by their military-intelligence sources. They received two postcards, both manufactured in Ethiopia but mailed from New Zealand, with cryptic messages directing them to Washington and the National Archives, where in July 1985 the two researchers found, amid other recently-declassified documents, a memo from President Eisenhower's assistant Gen. Robert Cutler referring to an "MJ-12 SSP [Special Studies Project] briefing" to "take place during the already scheduled White House meeting of July 16. . . ." Although nothing was said about the nature of MJ-12, this seemed clear confirmation that a project by that name did exist.

Moore and Shandera kept all this a secret, though they did show the document to fellow cover-up investigator Lee Graham, who described what he had seen to Bruce Maccabee. Maccabee wrote an article, "What the Admiral Knew: UFOs, MJ-12 and Roscoe Hillenkoetter" (*International UFO Reporter*, November/December 1986), repeating what Graham had told him, mentioning the interesting discovery in the National Archives

and relating these to other documents, claims and speculations. Maccabee's article, however, had little impact—certainly compared to what would happen when the "actual" document would be released.

In May 1987, according to Moore and Shandera, their sources informed them that a separate release of the MJ-12 document was about to take place in Europe. They learned that London ufologist Timothy Good had also been given a copy of it and would announce as much to the British press. So on May 29 Moore mailed copies to reporters and ufologists, but not before putting thick black ink through classification designations and even some of the text—a pointless endeavor for which he would be much criticized. At the same time Good released his copy. (Good has never revealed his source but insists it was *not* Moore and Shandera. In late 1989 a published account of uncertain reliability claimed it was an American CIA agent. Nonetheless, like Moore and Shandera's copy, Good's was missing all appendices except A, the alleged Truman executive order.)

The first major press article appeared on the front page of the *London Observer* on May 31. The article, which would be widely reprinted around the world, took note of the first stirrings of skepticism among ufologists, quoting Massachusetts-based investigator Barry Greenwood, a longtime student of official involvement in UFO study, as suggesting the document was a forgery. "A bitter debate is now likely to develop among UFO experts," reporter Martin Bailey wrote prophetically.

Even as ufologists were expressing wonder and doubt, such mainstream media as the *New York Times*, the *Washington Post*, *The New Republic* and ABC-TV's *Nightline* were picking up the story, sparking an expression of alarm about press credulity from the *Columbia Journalism Review* and other self-styled media watchdogs. On August 20 the **Committee for the Scientific Investigation of Claims of the Paranormal** (CSICOP) issued a widely-reported press release denouncing the document as a fake. "This represents one of the

CRASHES OF UFOS (*continued*)

most deliberate attacks of deception ever perpetrated against the news media and the public," chairman Paul Kurtz charged. Soon the J. Allen Hynek Center for UFO Studies issued its own press release, refuting CSICOP's point by point and urging that further investigation would have to be conducted before any conclusion, positive or negative, could be reached.

Pro and Con on Majestic-12: The debate about the MJ-12 briefing paper raged through the rest of the decade. The battles were fought mostly within the UFO community, which remained largely doubtful. The leading critics were Greenwood and Larry Fawcett of Citizens Against UFO Secrecy (CAUS), UFO lecturer Robert Hastings and British ufologist Christopher D. Allan. A particularly fierce antagonist was CSICOP's UFO debunker **Philip J. Klass**, who wrote articles, white papers and letters denouncing Moore and hinting, as discreetly as libel laws allowed, that Moore had forged the document—an accusation for which certain evidence has yet to be produced. The most energetic defender of the document (though he refused to call himself a "proponent") was Stanton Friedman, who wrote to refute critics' charges. In 1988 he received a $16,000 grant from the Fund for UFO Research to conduct the archival work and interviews that it would take to resolve the controversy. Friedman worked hard but by the end of 1989 acknowledged that he had been unable to settle the issue.

When the controversy began, it was thought that document analysis would make a conclusive determination. But document analysts, ufologists quickly learned, were less sure; they complained that their work was seriously handicapped by the fact that they had no actual document to work with, only a photograph of a document, and the process of photography caused distortions in the type. So the battles were fought on other grounds: on the rendering of dates (the "0" as in "07 July, 1947" and "06 December, 1950" was much remarked on), the wording of the classification stamps, the verifiable physical locations of

individuals versus their locations as claimed in the documents, and so on. In time the arguments became arcane and, except to the most committed defenders and detractors, tedious. Those with the stamina to follow it generally agreed that the debunkers had produced few objections so compelling that the defenders could not reasonably answer; at the same time the defenders had been able to make only the broadest of circumstantial cases for the document's authenticity.

Of all the claims made in the document, there was only one that could not have been concocted out of a careful reading of the UFO literature of the early 1980s. This was the allegation that Donald Menzel, despite his public posture as a fierce foe of beliefs about the reality of UFOs, was privy to the Ultimate Secret and, beyond that, had the security clearances and intelligence associations *to be* privy to it. So far as ufologists—or, for that matter, his biographers—knew, Menzel was a civilian scientist no more likely to know about deep national-security secrets than his modern-day counterpart Carl Sagan would be in later decades. Intrigued by the mention of Menzel in the MJ-12 document, Friedman launched an investigation in which, after gaining access to unpublished and heretofore-unexamined papers, he found that Menzel had led a double life, one so secret that not even his closest friends knew about it. It turned out that Menzel had long been associated with both the CIA and the National Security Agency, worked on numerous classified projects for industrial companies, and possessed a Navy TOP SECRET ULTRA security clearance. Moreover, since the 1930s he had been a good friend of Vannevar Bush. Friedman speculated that, besides contributing his scientific expertise to the study of UFO remains, Menzel had served to dissuade his scientific colleagues from becoming seriously interested in the UFO phenomenon.

To critics this suggested that the MJ-12 document had been forged by official sources cognizant of Menzel's secret history. Other phony UFO documents, some associated with a disinformation campaign run out of the AFOSI office at Kirtland AFB, are known or strongly suspected to be the creation of military-intelligence personnel. But this, like anything else related to the document, was speculation.

The strongest *prima facie* reason to question the document's authenticity came with the discovery that the signature on Truman's disputed September 24, 1947, executive order (Appendix A) and that on an unquestioned Presidential letter of October 1 to Bush seem not just suspiciously similar but identical. Benedict K. Zobrist, director of the Harry S Truman Library, says Truman never used a signature machine; so the only other possible conclusion, critics believe, is that a hoaxer with a copy machine appended a real signature to a fictitious executive order. If this in fact is the case, that hardly makes the MJ-12 document any less mysterious. If a hoax, as it almost certainly is, it is the most sophisticated in UFO history, and intriguing questions about the identities and motivations of the hoaxers remain.

Roswell Redux: In 1988 the J. Allen Hynek Center for UFO Studies decided to reopen the Roswell case, which had lain mostly dormant in recent years as the MJ-12 issue claimed the attention and energy of Moore and Friedman. CUFOS officials felt that it might still be possible to learn more and they were unhappy with some aspects of the earlier investigation. The new effort was spearheaded by Don Schmitt, CUFOS' Director of Special Investigations, and by writer and former Air Force intelligence officer Kevin D. Randle, with some help from Friedman. By the end of 1989 Schmitt and Randle had reinterviewed all still-living informants who originally had told their stories to Moore and Friedman; they also found over 60 additional persons who were close to the incident or to individuals who had participated in the recovery. In September 1989 CUFOS brought a 10-person team, including three scientists, to the crash site in an attempt, which proved unsuccessful, to recover material (however minute) that might have remained there undetected after 42 years.

Schmitt and Randle's investigation called into question some aspects of Moore and Friedman's

reconstruction of the incident but significantly strengthened the evidence for the event's extraordinary nature. Most spectacularly, they were able to pinpoint the location at which, according to their sources, the bodies of the occupants were found (on the Brazel property, not, as Moore and Berlitz had it in *The Roswell Incident*, on the Plains of San Augustin, many miles to the west) and to learn who had participated in the recovery and what had been done to the bodies. The results of their on-going research were to be reported in 1990, first in the *International UFO Reporter* and then in a book.

Before 1989 the Roswell story, despite occasional articles about it, was little known outside the UFO community. But in the fall of that year **Whitley Strieber**, a novelist who had written about his abduction experiences in two much-discussed books (*Communion: A True Story* [1987] and *Transformation: The Breakthrough* [1988]), produced an imaginary version of the Roswell incident in *Majestic* (1989). He made clear, both in an afterword to the novel and in media interviews, that the novel was based on a "factual reality that has been hidden and denied." In September NBC-TV's *Unsolved Mysteries* told an abbreviated version of the incident, with actors playing some of the key figures.

A Crash in South Africa?: The latter half of 1989 also saw the emergence of two other crash-related stories which seemed likely to be the focus of attention, investigation and controversy in 1990 and beyond.

In the first of these, documents purporting to be leaked from the South African Air Force claimed that on May 7, 1989, two Mirage fighter aircraft pursued a fast-moving UFO and shot it down with, as a document stamped CLASSIFIED TOP SECRET has it, an "experimental aircraft mounted thor 2 laser canon [sic]." The account goes on:

"Squadron leader [deleted] reported that several blinding flashes eminated [sic] from the object. The object started wavering whilst still heading in a northerly direction. At [illegible] it was

CRASHES OF UFOS (*continued*)

reported that the object was decreasing altitude at a rate of 3000 feet per minute. Then at great speed it dived at an angle of 25 degrees and impacted in desert terrain 80km north of South African border with Botswana, identified as the Central Kalahari Desert. Squadron leader [deleted] was instructed to circle the area until a retreival [sic] of the object was complete. A team of airforce intelligence officers, together with medical and technical staff[,] were promptly taken to area of impact for investigation and retreival [sic].

"The findings were as follows:

"1) A crater of 150 metres in diameter and 12 metres in depth.

"2) A silver coloured disc shaped object 45 degrees embedded in side of crater.

"3) Around object sand and rocks were fused together by the intense heat.

"4) An intense magnetic and radioactive environment around object resulted in electronic failure in air force equipment.

"5) It was suggested by team leader that object be moved to a classified air force base . . . for further investigation and this was done."

According to subsequent reports, though not from very reliable sources, occupants were found at the crash site. The wreckage and the bodies were shipped to Wright-Patterson AFB in Ohio in exchange for advanced American weapons technology. An informant claiming to be a South African Air Force man involved in the event surfaced and fled to England, then to an unnamed South American country. He was interviewed in hiding by a prominent American ufologist.

Details remained both murky and scant at year's end. Ufologists investigating the claim were intrigued but deeply suspicious. If a hoax, it appeared to be a complex and expensive one,

raising new concerns about the continuing spread of disinformation, apparently with official sponsorship, about crashed-disc claims.

Mystery in Nevada: An even more remarkable development came from outside the UFO community. In November KLAS-TV in Las Vegas devoted two nights to the astonishing testimony of one Robert Lazar.

Area 51 is situated at a corner of the Nevada Test Site, where highly-classified national-security work has been conducted for several decades. Spy planes such as the U-2 and the SR-71 were developed there. It is also the place where government scientists and engineers planned and experimented with the technology that brought the Stealth aircraft into being and where the technology of the Strategic Defense Initiative (popularly known as "Star Wars") was created. The CIA has developed sophisticated devices there. Area 51 is in a remote location ringed by the Groom Mountains and vast desert expanses.

It is also a place over which odd lights, maneuvering in ways conventional aircraft do not, flying at great speeds, stopping suddenly and hovering, have been reported for some time. These sightings, plus other stories from sources of varying credibility, have sparked rumors that the technology being developed at Area 51 is not entirely earthly in origin.

On November 11 and 13 KLAS reporter George Knapp told the story of Bob Lazar, allegedly a physicist who worked at Area 51 called S-4, where he saw, in Lazar's words, "nine . . . flying discs that are out there of extraterrestrial origin." Knapp said he had been employed by the Navy and when he went to S-4, he assumed he was to work on advanced propulsion systems. The first day he was there, he was given briefing papers to read and quickly realized that the propulsion systems were advanced beyond anything he could have imagined. "The power source is an anti-matter reactor," he told Knapp. "They run gravity amplifiers. There is [sic] actually two parts to the drive mechanism. It's a bizarre technology. There is [sic] no physical hookups between any of the systems in there. They use gravity as a wave, using wave guides that look like microwaves."

Lazar said the work areas were peppered with posters showing a disc-shaped craft lifted three feet off the ground, with the caption "They're here." Only later, however, did he see the real thing, when he was led into a hangar and directed to walk past the disc without looking directly at it or saying anything about it. But as he passed it, he could not resist the temptation to put his hand on it. Subsequently, he said, he was permitted to see the craft flown. He also saw the other eight craft in connecting hangars separated by large bay doors. All had a different shape, but all were generally discoid in form. One, he said, "looked new, if I knew what a new flying saucer looked like. One of them looked like it was hit with some sort of a projectile. It had a large hole in the bottom and a large hole in the top with the metal bent out like some sort of . . . large caliber four- or five-inch had gone through it."

Although Lazar was told nothing about the nature and origin of these vehicles, once he looked inside the "sport model" (as he called the craft that looked newest) and saw "it had really small chairs." He was shocked. Before this, he had been able to tell himself that the project he was working on was not so strange and unearthly as he sometimes suspected it was, but now "things began to click together just all too fast." When he got to see the craft actually being flown, he knew such achievements could not possibly have come solely from terrestrial knowledge, however advanced. Even more telling to him was his discovery that an element, called 115 and unknown to earthly science, was being used in the development of the gravity-harnessing technology. The U.S. government, he said, has 500 pounds of it stored in lead casings. He said it would be "impossible to synthesize an element that heavy here on earth. . . . The substance has to come from a place where super-heavy elements could have been produced naturally."

He speculated that not even Congress knew about the project ("they don't report to anyone") and that it was unlikely it would ever be an-nounced to the American people. In his view the funding probably came out of the Star Wars project.

Working at the site was not a pleasant occupation, according to Lazar. Security was enforced by constant fear in which "they did everything but physically hurt me," even putting a gun to his head. "They did that even in the original security briefing," he said. "Guards there with M-16s. Guys there slamming their fingers into my chest, screaming into my ear. They were pointing guns at me." He said security personnel even came to his house periodically and threatened his and his wife's lives, all as part of an effort to make sure they never talked.

Knapp interviewed Gene Huff, a Las Vegas real-estate appraiser and Lazar's neighbor, to whom Lazar eventually confided his story. At one point, according to Huff, he, Lazar and a few others managed over two consecutive weekends to film the maneuvers of a fast-moving, glowing object which rose up from the Groom Mountains and maneuvered in the sky for a period of time. The KLAS presentation showed the videotape.

"Checking out Lazar's credentials proved to be a difficult task," Knapp reported. Other investigators, notably Stanton T. Friedman, found the same thing. Lazar claimed, for example, to have degrees from the Massachusetts Institute of Technology, which denies ever having heard of him. A claimed association with the California Institute of Technology also failed to check out. Although claiming to be a physicist, he is not a member of the American Physical Society. A check with the Social Security Administration established that a card with the numbers Lazar gives was assigned to a Robert Lazar. Lazar also said he had worked with one of the world's largest particle-beam accelerators at the Los Alamos National Laboratories. But when Los Alamos later denied any knowledge of his employment there, Knapp found it was "either mistaken or . . . lying. A 1982 phone book from the lab lists Lazar right there among the other scientists and technicians. A 1982 news clipping from the Los Alamos news-paper profiled Lazar and his interest in jet cars.

71

CRASHES OF UFOS (*continued*)

It, too, mentioned his employment at the lab as a physicist."

Lazar says, "They're trying to make me look nonexistent . . . [at] the schools I went to; the hospital that I was born at; past jobs. Nothing comes up with my name on it."

As part of his investigation, Knapp had Lazar undergo a polygraph examination. One examiner gave him two tests, one of which indicated truthfulness, the other deception. A second examiner put Lazar through four tests and found no evidence of any attempt to deceive. A third polygrapher examined the charts and agreed with the second examiner's conclusions. A fourth examiner disagreed, saying it looked to him as if Lazar were reporting something he had heard, not something he had personally experienced. In his televised report Knapp said, "The polygraphers . . . decided they would not issue a final statement on truthfulness until more specific testing can be conducted. And that's where it stands." The second polygrapher expressed the opinion that the ambiguities in the test results were caused not by lies but by Lazar's fears and anxieties.

Knapp also arranged for Lazar to undergo hypnosis, in part because Lazar said he suspected mind-control techniques had been used on him to make him forget much of what he had seen or heard. The hypnotist, Layne Keck, was told only that Lazar wanted aid in recalling the contents of briefing papers (contents unspecified) he had seen. Keck later told Knapp, "I have no clue as to what we were getting into and he started saying that there were pictures of what I thought was [sic] desks on the wall. Well, as it turned out, it was discs that he was referring to. And at that moment I realized we were into something that was pretty heavy."

Keck concluded that Lazar was telling the truth as he saw it. He said it appeared that Lazar had been subjected to mind manipulation, including chemicals, both to frighten him and to dim his memory.

Lazar acknowledged that "I'm not going to change anyone's mind. . . . I don't expect anyone to believe it." But Knapp stated on the television program that he *does* believe Lazar for a number of reasons, not the least of them the man's reluctance to appear on the show, his unwillingness to profit from his experiences, and his neighbor's testimony. More important, Knapp said he had interviewed other individuals, all unnamed, who said it is "common knowledge among those with high-security clearances that recovered alien discs are stored at the Nevada Test Site," as a "technician in a highly-sensitive position" put it. Other sources—a "Las Vegas professional, who once served in the military and was stationed at the test site"; a "man who once worked at Groom Lake as a technician"; and an "airman who worked at Nellis [AFB] at a radar installation"—told Knapp stories of discs they had seen on the ground or in the air.

At year's end journalist Knapp was continuing his investigation, and ufologists were also following leads. The Lazar saga had just begun. It seems safe to say that the crashed-disc controversy would be at the forefront of 1990s ufology.

Sources:

Beckley, Timothy Green. *MJ-12 and the Riddle of Hangar 18*. New Brunswick, NJ: Inner Light Publications, 1989.

Berlitz, Charles, and William L. Moore. *The Roswell Incident*. New York: Grosset & Dunlap, 1980.

Cahn, J. P. "Flying Saucers and the Mysterious Little Men." *True* (September 1952): 17-19, 102-112.

Clark, Jerome. "Books, News & Reviews." *Fate* 34, 2 (February 1981): 111-15.

Clark, Jerome. "Crashed Saucers—Another View." *UFO Report* 8, 1 (February 1980): 28-31, 50, 52, 54-56.

Clark, Jerome. "Spaceship and Saltshaker." *International UFO Reporter* 11, 6 (November/December 1986): 12, 21.

Earley, George W. "Crashed Saucers and Pickled Aliens." *Fate* Pt. I. 34, 3 (March 1981): 42-48; Pt. II. 34, 4 (April 1981): 84-89.

Fawcett, Lawrence, and Barry J. Greenwood. *Clear Intent: The Government Coverup of the UFO Experience.* Englewood Cliffs, NJ: Prentice-Hall, Inc., 1984.

Friedman, Stanton T. "The Secret Life of Donald H. Menzel." *International UFO Reporter* 13, 1 (January/February 1988): 20-24.

Friedman, Stanton T. "Update on Operation Majestic-12." In Walter H. Andrus, Jr., ed. *MUFON 1989 International UFO Symposium Proceedings.* Seguin, TX: Mutual UFO Network, Inc., 1989. Pp. 81-112.

Good, Timothy. *Above Top Secret: The Worldwide UFO Cover-up.* New York: William Morrow and Company, Inc., 1988.

Hastings, Robert. "The MJ-12 Affair: Facts, Questions, Comments." *MUFON UFO Journal* 254 (June 1989): 3-11.

Jacobs, David M. "Crashed Discs—No." *International UFO Reporter* 10, 4 (July/August 1985): 4, 6.

Klass, Philip J. "Crash of the Crashed-Saucer Claim." *The Skeptical Inquirer* 10, 3 (Spring 1986): 234-237, 240-241.

Klass, Philip J. *"Smoking Gun" Confirms That MJ-12 Documents Are Counterfeit.* Washington: The Author, September 20, 1989.

Maccabee, Bruce. "What the Admiral Knew: UFOs, Mj-12 and Roscoe Hillenkoetter." *International UFO Reporter* 11, 6 (November/December 1986): 15-21.

Maccabee, Bruce, ed. *Documents and Supporting Information Related to Crashed Flying Saucers and Operation Majestic Twelve.* Mount Rainier, MD: Fund for UFO Research, 1987.

Moore, William L. "Crashed Saucers: Evidence in Search of Proof." In Walter H. Andrus, Jr., and Richard H. Hall, eds. *MUFON 1985 UFO Symposium Proceedings*, 130-179. Seguin, TX: Mutual UFO Network, Inc., 1985.

Moore, William L. "Phil Klass and the Roswell Incident: The Skeptics Deceived." *International UFO Reporter* 11, 4 (July/August 1986): 15-22.

Rodeghier, Mark. "Roswell, 1989." *International UFO Reporter* 14, 5 (September/October 1989): 3-8, 23.

Schmitt, Don, and Kevin D. Randle. "Roswell, July 9, 1947." *International UFO Reporter* 14, 6 (November/December 1988): 4-6, 23.

Scully, Frank. *Behind the Flying Saucers.* New York: Henry Holt, 1950.

Simmons, H. Michael. "Once Upon a Time in the West." *Magonia* 20 (August 1985): 3-6.

Steinman, William S., with Wendelle C. Stevens. *UFO Crash at Aztec: A Well Kept Secret.* Tucson, AZ: UFO Photo Archives, 1986.

Stringfield. Leonard H. *Situation Red, The UFO Siege!* Garden City, NY: Doubleday & Company, 1977.

Stringfield, Leonard H. *The UFO Crash/Retrieval Syndrome. Status Report II: New Sources, New Data.* Seguin, TX: Mutual UFO Network, Inc., 1980.

D

DELVAL UFO, INC.
948 Almshouse Road
Ivyland, Pennsylvania 18974

Delval UFO, Inc., "Dedicated to Universal Brotherhood," was formed in 1972. A **contactee**-oriented group which seeks to "commune with our Space Brothers and Sisters on all levels of existence" and to "prepare humankind for [its] place in this New Age that is now upon us," it meets on the second Wednesday of all months except July, August and December. It publishes *Awakening* 10 times a year to a readership in the United States, Canada and Japan. The directors are Anthony and Lynn Volpe.

Sources:

Volpe, Anthony, and Lynn Volpe. *Principles and Purposes of Delval UFO Inc.* Ivyland, PA: n.d.

Volpe, Lynn. Personal communication (October 19, 1989).

DRUFFEL, ANN (1929-)

Ufologist Ann Druffel dates her interest in UFOs from before the current "flying saucer" era began in 1947. In 1945, when she was a teenager, she sighted a UFO over Long Beach, California. She attended Immaculate Heart College where she earned her B.A. in sociology and did a year of graduate work at Catholic University. She married Charles K. Druffel. During the 1950s she combined an interest in psychic phenomena with her interest in UFOs. As early as 1957 she became a field investigator for the National Investigations Committee on Aerial Phenomena (NICAP). She remained with it until 1975 when she for a time became an investigator for the Center for UFO Studies (now the **J. Allen Hynek Center for UFO Studies**). Since 1972 she has also been associated with the **Mutual UFO Network** (MUFON), and has periodically contributed articles to both the *International UFO Reporter* and the *MUFON UFO Journal*.

Over the years Druffel has become convinced that UFOs have been a noticeable presence in human culture since prehistoric times. They have had a role to play in the past evolution of humankind, such as the change from Neanderthal to Cro-Magnon, and will play a role in the next evolutionary step for the race.

At the end of the 1970s, with Los Angeles writer D. Scott Rogo, she investigated a set of UFO encounters which resulted in one of the earlier case studies of the **abduction phenomenon**. Her and Rogo's investigation was reported in their book *The Tujunga Canyon Contacts* (1980). While her experience in the investigation did not lead to a definitive solution to the UFO question, it did confirm some longheld beliefs about the nature of UFOs and abductions. She finally concluded that whether or not the events reported by the abductees actually took place (as part of our

DRUFFEL, ANN (*continued*)

common reality) was of little ultimate importance. Rather, the abductions point toward the parapsychological aspect of the UFO experience, which often occurs in an altered state of consciousness. UFOs are probably not physical craft, but something from another space-time continuum.

J. Gordon Melton

Sources:

Boyd, Robert D. *International Who's Who in Ufology Directory*. Mobile, AL: The Author, 1988.

Druffel, Ann. "Resisting UFO 'Entities.'" *UFO* 4, 4 (1989): 16-19.

Druffel, Ann, and D. Scott Rogo. *The Tujunga Canyon Contacts*. Englewood Cliffs, NJ: Prentice-Hall, 1980.

Story, Ronald D. *The Encyclopedia of UFOs*. Garden City, NY: Doubleday & Company, 1980.

E

EARTHLIGHTS AND TECTONIC STRAIN THEORY

Natural phenomena have often been suggested as an explanation for UFOs, but such theories traditionally fail to account for the wide variety of traits reported by UFO sighters. A new theory, however, seeks to explain many heretofore-ignored UFO characteristics. This theory, called the Tectonic Strain Theory (TST), begins with the suggestion that strain fields within the earth's crust can produce an electromagnetic discharge which may manifest itself in one of two basic ways. One way is by the electric discharge's becoming visible as a moving body of light. The other way is by discharge's affecting the human brain so that the observer will believe he or she is viewing a moving body of light or otherwise having an anomalous experience. Both scenarios are consistent with the theory and are used to explain the reported appearances of UFOs.

Mostly, statistical evidence alone has been presented in support of this theory. This has been in the form of covariation of the number of reported UFOs in an area and the level of seismic activity in that area. Whether this is a real relationship or an artifact is not clear. Some studies have also attempted to correlate fluctuations in the earth's magnetic field with UFOs and other unusual phenomena. An early examination of this idea was presented by French ufologist Claude Poher in 1974, with limited success. Recently the idea has resurfaced in the context of the TST.

Papers dealing with certain aspects of the TST have been published in several journals covering various disciplines. The proposed mechanism is interdisciplinary in nature and carries with it some necessary qualifications to enable it to cope with a poorly-understood phenomenon in terms of better-known phenomena. The theory is best explained by its major proponent, Michael Persinger:

"Essentially . . . normal geophysical processes applied in unusual space-time configurations are responsible for electromagnetic phenomena that have direct physical and biological consequences. These processes involve normal alterations in tectonic (structural) stresses within the Earth's crust and are mediated by piezoelectric-like effects. The primary natural analog of this putative phenomena [sic] would be earthquake lightning. . . . Whereas earthquake-related luminosities appear contingent upon large releases of structural strain (seismic activities), the luminosities and electromagnetic correlates of alleged close encounters with UFOs are associated with highly localized, less intense changes in crustal structures not necessarily involving major seismic activity" (Persinger, 1980).

The TST draws on a number of processes for its mechanism, and it is best to examine each of them in some detail. The physical processes are linked implicitly by logical arguments, although the basis for these arguments needs examination. The major steps involved are:

EARTHLIGHTS AND TECTONIC STRAIN THEORY (*continued*)

(1) Strain is produced in the earth's crust.

(2) Strain produces an electromagnetic discharge.

(3a) The electromagnetic discharge produces a luminosity.

(4a) The luminosity is observed as a UFO.

Alternatively, steps 3a and 4a may be replaced by:

(3b) The electromagnetic discharge affects human perception.

(4b) A person believes that he or she has seen a UFO.

There are many types of reported earthquake precursors on record, including ground deformation, changes in well water, and unusual behavior in animals. A form of precursor that has received relatively little attention is that of the emission of electromagnetic (EM) radiation. Many such reports are spurious or represent other natural or man-made causes, but a significant number are well-documented.

For example, on March 31, 1980, anomalous EM emissions were recorded 30 minutes before a deep-focus magnitude 7 earthquake, 250 kilometers from an observatory near Tokyo. These emissions were widely separated at 10 Hz and 81 kHz. Other similar emissions were recorded for a magnitude 7.4 earthquake in Iran, 1200 km from the epicenter, at 27 kHz and 1.63 MHz.

It has been known for some time that the strain loading of rocks and minerals produces EM emission. The strength of the emission varies with the different types of substances; the strongest emission arises from quartz and other minerals with a high crystal lattice energy, while rocks such as sandstone have a very low ability to produce emission under strain. The actual mechanism for the production of the emission is not definitely known, although several theories have been proposed.

The term "piezoelectricity" comes from the Greek word *piezein*, meaning "to press." Piezoelectricity is an electrical charge produced when crystalline material is subjected to pressure. An example is the crystal in a crystal radio—a slight scratching of a needle upon the crystal's surface made the radio work. A better-known example is the luminous effect caused by biting down on a wintergreen candy or mint. In nature, crystalline rocks such as quartz will have a certain amount of piezoelectric potential when they are stressed by rocks above them or below.

Geologists have shown that a rapid drop in the piezoelectric field when stress is released (i.e., when fracturing occurs) can produce EM emission. Experiments have shown that the peak frequency for such a piezoelectric pulse is at about 1.7 kHz. There is some doubt, however, that piezoelectricity can produce earthquake lights because of its rapid decay and the possibility of its self-canceling nature as soon as it is generated.

An alternate theory for EM emission during fracturing is that of radio-frequency (RF) emission caused by a charge build-up across microcracks in the strained rock. During strain processes there will be discharges between walls of the microcracks which can give not only RF emission but also infrared and visible light as well.

The most plausible proposed mechanism involves the propagation of an elastic wave within rock, following fracture. Geophysicists have speculated that the wave would induce the growth of microcracks, and—in the case of semiconducting and piezoelectric minerals—the cracking would produce electrical discharges. But the piezoelectric field might also create "transistors" within the rock, using as barriers the layers of semiconducting minerals occurring naturally in the ore. These "transistors" could be coupled into "circuits," and an EM emission caused by the formation of microcracks could be amplified, in theory, by these piezoelectric and semiconducting minerals. It is immediately obvious that in this mechanism the frequency of the amplified EM wave would be dependent on several variables, especially the composition of the rock. This frequency could, depending on these variables, be represented at many points in the EM spectrum, including radio, infrared, visible and x-ray wavelengths.

If visible light is produced, its nature is not well understood. Luminescence has been reported in the geophysical literature, but only in the form of "comet tails" detected on photographic film close to the rock undergoing fracture. But small luminous bodies have been detected on a film of the fracturing of a core sample in the laboratory. These bodies have the reported appearance of sparks but are believed to be fracture- and not impact-related. Luminosities produced outside the laboratory will, it is thought, be much larger than those observed in the laboratory, perhaps reaching one meter or more in diameter.

If it is indeed possible that balls of light can be produced in nature by crystal stress, then it would seem likely that they would have been observed and reported. Many reports of seemingly inexplicable lights in the sky have been made. Further, there do exist rare natural phenomena that appear as lights in the night sky. These include ball lightning and earthquake lights, both of which are still not fully understood by scientists, but progress is being made in unraveling their mysteries.

In general, earthquake lights are luminous hemispheres, 20 to 200 meters in diameter, seen about the time of an earthquake and with a duration of a few seconds to a few minutes. In addition, radio interference is reported to occur after the luminescence, strongest at about 15 kHz, which is an order of magnitude from the peak emission for strain release under laboratory conditions.

Ball lightning has been reported infrequently, but enough cases are on record that some characteristics have been determined. The phenomenon is generally spherical, with a diameter of about 30 centimeters, and may contain a large amount of energy.

The TST proposes that many UFOs are produced by a strain field which is caused by crustal stress. This strain field is visibly indicated by a fracture (earthquake) which may occur many kilometers distant and many days or even months separated in time and space from the point at which the UFO was observed. It has been claimed that there is a statistical correlation between the numbers of UFO reports and earthquake activity. In effect, an increase in earthquake activity means an increase in UFO reports.

But the statistical correlation works best when UFO reports from large distances are included. This is described by TST proponents as choosing an "optimal space and time increment." For example, in a UFO/earthquake-correlation study in the New Madrid earthquake area, not only were the recognized New Madrid states included, but so were those surrounding them as well. The statistical study did find a good correlation for some years but also found a "lag" for others.

Hence, this is the source of the suggestion that UFO reports are related to earthquakes through a common strain field which may cover a large area. The UFOs may be observed hundreds of kilometers from the epicenter of an earthquake and still be related.

But what exactly is the strain field responsible for the UFOs and the earthquakes? It is known that crustal stress can build within rock through various processes, including tectonic and tidal force-related activities. This stress will accumulate in a certain area within the crust, the exact structure and dimensions of this area being dependent upon the local geology and the physical composition of the rocks involved.

Most sources agree that the size of the region strained to its breaking point prior to a fracture (earthquake) is about 20-50 kilometers in radius, but this depends on the magnitude. Rock outside this area will be under some strain but not

EARTHLIGHTS AND TECTONIC STRAIN THEORY (*continued*)

enough to cause fracture. There is no practical method for determining the exact extent of the strained region, since there will be some strain, even at large distances from the earthquake epicenter. Therefore the determination of a "strain field" is decidedly arbitrary.

TST advocates have argued that a strain field may travel extensively and be transmitted great distances through stable continental regions. In this way, for example, it has been claimed by TST advocates that the San Francisco earthquake of 1989 was linked to UFOs as far away as Manitoba, over 1500 kilometers away.

If a "strain field" is in existence, then the TST implies that its major visible indicator is an earthquake. Since this field is said to be responsible for the appearance of a UFO, critics have rightly asked why the UFO would not appear adjacent to the fracture site, where the most energy is released.

Earthquake lightning is often observed concurrently with earthquakes, and although it may be theorized that UFOs are indicators of smaller fractures, the use of "optimal temporal increments" to associate UFOs and earthquakes in a strain field tends to point out a lack of similarity between the two phenomena. Specifically, earthquake lightning is essentially simultaneous with an earthquake, while according to the TST UFOs can appear much before or later. Therefore, earthquake lights are probably not upscaled versions of UFOs.

What about energy produced within the crust at unknown depths? Radio wave propagation through rock is of the order of a few meters, unless one includes such things as "natural circuits" and energy tunneling. Even assuming that this energy could find its way to the surface, the method by which it would discharge into the atmosphere and exhibit UFO-like characteristics has not been adequately demonstrated.

In Britain a version of the TST is called earthlights and its principal proponent is Paul Devereux. He and his associates carried out experiments in which they crushed a specimen of rock and observed lights produced during this process. They went on to allege that they found the "best UFO-geology correlations yet published." For example, they found out that many UFO sightings in Wales occurred within a few hundred meters of a fault.

Devereux makes one distinction, however, in that he disagrees that piezoelectricity is the causative mechanism for UFOs. He suggests triboluminescence as a "more likely candidate." The two processes are different mechanisms, but both produce luminous phenomena in minerals. Piezoelectricity is created when certain crystals are subjected to pressure, while triboluminescence is the effect caused by mechanical friction upon two mineral surfaces.

The earthlight (EL) theory parallels the TST in many ways. A significant difference is that the EL theory restricts "earth energy" effects upon human systems to distances generally less than one kilometer, whereas the TST involves faults or events up to 200 kilometers away from an observer.

Rather than creating a physical luminosity through the production of visible photons, an alternate method to produce a UFO in the TST is the direct effect of EM radiation upon the human brain.

It has long been understood that both electric and magnetic fields affect physiological systems in various ways. Effects range from dizziness and irritation in weak fields to severe disruptive effects such as induced epilepsy in strong fields. Basically, it appears that the electrochemical responses within the body are interfered with by external fields, causing a confusion of signals received and originating from the brain. Experimental tests have shown that headaches are frequently reported by individuals exposed to electric fields for extended periods of time. Moreover, fatigue and sleepiness are reported to be symptoms of prolonged exposure to electric fields, although other studies fail to support this conclusion, possibly due to differing experimental conditions. Medical examinations of individuals exposed to electric fields have found changes in blood composition and cardiovascular function.

This has been further carried by TST proponents to an extreme situation where UFO witnesses and field investigators are thought to be at increased cancer risk. The reasoning is that if an area where UFOs are observed is indeed bathed in EM radiation from TST processes, then people living or working in the area for an extended period of time would receive large doses of this radiation. This is fundamentally similar to the current debate over cancer risk in people living near power-transmission lines, although the TST by definition is a natural rather than a man-made source of energy.

The perception of electric and magnetic fields by human beings has been a topic of interest for many years. Electric fields of about 10 kV/m can be consciously detected by human beings, usually by the erection of body hairs. Weaker fields of less than five V/m are claimed to produce behavioral effects, although this is being debated by psychologists.

The problem of magnetic-field exposure is not an easy one; few studies on this matter have been conducted. So far the actual effects are not fully known, although the strength at which magnetic fields are thought capable of influencing biological functions may be as low as one gauss. (For reference, a typical standard light bulb radiates a magnetic field of about two gauss, while a more complicated appliance such as a coffeemaker generates about 10 gauss.) Magnetic fields may be perceived as low as 10 gauss in strength. It has even been proposed that the detection of weak magnetic gradients can explain the "art" of dowsing in humans.

There is some evidence that electric and magnetic fields may operate directly upon the central nervous system, interfering with the normal transmission of information to and from the brain.

Because of the potential danger of exposure to EM radiation, limits were recently proposed for the maximum recommended level of human irradiation. (Interestingly, there are phenomena known as magnetic phosphenes which may be relevant to the subject of UFOs. Under the influence of an alternating magnetic field, an individual will sometimes observe flashes of light.)

Under extreme conditions, it has been speculated, at high voltages individuals may experience severe alterations in normal brain functions. "Dreamy conditions" and temporary paralysis may be experienced. Other suggested sensations are out-of-body experiences, religious "awakenings" and feelings of "cosmic significance." Analogies of these emotions can be produced by stimulating certain parts of the brain with electric currents. Such stimulation may also induce false memories of dreamed events, making a person believe that he or she has experienced something that never took place. These "artificial hallucinations" would seem real to the individual thus influenced. In this way aspects of UFO experiences such as seeing an alien entity and interacting with it may be explained in terms of interference in brain functions.

The temporal lobe in the brain is sensitive to EM radiation. TST advocates believe that reports in the psychological literature support their contention that all kinds of anomalous experiences can be ascribed to some sort of interference with the organ's function.

In fact, the TST has minimal supporting evidence but it does have wide appeal to individuals who wish to explain UFOs via known mechanisms. Although elements of the TST appear to include documented geophysical phenomena, the main thrust of the theory hinges on its unproved relationship with a controversial phenomenon, namely UFOs. For a theory of its kind, the TST has received a large amount of publicity and a generally-uncontested entrance into the scientific literature. This situation has resulted in an apparent acceptance of the theory's "principles" without much scientific comment.

81

EARTHLIGHTS AND TECTONIC STRAIN THEORY (*continued*)

Although statistics on UFO reports have been kept for over 40 years (and much earlier, if we include pre-1947 reports), the data are without many redeeming features. Data sources such as UFOCAT, a computerized catalog developed originally by psychologist David Saunders, contain many reports with poor investigation or insufficient information due to the methods used in obtaining data. For example, many entries in UFOCAT are from published articles or newspaper clippings, and not necessarily from an investigator's reports. Many reports are therefore anecdotal rather than factual. Problems with UFO data are found in all UFO-report listings. Problems such as these led Allan Hendry to observe that UFOCAT is not usable for statistical studies of UFO data because of inherent flaws in its design. Yet the TST uses several UFO-data sources, including UFOCAT, for statistical correlative studies, with vaguely-defined parameters.

There is no question that some of the geophysical processes invoked in the TST are sound. Rock undergoing strain can indeed give off EM radiation which can be detected by sensors near the event. There is also no question that earthquake lights exist and that their mechanism is not fully understood. The TST suggests that UFOs are essentially the same phenomenon and, as supporting evidence, proposes that the statistical correlation between UFOs and earthquakes supports the theory.

But the existence of UFO reports in seismically-inactive areas seems to contradict this correlation. To suggest that the seismic activity exists in these areas with magnitudes less than 2 (or even 1) on the Richter scale is perhaps grasping for straws.

Even a seismically-quiet area such as the American Midwest is apparently not immune to TST effects, according to the theory's advocates. The Carman, Manitoba, UFO wave of 1975-76 has been linked to a few minor earthquakes in southern Minnesota, hundreds of kilometers distant. Somehow, it is reasoned, the strain field wandered between the two points. Again, why the UFOs would not be observed closer to the earthquake epicenter is a question still in need of a proper answer. (Alternatively, it has been suggested that the flooding of the Carman area during the wave period may have contributed to the TST's effects through underground charging of the water in microcracks.)

Interestingly, Devereux himself asks of Persinger's research:

"Why attempt to explain other, possibly more complex and perhaps unrelated mechanisms under the same conceptual umbrella? . . . This approach to the UFO problem cannot sensibly be conducted over the entire USA in any case—the area is so vast that untenable numbers of UFO events would have to be involved. And how would one cope with the detailed geological data of such a continental area, even if it is available?"

He concludes, in what is perhaps the most succinct published criticism of the TST on record, that "despite all the scientific trappings [the] work displays, the conclusions drawn owe as much to intuition as to the computer" (Devereux, 1982).

One of the few other criticisms of the TST, this time directed at Devereux, was expressed by Steuart Campbell, who remarked in a *Magonia* article that "since Britain is criss-crossed with geological faults, it is not surprising that many reports of UFO sightings come from areas close to them." He cautioned that Devereux "should be as concerned with the UFO data as [he is] with geology" since in Devereux's own opinion Persinger's database is flawed. Campbell said that the "geological jargon conceals a poverty of hypotheses."

Devereux quickly countered by saying that surface faulting does not cover Britain as Campbell implied. Surely, he continued, the UFO/fault relationship could be no coincidence. He also has come close to Persinger's defense by calling his work "meticulous" and saying, "If [UFOs are] all hoaxes or hallucinations, then we had better start wondering why figments of the imagination correlate with faulting."

Of course the problem is not that UFOs are hoaxes or hallucinations (few are) but that the majority are misidentifications of other phenomena.

In the end, the major problem is the data themselves. We know that seismic activity exists and that earthquake lights exist and that UFO reports exist. But the data for these phenomena are taken from a variety of sources and cover a variety of disciplines. The handling of data is always a problem, regardless of the field of interest, and good statisticians always caution against the misinterpretation of data.

While the TST is appealing in its description of UFO phenomena in terms of terrestrial rather than extraterrestrial mechanisms, it provides little in the way of supportive evidence that its mechanism actually exists. As a hypothesis it cannot be discounted; only the evidence in its support can be evaluated as either favorable or not favorable. But using one poorly-understood phenomenon to explain another using an unknown mechanism is perhaps unwise at this point. Possibly the TST may explain some aspects of the UFO phenomenon, but the theory needs a great deal of refining and rethinking before it can be applied in general to UFOs and other anomalous phenomena.

Fortunately the continuing controversy over the TST and earthlights theories has spurred researchers to refine and rethink their approaches. There have been promising signs that the "energy connection" will face attempts to quantify it in the future. In his second book, *Earth Lights Revelation* (1989), Devereux lays out his theory in a much more succinct and structured manner than he did in his earlier writings. He and his associates have gone to greater lengths to show how balls of light seem to be linked to local faulting and seismic events and also how the lights appear to interact with observers. He believes that "we are dealing with a very sensitive energy form" and that it is an "energy manifestation that

is either an unfamiliar form of electromagnetism or is of a completely unknown order . . . a secret force." His research, though well documented by case studies and effusive praise of Persinger's findings, fails to mention *any* published criticisms such as those by Claude Mauge, Steuart Campbell or Chris Rutkowski. Although the *hypothesis* that the lights represent a kind of EM phenomenon is supported by some circumstantial and observational evidence, the empirical question of whether or not such energy can actually exist needs further study. Devereux does not seem to have considered the possibility that the observational evidence may involve more ordinary, explainable phenomena.

Similarly, recent work by Terence Meaden proposes that the geometrically-precise circles found in British fields throughout the 1980s are evidence of a plasmalike phenomenon which can emulate a silver disc-shaped craft, maneuver at high speeds and cause prominent physical effects upon the environment. Essentially a rephrasing of the TST in a slightly different context, the problem is once again that an energy-based explanation of UFO-related phenomena must be better supported. After all, explaining something as being due to a "mysterious and previously unknown phenomenon" is not explaining it at all and sounds suspiciously like the Condon Committee's much-criticized habit of "explaining" UFO sightings by inventing elaborate "natural phenomena" to keep reports out of the "unknown" category.

Chris Rutkowski

Sources:

Barnothy, M. F., ed. *Biological Effects of Magnetic Fields*. New York: Plenum Press, 1969.

Devereux, Paul. *Earth Lights: Towards an Understanding of the UFO Enigma.* Wellingborough, Northamptonshire, England: Turnstone Press Limited, 1982.

Devereux, Paul. *Earth Lights Revelation: UFOs and Mystery Lightform Phenomena: The Earth's*

EARTHLIGHTS AND TECTONIC STRAIN THEORY (*continued*)

Secret Energy Force. London: Blandford, 1989.

Hendry, Allan. *The UFO Handbook: A Guide to Investigating, Evaluating and Reporting UFO Sightings.* Garden City, NY: Doubleday & Company, Inc., 1979.

Persinger, Michael. "Earthquake Activity and Antecedent UFO Report Numbers." *Perceptual and Motor Skills* 50 (1980): 791-797.

Persinger, Michael, and Gyslaine F. Lafrenière. *Space-Time Transients and Unusual Events.* Chicago: Nelson-Hall, 1977.

Rikitake, T. *Earthquake Prediction.* New York: Elsevier, 1976.

Rutkowski, Chris A. "Geophysical Variables and Human Behavior: Some Criticisms." *Perceptual and Motor Skills* 58 (1984): 840-842.

EBERHART, GEORGE MARTIN (1950-)

George Martin Eberhart is ufology's premier bibliographer, best known as the compiler of such major reference tools as *A Geo-Bibliography of Anomalies* (1980) and the two-volume *UFOs and the Extraterrestrial Contact Movement* (1986). He is also a member of the board of directors of the **J. Allen Hynek Center for UFO Studies,** CUFOS' librarian, managing editor of the *Journal of UFO Studies,* and a contributing editor to *International UFO Reporter.* Besides being perhaps the leading authority on the UFO and extraterrestrial contact literature, he has also become an expert on the pre-1945 UFO cases, with which he has developed a particular fascination.

Eberhart was born on June 6, 1950, in Hanover, Pennsylvania. His degrees are in journalism (B.A., Ohio State University, 1973) and library science (M.A., University of Chicago, 1976). Since 1980 he has been editor of *College & Research Libraries News,* a monthly news magazine

published by the American Library Association.

He says, "It is my opinion that some variety of anomalous plasma akin to ball lightning or earthquake lights is responsible for many unexplained observations of nocturnal lights. Close encounters with structured objects and daylight discs are another matter entirely, however, and it is still unclear (in late 1989) whether abduction narratives, whether inspired by some traumatic event or anomalous mental process, have any direct relation to extraterrestrial UFOs. Before the extraterrestrial, psychosocial or any other hypothesis can be substantiated, far more systematic and coherent observational, statistical, and physical data need to be gathered. Because of the elusive and seemingly unpredictable nature of the UFO phenomenon, such an effort may have to be both international and interdisciplinary."

Sources:

Boyd, Robert D. *International Who's Who in Ufology Directory.* Mobile, AL: The Author, 1988.

Eberhart, George M. *A Geo-Bibliography of Anomalies: Primary Access to Observations of UFOs, Ghosts, and Other Mysterious Phenomena.* Westport, CT: Greenwood, 1980.

Eberhart, George M. "UFO Literature for the Serious Ufologists." *RQ* 20 (Winter 1980): 144-48.

Eberhart, George M. *UFOs and the Extraterrestrial Contact Movement. Vol. 1: Unidentified Flying Objects. Vol. 2: The Extraterrestrial Contact Movement.* Metuchen, NJ: The Scarecrow Press, Inc., 1986.

Eberhart, George M. "UFOs, Ufologists and the Library." *Wilson Library Bulletin* 52 (1978): 489-93.

EVANS, HILARY (1929-)

Hilary Evans is a prominent and articulate proponent of what has been called the

psychosocial hypothesis, which seeks to explain reports of UFO and other anomalous encounters as culturally-shaped visionary experiences.

Born in Shrewsbury, England, on March 6, 1929, Evans was educated at Cambridge and Birmingham Universities. He works as curator at the Mary Evans Picture Library in London. His major interests are in UFOs, psychical research, folklore and mythology. A frequent contributor to magazines and journals dealing with anomalies, he is the author of such important books as *Visions, Apparitions, Alien Visitors* (1984) and *Gods, Spirits, Cosmic Guardians* (1987). He is a member of the Society for Psychical Research (SPR), the British UFO Research Association, the Folklore Society and the **Society for Scientific Exploration** (SSE).

He says, "Of course I believe there are objects, apparently flying, which are unidentified; but I doubt if there is one specific phenomenon which has given rise to the tens of thousands of unexplained sightings. Rather, I would account for quite a high proportion (and this includes all cases of alleged contact with extraterrestrial entities, whether physical or mental) in terms of psychosocial processes—which is not by any means to belittle their importance to the witness or their value to the researcher, but simply to see them as a different kind of phenomenon from that suggested by their ostensible nature.

"In addition, I suspect there are 'natural' phenomena whose existence is unrecognized by conventional science and whose nature has yet to be established. Furthermore, I am impressed by evidence for interaction between humans and their physical environment leading to events currently classified as 'paranormal.'

"I am skeptical as regards the extraterrestrial hypothesis. While accepting the possibility of extraterrestrial life and consequently of extraterrestrial contact, I doubt that any such contact has occurred or is occurring. I am skeptical of programmed conspiracies to conceal government involvement (though this has surely occurred on an unorganized basis) and I tend to see this, along with many activities associated with

the UFO phenomenon, as secondary social artifacts rather than as primary features of the phenomenon per se.

"But for this reason alone—even apart from the intrinsic scientific puzzle and its sheer entertainment value—I believe investigation of the UFO phenomenon to be of the greatest value in helping us to understand not only human behavior but also many other aspects of the universe we live in."

Sources:

Boyd, Robert D. *International Who's Who in Ufology Directory*. Mobile, AL: The Author, 1988.

Evans, Hilary. *Alternate States of Consciousness: Unself, Otherself, and Superself*. Wellingborough, Northamptonshire, England: The Aquarian Press, 1989.

Evans, Hilary. *Gods, Spirits, Cosmic Guardians: A Comparative Study of the Encounter Experience*. Wellingborough, Northamptonshire, England: The Aquarian Press, 1987.

Evans, Hilary. "The Myth of the Authorized Myth." *Magonia* 16 (July 1984): 15-16.

Evans, Hilary. *Visions, Apparitions, Alien Visitors*. Wellingborough, Northamptonshire, England: The Aquarian Press, 1984.

Evans, Hilary, and John Spencer, eds. *Phenomenon: Forty Years of Flying Saucers*. New York: Avon Books, 1989.

EXTRATERRESTRIAL BIOLOGICAL ENTITIES

Perhaps the strangest and most convoluted UFO story of the 1980s concerns allegations from various sources, some of them individuals connected with military and intelligence agencies, that the U.S. government not only has communicated with but has an ongoing

EXTRATERRESTRIAL BIOLOGICAL ENTITIES
(*continued*)

relationship with what are known officially as "extraterrestrial biological entities," or EBEs.

The Emenegger/Sandler Saga: The story begins in 1973, when Robert Emenegger and Allan Sandler, two well-connected Los Angeles businessmen, were invited to Norton Air Force Base in California to discuss a possible documentary film on advanced research projects. Two military officials, one the base's head of the Air Force Office of Special Investigations, the other, the audio-visual director Paul Shartle, discussed a number of projects. One of them involved UFOs. This one sounded the most interesting and plans were launched to go ahead with a film on the subject.

Emenegger and Sandler were told of a film taken at Holloman AFB, New Mexico, in May 1971. In October 1988, in a national television broadcast, Shartle would declare that he had seen the 16mm film showing "three disc-shaped craft. One of the craft landed and two of them went away." A door opened on the landed vehicle and three beings emerged. Shardle said, "They were human-size. They had an odd, gray complexion and a pronounced nose. They wore tightfitting jump suits, [and] thin headdresses that appeared to be communication devices, and in their hands they held a 'translator.' A Holloman base commander and other Air Force officers went out to meet them" (Howe, 1989).

Emenegger was led to believe he would be given the film for use in his documentary. He was even taken to Norton and shown the landing site and the building in which the spaceship had been stored and others (Buildings 383 and 1382) in which meetings between Air Force personnel and the aliens had been conducted over the next several days. According to his sources, the landing had taken place at 6 a.m. The extraterrestrials were "doctors, professional types." Their eyes had "vertical slits like a cat's and their mouths were thin and slitlike, with no chins." All that Emenegger was told of what occurred in the

meetings was a single stray "fact": that the military people said they were monitoring signals from an alien group with which they were unfamiliar, and did their ET guests know anything about them? The ETs said no.

Emenegger's military sources said he would be given 3200 feet of film taken of the landing. At the last minute, however, permission was withdrawn, although Emenegger and Sandler were encouraged to describe the Holloman episode as something hypothetical, something that could happen or might happen in the future. Emenegger went to Wright-Patterson AFB, where Project Blue Book had been located until its closing in 1969, to ask Col. George Weinbrenner, one of his military contacts, what had happened. According to Emenegger's account, the exchange took place in Weinbrenner's office. The colonel stood up, walked to a chalkboard and complained in a loud voice, "That damn MIG 25! Here we're so public with everything we have. But the Soviets have all kinds of things we don't know about. We need to know more about the MIG 25!" Moving to a bookshelf and continuing his monologue about the Russian jet fighter, he handed Emenegger a copy of **J. Allen Hynek's** *The UFO Experience* (1972), with the author's signature and dedication to Weinbrenner. "It was like a scene from a Kafka play," Emenegger would recall, inferring from the colonel's odd behavior that he was confirming the reality of the film while making sure that no one overhearing the conversation realized that was what he was doing.

The documentary film *UFO's Past, Present & Future* (Sandler Institutional Films, Inc.) was released in 1974 along with a paperback book of the same title. The Holloman incident is recounted in three pages (127-29) of the book's "Future" section. Elsewhere, in a section of photos and illustrations, is an artist's conception of what one of the Holloman entities looked like, though it, along with other alien figures, is described only as being "based on eyewitness descriptions" (Emenegger, 1974). Emenegger's association with the military and intelligence he had met while doing the film would continue for years. At one point in the late 1980s his sources told him that he was about to be invited to film an interview with a live extraterrestrial in a Southwestern state, he says, but nothing came of it.

The Suffern Story: On October 7, 1975, a 27-year-old carpenter, Robert Suffern, of Bracebridge, Ontario, got a call from his sister who had seen a "fiery glow" near his barn and concluded it was on fire. Suffern drove to the spot and, after determining that there was no problem, got back on the road. There, he would testify, he encountered a large disc-shaped object resting in his path. "I was scared," he said. "It was right there in front of me with no lights and no sign of life." But even before his car could come to a complete stop, the object abruptly ascended out of sight. Suffern turned his car around and decided to head home rather than to his sister's place, his original intended destination. At that point a small figure wearing a helmet and a silver-gray suit stepped in front of the car, causing Suffern to hit the brakes and skid to a stop. The figure ran into a field. Then, according to Suffern, "When he got to the fence, he put his hands on a post and went over it with no effort at all. It was like he was weightless" (UFOIL, n.d.).

Within two days Suffern's report was on the wire services, and Suffern was besieged by UFO investigators, journalists, curiosity-seekers, and others. Suffern, who made no effort to exploit his story and gave every appearance of believing what he was saying, soon tired of discussing it. A year later, however, Suffern and his wife told a Canadian investigator that a month after the encounter, they were informed that some high-ranking officials wished to speak with them. Around this time, so they claimed, they were given thorough examinations by military doctors. After that an appointment was set up for December 12 and on that day an Ontario Provincial Police cruiser arrived with three military officers, one Canadian, two American. They were carrying books and other documents. In the long conversation that followed, the officers apologized for the UFO landing, claiming it was a "mistake" caused by the malfunctioning of an extraterrestrial spaceship.

The officers produced close-up pictures of UFOs, claiming that the U.S. and Canadian governments had had intimate knowledge of aliens since 1943 and were cooperating with them. The officers even knew the exact dates and times of two previous but unreported UFO sightings on the Suffern property. The Sufferns said the officers had answered all their questions fully and frankly, but they would not elaborate on what they were told. Reinterviewed about the matter some months later, the couple stuck by their story but added few further details.

The investigator, Harry Tokarz, would remark, "Robert Suffern strikes one as an individual who carefully measures his thoughts. His sincerity comes through clearly as he slowly relates his concepts and ideas. His wife, a home-bred country girl, is quick to air her views and state unequivocally what she believes to be fact" (CUFORN, 1983).

EBEs in South Dakota: On February 9, 1978, a curious document—an apparent carbon copy of an official U.S. Air Force incident report—arrived at the office of the *National Enquirer* in Lantana, Florida. Accompanying the document was an unsigned letter dated "29 Jan." It read: "The incident stated in the attached report actually occurred. The Air Force appointed a special team of individuals to investigate the incident. I was one of those individuals. I am still on active duty and so I cannot state my name at this time. It is not that I do not trust the Enquirer (I sure [sic] you would treat my name with [sic] confidence but I do not trust others.) The incident which occurred on 16 Nov 77, was classified top secret on 2 Dec 77. At that time I obtained a copy of the original report. I thought at that time that the Air Force would probably hush the whole thing up, and they did. The Air Force ordered the silence on 1 Dec 77, after which, the report was classified. There were 16 pictures taken at the scene. I do not have access to the pictures at this time" (Pratt, 1984).

The report, stamped FOR OFFICIAL USE ONLY, purported to be from the commander of the 44th Missile Security Squadron at Ellsworth

EXTRATERRESTRIAL BIOLOGICAL ENTITIES
(*continued*)

AFB near Rapid City, South Dakota. The incident was described as a "Helping Hand (security violation)/Covered Wagon (security violation) at Lima 9 (68th SMSq Area), 7 miles SW of Nisland, SD, at 2100 hours on 16 Nov. 77." The recipient of the report was identified as "Paul D. Hinzman, SSgt, USAF, Comm/Plotter, Wing Security Control." Two security men, Airmen 1st Class Kenneth Jenkins and Wayne E. Raeke, experienced and reported the incident, which was investigated by Capt. Larry D. Stokes and TSgt. Robert E. Stewart.

The document told an incredible story. At 10:59 on the evening of November 16 an alarm sounded from the Lima Nine missile site. Jenkins and Raeke, at the Lima Launch Control Facility 35 miles away, were dispatched to the scene. On their arrival Raeke set out to check the rear fence line. There he spotted a helmeted figure in a glowing green metallic suit. The figure pointed a weapon at Raeke's rifle and caused it to disintegrate, burning Raeke's hands and arms in the process. Raeke summoned Jenkins, who carried his companion back to their Security Alert Team vehicle. When Jenkins went to the rear fence line, he saw two similarly-garbed figures. He ordered them to halt, but when they ignored his command, he opened fire. His bullets struck one in the shoulder and the other in the helmet. The figures ran over a hill and were briefly lost to view. Jenkins pursued them and when he next saw them, they were entering a 20-foot-in-diameter saucer-shaped object, which shot away over the horizon.

As Raeke was air-evacuated from the scene, investigators discovered that the missile's nuclear components had been stolen.

Enquirer reporters suspected a hoax but when they called Rapid City and Ellsworth to check on the names, they were surprised to learn that such persons did exist. Moreover, all were on active duty. The *Enquirer* launched an investigation, sending several reporters to Rapid City. Over

the course of the next few days they found that although the individuals were real, the document inaccurately listed their job titles, the geography of the alleged incident was wrong (there was no nearby hill over which intruders could have run), Raeke had suffered no injuries, he and Jenkins did not even know each other, and no one (including Rapid City civilian residents and area ranchers) had heard anything about such an encounter. As one of the reporters, Bob Pratt, wrote in a subsequent account, "We found more than 20 discrepancies or errors in the report—wrong names, numbers, occupations, physical layouts and so on. Had the Security Option alert mentioned in the report taken place, it would have involved all security personnel at the base, and everyone at the base and in Rapid City (population 45,000 plus) would have known about it."

The Bennewitz Affair: In the late 1970s Paul Bennewitz, an Albuquerque businessman trained as a physicist, became convinced that he was monitoring electromagnetic signals which extraterrestrials were using to control persons they had abducted. Bennewitz tried to decode these signals and believed he was succeeding. At the same time he began to see what he thought were UFOs maneuvering around the Manzano Nuclear Weapons Storage Facility and the Coyote Canyon test area, located near Kirtland AFB, and he filmed them.

Bennewitz reported all this to the Tucson-based Aerial Phenomena Research Organization (APRO), whose directors were unimpressed, judging Bennewitz to be deluded. But at Kirtland, Bennewitz's claims, or at least some of them, were being taken more seriously. On October 24, 1980, Bennewitz contacted Air Force Office of Special Investigations (AFOSI) agent Sgt. Richard Doty (whose previous tour of duty had been at Ellsworth) after being referred to him by Maj. Ernest Edwards, head of base security, and related that he had evidence that something potentially threatening was going on in the Manzano Weapons Storage Area. A "Multipurpose Internal OSI Form," signed by Maj. Thomas A. Cseh (Commander of the Base Investigative

Detachment), dated October 28, 1980, and subsequently released under the Freedom of Information Act, states:

"On 26 Oct 80, SA [Special Agent] Doty, with the assistance of JERRY MILLER, GS-15, Chief, Scientific Advisor for Air Force Test and Evaluation Center, KAFB, interviewed Dr. BENNEWITZ at his home in the Four Hills section of Albuquerque, which is adjacent to the northern boundary of Manzano Base. (NOTE: MILLER is a former Project Blue Book USAF Investigator who was assigned to Wright-Patterson AFB (W-PAFB), OH, with FTD [Foreign Technology Division]. Mr. MILLER is one of the most knowledgeable and impartial investigators of Aerial Objects in the southwest.) Dr. BENNEWITZ has been conducting independent research into Aerial Phenomena for the last 15 months. Dr. BENNEWITZ also produced several electronic recording tapes, allegedly showing high periods of electrical magnetism being emitted from Manzano/Coyote Canyon area. Dr. BENNEWITZ also produced several photographs of flying objects taken over the general Albuquerque area. He has several pieces of electronic surveillance equipment pointed at Manzano and is attempting to record high frequency electrical beam pulses. Dr. BENNEWITZ claims these Aerial Objects produce these pulses. . . . After analyzing the data collected by Dr. BENNEWITZ, Mr MILLER related the evidence clearly shows that some type of unidentified aerial objects were caught on film; however, no conclusions could be made whether these objects pose a threat to Manzano/Coyote Canyon areas. Mr MILLER felt the electronical [sic] recording tapes were inconclusive and could have been gathered from several conventional sources. No sightings, other than these, have been reported in the area."

On November 10 Bennewitz was invited to the base to present his findings to a small group of officers and scientists. Exactly one week later Doty informed Bennewitz that AFOSI had decided against further consideration of the matter. Subsequently Doty reported receiving a call from then-New Mexico Sen. Harrison Schmitt, who wanted to know what AFOSI was planning to do about Bennewitz's allegations. When informed that no investigation was planned, Schmitt spoke with Brig. Gen. William Brooksher of base security. The following July New Mexico's other senator, Pete Domenici, looked into the matter, meeting briefly with Doty before dashing off to talk with Bennewitz personally. Domenici subsequently lost interest and dropped the issue.

Bennewitz was also aware of supposed cattle mutilations being reported in the western United States. At one point he met a young mother who told him that one evening in May 1980, after she and her six-year-old son saw several UFOs in a field and one approached them, they suffered confusion and disorientation, then a period of amnesia which lasted as long as four hours. Bennewitz brought the two to University of Wyoming psychologist **R. Leo Sprinkle**, who hypnotized them and got a detailed abduction story from the mother and a sketchy one from the little boy. Early in the course of the abduction they observed aliens take a calf aboard the UFO and mutilate it while it was still alive, removing the animal's genitals. At one point during the alleged experience, the mother said, they were taken via UFO into an underground area which she believed was in New Mexico. She briefly escaped her captors and fled into an area where there were tanks of water. She looked into one of them and saw body parts such as tongues, hearts and internal organs, apparently from cattle. But she also observed a human arm with a hand attached. There was also the "top of a bald head," apparently from one of the hairless aliens, but before she could find out for sure, she was dragged away. The objects in the tank, she said, "horrified me and made me sick and frightened me to death" (Howe, 1989). Later she wondered about the other tanks and about their contents.

The William Moore/MJ-12 Maze: Late in the summer of 1979 **William L. Moore** had left a teaching job in a small Minnesota town to relocate in Arizona, where he hoped to pursue a writing career. Moore was deeply involved in the investigation of an apparent UFO crash in New Mexico in July 1947, a case he and Charles Berlitz

EXTRATERRESTRIAL BIOLOGICAL ENTITIES
(*continued*)

would recount in their *The Roswell Incident* the following year. After his move to the Southwest Moore became close to **Coral and James Lorenzen** of the Aerial Phenomena Research Organization (APRO) and in due course Moore was asked to join the APRO board. The Lorenzens told him about Bennewitz's claims. Bennewitz, Jim Lorenzen thought, was "prone to make great leaps of logic on the basis of incomplete data" (Moore, 1989a).

The Roswell Incident was published in the summer of 1980 and in September a debate on UFOs at the Smithsonian Institution was scheduled to take place. Moore set off from his Arizona home to Washington, D.C., to attend the debate and along the way promoted his new book on radio and television shows. According to an account he would give seven years later, an extraordinary series of events began while he was on this trip.

He had done a radio show in Omaha and was in the station lobby, suitcase in hand, on his way to catch a plane which was to leave within the hour when a receptionist asked if he was Mr. Moore. He had a phone call. The caller was a man who claimed to be a colonel at nearby Offutt AFB. He said, "We think you're the only one we've heard who seems to know what he's talking about." He asked if he and Moore could meet and discuss matters further. Moore said that since he was leaving town in the next few minutes, that would not be possible, though he wrote down the man's phone number.

Moore went on to Washington. On September 8, on his way back, he did a radio show in Albuquerque. On the way out of the studio the receptionist told him he had a phone call. The caller, who identified himself as an individual from nearby Kirtland AFB, said, "We think you're the only one we've heard about who seems to know what he's talking about." Moore said, "Where have I heard that before?"

Soon afterwards Moore and the individual he would call "Falcon" met at a local restaurant. Falcon, later alleged (though denied by Moore) to be U.S. Air Force Sgt. Richard Doty, said he would be wearing a red tie. This first meeting would initiate a long-running relationship between Moore (and, beginning in 1982, partner Jaime Shandera) and 10 members of a shadowy group said to be connected with military intelligence and to be opposed to the continuation of the UFO cover-up. The story that emerged from this interaction goes like this:

The first UFO crash, involving bodies of small, gray-skinned humanoids, occurred near Corona, New Mexico, in 1947 (the "Roswell incident"). Two years later a humanoid was found alive and it was housed at Los Alamos until its death in the early 1950s. It was called EBE, after "extraterrestrial biological entity," and it was the first of three the U.S. government would have in its custody between then and now. An Air Force captain, now a retired colonel, was EBE-1's constant companion. At first communication with it was almost impossible; then a speech device which enabled the being to speak a sort of English was implanted in its throat. It turned out that EBE-1, the equivalent of a mechanic on a spaceship, related what it knew of the nature and purpose of the visitation.

In response to the Roswell incident, MJ-12—the MJ stands for "Majestic"—was set up by executive order of President Harry Truman on September 24, 1947. MJ-12 operates as a policy-making body. Project Aquarius is an umbrella group in which all the various compartments dealing with ET-related issues perform their various functions. Project Sigma conducts electronic communication with the extraterrestrials, part of an ongoing contact project run through the National Security Agency since 1964, following a landing at Holloman AFB in late April of that year.

Nine extraterrestrial races are visiting the earth. One of these races, little gray-skinned people from the third planet surrounding Zeta Reticuli, have been here for 25,000 years and influenced the direction of human evolution. They also help in the shaping of our religious beliefs. Some important individuals within the cover-up want it to end and are preparing the American people for the reality of the alien presence through the vehicle of popular entertainment, including the films *Close Encounters of the Third Kind*, whose climax is a thinly-disguised version of the Holloman landing, and *ET*.

At CIA headquarters in Langley, Virginia, there is a thick book called "The Bible," a compilation of all the various project reports.

According to his own account, which he would not relate until 1989, Moore cooperated with his AFOSI sources—including, prominently, Richard Doty—and provided them with information. They informed him that there was considerable interest in Bennewitz. Moore was made to understand that as his part of the bargain he was to spy on Bennewitz and also on APRO as well as, in Moore's words, "to a lesser extent, several other individuals" (Moore, 1989a). He learned that *several* government agencies were interested in Bennewitz's activities and they wanted to inundate him with false information—disinformation, in intelligence parlance—to confuse him. Moore says he was not one of those providing the disinformation, but he knew some of those of who were, such as Doty.

Bennewitz on his own had already begun to devise a paranoid interpretation of what he thought he was seeing and hearing, and the disinformation passed on to him built on that foundation. His sources told him that the U.S. government and malevolent aliens are in an uneasy alliance to control the planet, that the aliens are killing and mutilating not only cattle but human beings, whose organs they need to lengthen their lives, and that they are even *eating* human flesh. In underground bases at government installations in Nevada and New Mexico human and alien scientists work together on ghastly experiments, including the creation of soulless androids out of human and animal body parts. Aliens are abducting as many as one American in 40 and implanting devices which control human behavior. CIA brainwashing and other control

techniques are doing the same, turning life on earth into a nightmare of violence and irrationality. It was, as Moore remarks, "the wildest science fiction scenario anyone could possibly imagine."

But Bennewitz believed it. He grew ever more obsessed and tried to alert prominent persons to the imminent threat, showing photographs which he held showed human-alien activity in the Kirtland area but which dispassionate observers thought depicted natural rock formations and other mundane phenomena. Eventually Bennewitz was hospitalized, but on his release resumed his activities, which continue to this day. Soon the ghoulish scenario would spread into the larger UFO community and beyond and command a small but committed band of believers. But that would not happen until the late 1980s and it would not be Bennewitz who would be responsible for it.

In 1981 the Lorenzens received an anonymous letter from someone identifying himself as a "USAF Airman assigned to the 1550th Aircrew Training and Testing Wing at Kirtland AFB." The "airman" said, "On July 16, 1980, at between 10:30-10:45 A.M., Craig R. Weitzel . . . a Civil Air Patrol Cadet from Dobbins AFB, Ga., visiting Kirtland AFB, NM, observed a dull metallic colored UFO flying from South to North near Pecos New Mexico. Pecos has a secret training site for the 1550th Aircrew Training and Testing Wing, Kirtland AFB, NM. WEITZEL was with ten other individuals, including USAF active duty airmen, and all witnessed the sighting. WEITZEL took some pictures of the object. WEITZEL went closer to the UFO and observed the UFO land in a clearing approximately 250 yds, NNW of the training area. WEITZEL observed an individual dressed in a metallic suit depart the craft and walk a few feet away. The individual was outside the craft for just a few minutes. When the individual returned the craft took off towards the NW." The letter writer said he had been with Weitzel when the UFO flew overhead, but he had not been with him to observe the landing.

UFOs in the 1980s

EXTRATERRESTRIAL BIOLOGICAL ENTITIES
(*continued*)

The letter went on to say that late on the evening of the next day a tall, dark-featured, black-suited man wearing sunglasses called on Weitzel at Kirtland. The stranger claimed to be "Mr. Huck" from Sandia Laboratories, a classified Department of Energy contractor on the base. Mr. Huck told Weitzel he had seen something he should not have seen, a secret aircraft from Los Alamos, and he demanded all of the photographs. Weitzel replied that he hadn't taken any, that the photographer was an airman whose name he did not know. "The individual warned Weitzel not to mention the sighting to anyone or Weitzel would be in serious trouble," the writer went on. "After the individual left Weitzel[']s room, Weitzel wondered how the individual knew of the sighting because Weitzel didn't report the sighting to anyone. Weitzel became scared after thinking of the threat the individual made. Weitzel call [sic] the Kirtland AFB Security Police and reported the incident to them. They referred the incident to the Air Force Office of Special Investigations (AFOSI), which investigates these matters according to the security police. A Mr. Dody [sic], a special agent with OSI, spoke with Weitzel and took a report. Mr. Dody [sic] also obtained all the photographs of the UFO. Dody [sic] told Weitzel he would look into the matter. That was the last anyone heard of the incident."

But that was not all the correspondent had to say. He added, "I have every reason to believe [sic] the USAF is covering up something. I spent a lot of time looking into this matter and I know there is more to it than the USAF will say. I have heard rumors, but serious rumors here at Kirtland that the USAF has a crashed UFO stored in the Manzano Storage area, which is located in a remote area of Kirtland AFB. This area is heavily guarded by USAF Security. I have spoke [sic] with two employees of Sandia Laboratories, who also store classified objects in Manzano, and they told me that Sandia has examined several UFO's during the last 20 years. One that crashed near Roswell NM in the late 50's was examined by Sandia scientists. That craft

is still being store [sic] in Manzano.

"I have reason to beleive [sic] OSI is conducting a very secret investigation into UFO sightings. OSI took over when Project Blue Book was closed. I was told this by my commander, COL Bruce Purvine. COL Purvine also told me that the investigation was so secret that most employees of OSI doesn't [sic] even know it. But COL Purvine told me that Kirtland AFB, AFOSI District 17 has a special secret detachment that investigates sightings around this area. They have also investigated the cattle mutilations in New Mexico."

In 1985 investigator Benton Jamison located Craig Weitzel, who confirmed that he had indeed seen a UFO in 1980 and reported it to Sgt. Doty. But his sighting, while interesting, was rather less dramatic than the CE3 reported in the letter; Weitzel saw a silver-colored object some 10,000 to 15,000 feet overhead. After maneuvering for a few minutes, he told Jamison, it "accelerated like you never saw anything accelerate before" (Hastings, 1985). He also said he knew nothing of a meeting with anyone identified as "Mr. Huck."

In December 1982, in response to a Freedom of Information request from Barry Greenwood of **Citizens Against UFO Secrecy** (CAUS), Air Force Office of Special Investigations released a two-page OSI Complaint Form stamped "For Official Use Only." Dated September 8, 1980, it was titled "Kirtland AFB, NM, 8 Aug-3 Sept 80, Alleged Sightings of Unidentified Aerial Lights in Restricted Test Range." The document described several sightings of UFOs in the Monzano Weapons Storage Area, at the Coyote Canyon section of the Department of Defense Restricted Test Range. One of the reports cited was a New Mexico State Patrolman's August 10 observation of a UFO landing. (A later check with state police sources by Larry Fawcett, a Connecticut police officer and UFO investigator, uncovered no record of such a report. The sources asserted that the absence of a report could only mean that no such incident had ever happened.) This intriguing document is signed by then OSI Special Agent Richard C. Doty.

92

In 1987, after comparing three documents (the anonymous letter to APRO, the September 8, 1980, AFOSI Complaint Form, and a purported AFOSI document dated August 14, 1980, and claiming "frequency jamming" by UFOs in the Kirtland area), researcher Brad Sparks concluded that Doty had written all three. In 1989 Moore confirmed that Doty had written the letter to APRO. "Essentially it was 'bait,'" he says. "AFOSI knew that Bennewitz had close ties with APRO at the time, and they were interested in recruiting someone within . . . APRO . . . who would be in a position to provide them with feedback on Bennewitz'[s] activities and communications. Since I was the APRO Board member in charge of Special Investigations in 1980, the Weitzel letter was passed to me for action shortly after it had been received." According to **Bruce Maccabee**, Doty admitted privately that he had written the Ellsworth AFB document, basing it on a real incident which he wanted to bring to public attention. Doty has made no public comment on any of these allegations. Moore says Doty "was almost certainly a part of [the Ellsworth report], but not in a capacity where he would have been responsible for creating the documents involved" (Moore, 1989a).

Doty was also the source of an alleged AFOSI communication dated November 17, 1980, and destined to become known as the "Aquarius document." Allegedly sent from AFOSI headquarters at Bolling AFB in Washington, D.C., to the AFOSI District 17 office at Kirtland, it mentions, in brief and cryptic form, analyses of negatives from a UFO film apparently taken the previous month. The version that circulated through the UFO community states in its penultimate paragraph: "USAF NO LONGER PUBLICLY ACTIVE IN UFO RESEARCH, HOWEVER USAF STILL HAS INTEREST IN ALL UFO SIGHTINGS OVER USAF INSTALLATION/TEST RANGES. SEVERAL OTHER GOVERNMENT AGENCIES, LED BY NASA, ACTIVELY INVESTIGATES [sic] LEGITIMATE SIGHTINGS THROUGH COVERT COVER. . . . ONE SUCH COVER IS UFO REPORTING CENTER, US COAST AND GEODETIC SURVEY, ROCKVILLE, MD

20852. NASA FILTERS RESULTS OF SIGHTINGS TO APPROPRIATE MILITARY DEPARTMENTS WITH INTEREST IN THAT PARTICULAR SIGHTING. THE OFFICIAL US GOVERNMENT POLICY AND RESULTS OF PROJECT AQUARIUS IS [sic] STILL CLASSIFIED TOP SECRET WITH NO DISEMINATION [sic] OUTSIDE OFFICIAL INTELLIGENCE CHANNELS AND WITH RESTRICTED ACCESS TO 'MJ TWELVE'."

This is the first mention of "MJ-12" in an allegedly official government document. Moore describes it as an "example of some of the disinformation produced in connection with the Bennewitz case. The document is a retyped version of a real AFOSI message with a few spurious additions." Among the most significant additions, by Moore's account, are the bogus references to the U.S. Coast and Geodetic Survey and to NASA, which he says was NSA (National Security Agency) in the original.

According to Moore, Doty got the document "right off the teletype" (Moore, 1990) and showed it to Moore almost immediately. Later Doty came by with what purported to be a copy of it, but Moore noticed that it was not exactly the same; material had been added to it. Doty said he wanted Moore to give the doctored copy to Bennewitz. Reluctant to involve himself in the passing of this dubious document, Moore sat on it for a while, then finally worried that the sources he was developing, the ones who were telling him about the U.S. government's alleged interactions with EBEs, would dry up if he did not cooperate. So eventually he gave the document to Bennewitz but urged him not to publicize it. Bennewitz agreed and kept his promise.

As of September 1982 Moore knew of three copies of the document: the one Bennewitz had, one Moore had in safekeeping, and one he had in his briefcase during a trip he made that month to meet someone in San Francisco. He met the man in the morning and that afternoon someone broke into his car and stole his briefcase. Four months later a copy of the document showed up in the hands of a New York lawyer interested in UFOs,

EXTRATERRESTRIAL BIOLOGICAL ENTITIES
(*continued*)

and soon the document was circulating widely. Moore himself had little to say on the subject until he delivered a controversial and explosive speech to the annual conference of the **Mutual UFO Network** (MUFON) in Las Vegas in 1989.

In late 1982, "during," he says, "one of the many friendly conversations I had with Richard Doty," Moore mentioned that he was looking into the old (and seemingly discredited) story that a UFO had crashed in Aztec, New Mexico, in 1948. This tale was the subject of Frank Scully's 1950 book *Behind the Flying Saucers*. (Moore's long account of his investigation into the affair, which he found to be an elaborate hoax, would appear in the 1985 MUFON symposium proceedings.) Doty said he had never heard the story and asked for details, taking notes as Moore spoke.

On January 10 and 11, 1983, attorney Peter Gersten, director of CAUS, met with Doty in New Mexico. There were two meetings, the first of them also attended by Moore and San Francisco television producer Ron Lakis, the second by Gersten alone. During the first meeting Doty was guarded in his remarks. But at the second he spoke openly about what ostensibly were extraordinary secrets. He said the Ellsworth case was the subject of an investigation by AFOSI and the FBI; nuclear weapons were involved. The *National Enquirer* investigation, which had concluded the story was bogus, was "amateurish." At least two civilians, a farmer and a deputy sheriff, had been involved, but were warned not to talk. The government knows why UFOs appear in certain places, Doty said, but he would not elaborate. He added, however, that "beyond a shadow of a doubt they're extraterrestrial" (Greenwood, 1988) and from 50 light years from the earth. He knew of at least three UFO crashes, the Roswell incident and two others, one from the 1950s, the other from the 1960s. Bodies had been recovered. A spectacular incident, much like the one depicted in the ending of the film *Close Encounters of the Third Kind*, took place in 1966. The NSA was involved in

communications with extraterrestrials; the effort is called Project Aquarius. Inside the UFO organizations government moles are collecting information and spreading disinformation. Doty discussed the Aquarius document and said the really important documents are impossible to get out of the appropriate files. Some are protected in such a way that they will disintegrate within five seconds' exposure to air. These documents tell of agreements between the U.S. government and extraterrestrials under which the latter are free to conduct animal mutilations (especially of cattle) and to land at a certain base, in exchange for information about advanced UFO technology. Doty also claimed that via popular entertainment the American people are being prepared to accept the reality of visitation by benevolent beings from other worlds.

At one point in the conversation Doty asked Gersten, "How do you know that I'm not here to either give you misinformation or to give you information which is part of the programming, knowing you are going to go out and spread it around?" (Howe, 1989).

In the 1970s, as director of special projects for the Denver CBS-TV affiliate, Linda Moulton Howe had produced 12 documentaries, most of them dealing with scientific, environmental and health issues. But the one that attracted the most attention was *Strange Harvest*, which dealt with the then-widespread reports that cattle in Western and Midwestern states were being killed and mutilated by persons or forces unknown. Most veterinary pathologists said the animals were dying of unknown causes. Farmers, ranchers and some law-enforcement officers thought the deaths were mysterious. Some even speculated that extraterrestrials were responsible. This possibility intrigued Howe, who had a lifelong interest in UFOs, and *Strange Harvest* argues for a UFO-mutilation link.

In the fall of 1982, as Howe was working on a documentary on an unrelated matter, she got a call from Home Box Office (HBO). The caller said the HBO people had been impressed with *Strange Harvest* and wanted to know if Howe would do a film on UFOs. In March 1983 she went to New York to sign a contract with HBO for a show to be titled *UFOs–The ET Factor.*

The evening before her meeting with the HBO people, Howe had dinner with Gersten and science writer Patrick Huyghe. Gersten told Howe that he had met with Sgt. Doty, an AFOSI agent at Kirtland AFB, and perhaps Doty would be willing to talk on camera or in some other helpful capacity about the incident at Ellsworth. Gersten would call him and ask if he would be willing to meet with Howe.

Subsequently arrangements were made for Howe to fly to Albuquerque on April 9. Doty would meet her at the airport. But when she arrived that morning, no one was waiting. She called his home. A small boy answered and said his father was not there. Howe then phoned Jerry Miller, Chief of Reality Weapons Testing at Kirtland and a former Blue Book investigator. (He is mentioned in the October 28, 1980, "Multipurpose Internal OSI Form" reporting on Doty and Miller's meeting with Bennewitz.) She knew Miller from an earlier telephone conversation, when she had called to ask him about Bennewitz's claims, in which she had a considerable interest. Miller asked for a copy of *Strange Harvest.* Later he had given Howe his home phone number and said to contact him if she ever found herself in Albuquerque. So she called and asked if he would pick her up at the airport.

Miller drove Howe to his house. On the way Howe asked him a number of questions but got little in the way of answers. One question he did not answer was whether he is the "Miller" mentioned in the Aquarius document. When they got to Miller's residence, Miller called Doty at his home, and Doty arrived a few minutes later, responding aggressively to Howe's question about where he had been. He claimed to have been at the airport all along; where had she been? "Perhaps," Howe would write, "he had decided he didn't want to go through with the meeting, and it was acceptable in his world to leave me stranded at the airport—until Jerry Miller called his house" (Howe, 1989).

On the way to Kirtland, Howe asked Doty, whose manner remained both defiant and nervous, if he knew anything about the Holloman landing. Doty said it happened but that Robert Emenegger had the date wrong; it was not May 1971 but April 25, 1964—12 hours after a much-publicized CE3 reported by Socorro, New Mexico, policeman Lonnie Zamora. (Zamora said he had seen an egg-shaped object on the ground. Standing near it were two child-sized beings in white suits.) Military and scientific personnel at the base knew a landing was coming, but "someone blew the time and coordinates" and an "advance military scout ship" had come down at the wrong time and place, to be observed by Zamora. When three UFOs appeared at Holloman at six o'clock the following morning, one landed while the other two hovered overhead. During the meeting between the UFO beings and a government party, the preserved bodies of dead aliens had been given to the aliens, who in turn had returned something unspecified. Five ground and aerial cameras recorded this event.

At the Kirtland gate Doty waved to the guard and was let through. They went to a small white and gray building. Doty took her to what he described as "my boss' office." Doty seemed unwilling to discuss the Ellsworth case, the ostensible reason for the interview, but had much to say about other matters. First he asked Howe to move from the chair on which she was sitting to another in the middle of the room. Howe surmised that this was to facilitate the surreptitious recording of their conversation, but Doty said only, "Eyes can see through windows."

"My superiors have asked me to show you this," he said. He produced a brown envelope he had taken from a drawer in the desk at which he was sitting and withdrew several sheets of white paper. As he handed them to Howe, he warned her that they could not be copied; all she could do was read them in his presence and ask questions.

The document gave no indication anywhere as to which government, military or scientific agency (if any) had prepared the report, titled *A Briefing Paper for the President of the United States on*

EXTRATERRESTRIAL BIOLOGICAL ENTITIES
(*continued*)

the Subject of Unidentified Flying Vehicles. The title did not specify which President it had in mind, nor did the document list a date (so far as Howe recalls today) which would have linked it to a particular administration.

The first paragraph, written—as was everything that followed—in what Howe characterizes as "dry bureaucratese," listed dates and locations of crashes and retrievals of UFOs and their occupants. The latter were invariably described as 3½ to four feet tall, gray-skinned and hairless, with oversized heads, large eyes and no noses. It was now known, the document stated on a subsequent page, that these beings, from a nearby solar system, have been here for many thousands of years. Through genetic manipulation they influenced the course of human evolution and in a sense created us. They had also helped shape our religious beliefs.

The July 1947 Roswell crash was mentioned; so, however, was another one at Roswell in 1949. Investigators at the site found five bodies and one living alien, who was taken to a safe house at the Los Alamos National Laboratory north of Albuquerque. The aliens, small gray-skinned humanoids, were known as "extraterrestrial biological entities" and the living one was called "EBE" (ee-*buh*). EBE was befriended (if that was the word) by an Air Force officer, but the being died of unknown causes on June 18, 1952. (EBE's friend, by 1964 a colonel, was among those who were there to greet the aliens who landed at Holloman.) Subsequently, it would be referred to as EBE-1, since in later years another such being, EBE-2, would take up residence in a safe house. After that, a third, EBE-3, appeared on the scene and was now living in secret at an American base.

The briefing paper said other crashes had occurred, one near Kingman, Arizona, another just south of Texas in northern Mexico. It also mentioned the Aztec crash. The wreckage and bodies had been removed to such facilities as Los Alamos laboratory and Wright-Patterson AFB. A number of highly classified projects dealt with these materials. They included Snowbird (research and development from the study of an intact spacecraft lcft by the aliens as a gift) and Aquarius (the umbrella operation under which the research and contact efforts were coordinated). Project Sigma was the ongoing electronic-communications effort. There was also a defunct Project Garnet, intended to investigate extraterrestrial influence on human evolution. According to the document, extraterrestrials have appeared at various intervals in human history— 25,000, 15,000, 5000 and 2500 years ago as well as now—to manipulate human and other DNA.

One paragraph stated briefly, "Two thousand years ago extraterrestrials created a being" who was placed here to teach peace and love. Elsewhere a passing mention was made of another group of EBEs, called the "Talls."

The paper said Project Blue Book had existed solely to take heat off the Air Force and to draw attention away from the real projects. Doty mentioned an "MJ-12," explaining that "MJ" stood for "Majority." It was a policy-making body whose membership consisted of 12 very high-ranking government scientists, military officers and intelligence officials. These were the men who made the decisions governing the cover-up and the contacts.

Doty said Howe would be given thousands of feet of film of crashed discs, bodies, EBE-1 and the Holloman landing and meeting. She could use this material in her documentary to tell the story of how U.S. officials learned that the earth is being visited and what they have done about it. "We want you to do the film," Howe quotes him as saying.

When Howe asked why she, not the *New York Times*, the *Washington Post* or *60 Minutes*, was getting this, the story of the millennium, Doty replied bluntly that an individual media person is easier to manipulate and discredit than a major organization with expensive attorneys. He said that another plan to release the information, through Emenegger and Sandler, had been halted because political conditions were not right.

Over the next weeks Howe had a number of phone conversations with Doty, mostly about technical problems related to converting old film to videotape. She spoke on several occasions with three other men but did not meet them personally.

Doty suggested that eventually she might be allowed to film an interview with EBE-3. But the current film project was to have a historical emphasis; it would deal with events between 1949 and 1964. If at some point she did meet EBE-3, however, there was no way she could prepare herself for the "shock and fear" of meeting an alien being.

Howe, of course, had informed her HBO contacts, Jean Abounader and her superior Bridgett Potter, of these extraordinary developments. Howe urged them to prepare themselves, legally and otherwise, for the repercussions that would surely follow the release of the film. The HBO people told her she would have to secure a letter of intent from the U.S. government with a legally-binding commitment to release the promised film footage. When Howe called Doty about it, he said, "I'll work on it." He said he would mail the letter directly to HBO.

Then HBO told her it would not authorize funds for the film production until all the evidence was in hand and, as Potter put it, Howe had the "President, Secretary of Defense, Secretary of State and Joint Chiefs of Staff to back it up" (Howe, 1989). But proceed anyway, Howe was told. Now she was furious at both HBO and Doty.

When she called him at the base, he remarked that he had good news and bad news. She and a small crew would soon be able to interview the retired colonel (then a captain) who had spent three years with EBE-1. The bad news was that it would be three months before the thousands of feet of film of EBE-1 and the Holloman landing/contact would be available. Meanwhile,

before she could screen the footage, Howe would have to sign three security oaths and undergo a background check. She would also have to supply photographs of all the technical assistants who would accompany her to the interview.

The interview was repeatedly set up and canceled. Then in June Doty called to say he was officially out of the project. This was a blow because Doty was the only one she could call. She did not know how to get in touch with the others and always had to wait for them to contact her.

By October the contacts had decreased. The same month her contract with HBO expired. All she had was the name of the Washington contact. In March 1984 this individual called her office three times, although she was out of town working on a non-UFO story at the time. "Upon returning home," she writes, "I learned the man was contacting me to explain there would be further delays in the film project after the November 1984 election" (Howe, 1989).

For Howe that was the end of the matter, except for a brief sequel. On March 5, 1988, Doty wrote ufologist **Larry W. Bryant,** who had unsuccessfully sought access to Doty's military records through the Freedom of Information Act, and denied that he had ever discussed government UFO secrets or promised footage of crashed discs, bodies and live EBEs. Howe responded by making a sworn statement about the meeting and producing copies of her correspondence from the period with both Doty and HBO.

In 1989 Moore said that "in early 1983 I became aware that Rick [Doty] was involved with a team of several others, including one fellow from Denver that I knew of and at least one who was working out of Washington, D.C., in playing an elaborate disinformation scheme against a prominent UFO researcher who, at the time, had close connections with a major television film company interested in doing a UFO documentary." He was referring to Howe, of course. The episode was a counterintelligence sting operation, part of the "wall of disinformation" intended to

EXTRATERRESTRIAL BIOLOGICAL ENTITIES
(*continued*)

"confuse" the Bennewitz issue and to "call his credibility into question." Because of Howe's interest in Bennewitz's work, according to Moore, "certain elements within the intelligence community were concerned that the story of his having intercepted low frequency electromagnetic emissions from the Coyote Canyon area of the Kirtland/Sandia complex would end up as part of a feature film. Since this in turn might influence others (possibly even the Russians) to attempt similar experiments, someone in a control position apparently felt it had to be stopped before it got out of hand." In his observation, Moore said, "the government seemed hell bent on severing the ties that existed between [Howe] and [HBO]" (Moore, 1989b).

Doty's assertion that Howe had misrepresented their meeting was not to be taken seriously, according to Moore, since Doty was bound by a security oath and could not discuss the matter freely. Moore said that the Aztec crash, known beyond reasonable doubt never to have occurred, was something Doty had added to the document after learning from Moore of his recent investigation of the hoax.

In December 1984, in the midst of continuing contact with their own sources (Doty and a number of others) who claimed to be leaking the secrets of the cover-up, Moore's associate Jaime Shandera received a roll of 35mm film containing, it turned out, what purported to be a briefing paper, dated November 18, 1952, and intended for President-elect Eisenhower. The purported author, Adm. Roscoe H. Hillenkoetter, reported that an "Operation Majestic-12," consisting of a dozen top scientists, military officers and intelligence specialists, had been set up by Presidential order on September 24, 1947, to study the Roswell remains and the four humanoid bodies that had been recovered nearby. The document reports that the team directed by MJ-12 member and physiologist Detlev Bronk "has suggested the term 'Extra-terrestrial Biological Entities', or 'EBEs', be adopted as the standard

term of reference for these creatures until such time as a more definitive designation can be agreed upon." Brief mention is also made of a December 6, 1950, crash along the Texas-Mexico border. Nothing is said, however, about live aliens or communications with them.

In July 1985 Moore and Shandera, acting on tips from their sources, traveled to Washington and spent a few days going through recently-declassified documents in Record Group 341, including Top Secret Air Force intelligence files from USAF Headquarters. In the 126th box whose contents they examined, they found a brief memo, dated July 14, 1954, from Robert Cutler, Special Assistant to the President, to Gen. Nathan Twining. It says, "The president has decided that the MJ-12/SSP [Special Studies Project] briefing should take place *during* the already scheduled White House meeting of July 16 rather than following it as previously intended. More precise arrangements will be explained to you upon your arrival. Your concurrence in the above change of arrangements is assumed" (Friedman, 1987).

The Cutler/Twining memo, as it would be called in the controversies that erupted after Moore released the MJ-12 document to the world in the spring of 1987, is the only official document—not to be confused with such disputed ones as the November 17, 1980, Aquarius document—to mention MJ-12. (Several critics of the MJ-12 affair have questioned the memo's authenticity as well, but so far without unambiguous success.) The memo does not, of course, say what the MJ-12 Special Studies Project was.

MJ-12 Goes Public: Just prior to Moore's release of the MJ-12 briefing paper, another copy was leaked to British ufologist Timothy Good, who took his copy to the press. The first newspaper article on it appeared in the *London Observer* of May 31, 1987, and soon it was the subject of pieces in the *New York Times, Washington Post* and ABC-TV's *Nightline*. It was also denounced, not altogether persuasively, both by professional debunkers and by many ufologists. The dispute would rage without resolution well into 1989, when critics discovered that President Truman's signature on the September 24, 1947, executive order (appended to the briefing paper) was exactly like his signature on an undisputed, UFO-unrelated October 1, 1947, letter to his science adviser (and supposed MJ-12 member) Vannevar Bush. To all appearances a forger had appended a real signature to a fake letter. The MJ-12 document began to look like another disinformation scheme.

Although acutely aware of the mass of disinformation circulating throughout the UFO community, Moore remained convinced that at least some of the information his own sources were giving him was authentic. In 1988 he provided two of his sources, "Falcon" (Sgt. Doty according to some) and "Condor" (later claimed to be former U.S. Air Force Capt. Robert Collins), to a television production company. (Moore and Shandera had given them avian names and called the sources collectively "the birds.") *UFO Cover-up . . . Live*, a two-hour program, aired in October 1988, with Falcon and Condor, their faces shaded, their voices altered, relating the same tales with which they had regaled Moore and Shandera. The show, almost universally judged a laughable embarassment, was most remembered for the informants' statements that the aliens favored ancient Tibetan music and strawberry ice cream. Critics found the latter allegation especially hilarious.

Lear's Conspiracy Theory: Events on the UFO scene were taking a yet more bizarre turn that same year as even wilder tales began to circulate. The first to tell them was John Lear, a pilot with a background in the CIA and the estranged son of aviation legend William P. Lear. Lear had surfaced two or three years earlier, but aside from his famous father there seemed little to distinguish him from any of hundreds of other UFO buffs who subscribe to the field's publications and show up at its conferences. But then he started claiming that unnamed sources had told him of extraordinary events which made those told by Doty and the birds sound like bland and inconsequential anecdotes.

According to Lear, not just a few but *dozens* of

flying saucers had crashed over the years. In 1962 the U.S. government started Project Redlight to find a way to fly the recovered craft, some relatively intact. A similar project exists even now and is run out of supersecret military installation; one is Area 51 (specifically at a facility called S4) at the Nevada Test Site and the other is set up near Dulce, New Mexico. These areas, unfortunately, may no longer be under the control of the government or even of the human race. In the late 1960s an official agency so secret that not even the President may know of it had made an agreement with the aliens. In exchange for extraterrestrial technology the secret government would permit (or at least not interfere with) a limited number of abductions of human beings; the aliens, however, were to provide a list of those they planned to kidnap.

All went relatively well for a few years. Then in 1973 the government discovered that thousands of persons who were not on the alien's list were being abducted. The resulting tensions led to an altercation in 1978 or 1979. The aliens held and then killed 44 top scientists as well as a number of Delta force troops who had tried to free them. Ever since, frantic efforts, of which the Strategic Defense Initiative ("Star Wars") is the most visible manifestation, have been made to develop a defense against the extraterrestrials, who are busy putting implants into abductees (as many as one in 10 Americans) to control their behavior. At some time in the near future these people will be used for some unknown, apparently sinister, alien purpose. Even worse than all this, though, is the aliens' interest in human flesh. Sex and other organs are taken from both human beings and cattle and used to create androids in giant vats located in underground laboratories at Area 51 and Dulce. The extraterrestrials, from an ancient race near the end of its evolution, also use materials from human body parts as a method of biological rejuvenation. ("In order to sustain themselves," he said, "they use an enzyme or hormonal secretion obtained from the tissue that they extract from humans and animals. The secretions are then mixed with hydrogen peroxide and applied on the skin by spreading or dipping parts of their bodies in the solution. The body

EXTRATERRESTRIAL BIOLOGICAL ENTITIES
(*continued*)

absorbs the solution, then excretes the waste back through the skin" [Berk and Renzi, 1988].)

One of Lear's major sources was Bennewitz, who had first heard these scary stories from AFOSI personnel at Kirtland in the early 1980s. By this time Bennewitz had become something of a guru to a small group of UFO enthusiasts, Linda Howe among them, who believed extraterrestrials were mutilating cattle and had no trouble believing they might do the same thing to people. Also Lear, whose political views are far to the right of center, was linking his UFO beliefs with conspiracy theories about a malevolent secret American government which was attempting to use the aliens for its own purposes, including enslavement of the world's people through drug addiction. A considerable body of rightwing-conspiracy literature, some with barely-concealed anti-Semitic overtones, was making similar charges. Lear himself was not anti-Semitic, but he did share conspiracy beliefs with those who were.

Another of his claimed sources was an unnamed physicist who, Lear claimed, had actually worked at S4. To the many ufologists who rejected Lear's stories as paranoid, lunatic or fabricated (though not by the patently-sincere Lear), there was widespread skepticism about this physicist's existence. It turned out that he did indeed exist. His name is Robert Lazar, who, according to a story broken by reporter George Knapp on KLAS-TV, the ABC affiliate in Las Vegas, on November 11 and 13, 1989, claims to have worked on alien-technology projects at Area 51. Lazar, whose story is being investigated by both ufologists and mainstream journalists, has not endorsed Lear's claims about human-alien treaties, man-eating ETs or any of the rest and has distanced himself from Lear and his associates. His claims, while fantastic by most standards, are modest next to Lear's.

Cooper's Conspiracy Theory: Soon Lear was joined by someone with an even bigger supply of fabulous yarns: one Milton William Cooper.

Cooper surfaced on December 18, 1988, when his account of the fantastic secrets he learned while a Naval petty officer appeared on a computer network subscribed to by ufologists and others interested in anomalous phenomena. Cooper said that while working as a quartermaster with an intelligence team for Adm. Bernard Clarey, Commander in Chief of the Pacific Fleet, in the early 1970s he saw two documents, *Project Grudge Special Report 13* and a Majority briefing. (In conventional UFO history, Grudge was the second public Air Force UFO project, superseding the original, Sign, in early 1949 and lasting until late 1951, when it was renamed Blue Book. Whereas Sign investigators at one time concluded UFOs were of extraterrestrial origin—a conclusion the Air Force leadership found unacceptable—Grudge, as its name suggests coincidentally or otherwise, was known for its hostility to the idea of UFOs and for its eagerness to assign conventional explanations, warranted or otherwise, to the sighting reports that came its way.) Cooper's account of what was in these reports is much like the by-now familiar story of crashes, bodies, contacts and projects, with some elaborations. Moreover, he said the aliens were called "ALFs" (which, as any television viewer knows, stands for Alien Life Forms) and the "M" in MJ-12 is for Majority, not Majestic. Later he would say he had seen photographs of aliens, including a type he called the "big-nosed grays"—like those that supposedly landed at Holloman in 1964 or 1971. The U.S. government was in contact with them and alien-technology projects were going on at Area 51.

If this sounded like a rehash of Moore and Lear, that was only because Cooper had yet to pull out all the stops. On May 23, 1989, Cooper produced a 25-page document titled *The Secret Government: The Origin, Identity and Purpose of MJ-12.* He presented it as a lecture in Las Vegas a few weeks later. In Cooper's version of the evolving legend, the "secret government," an unscrupulous group of covert CIA and other intelligence operatives who keep many of their activities sealed from even the President's knowledge, runs the country. One of its first acts was to murder one-time Secretary of Defense (and alleged early MJ-12 member) James Forrestal—the death was made to look like suicide—because he threatened to expose the UFO cover-up. Nonetheless, President Truman, fearing an invasion from outer space, kept other nations, including the Soviet Union, abreast of developments. But keeping all this secret was a real problem, so an international secret society known as the Bilderbergers, headquartered in Geneva, Switzerland, was formed. Soon it became a secret world government and "now controls everything," Cooper said.

All the while flying saucers were dropping like flies out of the heavens. In 1953 there were 10 crashes in the United States alone. Also that year, astronomers observed huge spaceships heading toward the earth and in time entering into orbit around the equator. Project Plato was established to effect communication with these new aliens. One of the ships landed and a face-to-face meeting took place, and plans for diplomatic relations were laid. Meanwhile a race of human-looking aliens warned the U.S. government that the new visitors were not to be trusted and that if the government got rid of its nuclear weapons, the human aliens would help us in our spiritual development, which would keep us from destroying ourselves through wars and environmental pollution. The government rejected these overtures.

The big-nosed grays, the ones who had been orbiting the equator, landed again, this time at Holloman AFB, in 1954 and reached an agreement with the U.S. government. These beings stated that they were from a dying planet that orbits Betelguese. At some point in the not too distant future, they said, they would have to leave there for good. A second meeting took place not long afterwards at Edwards AFB in California. This time President Eisenhower was there to sign a formal treaty and to meet the first alien ambassador, "His Omnipotent Highness Krlll," pronounced Krill. He, in common with his fellow space travelers, wore a trilateral insignia on his uniform; the same design appears on all Betelguese spacecraft.

According to Cooper's account, the treaty's provisions were these: Neither side would interfere in the affairs of the other. The aliens would abduct humans from time to time and would return them unharmed, with no memory of the event. It would provide a list of names of those it was going to take. The U.S. government would keep the aliens' presence a secret and it would receive advanced technology from them. The two sides would exchange 16 individuals each for the purpose of learning from and teaching each other. The aliens would stay on earth and the humans would go to the other planet, then return after a specified period of time. The two sides would jointly occupy huge underground bases which would be constructed at hidden locations in the Southwest.

(It should be noted that the people listed as members of MJ-12 are largely from the Council on Foreign Relations and the Trilateral Commission. These organizations play a prominent role in conspiracy theories of the far right. In a book on the subject George Johnson writes, "After the Holocaust of World War II, anti-Semitic conspiracy theories became repugnant to all but the fringe of the American right. Populist fears of the power of the rich became focused instead on organizations that promote international capitalism, such as the Trilateral Commission, the Council on Foreign Relations, and the Bilderbergers, a group of world leaders and businesspeople who held one of their early conferences on international relations at the Bilderberg Hotel in the Netherlands" [Johnson, 1983]. According to Cooper, the trilateral emblem is taken directly from the alien flag. He adds that under Presidents Nixon, Ford and Carter MJ-12 became known as the 50 Committee. Under Reagan it was renamed the PI-40 Committee.)

By 1955, during the Eisenhower years, Cooper charged, officials learned for certain what they had already begun to suspect a year earlier: that the aliens had broken the treaty before the ink on it had time to dry. They were killing and mutilating both human beings and animals, failing to supply a complete list of abductees, and not returning some of those they had taken. On top

EXTRATERRESTRIAL BIOLOGICAL ENTITIES
(*continued*)

of that, they were conspiring with the Soviets, manipulating society through occultism, witchcraft, religion and secret organizations. Eisenhower prepared a secret executive memo, NSC 5411, ordering a study group of 35 top members (the "Jason Society") associated with the Council on Foreign Relations to "examine all the facts, evidence, lies, and deception and discover the truth of the alien question" (Cooper, 1989). Because the resulting meetings were held at Quantico Marine Base, they were called the Quantico meetings. Those participating included Edward Teller, Zbigniew Brzezinski, Henry Kissinger and Nelson Rockefeller.

The group decided that the danger to established social, economic, religious and political institutions was so grave that no one must know about the aliens, not even Congress. That meant that alternative sources of funding would have to be found. It also concluded that the aliens were using human organs and tissue to replenish their deteriorating genetic structure.

Further, according to Cooper, overtures were made to the Soviet Union and other nations so that all the earth could join together to deal with the alien menace. Research into sophisticated new weapons systems commenced. Intelligence sources penetrated the Vatican hoping to learn the Fatima prophecy which had been kept secret ever since 1917. It was suspected that the Fatima, Portugal, "miracle" was an episode of alien manipulation. As it turned out, the prophecy stated that in 1992 a child would unite the world under the banner of a false religion. By 1995 people would figure out that he was the Anti-Christ. That same year World War III would begin when an alliance of Arab nations invaded Israel. This would lead to nuclear war in 1999. The next four years would see horrible death and suffering all over the planet. Christ would return in 2011.

When confronted about this, claimed Cooper, the aliens candidly acknowledged it was true.

They knew it because they had traveled into the future via time machine and observed it with their own eyes. They added that they created us through genetic manipulation. Later the Americans and the Soviets also developed time travel and confirmed the Fatima/ET vision of the future.

In 1957 the Jason group met again, by order of Eisenhower, to decide what to do. It came up with three alternatives: (1) Use nuclear bombs to blow holes in the stratosphere so that pollution could escape into space. (2) Build a huge network of tunnels under the earth and save enough human beings of varying cultures, occupations and talents so that the race could reemerge after the nuclear and environmental catastrophes to come. Everybody else—i.e., the rest of humanity—would be left on the surface presumably to die. (3) Employ alien and terrestrial technology to leave earth and colonize the moon (code name "Adam") and Mars ("Eve"). The first alternative was deemed impractical, so the Americans and the Soviets started working on the other two. Meanwhile they decided that the population would have to be controlled, which could be done most easily by killing off as many "undesirables" as possible. Thus AIDS and other deadly diseases were introduced into the population. Another idea to raise needed funds was quickly acted on: sell drugs on a massive scale. An ambitious young member of the Council on Foreign Relations, a Texas oil-company president named George Bush, was put in charge of the project, with the aid of the CIA. "The plan worked better than anyone had thought," Cooper said. "The CIA now controls all the worlds [sic] illegal drug markets" (Cooper, 1989).

Unknown to just about everybody, a secret American/Soviet/alien space base existed on the dark side of the moon. By the early 1960s human colonies were thriving on the surface of Mars. All the while the naive people of the earth were led to believe the Soviets and the Americans were something other than the closest allies. But Cooper's story got even more bizarre and byzantine.

He claimed that in 1963, when President Kennedy found out some of what was going on, he gave an ultimatum to MJ-12: get out of the drug business. He also declared that in 1964 he would tell the American people about the alien visitation. Agents of MJ-12 ordered his assassination. Kennedy was murdered in full view of many hundreds of onlookers, none of whom apparently noticed, by the Secret Service agent driving the President's car in the motorcade.

In 1969, reported Cooper, a confrontation between human scientists and aliens at the Dulce laboratory resulted in the former's being taken hostage by the latter. Soldiers who tried to free the scientists were killed, unable to overcome the superior alien weapons. The incident led to a two-year rupture in relations. The alliance was resumed in 1971 and continues to this day, even as a vast invisible financial empire run by the CIA, the NSA and the Council on Foreign Relations runs drugs, launders money and encourages massive street crime so that Americans will be susceptible to gun-control legislation. The CIA has gone so far as to employ drugs and hypnosis to cause mentally-unstable individuals to commit mass murder of schoolchildren and other innocents, the point being to encourage anti-gun hysteria. All of this is part of the plot, aided and abetted by the mass media (also under the secret government's control), to so scare Americans that they will soon accept the declaration of martial law. When that happens, people will be rounded up and put in concentration camps already in place. From there they will be flown to the moon and Mars to work as slave labor in the space colonies.

The conspirators already run the world. As Cooper put it, "Even a cursory investigation by the most inexperienced researcher will show that the members of the Council on Foreign Relations and the Trilateral commission control the major foundations, all of the major media and publishing interests, the largest banks, all the major corporations, the upper echelons of the government, and many other vital interests."

Reaction to Lear and Cooper: Whereas Lear had felt some obligation to name a source or two, or at least to mutter something about "unnamed sources," Cooper told his lurid and outlandish tale as if it were so self-evidently true that sources or supporting data were irrelevant. And to the enthusiastic audiences flocking to Cooper's lectures, no evidence was necessary. By the fall of the year Cooper was telling his stories—whose sources were, in fact, flying-saucer folklore, AFOSI disinformation unleashed during the Bennewitz episode, conspiracy literature, and outright fiction-—to large crowds of Californians willing to pay $10 or $15 apiece for the thrill of being scared silly.

Lear and Cooper soon were joined by two other tellers of tales of UFO horrors and Trilateral conspiracies, William English and John Grace (who goes under the pseudonym "Val Valarian" and heads the **Nevada Aerial Research Group** in Las Vegas).

Few if any mainstream ufologists took these stories seriously and at first treated them as something of a bad joke. But when it became clear that Lear, Cooper and company were commanding significant media attention and finding a following among the larger public interested in ufology's fringes, where a claim's inherent improbability had never been seen as an obstacle to believe in it, the leaders of the UFO community grew ever more alarmed.

One leader who was not immediately alarmed was **Walter H. Andrus, Jr.**, director of the Mutual UFO Network (MUFON), one of the two largest UFO organizations in the United States (the other being the **J. Allen Hynek Center for UFO Studies** [CUFOS]). In 1987, before Lear had proposed what some wags would call the Dark Side Hypothesis, he had offered to host the 1989 MUFON conference in Las Vegas. Andrus agreed. But as Lear's true beliefs became known, leading figures within MUFON expressed concern about Lear's role in the conference. When Andrus failed to respond quickly, MUFON officials were infuriated.

EXTRATERRESTRIAL BIOLOGICAL ENTITIES
(*continued*)

Facing a possible palace revolt, Andrus informed Lear that Cooper, whom Lear had invited to speak at the conference, was not an acceptable choice. But to the critics on the MUFON board and elsewhere in the organization, this was hardly enough. One of them, longtime ufologist **Richard Hall**, said this was "like putting a Band-Aid on a hemorrhage" (Hall, 1989). In a heated telephone exchange Andrus called Hall's objections to Lear "just one man's opinion" and claimed support, which turned out not to exist, from other MUFON notables. In a widely-distributed open letter to Andrus, Hall wrote, "Having Lear run the symposium and be a major speaker at it is comparable to NICAP in the 1960's having George Adamski run a NICAP conference!" (NICAP, the National Investigations Commitee on Aerial Phenomena, of which Hall was executive secretary in the late 1950s and much of the 1960s, was a conservative UFO-research organization which attacked as fraudulent the claims of Adamski, who wrote books about his meetings with Venusians and distributed photographs of what he said were their spaceships.) Hall went on, "You seem to be going for the colorful and the spectacular rather than for the critical-minded approach of science; you even expressed the view—in effect—that having a panel to question Lear critically would be good show biz and the 'highlight' of the symposium. Maybe so, but it obviously would dominate the entire program, grab off all major news media attention, and put UFO research in the worst possible light." Hall declared, "I am hereby resigning from the MUFON Board and I request that my name be removed from all MUFON publications or papers that indicate me to be a Board Member."

Fearing more resignations, Andrus moved to make Lear barely more than a guest at his own conference. He was not to lecture there, as previously planned, and hosting duties would be handled, for the most part, by others. Lear ended up arranging an "alternative conference" at which he, Cooper, English and Don Ecker presented the latest elaborations on the Dark Side Hypothesis.

Meanwhile another storm was brewing. On March 1, 1989, an Albuquerque ufologist, Robert Hastings, issued a 13-page statement, with 37 pages of appended documents, and mailed it to many of ufology's most prominent individuals. Hastings opened with these remarks:

"First, it has been established that 'Falcon,' one of the principle [sic] sources of the MJ-12 material, is Richard C. Doty, formerly attached to District 17 Air Force Office of Special Investigations (AFOSI) at Kirtland Air Force Base, Albuquerque, New Mexico. Sgt. Doty retired from the U.S. Air Force on October 1, 1988.

"How do I know that Doty is 'Falcon?' During a recent telephone conversation, Linda Moulton Howe told me that when Sgt. Doty invited her to his office at Kirtland AFB in early April 1983, and showed her a purportedly authentic U.S. government document on UFOs, he identified himself as code-name 'Falcon' and stated that it was Bill Moore who had given him that name.

"Also, in early December 1988, a ranking member of the production team responsible for the 'UFO Cover Up?—Live' television documentary confirmed that Doty is 'Falcon.' This same individual also identified the second MJ-12 source who appeared on the program, 'Condor,' as Robert Collins who was, until recently, a Captain in the U.S. Air Force. Like Doty, he was stationed at KAFB when he left the service late last year." (Collins, a scientist, was assigned to the plasma physics group at Sandia National Laboratories on the Kirtland Air Force Base. Following his retirement he moved to Indiana and remains actively interested in UFOs.)

Hastings reviewed evidence of Doty's involvement in the concoction of various questionable documents and stories, including the Ellsworth tale and the Weitzel affair. He also noted important discrepancies between the paper Howe saw and the MJ-12 briefing document. For example, while the first mentioned the alleged Aztec crash, the second said nothing about it at all. Hastings wondered, "[I]f the briefing paper that Sgt. Doty showed to Linda Howe was genuine, what does that say about the accuracy (and authenticity) of the Eisenhower document? If, on the other hand, the former was bogus and was meant to mislead Howe for some reason, what does that say about Richard 'Falcon' Doty's reliability as a source for MJ-12 material as a whole?" (Hastings, 1989). Hastings also had much critical to say about Moore, especially about an incident in which Moore had flashed a badge in front of ufologist/cover-up investigator Lee Graham and indicated he was working with the government on a project to release UFO information. (Moore would characterize this as a misguided practical joke.)

Both Moore and Doty denied that the latter was Falcon. They claimed Doty had been given that pseudonym long after the 1983 meeting with Howe. Howe, however, stuck by her account. Moore and Doty said the real Falcon, an older man than Doty, had been in the studio audience as the video of his interview was being broadcast on *UFO Cover-up . . . Live*. Doty himself was in New Mexico training with the state police.

Moore's Confession: By mid-1989 the two most controversial figures in ufology were Moore and Lear. Moore's MUFON lecture on July 1 did nothing to quiet his legion of critics. On his arrival in Las Vegas, Moore checked into a different hotel from the one at which the conference was being held. He already had refused to submit his paper for publication in the symposium proceedings, so no one knew what he would say. He had also stipulated that he would accept no questions from the floor.

Moore's speech stunned and angered much of the audience. At one point the shouts and jeers of Lear's partisans brought proceedings to a halt until order was restored. Moore finished and exited immediately. He left Las Vegas not long afterwards.

In his lecture Moore spoke candidly, for the first time, of his part in the counterintelligence operation against Bennewitz. "My role in the affair," he said, "was largely that of a freelancer

providing information on Paul's current thinking and activities." Doty, "faithfully carrying out orders which he personally found distasteful," was one of those involved in the effort to confuse and discredit Bennewitz. Because of his success at this effort, Moore suggested, Doty was chosen by the real "Falcon" as "liaison person, although I really don't know. Frankly, I don't believe that Doty does either. In my opinion he was simply a pawn in a much larger game, just as I was."

From disinformation passed on by AFOSI sources, and his own observations and guesses, according to Moore, "by mid-1982" Bennewitz had put together a story that "contained virtually all of the elements found in the current crop of rumors being circulated around the UFO community." Moore was referring to the outlandish tales Lear and Cooper were telling. Moore said that "when I first ran into the disinformation operation . . . being run on Bennewitz . . . [i]t seemed to me . . . I was in a rather unique position. There I was with my foot . . . in the door of a secret counterintelligence game that gave every appearance of being somehow directly connected to a high-level government UFO project, and, judging by the positions of the people I knew to be directly involved with it, definitely had something to do with national security! There was no way I was going to allow the opportunity to pass me by without learning at least something about what was going on. . . . I would play the disinformation game, get my hands dirty just often enough to lead those directing the process into believing that I was doing exactly what they wanted me to do, and all the while continue to burrow my way into the matrix so as to learn as much as possible about who was directing it and why." Some of the same people who were passing alleged UFO secrets on to Moore were also involved in the operation against Bennewitz. Moore knew that some of the material he was getting—essentially a mild version of the Bennewitz scenario, without the horror, paranoia and conspiracy—was false, but he (along with Jaime Shandera and **Stanton Friedman**, to whom he confided the cover-up story in June 1982; Friedman, however, would not learn of Moore's

EXTRATERRESTRIAL BIOLOGICAL ENTITIES
(*continued*)

role in the Bennewitz episode until seven years later) felt that some of it was probably true, since an invariable characteristic of disinformation is that it contains *some* facts. Moore also said that Linda Howe had been the victim of one of Doty's disinformation operations.

Before he stopped cooperating with such schemes in 1984, Moore said, he had given "routine information" to AFOSI about certain other individuals in the UFO community. Susequently he claimed that during this period (his emphasis) "*three* other members of the UFO community . . . were actively doing the same thing. I have since learned of a fourth. . . . All four are prominent individuals whose identities, if disclosed, would cause considerable controversy in the UFO community and bring serious embarrassment to two of its major organizations. To the best of my knowledge, at least two of these people are still actively involved" (Moore, 1989b).

Although he would not reveal the identities of the government informants within ufology, Moore gave the names of several persons "who were the subject of intelligence community interest between 1980 and 1984." They were:

(1) Len Stringfield, a ufologist known for his interest in crashed-disc stories; in 1980 he had been set up by a counterintelligence operative who gave him phony pictures of what purported to be humanoids in cold storage.

(2) The late Pete Mazzola, whose knowledge of film footage from a never-publicized Florida UFO case was of great interest to counterintelligence types. Moore was directed to urge Mazzola to send the footage to ufologist Kal Korff (who knew nothing of the scheme) for analysis; then Moore would make a copy and pass it on to Doty. But Mazzola never got the film, despite promises, and the incident came to nothing. "I was left with the impression," Moore wrote, "that the file had been intercepted and the witnesses somehow persuaded to cease communication with Mazzola."

(3) Peter Gersten, legal counsel for Citizens Against UFO Secrecy (CAUS), who had spearheaded a (largely unsuccessful) legal suit against the NSA seeking UFO information.

(4) Larry Fawcett, an official of CAUS and coauthor of a book on the cover-up, *Clear Intent* (1984).

(5) James and Coral Lorenzen, the directors of the Aerial Phenomena Research Organization (APRO), periodically "subjects of on-again, off-again interest . . . mostly passive monitoring rather than active meddling," according to Moore. Between 1980 and 1982 APRO employed a "cooperative" secretary who passed on confidential material to counterintelligence personnel.

(6) Larry W. Bryant, who was battling without success in the courts to have UFO secrets revealed. Moore said, "His name came up often in discussions, but I never had any direct involvement in whatever activities revolved around him."

These revelations sent shock waves through the UFO community. In September CAUS devoted virtually all of an issue of its magazine *Just Cause* to a harshly critical review of Moore's activities. Barry Greenwood declared that the "outrageousness" of Moore's conduct "cannot be described. Moore, one of the major critics of government secrecy on UFOs, had covertly informed on people who thought he was their friend and colleague. Knowing full well that the government people with whom he was dealing were active disinformants, Moore pursued a relationship with them and observed the deterioration of Paul Bennewitz'[s] physical and mental health. . . . Moore reported the effects of the false information regularly to some of the very same people who were 'doing it' to Paul. And Moore boasted in his speech as to how effective it was" (Greenwood, 1989). Greenwood complained further about Moore's admission that on the disastrous *Cover-up . . . Live* show Falcon and Condor had said things that they knew were untrue. "In the rare situation where two hours of prime time television are given over to a favorable

106

presentation of UFOs, here we have a fair portion of the last hour wasted in presenting what Moore admits to be false data. . . . Yet he saw fit to go ahead and carry on a charade, making UFO research look ridiculous in the process. Remarks by Falcon and Condor about the aliens' lifestyle and preference for Tibetan music and strawberry ice cream were laughable." So far as Greenwood and CAUS, skeptical of the MJ-12 briefing document from the first, were concerned, "July 1, 1989, may well be remembered in the history of UFO research as the day when the 'Majestic 12' story came crashing to Earth in a heap of rubble. Cause of death: Suicide!"

Nonetheless it seemed unlikely that MJ-12, EBEs, and other cover-up matters would pass away soon. The Dark Siders appeared well on their way to starting a new occult movement in America and elsewhere. Among more conservative ufologists many legitimate questions about conceivably more substantive matters remained to be answered. A reinvestigation of the Roswell incident by Don Schmitt and Kevin D. Randle of CUFOS produced what appeared to be solid new evidence of a UFO crash and cover-up. The emergence of Robert Lazar, who even a mainstream journalist such as television reporter George Knapp concluded is telling the truth as he knows it, possibly suggested a degree of substance to recurrent rumors about developments in Area 51 and S4. Even Moore's critics were puzzled by the extraordinary interest of intelligence operatives in ufologists and the UFO phenomenon, going back in time long before Bennewitz's interception of low-frequency signals at Kirtland and ahead to the present. Why go to all this trouble and expense, with so many persons over such a period of time, if there are no real UFO secrets to protect?

Moore says he is still working with the "birds," who are as active as ever. The birds tell him, he says, that disinformation is used not only against ufologists but even against those insiders like themselves who are privy to the cover-up. Those in charge are "going to great lengths to mislead their own people." At one point the birds were told that there is no substance to abduction reports, only to learn later, by accident, that a major high-level study had been done. "Even people with a need to know didn't know about it," he says. "The abduction mess caused a lot of trouble. There may have been an official admission of the cover-up by now if the abductions had not come into prominence in the 1980s."

As for the stories of ongoing contact between the U.S. government and extraterrestrial biological entities, he says there is, in his observation, a "pretty good possibility, better than three to one," that such a thing is happening. "But I don't think we can communicate with them. Perhaps we only intercept their communications. Or maybe they communicate with *us*."

He thinks he has found MJ-12. "It's not in a place anybody looked," he says. "Not an agency one would have expected. But when you think about it, it fits there" (Moore, 1990).

Doty, now a New Mexico State Police officer, was decertified as an AFOSI agent on July 15, 1986, for "misconduct" related to an incident (not concerned with UFOs) that occurred while he was stationed in West Germany. In August Doty requested a discharge from the Air Force and was sent to New Jersey to be separated from the service. But then, Doty says, the Senior Enlisted Advisor for AFOSI made a trip to the Military Personnel Center at Randolph AFB, Texas, and asked that Doty be reassigned to Kirtland, where his son lived. In September Col. Richard Law, Commander of AFOSI District 70, rescinded Doty's decertification and assigned him to Kirtland as a services career specialist (i.e., an Air Force recruiter). When he left the Air Force in October 1988, he was superintendent of the 1606 Services Squadron. Doty remains close to Moore and uncommunicative with nearly everyone else. All he will say is that one day a book will tell his side of the story and back it up with "Official Government Documents" (Doty, 1989).

Sources:

Berk, Lynn, and David Renzi. "Former CIA

EXTRATERRESTRIAL BIOLOGICAL ENTITIES
(*continued*)

Pilot, Others Say Aliens Are Among Us." *Las Vegas Sun* (May 22, 1988).

Cannon, Martin. "Earth Versus the Flying Saucers: The Amazing Story of John Lear." *UFO Universe* 9 (March 1990): 8-12.

Clark, Jerome. "Editorial: Flying Saucer Fascism." *International UFO Reporter* 14, 4 (July/August 1989): 3, 22-23.

Cooper, Milton William. *The Secret Government: The Origin, Identity, and Purpose of MJ-12*. Fullerton, CA: The Author, May 23, 1989.

Doty, Richard. Letter to Philip J. Klass (May 24, 1989).

Emenegger, Robert. *UFO's Past, Present and Future*. New York: Ballantine Books, 1974.

Friedman, Stanton T. "MJ-12: The Evidence So Far." *International UFO Reporter* 12, 5 (September/October 1987): 13-20.

Govt.-Alien Liaison? Top-Secret Documents. New Brunswick, NJ: UFO Investigators League, n.d.

Greenwood, Barry. "A Majestic Deception." *Just Cause* 20 (September 1989): 1-14.

Greenwood, Barry. "Notes on Peter Gersten's Meeting with SA Richard Doty, 1/83." *Just Cause* 16 (June 1988): 7.

Hall, Richard H. Letter to Walter H. Andrus, Jr. (March 18, 1989).

Hastings, Robert. *The MJ-12 Affair: Facts, Questions, Comments*. Albuquerque: The Author, March 1, 1989.

Howe, Linda Moulton. *An Alien Harvest: Further Evidence Linking Animal Mutilations and Human Abductions to Alien Life Forms*. Littleton, CO: Linda Moulton Howe Productions, 1989.

Information Originally Intended for Those in the Intelligence Community Who Have a "Need to Know" Clearance Status. Canadian U.F.O. Research Network: Toronto, n.d.

Johnson, George. *Architects of Fear: Conspiracy Theories and Paranoia in American Politics*. Los Angeles: Jeremy P. Tarcher, Inc., 1983.

Maccabee, Bruce, ed. *Documents and Supporting Information Related to Crashed Flying Saucers and Operation Majestic Twelve*. Mount Rainer, MD: Fund for UFO Research, 1987.

Moore, William L. "Crashed Saucers: Evidence in Search of Proof." In Walter H. Andrus, Jr., and Richard H. Hall, eds. *MUFON 1985 UFO Symposium Proceedings*, 130-79. Seguin, TX: Mutual UFO Network, Inc., 1985. Rept.: Burbank: The Author, 1985.

Moore, William L. Interview with Jerome Clark (January 5, 1990).

Moore, William L. *The Roswell Investigation: Update and Conclusions 1981*. Prescott, AZ: The Author, 1981. Rev. ed.: *The Roswell Investigation: New Evidence in the Search for a crashed UFO*. Prescott, AZ: The Author, 1982.

Moore, William L. "UFOs and the U.S. Government, Part I." *Focus* 4, 4-5-6 (June 30, 1989a): 1-18.

Moore, William L. "UFOs and the U.S. Government, Part II." *Focus* 4, 7-8-9 (September 30, 1989b): 1-3.

Pratt, Bob. "The Truth About the 'Ellsworth Case.'" *MUFON UFO Journal* 191 (January 1984): 6-9.

Scully, Frank. *Behind the Flying Saucers*. New York: Henry Holt, 1950.

Scully, Frank. "What I've Learned Since Writing 'Behind the Flying Saucers.'" *Pageant* 6 (February 1951): 76-81.

Steinman, William S., with Wendelle C. Stevens. *UFO Crash at Aztec: A Well Kept Secret.* Tucson, AZ: UFO Photo Archives, 1986.

Stringfield, Leonard H. "Status Report on Alleged Alien Cadaver Photos." *MUFON UFO Journal* 154 (December 1980): 11-16.

Todd, Robert G. "MJ-12 Rebuttal." *MUFON UFO Journal* 261 (January 1990): 17-20.

F

FANTASY-PRONE PERSONALITY HYPOTHESIS

A noteworthy contribution to the debate about the **abduction phenomenon** appeared in two articles in *International UFO Reporter* (*IUR*) in 1988. The authors were Keith Basterfield, a longtime Australian ufologist, and Robert E. Bartholomew, an American pursuing graduate studies in sociology at an Australian university. According to Basterfield and Bartholomew, individuals who believe they have had these experiences are "fantasy-prone personalities" whose mental lives are so filled with imaginary images that at times these images are mistaken for reality. They write, "There seem to us to be an entire class of what psychologists would classify as normal, healthy individuals who are prone to experiencing a variety of [altered states of consciousness (ASC)], without conscious intent to deceive. This group perceive ASCs—fugues, transient memory losses, road hypnosis, amnesias, lucid dreams, out-of-body experiences and imaginary companions—within the context of their supernatural worldview."

Drawing on ideas proposed by Josephine Hilgard in 1970 and later by T. X. Barber and S. C. Wilson, though acknowledging they are "tentative and need replication," Basterfield and Bartholomew noted the latter's assertion that as much as four percent of the population may be fantasy-prone. Fantasy-prone personalities (FPPs) share such characteristics as susceptibility to hypnosis, vivid dreams and psychic experiences.

As children they had imaginary friends and believed in fairies. After reviewing aspects of **Whitley Strieber**'s account in *Communion: A True Story* (1987) and finding evidence of fantasy-proneness, Basterfield and Bartholomew theorize that Strieber "may be within this four percent" of FPPs.

In a follow-up article the authors declare that "UFO contacts/abductions . . . are events generated within the minds of fantasy-prone individuals." Further, "They appear to be a real physical event to the individuals concerned. . . . Physical effects may occur to the percipients. . . . If other fantasy-prone personalities are also present, the experience may be shared by them." Basterfield and Bartholomew reject the generally-held view of ufologists that **contactees** and abductees are fundamentally unalike, holding both to be participants in events that only appear real because "some of the brain's neural inputs from the normal five senses are also used when generating imagery/fantasy." Physical effects, such as wounds and scars, are generated by the human mind. They add, referring to multiple-witness abduction accounts, that "we believe all multiple percipients will be found to be FPP thus explaining how several persons can be involved."

Abduction investigators, while expressing admiration for the ingenuity of the fantasy-prone personality hypothesis, responded mostly with caution and often open skepticism. One critic was sociologist Ron Westrum, who wrote in a

111

FANTASY-PRONE PERSONALITY HYPOTHESIS
(*continued*)

letter published in *IUR* (September/October 1988), "According to the authors, the general incidence of the fantasy-prone personality (FPP) in the population is four percent (.04) or one out of 25. This has some implications for how likely a group of persons with two or more members is to have only FPPs in it. If we start with a two-person group and one person is FPP, the chance that a second person, taken at random, is FPP is one out of 25. If we take a three-person group, the chance that all three are FPP, if one person is, is .0016, or one in 625. Even considering that FPPs may be likely to be the spouses or friends of FPPs—a point not yet proved—these numbers imply that most FPPs, if part of a group, are very likely to have another member of that group be a non-FPP. This is important for multiple-person abduction cases, because the implication is that during most 'abductions' when another is present, usually that other person present will not be another FPP."

Westrum went on to argue, "Most of the symptomatology of abductees is perfectly consistent with the hypothesis of post-traumatic stress syndrome."

Another *IUR* correspondent (July/August 1988), writer D. Scott Rogo, noting public-opinion surveys indicating that paranormal and psychic experiences are surprisingly widespread, said, "We have no way of determining whether close-encounter percipients report psychic experiences any more frequently than the general public (which would serve as a hypothetical baseline)." Rogo also objected to Basterfield and Bartholomew's suggestion that scars on abductees are psychosomatically generated through hypnosis, saying that no medical or psychological evidence supports the notion that the mind alone can cause deep cuts such as those abductees report. "To compare these marks to the peripheral sorts of phenomena seen in hypnosis," he says, "is like comparing a bee sting to heart surgery."

In responding to critics, Basterfield and

Bartholomew urged that abductees be subjected to "psychological tests designed to assess hypnotic susceptibility, absorption, vividness of mental imagery, response to waking suggestion, creativity and social desirability. . . . The subjectivity involved in abductees' accounts is often ignored by those proposing an extraterrestrial explanation."

The first formal test of the fantasy-prone personality hypothesis was conducted in 1989 by University of Connecticut psychologist Kenneth Ring. Ring found no correlation between fantasy proneness and UFO experiences, including abductions.

Sources:

Bartholomew, Robert E., and Keith Basterfield. "Abduction States of Consciousness." *International UFO Reporter* 13, 2 (March/April 1988): 7-9, 15.

Basterfield, Keith, and Robert E. Bartholomew. "Abductions: The Fantasy-Prone-Personality Hypothesis." *International UFO Reporter* 13, 3 (May/June 1988): 9-11.

FRENCH UFOLOGY

A major event in the evolution of ufology (and popular interest in UFOs generally) in France was a series of France-Inter radio shows broadcast between January and March 1974. Reporter Jean-Claude Bourret interviewed a number of witnesses and authorities. The most prominent of the latter was Robert Galley, then the Minister of Defense, who declared, "I am sincerely convinced that we must have a very open mind about these phenomena." He reported that French pilots had tracked UFOs on radar and observed them visually. "These cases are unexplained," he said. "Similar phenomena do occur abroad" (Bourret, 1974). Although he cautioned that it would be premature to come to firm conclusions about what these cases mean, he said that the government had ordered the airborne Gendarmerie to channel the reports it received to Claude Poher, an aerospace engineer with the Centre National d'Etudes Spatiales (CNES, National Space Study Center). (In 1977 Poher would be appointed head of **Groupe d'Etude des Phénomènes Aérospatiaux Non-Identifiés** [GEPAN, Study Group Into Unidentified Aerospace Phenomena], an official project under CNES' direction). Galley remarked that if people saw the impressive UFO material Poher had received, they would find it "actually rather perturbing."

Such statements, British ufologist **Jenny Randles** has written, were "literally the equivalent of a British or American minister such as Michael Heseltine or Caspar Weinberger, whilst still in office, broadcasting to the nation the news that UFOs exist, are being studied by the correct authorities and remain utterly perplexing" (Randles, 1987).

The French-Inter series and Galley's remarks sparked fascination with UFOs, although ufology and ufologists were hardly unknown in France before this time. In the 1950s Aimé Michel had written two widely-read books, translated into English as *The Truth About Flying Saucers* (1956) and *Flying Saucers and the Straight-Line Mystery* (1958), and was one of the world's best-known ufologists. Although **Jacques Vallee**, an enormously influential figure in the field, left France in the early 1960s, he was a product of French ufology and his books, beginning with *Anatomy of a Phenomenon* (1965) and the books that followed and continuing with his latest, *Confrontations* (1990), contain many references to cases, books and investigators from his native country. But the publicity given the UFO phenomenon in the early months of 1974 had a special impact, leading to the creation of a number of UFO groups. Most were not important and are now gone, but their presence, however brief, gave French ufology new life.

During the 1970s the extraterrestrial hypothesis (ETH) of UFO origin was the prevailing view. But in 1975 two new approaches came to the fore. They were associated with individuals who published in the magazine *Lumières Dans la Nuit*,

which otherwise had an orthodox ETH orientation. One of these tendencies, which proved to be short-lived, was called "psycho-ufology," an attempt to explain UFO phenomena by parapsychological theories. The major expression of this view appeared in Pierre Vieroudy's *Ces OVNI Qui Annoncent le Surhomme* (1977). Far more influential was the emerging **psychosocial hypothesis**, suggested for the first time in France in two books by Michel Monnerie, *Et si les OVNIs N'existaient pas?* (1977) and *Le Naufrage des Extraterrestres* (1979), which treated UFO reports skeptically but differed from other debunking books in suggesting unusual psychological states rather than hoaxes as the explanation for extraordinary close-encounter claims. Gérard Barthel and Jacques Brucker's *La Grande Peur Martienne* (1979), in debunking the fall 1954 UFO wave which had been the subject of Michel's *Straight-Line Mystery*, contributed further to a climate in which hypotheses focused on more mundane cultural and mental processes rather than extraterrestrial visitation would receive a sympathetic hearing.

For many years *Lumières Dans la Nuit* (*LDLN*) was the major magazine in the field. In the 1970s, when it was published ten times a year as a commercial venture, it even had a network of local investigators and groups that conducted field investigations and archival searches. (These groups went into decline and had all but disappeared by the early 1980s.) Under the editorship of Raymond Veillith *LDLN* covered the whole range of the literature: case studies, catalogs, historical reports, theoretical views. In 1988 Veillith sold the magazine to Joel Mesnard. Under Mesnard's editorship, the publication continues to be a significant force in French ufology. Nevertheless, the quality of the magazine seems on the decline and some recent articles are of a decidedly paranoid nature.

Most of the other periodicals are associated with organizations that thrive or falter as the leadership's and membership's enthusiasms rise or fall. Today there are fewer than ten active groups. The reasons are several. One is that some ufologists, owing to Monnerie's book,

FRENCH UFOLOGY (*continued*)

became convinced that UFOs are not extra-terrestrial devices, the idea that had brought them into ufology in the first place, and they saw no reason to continue an involvement with the subject. Most left quietly, but one who did not was Pascal Grousset, who declared his newfound skepticism in an editorial in the last issue of *CPCGU Bulletin*, the publication of the Comité Poitou-Charente des Groupements Ufologiques.

Among the groups that survive, one of the most notable is Association d'Etude Sur les Soucoupes Volantes (AESV), founded in 1974 by Perry Petrakis. For its first few years it was a mundane, ordinary flying-saucer club, but in the early 1980s, thanks largely to Yves Bosson, it began to mature. Its quarterly review *AESV* was renamed *OVNI-Presence* (*OP*) starting with the September 1981 issue and it adopted a more serious-minded, critical approach, including articles with skeptical or psychosociological points of view. In February 1984 AESV created "S.O.S. OVNI," a UFO hot line on which witnesses could phone in reports. AESV's greatest success in this department was in establishing good contacts among France's air-traffic controllers, through whom they received sightings reports from airline personnel and pilots. By the end of the decade, however, *OP* was appearing less and less frequently, and AESV's future seems clouded.

The Comité Nord-Est des Groupements Ufologiques (CNEGU), a federation of four groups (once ten, the other six having ceased to exist), is concerned mainly with field investigations. It has no corporate opinion about the nature of the UFO phenomenon. Another federation, Comité Ile-de-France des Groupements Ufologiques (CIGU), conducts investigations, reports on them and other matters in a thick annual review (the last issue of which appeared in 1987) and runs a news clipping service (from which we learn 642 articles on UFOs were published in French media between July 1987 and June 1989). A somewhat atypical group is Crashes Réalité, a tiny organization devoted to the "raising of the secrecy on UFO crashes world-wide." Two other small groups promote the sinister speculations of American John Lear, who combines conspiracy theories with a nightmarish vision of evil aliens manipulating earthly life and performing hideous experiments on human beings.

French ufologists meet annually in Lyons at a conference organized by Perry Petrakis of AESV. The First European Conference on Anomalous Aerial Phenomena: Physical and Psychosocial Aspects was held in November 1988 in Belgium, though it was organized by Thierry Pinvidic and Jacques Scornaux of France. From 1983 to 1986 French and British ufologists met on four occasions, twice in each country, to compare ideas, largely of a psychosocial nature. The organizers were Pinvidic and **Hilary Evans**.

Such figures from French ufological history as René Fouéré, Aimé Michel and astronomer Pierre Guérin are no longer active, Fouéré because of age and illness, Michel and Guérin because of feelings that the UFO phenomenon is beyond human comprehension and therefore futile to contemplate. Jimmy Guieu, a figure in French ufology since the 1950s, suffered from a loss of credibility because of his involvement with questionable individuals on the margins of ufology and his authorship of a book endorsing the **Cergy-Pontoise hoax**; he now is a leading promoter of John Lear's ideas (see p. 99). Michel Monnerie left ufology after he became convinced that UFO reports represent nothing truly anomalous. Younger, active ufologists include Claude Mauge, largely sympathetic to the psychosocial hypothesis; Pierre Lagrange and Bertrand Méheust, who favor no particular interpretation but have an intellectual interest in the sociological and historical phenomena associated with UFO reports—Méheust wrote *Soucoupes Volantes et Folklore* (1985), relating modern UFO lore to traditional supernatural beliefs; and Jean Sider, a supporter of the ETH, with a keen interest in cover-up issues.

The major event of the decade was the January 8, 1981, **Trans-en-Provence CE2**, which GEPAN investigated and on which it produced a detailed *Technical Note 16*. In July 1983 an abduction was reported at Sommerecourt, where Stephane Gasparovic and members of his family saw a bright luminous object. In time everyone but Gasparovic tired of watching the object. After they left, Gasparovic allegedly was paralyzed and drawn into the air, at which point he lost consciousness. He was later found wandering around like a robot and taken to a hospital, where he murmured he had encountered small beings with pointed ears. This remarkable incident was investigated by CNEGU. In the summer of 1989 GEPAN investigated three landing-trace cases but has yet to release results.

The **contactee** movement in France is small. Best known to the public (outside France as well as inside the country) are the Raelians, founded by Claude Vorilhon ("Caude Rael"), who has claimed contacts with the Elohim (literally, the Gods) since December 1973. (He subsequently wrote two books, in 1974 and 1975. These were published in English in one volume as *Space Aliens Took Me to Their Planet: The Most Important Revelation in the History of Mankind* [1978].) Jean-Paul Appel leads a contactee group first known as Iso Zen, then as Futura, now as Galacteus. Its members include Jean Giraud, alias Gir, alias Moebius, a prominent science-fiction illustrator. These are going concerns, but the early-1980s groups La Grand Contact (Jean-Pierre Prevost) and Spirale (Patrick Marsili), both of which grew out of the Cergy-Pontoise hoax (Prevost claimed to be one of the original "witnesses" before meeting extraterrestrials himself), are long gone.

Claude Mauge and Jerome Clark

Sources:

Bourret, Jean-Claude. *The Crack in the Universe: What You Have Not Been Told About Flying Saucers*. Jersey: Neville Spearman, Ltd., 1974.

Guérin, Pierre. "Thirty Years After Kenneth Arnold: The Situation Regarding UFOs." *Zetetic Scholar* 5 (1979): 35-49.

Méheust, Bertrand. *Science-Fiction et Soucoupes Volantes: Une Réalité Mythico-Physique*. Paris: Editions Mercure de France, 1978.

Méheust, Bertrand. *Soucoupes Volantes et Folklore*. Paris: Editions Mercure de France, 1985.

Monnerie, Michel. *Et si les OVNIs N'existaient pas?* Paris: Les Humanoides Associés, 1977.

Randles, Jenny. *The UFO Conspiracy: The First Forty Years*. Poole, England: Blandford Press, 1987.

FRIEDMAN, STANTON TERRY (1934-)

Stanton Terry Friedman is a nuclear physicist and an active UFO lecturer and investigator. He is best known in ufology as an aggressive proponent of the extraterrestrial hypothesis and outspoken critic of UFO debunkers.

Friedman was born on July 29, 1934, in Elizabeth, New Jersey, the second son of Louis and Florence Friedman. He was graduated as a valedictorian of his high school class in 1951. Although he was admitted to MIT, he could not afford to attend. He took advantage of a scholarship to attend Rutgers University, majoring in physics, for two years. Another scholarship took him in 1953 to the University of Chicago. In 1956 he received his M.S. in physics.

"I have had three successive careers," Friedman says. "First I spent 14-plus years as an itinerant nuclear physicist going from canceled program to canceled program. I worked for the Aircraft Nuclear Propulsion department of General Electric just outside Cincinnati from 1956 through 1959 and became an expert on the design, development and testing of advanced radiation-shielding systems for various high-performance nuclear and space systems. All the programs were classified." While at GE, he first became interested in UFOs, somewhat by accident. He was ordering books from a catalogue and needed just one more to save shipping costs. He

FRIEDMAN, STANTON TERRY (*continued*)

happened to see former Project Blue Book head Capt. Edward J. Ruppelt's book *The Report on Unidentified Flying Objects* and figuring that it might at least be good for a laugh, he ordered a copy. He also hoped that it might have some insights into advanced propulsion systems similar to the nuclear-powered aircraft he was working on at the time. As he read the book, he was surprised to find himself intrigued.

"I moved to Northern California in late 1959 to work on the shielding aspects of compact nuclear reactors for space applications for Aerojet General," he says. "I wound up as a project engineer on a one-person contract with the Air Force's Foreign Technology Division . . . at Wright-Patterson Air Force Base in Ohio. My contract was 'Analysis and Evaluation of Fast and Intermediate Reactors for Space Vehicle Applications.' Basically I reviewed loads of Soviet technical publications at the Battelle Memorial Institute in Columbus, Ohio, and made a bunch of trips back there and to Air Technical Intelligence Center. ATIC was also the home of Project Blue Book and I met with Lt. Col. Robert Friend several times.

"A California librarian got me over a dozen UFO books, some of which if I had read first I would never have read another UFO book. A turning point was finding a copy of Leon Davidson's privately-published version of *Project Blue Book Special Report 14* and the contrasts between the Air Force press release about it and the data in it. I have mentioned that seminal volume in every one of the more than 600 lectures I have presented at colleges and professional groups in all 50 states, eight provinces, Puerto Rico, England and other places.

"I also worked on the design of the shielding for a deep-space fusion-propulsion system using the new 'hard' superconductors and able to get man to the stars. While at Aerojet General Nucleonics I joined the American Institute of Aeronautics and Astronautics as well as the Aerial Phenomena Research Organization [APRO] and the National

Investigations Committee on Aerial Phenomena [NICAP]. . . . When the AGN programs collapsed, I went to General Motors in Indianapolis in 1963 to work on compact nuclear reactors for mobile applications. . . . In 1966 I moved to Pittsburgh to work for the Westinghouse AstroNuclear Lab on the Nerva nuclear-rocket development program. As I had been in my other jobs, I served as a bridge between experimentalists and theoreticians, trying to make sense out of the work of both groups." During this period he did a considerable amount of traveling to advanced test facilities, including the nuclear-test site in Nevada, Los Alamos Scientific Lab, Oak Ridge National Lab, and the Idaho Nuclear Test Station.

"Frank Edwards sent me a copy of his best-selling book *Flying Saucers: Serious Business* [1966]. After reading it I contacted Frank to see how I might do more to make the public aware of the facts about flying saucers. He gave me some tips, including somebody to call at KDKA radio in Pittsburgh. I called the talk show, and their attitude was, 'Don't call us, we'll call you.' But one day the station called me at about 6:30 p.m. to do the 7:00 p.m. talk show. That was my first talk show. . . .

"Lots of people heard the show and a technician at work asked me to give a talk to her book-review club about Edwards' *Serious Business*. That was my first UFO lecture."

Soon Friedman was lecturing to scientific and popular groups, writing on UFOs and investigating reports. In due course, as money for the nuclear-rocket program was cut back, he decided to lecture full time. Now divorced and remarried, he moved to the San Francisco area, then in the early 1980s to his wife's native Canada. After settling in Fredericton, New Brunswick, Friedman relates, "I wound up working on the commissioning of the Point Lepreau nuclear power plant 75 miles away and when that was finished, I got involved with a local company in various studies such as food irradiation, seed stimulation with radiation, and so on. I had various research ideas and managed to get them funded. Among them were studies of waste heat recovery from power plants, the use of accelerators for industrial applications, treatment of flue gas with electron beams to get rid of acid rain, and all aspects of the radon problem. Since 1982 I have mixed the technical work with my UFO-lecturing, writing and investigating."

In the late 1970s and into the 1980s Friedman, along with writer/researcher **William L. Moore**, interviewed persons connected with the Roswell incident, the alleged crash of a UFO in Lincoln County, New Mexico, in July 1947. In 1988, after securing a $16,000 grant from the **Fund for UFO Research**, he devoted considerable effort, through archival work and interviews, to the investigation of the MJ-12 briefing document. Friedman's monographs have dealt with such issues as debunkers, UFO propulsion, the Betty Hill star map and extraterrestrial intelligence. He says, "The evidence is overwhelming that *some* UFOs are alien spacecraft. . . . There is no question that the subject of UFOs represents a kind of Cosmic Watergate and that small groups of people within the U.S., Canadian and other governments have known since 1947 that indeed some UFOs are alien spacecraft. . . . The UFO story is the most important story of the past millennium."

Sources:

Friedman, Stanton T. *Flying Saucers: Four Scientific Papers*. Union City, CA: UFORI, 1980.

Friedman, Stanton T. "MJ-12 Debunking Fiasco." *International UFO Reporter* 13, 3 (May/June 1988): 12-17.

Friedman, Stanton T. "UFO Propulsion Systems." In Curtis G. Fuller, ed. *Proceedings of the First International UFO Congress*, 95-103. New York: Warner Books, 1980.

Friedman, Stanton T. "UFOs and Science." In U.S. Congress, House. Committee on Science and Astronautics. *Symposium on Unidentified Flying Objects*. Hearings, 90th Congress, second session, July 29, 1968. Washington, DC: Government Printing Office, 1968. 214-23.

FUND FOR UFO RESEARCH, INC.
Box 227
Mount Rainier, Maryland 20712

The Fund for UFO Research, Inc., established as a nonprofit corporation in the District of Columbia on August 1, 1979, raises money to support scientific research and public-information projects. **Bruce Maccabee**, a physicist, was appointed chairman and holds that position today.

The Fund's first grant went to support an on-site investigation of the December 1978 air-to-air filming of a UFO over New Zealand. In 1981 the Fund published the first of three volumes of recently-declassified government documents. With the rising interest in the **abduction phenomenon**, later that same year it supported the first psychological study of a group of UFO abductees. Other funded projects included studies of historical UFO sightings, investigation of the MJ-12 briefing document, computer analyses of 400 abduction reports, further psychological surveys of UFO witnesses, the analysis of a daylight video-tape of a Japanese UFO, and more. In 1987 the Fund sponsored the annual **Mutual UFO Network** (MUFON) symposium, held this time at American University in Washington, D.C., and in 1989 it gave financial support to the first meeting of **Treatment and Research on Experienced Anomalous Trauma** (TREAT), which brought ufologists and mental-health professionals to Fairfield University in Connecticut in May to discuss methodological questions related to the abduction phenomenon. In its first decade the Fund disbursed more than $50,000 for scientific research on UFO matters.

The Fund is not a membership organization. It does not publish a magazine or investigate UFO reports, though it works closely with groups that do. Grant proposals must be supported by a majority of the national board to be approved.

The Fund's executive committee currently consists of Bruce Maccabee; Craig Phillips, a biologist; Don Berliner, an aviation and science writer; Rob Swiatek, a physicist at the U.S. Patent Office; and Fred Whiting, a public-relations

FUND FOR UFO RESEARCH (*continued*)

consultant. Serving on the national board are John B. Carlson, University of Maryland astronomer; Thomas P. Deuley, a retired Naval officer; Barry Downing, a pastor and theologian; **Richard Hall**, a writer and veteran figure in ufology; Robert Hall, a sociologist recently retired from the University of Illinois at Chicago; **Richard F. Haines**, an aviation psychologist; Richard C. Henry, an astrophysicist at Johns Hopkins University; Herbert E. Roth, a pilot and aviation trainer; David W. Schwartzman, a Howard University geologist; and Ron Westrum, a sociologist of science at Eastern Michigan University.

Sources:

Bloecher, Ted, Aphrodite Clamar, and Budd Hopkins. *Final Report on the Psychological Testing of UFO "Abductees."* Mount Rainier, MD: Fund for UFO Research, 1985.

A Brief History of the Fund for UFO Research. Washington: Fund for UFO Research, n.d.

The Government UFO Collection: A Collection of UFO Documents from the Governments of the USA and Canada. Mount Rainier, MD: Fund for UFO Research, 1981-1985.

Winkler, Louis. *Catalog of UFO-Like Data Before 1947.* Mount Rainier, MD: Fund for UFO Research, 1984.

G

GROUPE D'ETUDES DES PHENOMENES AEROSPATIAUX NON IDENTIFIES

Groupe d'Etudes des Phénomènes Aérospatiaux Non Identifiés (GEPAN)—Study Group into Unidentified Aerospace Phenomena, France's official UFO-investigation agency—was founded on May 1, 1977, as a section of the Centre National d'Etudes Spatiales (CNES), the French equivalent of America's National Aeronautics and Space Administration, headquartered in Toulouse. Its first director was Claude Poher, an aeronautical engineer who between 1969 and 1971 had conducted extensive statistical studies of world-wide UFO reports. GEPAN set up an advisory body of astronomers, physicists and other scientists and professionals, and has remained the most important organization to figure in **French ufology**.

GEPAN's first goals were to put into place data-collection systems whereby the agency could receive reports from the Air Force, civil-aviation authorities, the Gendarmerie, weather services and national police; conduct statistical analyses of sightings; and investigate cases already reported. When these initial inquiries were completed, GEPAN concluded that "(a) the appearance of certain unidentified phenomena cannot be accommodated by conventional physical, psychological, or psychosocial models; (b) a physical component in the phenomena reported is extremely likely; and (c) the spatial and temporal dimensions of the events are of a very low order."

The organization then sought to develop a scientific methodology which would govern collection and investigation of reports. The resultant model yielded, according to GEPAN's current director, Jean-Jacques Velasco, "a quantifiable body of information revolving around two major axes, namely data of a physical nature and those of a psychological nature. Since communication of information by the witness(es) represents a reaction to the stimulus of an event, the first observable dimension is the witness(es).

"The information appears in the form of the witness' narration, and the duly constituted witness report represents the second observable dimension. However, these conditions are not in themselves sufficient to analyze the whole case; they must be set against their background, a tangible physical environment. This gives us the third observable dimension. Our view would, however, be incomplete if the report, the most subjective element, were not seen in the light of the social, cultural, and ideological system in which the witness interacts, and so we arrive at the fourth observable dimension, the psychosocial environment." GEPAN uses a tetrahedron to illustrate and to represent a "complex system in which variables can be analyzed globally and symmetrically, in contrast with partial or reductive methods" (Velasco, 1987).

By November 1985 GEPAN had received 1615 Gendarmerie reports dating back to 1974. Researchers set about the task of classifying them

GROUPE D'ETUDES DES PHENOMENES AEROSPATIAUX NON IDENTIFIES (*continued*)

as follows, using as a criterion, in Velasco's words, "the level of difficulty in understanding the witness reports:

"Type A: Phenomena are fully and unambiguously identified.

"Type B: Nature of phenomena seems to have been identified but doubts remain.

"Type C: Witness report cannot be analyzed, i.e., no opinion can be formulated because the report is not sufficiently precise.

"Type D: Witness report is consistent and precise and cannot be interpreted [as] . . . conventional phenomena. . . ."

Velasco writes that GEPAN conducts two types of investigations: "mini-investigations, where the aim is to study cases that are significant from, say, a physical or psychological point of view, allowing a particular category of phenomenon to be isolated; [and] full investigations, concerning unexplained cases and checking on all the observable elements, in particular the gathering and examination of physical and biological evidence." Eighteen full investigations have been conducted, each published in a monograph titled *Technical Note* (the last appearing in 1983), resulting in three cases for which no explanation could be found. The most impressive and evidential of these was a landing-trace case at **Trans-en-Provence** in early 1981 (*Technical Note 16*). Nineteen eighty-one was also a year in which the number of reports coming to GEPAN declined precipitously, reflecting a worldwide sighting dip which lasted until the last year or two of the decade.

Poher resigned from GEPAN in October 1978, designating Alain Esterle, an American with a Ph.D. in statistics, as his successor. Esterle was left to deal with growing political and scientific opposition to the project. Although GEPAN's governing scientific council regularly reviewed and approved GEPAN's methodology and conclusions, a number of attempts to disband the group have been made. GEPAN's imminent demise was widely rumored late in 1982 and early 1983. On February 11, 1983, the newspaper *Le Figaro* cited unnamed "specialists" who said GEPAN existed only because it reflected an enthusiasm of former president Valéry Giscard d'Estaing. They also asserted that GEPAN cost too much. In fact, it claimed only a small percentage of the CNES budget. (Physicist-ufologist Jean-Pierre Petit, GEPAN's harshest critic, says, on the other hand, that Roger Lesgard, the CNES secretary general who helped bring GEPAN into being, told him, "The Army and CNES were furious about all the noise made about UFOs. Then we created GEPAN to cool and extinguish the problem and it worked perfectly" [Petit, 1988].)

When Jean-Jacques Velasco was appointed head of GEPAN on September 1, 1983, GEPAN was "reorganized." It was transferred to CNES' department of Environnement Spatial Terrestre (ESO), and its eight-person team was given different assignments within CNES, leaving Velasco, who is not a scientist, with only himself and a secretary. According to Petit, Esterle and his colleagues were ordered "never to deal again with UFOs." It is rumored at the same time, however, that Esterle maintains a behind-the-scenes role within GEPAN. (In *The UFO Conspiracy* [1987] **Jenny Randles** writes, "Esterle visited Britain in May 1981, when he attended the International UFO Congress. He did not address the meeting and few realized who he was. However, in a nearby cafe he told some of us that the work of GEPAN was proving the alien reality of UFOs." This account, of course, directly contradicts Lesgard's account as reported by Petit. Petit says, however, that Velasco complained to him in 1984, "We are collecting UFO reports, but we don't know what to do with them. Once a case has been investigated, we publish a note on it, and that is that. We have no scientific structure behind GEPAN.")

On November 25, 1988, GEPAN got two additional staff persons, one a computer expert, and the additional task of tracking orbiting objects (conventional ones, not UFOs). It also got the go-ahead to perform physical experiments related to its assignments. The following summer it investigated three landing-trace cases but had not published the results by the end of the year.

Sources:

Creighton, Gordon. "Another French Report on G.E.P.A.N." *Flying Saucer Review* 30, 3 (February 1985): 27.

Mauge, Claude. *Some Notes About the History of GEPAN.* Aubervilliers, France: The Author, August 8, 1989.

Mauge, Claude. *Some Notes About the History of GEPAN: (2) Complements and Corrections.* Aubervilliers, France: The Author, October 18, 1989.

Petit, Jean-Pierre. "The UFO Impact." *Pursuit* 21, 1 (First Quarter 1988): 10-13.

Petit, Jean-Pierre. "Where Have the Flying Saucers Gone?" *Pursuit* 17, 4 (Fourth Quarter 1984): 153-156.

Velasco, Jean-Jacques. "Scientific Approach and Results of Studies Into Unidentified Aerospace Phenomena in France." In Walter H. Andrus, Jr., and Richard H. Hall, eds. *MUFON 1987 UFO Symposium Proceedings*, 51-67. Seguin, TX: Mutual UFO Network, Inc., 1987.

GULF BREEZE SIGHTINGS

On November 11, 1987, as the story has it, Edward Walters, a prominent businessman in the small city (pop. 6000) of Gulf Breeze, in west Florida's panhandle, had his first encounter with a UFO. At 5 p.m. he was working in his office at home when he saw something glowing behind a 30-foot pine tree in the front yard. Curious, he stepped outside, where he got a clearer view of the source: a top-shaped craft with a row of dark squares and smaller openings between them ("portholes") across the midsection. There was a bright, luminous ring on the bottom. Walters stepped back into his office, grabbed an old Polaroid camera, went outside again and snapped a picture just as the craft moved from behind the tree. He took three more pictures as the object, about 150 feet away, continued to drift in a northeasterly direction.

Walters got some more film and took another picture. Now the object was moving closer, apparently about to cross the road in front of his house. He ran out to the street intending to snap yet more pictures. Suddenly the UFO was above him and something hit him, a blue beam which paralyzed him and lifted him several feet off the ground. A foul odor, like ammonia heavily laced with cinnamon, enveloped him and stuck to the back of his throat. Then a "computerlike" voice inside his head said, "We will not harm you." He managed to scream. Then a female voice began to speak and images of dogs appeared, "flashing . . . just as if they were turning the pages of a book," Walters would recall (Walters, 1990). Then he fell hard on the pavement, the blue beam gone. He turned around on his back and looked for the UFO. It, too, was gone.

Walters' teenaged son, Dan, in the house watching television, had missed the episode. When Walters' wife Frances came home, her husband told her what had happened. She noted both his obvious fear and the strange odor on him. The couple discussed at length what they ought to do. After dinner they told their children.

On the 17th Walters went to Duane Cook, editor of the *Gulf Breeze Sentinel*, and showed the pictures to him. He told Cook that the photos had been given to him by a Mr. X, who desired no publicity. Walters also produced a letter allegedly from X, but really from Walters himself. The photographs and letter were run in the paper two days later, along with an editorial plea that those who knew more come forward.

At about 4 p.m. on the 20th Walters came home and as he walked in the door he became aware of

GULF BREEZE SIGHTINGS (*continued*)

a humming sound in his ear. At first it was barely noticeable. Then it rose in pitch until it was unbearable. Walters went through the house and into the backyard, followed by his alarmed wife. Walters recognized the hum as the same one he had heard while entrapped in the blue beam. The couple returned to the house and went to the front porch, where they scanned the sky looking for the UFO. Seeing nothing, they resumed their normal activities, though the hum was continuing inside Walters' head.

As Walters sat in his office, he heard a "blast of air," then a voice inside his head. The hum had now stopped, replaced by a mechanical voice speaking in what sounded like one part of a conversation, the audible part of it spoken in something like an "African dialect." This went on for some minutes and Walters said nothing about it to his wife when she came in to say she and their daughter, Laura, were off to a football game. After they left, Walters picked up his camera and went out the front door. The neighborhood, as it had been during his earlier encounter, was quiet.

Frightened and drenched with sweat, Walters said, "I hear you, you bastard." Another rush of air filled his head as the voice stopped. It resumed some moments later to say, "Be calm. Step forward." A speck of light appeared high in the sky and was falling downward at a rapid rate. Walters raised his camera, only to hear the voice tell him not to do that. It was followed by a "distorted" female voice repeating the message, and then by a male voice speaking in Spanish: *"Los fotos son prohibidio."* The female voice added, "You can't expose them. They won't hurt you. Just a few tests. That's all."

Ignoring the warnings, Walters took a picture of the UFO, hovering above a power pole at the front end of the lawn. All the voices were speaking in his head at once, all sounding "somewhat computerlike." When the UFO shot to his right, Walters took another picture. The first voice, the "UFO voice" as Walters would call it, directed him to step forward so that he could

be brought aboard. When Walters said they had no right to do that, the voice replied, "We have the right." The female voice said, "You must do what they say. They haven't hurt us and we are going back home now."

At that moment visions of naked women of all types, ages and weights flashed through Walters' brain. Then the UFO voice said, "We will come for you." In response Walters took one more picture and with that the UFO moved forward slightly, then ascended abruptly and vanished almost instantly.

At 3 a.m. on December 2 Walters awoke to the sound of a baby's crying. Since there was no baby in either his house or his neighbors', Walters felt uneasy. A few minutes later he heard the same "distorted" voices in his head. They were speaking in Spanish and referring to the crying baby and also to apparent abductors who were feeding them nothing but bananas. Walters, who had lived in Central America at one point in his life, thought the speakers were a young Costa Rican or Nicaraguan couple. Accompanied by Frances, Walters took a .32-caliber pistol and checked the front yard. He then went through the house to the backyard, where he saw the UFO descending at a blinding speed. It stopped about 100 feet above the pool, then drifted a short distance from the house.

Meanwhile Walters had fled inside, to join Frances, who was seeing the UFO for the first time. They watched the object from behind the door. Then, as Walters pushed the door slightly ajar, the "UFO voice" said in a commanding tone, "Step forward now."

Instead Walters picked up the Polaroid camera, holding it in his right hand and the pistol in his left. After dashing to the far end of the pool, he snapped a picture, feeling exposed as the flash went off. He ran back to the kitchen door and he and Frances saw the UFO shoot off. The hum in his head faded.

But the night was not over. The couple had been back in bed for no more than a few minutes when they heard their dog bark—once. This was strange because typically the dog let loose with a string of barks.

Again with pistol and camera in hand, Walters walked to the French doors that connected the bedroom to a screened-in porch overlooking the pool, where he expected the UFO would be again. But when he pulled the curtains open, he saw a "creature" on the other side of the glass, just inches from him. It was a four-foot humanoid with big black eyes. It was wearing a helmet with a transparent insert which allowed the eyes to see out. A grayish "box" or shield covered its trunk and another, similar (though slightly smaller) device covered it from its hips to its knees. A glowing silver rod was in its right hand.

Shocked and frightened, Walters screamed, reeled backwards and tripped. The being simply stood and watched. As Frances crawled over the bed to her husband, she saw it, too. Walters raised his gun and pointed it, thinking he would shoot if the being tried to enter. But it did not. According to Walters' account, the being "stared at me with eyes that showed no fear. Eyes that were calm. Eyes that were almost sad. Eyes that somehow seemed curious" (Walters, 1990).

Walters rose to his feet and struggled with the lock on the doors, having to put aside the gun and camera in the process. The being was retreating toward the porch stairs, but it was only about 20 feet away and Walters was certain he could capture it. He opened the screen door and stepped out on to the wooden deck, where a blue beam hit him in the right leg. From his knee down the leg was "frozen" as if, in Walters' words, "nailed to the floor." Then the beam started to *lift* his leg. Walters leaned back and clasped the screendoor jamb. As he did so, he saw the bottom of the UFO some 50 feet up. Frances held on to him from behind and soon his leg came out of the beam. He was free.

The UFO hovered over a field—the one into which the being had fled—behind the house. Walters reclaimed his camera and shot a picture (his 11th UFO photo) as the object shot out the

blue beam, apparently, Walters thought, to pick up the crew member in the field.

There would be other UFO incidents, enough to fill the book the couple one day would write. They are summarized briefly:

December 5, 6 a.m.: Walters sees and photographs a large UFO behind the house. The "UFO voice" addresses him as "Zehaas" and says that "we have come for you." Walters refuses to "step forward," as he is told to do, and the object departs in the usual manner, quickly and straight upward.

December 17, 1 a.m.: Two hours after retiring, Walters is awakened by a noise like a waterfall. He goes outside and takes a picture of a UFO hovering at 80 feet. Inside his head he hears sounds of "whooshing" and of liquid hitting the ground and with his eyes sees smoke or steam being expelled from the object. Later that day he finds a plastic butter tub his children had left in the yard. It contains an unusual bubbling liquid which he saves for analysis. The UFO recedes in the darkness. A few minutes later a UFO in the back of the field beyond Walters' property suddenly lights up, ascends and disappears. Walters takes four pictures of its departure, for a total now of 17 photographs.

A year later, after investigators find that Walters' photo 17 actually precedes 16, Walters undergoes hypnotic regression with psychologist Dan Overlade. Under hypnosis Walters recalls seeing dark figures in the bedroom. When he tries to grab one, a "waterfall" sound—the one he consciously remembers—explodes in his head. Frances awakens as sounds "like the high and low tones of music being fast-forwarded on a reel-to-reel tape recorder" echo through Ed's head. He sees and photographs the UFO, which disappears into the field. Another, bigger and differently-shaped UFO appears and positions itself above him. Walters takes photo 15, hands it to Frances and takes 16 of the UFO going over the house. He pulls the film (photo 16) and intends to hand it to Frances but finds that she is no longer behind him. So he puts it under the elastic waist

123

GULF BREEZE SIGHTINGS (*continued*)

band of his pajamas. A voice says, "We are here for you," and a white flash fills his head and he falls headfirst into a chain-link fence. Back on his feet, Walters takes one more picture.

December 23, 5:55-6:00 a.m.: Walters photographs three UFOs just above the trees at the edge of his back yard.

December 27, 8:15 p.m.: While visiting the Walterses, Patrick Hanks, a college student and friend of the family, sees a UFO like those Walters has photographed. Ed and Frances see it, too.

December 28, evening: Walters takes a one-minute, 38-second video of a UFO passing behind a tree. Frances, son Dan and daughter Laura observe the object and the filming.

January 12, 1988: While driving on County Road 191B, Walters sees a brilliant white flash. Some of it hits his arms. Then a second white flash hits and briefly blinds him. His arms and hands have no feeling except of "pin pricks." A UFO hovers in the road 500 feet ahead. Walters hits the brakes, hoping to execute a U-turn, but fails because his numb hands cannot control the turn. The truck stops 200 feet from the UFO. Walters manages to take one picture; then, camera in hand, he crawls under the truck because the UFO seems to be approaching. Halfway under the truck, he feels his legs being hit and going numb. He looks forward (his head is below the oil pan) and sees the UFO again just above the road. He takes a picture and a voice delivers a peculiar message: "You are in danger. We will not harm you. Come forward."

As Walters ignores the command, five blue beams shoot down from the UFO, each depositing one of the rod-bearing creatures, which then move toward him in lock-step as Walters, in a state of shock, screams obscenities. He crawls out behind the truck, gets in and roars away, not looking back.

January 16, 2 a.m.: A humming sound in Ed's head brings the Walterses outside. Two UFOs—one a small disc unlike the globe-shaped UFOs of the earlier sightings—are observed. Walters takes a picture.

January 21, 10:20 p.m.: Walters hears a hum and sees a distant UFO. With a walkie-talkie he calls investigator Bob Reid, about a block away on stakeout with a video camera. Reid says he is seeing something, but it is a low-flying airplane. Walters concludes Reid "must have been looking the wrong way."

January 24: Driving home from work on a wet, overcast day, Walters hears the humming. Once home, he tries to get investigator Gary Watson on the walkie-talkie but gets no answer. Walters goes to the *Sentinel* office and he and editor Duane Cook go to a secluded area hoping the UFO will appear so that they can record it on video equipment. On the way, as the humming inside the head continues, Walters hears a voice say cryptically, "In sleep you know." He grows increasingly rattled as sensations of acute pain shoot through his body. Suddenly he senses that something is about to happen. He stops the truck and gets out but sees nothing. Cook is filming him as he steps back into the truck. At 200 feet behind Cook, and about six feet above the ground, the UFO appears. Walters grabs his Polaroid camera and takes a picture. An instant later the UFO is gone. Cook has not seen it. Cook takes the camera and peels off the developed picture, which shows the UFO.

January 26: Late in the evening, as Walters is taking a shower, Frances bangs on the bathroom door and tells him the UFO is outside. He grabs a towel and rushes to the back of the house, where he sees the UFO approaching. It is the small one he saw on the 16th. He steps out on the pool deck and shouts, "What the hell do you want?" A rush of air fills his head and a voice says, "Zehaas, we are here for you." Walter raises his fists and shouts, "Land or get the hell out of my life!" "Zehaas," the voice replies, "in sleep you know . . . we are here for you." To Walters' derisive response the voice replies, "Zehaas . . .

sleep and know." The UFO vanishes. Frances has taken a picture of the scene, with her husband clad only in a towel challenging the object.

February 7: In the early evening Walters, summoned by his daughter's shouts, grabs his Polaroid and runs to the back of the house. Laura is pointing to her mother, who is running from the steps near the pool to the open kitchen door. "Watch out!" she yells. "It's back there!" Because the house blocks the part of the sky behind Frances, her husband can see nothing. But as he steps even with the kitchen door frame, a blue beam shoots down at an angle across the door and hits the concrete pool deck at the bottom of the step. He hits the trigger of the camera and the flash goes off just as Frances flies into the house to the right of the beam. Ten minutes later Walters hears the voice say, "Do not deny us. We are here. Remember."

February 26: Earlier in the month investigators from the **Mutual UFO Network** (MUFON) had given Walters a special four-lens camera (known as a Nimslo) so that there could be four independent negatives of each picture. Another advantage, as principal investigator **Bruce Maccabee** would explain, would be that it "would also provide a parallax effect since the outer two lenses were separated by about two inches allowing for a calculation of the distance to the object if it weren't too far away" (Maccabee, 1988).

On the evening of the 26th Walters takes pictures of "three rows of lights with a trailing light. The lights were definitely not those of an airplane, and there was no sound. This was not what I had expected to see, but it was a UFO of some kind" (Walters, 1990). Ed thinks the object is large and distant, but Frances thinks it is small and close.

March 8: Using a new and different kind of Polaroid camera (a Sun 600 LMS, which ejects pictures virtually as soon as the exposure is made), Walters photographs a UFO hovering 300 feet beyond two pine trees which are 50 feet away.

March 17: As Ed and Frances discuss whether to take up an invitation by Cook and reporter Dari Holston to go UFO-hunting, Ed hears the humming sounds. Shortly after 8 p.m. the Walterses arrive at the park, where they are to meet the two from the *Sentinel*. Walters has brought with him a "self-referenced stereo" (SRS) camera, which he has built at investigator Maccabee's suggestion. It consists of two Polaroid cameras set about two feet apart on top of a tripod. The couple waits in the park with Cook and Holston (and others, who after two hours announce they are going to leave and do so). A minute later Walters hears a hum and within four minutes a UFO is seen in the southwestern sky. Walters takes pictures and the UFO vanishes, after being visible for only about ten seconds. Cook and the others are on the scene shortly, having seen the flashes of light but not the UFO, the view of which was obstructed by the thick growth of trees. They confess they were playing a trick on Walters and did not really intend to depart permanently. Brenda Pollak, wife of one of the other UFO-watchers, arrives, announcing she has seen a UFO while on her way to the park. (According to Maccabee, "A daylight photograph taken from the location where Ed had the SRS camera shows that he was looking over the shoreline southwestward of the park when he took the UO [unidentified object] photos. That is, he was looking in the general direction that Brenda's object was traveling. Considering the close coincidence between Brenda's and Ed's sightings, it seems quite plausible that Ed photographed what Brenda saw" [Maccabee, 1988]).

March 20: At 10:50 Walters hears a voice say, "Zehaas, Zehaas, sleep and know." He steps outside and sets up the SRS near the gate in the back fence. A UFO, resembling the one he saw and photographed on the 17th, appears briefly and Walters takes pictures.

May 1: At around 1:15 a.m. Walters is alone in the park with the SRS camera (Frances is out of town on a school trip with Dan) when he senses a faint humming. He shouts, "Here I am! I want you out of my life!" Two UFOs appear in

GULF BREEZE SIGHTINGS (*continued*)

succession and as Walters is photographing one, his eyes go "completely white, just as if a flashcube had gone off in my brain." He loses all sensation in his body except a vague sense of falling. The next thing he knows, he is waking up in the sand at the edge of the water that borders the park. It is 2:25 a.m. Concerned about his daughter, who is home alone, he gets in his van and races to his house, where he finds her sleeping peacefully. Nonetheless he stands guard by her door until dawn. He wakes up at noon. His right hand has a foul odor, which he finds is emanating from black material under his fingernails. He has a big bruise, with a red dot in the center, between his eyes at the bridge of his nose. At the center of each temple is a similar mark. This is Walters' final encounter.

The Walterses' sightings were not occurring in a vacuum. In the six months between November 1987 and May 1988 over 100 persons in the Gulf Breeze area reported UFOs. On November 11, for example, there were seven sightings besides Walters'. In one of these a witness, Jeff Thompson, reported seeing an object with a bluish beam. Another sighting, by Charlie and Dori Somerby, occurred just minutes before Walters'. Many of the witnesses (a number of the reports were published in the *Sentinel* and elsewhere) maintained that they had seen UFOs identical to those depicted in the newspapers (Walters' photographs, plus others from two anonymous correspondents, never identified; one signed his name "Believer Bill").

The Debate: Yet the Gulf Breeze affair ignited a furious controversy among ufologists. MUFON, whose investigators (notably Don Ware and Charles Flannigan) were first on the scene, championed the case practically from its onset. The **J. Allen Hynek Center for UFO Studies** was harshly critical, also practically from the onset, because its investigator in the area, Robert D. Boyd (who has since left the organization), was certain Walters was lying. (Boyd began to suspect as much, he says, when he visited Walters and watched him as he spoke. Walters, in Boyd's

view, did not have the "convincing atmosphere [sic] of someone that had been put through the trying times he was relating to us" [Boyd, 1988].) While retaining reservations, CUFOS would moderate its rhetoric as new evidence demonstrated that the issues were not nearly so clear-cut as first they seemed. Still, many ufologists remain skeptical of the Walterses' claims and photographs, despite a body of evidence that probably would have been considered adequate to make the case if this had been a different, more "conventional" kind of UFO story. The problem some ufologists had immediately was that the episode was outside the pattern of acceptable UFO reports. The only cases in which claimants had repeated encounters and took numerous close-up photographs were known or strongly-suspected hoaxes, usually associated with the sorts of **contactee** charlatans ufologists had long despised. To students of the UFO phenomenon it is patterns as much as anything that indicate UFOs are a true phenomenon, not an assortment of random fantasies, delusions and lies. Investigators had found time and again that reports outside the pattern tend to fall apart under hard scrutiny. They were certain that this would happen with the Gulf Breeze case.

That it did not had nothing to do with lack of effort. But if the Gulf Breeze incident fell outside the pattern of apparently authentic UFO cases, it also fell outside the pattern of hoaxes. To begin with, the Walterses' motive was obscure at best. They certainly were not seeking publicity. In fact, they went to some lengths to keep their names from getting out, even though the newspaper editor and a handful of locals knew who they were. (Walters was referred to only as "Ed" or [somewhat oddly] as "Mr. Ed" in published accounts.) Not until well into 1989 did the Walterses allow their names to appear in print. Moreover, unlike many hoaxers in UFO history, they seemed to have no financial interest in perpetrating UFO fraud. Walters was, and is, the president of a construction company and occupies a secure position in the upper middle class. He says he remained anonymous for so long because he was afraid UFO publicity would *hurt* him financially. Nor, like many hoaxers, was he some kind of marginal or eccentric figure; he was, and is, one of the community's most active and respected citizens.

Furthermore, on February 18 and 23 Walters underwent polygraph examinations (the second of them given to him by surprise, without prior warning) by Harvey W. McLaughlin, Jr., a professional with no previous involvement in UFO controversies. The tests, which lasted several hours, covered both his sightings and his photographs. McLaughlin concluded that Walters was telling the truth as he saw it. In June a prominent Florida clinical psychologist, the late Dan Overlade, met Walters and administered a battery of psychological tests (Wechsler Adult Intelligence Scale [Revised], Minnesota Multiphasic Personality Inventory, Thematic Apperception Test, Draw-a-Person Test, and Rorschach). Overlade later concluded that his psychological examination and the subsequent sessions with Ed elicited no evidence that he possessed any psychopathologies or any other mental disorders. Debunkers in the UFO community had suggested that Walters probably had a sociopathic personality, which would explain why he had passed the polygraph tests. Overlade did not think this was the case and no other, independent evidence has emerged to support this reading of Walters' personality. All critics were able to find was a youthful scrape with the law, including time in jail, but no subsequent adult patterns of antisocial behavior.

By far the most comprehensive investigation of the photographs was performed by Bruce Maccabee, an optical physicist employed by the U.S. Navy and ufology's foremost photoanalyst. Maccabee found Walters to be entirely cooperative, willing to perform any experiment asked of him, including ones that Maccabee had devised as a method of proving fraud, if fraud was there. Besides an enormous amount of time in the laboratory, Maccabee spent time on-site with Walters and other witnesses, trying to determine the precise conditions under which the photographs had been taken. In the end, for many technical and other reasons (including Walters' apparent lack of technical expertise),

Maccabee concluded that it would have been extremely difficult for Walters—or even an expert in trick photography—to fake the photographs. So far there has been no serious challenge to Maccabee's analysis.

Yet debunkers could always argue that absence of evidence of a hoax is not evidence of absence of evidence out there somewhere, yet to be uncovered. Skeptics within the UFO community are still troubled by the bizarre and anomalous UFO behavior so central to the story. One of ufology's most respected figures, **Richard Hall**, posed the hard question, "*How do the Gulf Breeze incidents fit in with UFO history?*" And he offered a tentative answer: "Basically, they don't fit very well. . . . [I]f the Gulf Breeze events are genuine, then the entire character of the UFO phenomenon has suddenly changed. (Not impossible, but if so, we should begin seeing other confirmatory signs elsewhere in the country and around the world.) No precedent exists in the literature for a six-month siege by one individual by UFOs, or the taking of dozens of photographs—almost at will—by one individual (other than Billy Meier, whom MUFON rates as a hoaxer)" (Hall, 1988).

Debunkers could also claim that the Walterses were after money, after all. Although early in the affair Walters reportedly turned down a six-figure book offer from a paperback publisher, *Publishers Weekly* announced in its April 7, 1989, issue that William Morrow, publisher of **Whitley Strieber's** best-selling *Communion: A True Story* (1987), had paid the Walterses $200,000 for a book, and a production company had put $100,000 down against $450,000 for miniseries rights. (The book, *The Gulf Breeze Sightings*, was released in February 1990.)

To those who felt no immediate need to take a position one way or the other, the issues seemed most likely to be sorted out in the passing of time and the cooling of emotions. All sides could agree with Hall's suggestion that future patterns of Gulf Breeze-like episodes, with good supporting evidence, would make the Walterses' story more palatable as well as confirm that patterns, even

GULF BREEZE SIGHTINGS (*continued*)

ones that show up rather late in the game, are still what the UFO phenomenon is all about.

Sources:

Boyd, Robert D. *Failure at Science*. Mobile, AL: The Author, 1988.

Hall, Richard, and Willy Smith. "Balancing the Scale: Unanswered Questions About Gulf Breeze." *MUFON UFO Journal* 248 (December 1988): 3-7.

Maccabee, Bruce. "A History of the Gulf Breeze, Florida, Sighting Events." In Walter H. Andrus, Jr., and Richard H. Hall, eds. *MUFON 1988 International UFO Symposium Proceedings*, 113-204. Seguin, TX: Mutual UFO Network, Inc., 1988.

Overlade, Dan C. "Psychological Evaluation of Mr. Ed." *MUFON UFO Journal* 248 (December 1988): 7-8.

Rodeghier, Mark. "Gulf Breeze: A Note to the Committed." *International UFO Reporter* 13, 2 (March/April 1988): 12-13, 23.

Stacy, Dennis. "Gulf Breeze: A Note to the Skeptical." *International UFO Reporter* 13, 2 (March/April 1988): 10-11.

Walters, Ed, and Frances Walters. *The Gulf Breeze Sightings: The Most Astounding Multiple Sightings of UFOs in U.S. History*. New York: William Morrow and Company, 1990.

H

HAINES, RICHARD FOSTER (1937-)

Richard Foster Haines is known as a careful, scientifically-grounded writer and investigator. His UFO study has centered on photographic analysis, methodology for researching the UFO **abduction phenomenon,** behavioral-science aspects, and pilot sightings. He lives in northern California.

He was born on May 19, 1937, in Seattle. He received a B.A. in psychology from Pacific Lutheran College in 1960, an M.A. in experimental psychology from Michigan State University in 1962, and a Ph.D. from the same institution two years later for experimental psychology and physiology. Between 1964 and 1988 he worked in varying capacities as a scientist employed at the NASA-Ames Research Center at Moffett Field in California. When he retired from government service in 1988, he was chief of the Space Human Factors Office at NASA-Ames. Currently he is a research scientist for the Research Institute for Advanced Computer Science, at Ames Research Center. He is cited in such major biographical reference works as *Who's Who in America, American Men and Women of Science, Dictionary of International Biography* and many others.

He has published 35 major articles on various aspects of UFO investigation and is a contributing editor to **International UFO Reporter**, the magazine of the **J. Allen Hynek Center for UFO Studies.**

He is the author of two UFO-related books, *Observing UFOs* (1980) and *Melbourne Episode* (1987), and editor of the anthology *UFO Phenomena and the Behavioral Scientist* (1979).

Haines says, "The UFO phenomenon represents one of the truly important challenges of our times and holds promise for numerous advancements in science, technology, the social sciences, and religion. The preponderance of evidence seems to point toward an advanced intelligence source. Where this intelligence originates, however, is not yet clear. It is likely that traditional science will not be able to adequately explain the phenomenon in all of its dimensions. Nevertheless, a multidimensional and interdisciplinary team approach, involving all nations of the earth, is called for."

Sources:

Haines, Richard F. *Melbourne Episode: Case Study of a Missing Pilot.* Los Altos, CA: L.D.A. Press, 1987.

Haines, Richard F. *Observing UFOs: An Investigative Handbook.* Chicago: Nelson-Hall, 1980.

Haines, Richard F., ed. *UFO Phenomena and the Behavioral Scientist.* Metuchen, NJ: Scarecrow Press, 1979.

HALL, RICHARD HARRIS (1930-)

Richard Harris Hall has had a long, distinguished career in ufology, beginning in the mid-1950s and continuing to the present.

He was born on Christmas Day 1930 in Hartford, Connecticut. While serving as an Air Force enlisted man, he read Donald E. Keyhoe's *The Flying Saucers Are Real* (1950) and got interested in the UFO phenomenon. He received a B.A. in philosophy from Tulane University in 1958. During his college years he published a UFO newsletter titled *Satellite*, which he describes as "little known nor long remembered." One day in 1957 Hall saw a letter addressed to Fraser Thompson, the university's one astronomer, from Keyhoe, announcing the formation of the National Investigations Committee on Aerial Phenomena (NICAP) and soliciting support from scientists. Hall entered into correspondence with Keyhoe and the next year moved to Washington, D.C., where NICAP was headquartered. Soon he was working full time for the organization, starting as first (executive) secretary, then becoming assistant director and finally acting director.

"For about the first six years it was tough sledding," Hall wrote in a memoir of that period in the *MUFON UFO Journal*, published by the **Mutual UFO Network** (MUFON). "UFO sightings faded to an all-time low and NICAP grew only slowly. Then the UFO waves of 1964-67 turned things around and NICAP reached its peak of activity and influence." During that period Hall cowrote *The Challenge of Unidentified Flying Objects* (1961) and edited one of the major early works on the phenomenon, *The UFO Evidence* (1964). He also contributed to *Mysteries in the Skies* (1968) by Gordon I. R. Lore, Jr., and Harold H. Deneault, Jr. He left NICAP in 1968 for employment in science writing, abstracting and editing, including a six-year stint with the American Psychological Association. In the 1970s, as a technical editor for a consulting firm, he worked on various projects for NASA, the Department of Transportation, the Department of Energy, the Navy, and the National Science Board. Since 1980 he has been employed by the Congressional Information Service, a Maryland-based publisher of abstracts and statistics culled from government and foreign printed material.

From the late 1970s into the early 1980s he edited the *MUFON UFO Journal* and through 1988 he coedited the annual *MUFON UFO Symposium Proceedings*. He is currently consulting editor of **International UFO Reporter** and a board member of the **Fund for UFO Research**. His book *Uninvited Guests* was published in 1988.

Hall believes that "the evidence is overwhelming that earthlings are having encounters with beings from elsewhere and that craftlike UFOs and humanoid beings are integral to the body of evidence that requires an explanation. Thus the only remaining question of interest (though one with momentous implications for humanity) is the location of 'elsewhere.'" Hall adds, "In my present view, the more exotic alternatives to 'nuts and bolts' are not necessary in order to fit UFO phenomena into a conceptual scheme that would account for all reliably reported data. Unless the presumed intelligence behind the phenomena chooses to provide the necessary evidence, the alternatives are essentially untestable and therefore, in the scientific sense, meaningless. The ETH [extraterrestrial hypothesis] itself is not easily testable, but it is testable in principle because our space probes and increasingly sophisticated sensors in earth satellites could conceivably find evidence of extraterrestrial life entering or leaving our solar system, or the lack of evidence, if systematically applied in search of UFOs. . . .

"If we are being examined by extraterrestrial anthropologists who are scientifically far advanced over us, we are not likely to understand their comings and goings, the technological means of it, their cultural values and beliefs, or their ultimate intentions. A cultural/technological gap, rather than a more exotic origin, could easily account for the baffling behavior and incomprehensible technology we are seeing."

Sources:

Hall, Richard. "Major Donald E. Keyhoe: An Appreciation." *MUFON UFO Journal* 250 (February 1989): 12-13.

Hall, Richard. *Uninvited Guests: A Documented History of UFO Sightings, Alien Encounters and Coverups.* Santa Fe, NM: Aurora Press, 1988.

Hall, Richard, ed. *The UFO Evidence.* Washington: National Investigations Committee on Aerial Phenomena, 1964.

Hall, Richard, and Charles A. Maney. *The Challenge of Unidentified Flying Objects.* Washington: privately published, 1961.

HESSDALEN LIGHTS

The Hessdalen Valley stretches over 12 kilometers of a thinly-populated area of central Norway near the border of Sweden. Only about 150 persons live there, but a series of strange events which began in November 1981 and ended in 1986 brought the region to the attention of ufologists, including no less than **J. Allen Hynek**, who came to the area in January 1985 to investigate.

Residents of the valley were reporting frequent sightings of unusual lights which hovered (sometimes for as long as an hour) and sometimes streaked off at speeds that rendered the objects all but invisible. On many occasions, the lights were below the horizon, either just beneath the tops of nearby mountains or not far from the ground or the rooftops of houses. The lights came in various shapes, but three predominated: a bullet or cigar, a sphere, and an "upside-down Christmas tree." The lights were usually white or yellowish-white. Sometimes a small red light appeared in front of the others, the various lights maintaining a fixed position which led observers to suspect that they were attached to a single, invisible object. More often than not they were moving from north to south, and at night; yet daylight

sightings also occurred, usually during the winter (possibly because in summer Hessdalen is in almost constant daylight). The phenomena sometimes appeared as many as four times a day.

Local people also reported anomalous sounds. In 1981 they heard something that sounded like a train passing through a tunnel under their feet. At other times there were loud "banging" sounds which seemed to be moving through the mountains, but no source was apparent.

On March 26, 1982, investigators from UFO-Norge, Norway's leading UFO group, held a town meeting in nearby Alen. Of the 130 residents who attended, 17 said they had seen a yellow spherical light, 12 a cigar-shaped object, and six an oblong object with one red and two yellow lights. That same week two officers from Vaernes Air Force base made a short visit and interviewed some witnesses. Afterwards they told the press that the "people of Hessdalen have been seeing luminous objects since 1944, but many years passed before they dared to talk about the sightings. But the accounts are credible, and we in the Defense [Department] must take them seriously. There are more things between heaven and earth than can be explained at first sight" (Stacy, 1988). This, however, is the extent of known official interest in the Hessdalen lights, the investigation of which would be taken up (to all appearances) solely by ufologists and civilian scientists. No one besides the officers has reported a pre-1981 tradition of anomalous lights in the region.

Despite a steep decline in sightings in the spring and summer of 1983, Norwegian ufologists, aided by Swedish and Finnish colleagues, decided that a formal investigation, with the proper instrumentation and personnel, was merited. In June 1983 they announced the formation of Project Hessdalen, under the directorship of Leif Havik, Odd-Gunnar Roed, Erling Strand, Haken Ekstrand and Jan Fjellander. The ufologists secured technical assistance from scientists from the Universities of Oslo and Bergen as well as cameras with grating filters, a seismograph, Geiger-counter, radar, infrared viewer,

HESSDALEN LIGHTS (*continued*)

magnetograph and spectrum-analyzer. In November investigators went to Hessdalen and explained the project to locals and two months later sent out a report form to 3300 households. The field work started on January 21, 1984, and ended on February 26. Three stations were set up, the primary one located at Aspaskjolen mountain, and two smaller ones at Hersjoen and Litfjellet.

In the course of the month's observations (made under the harshest possible winter conditions), the investigators saw numerous lights, took photographs of many of them, and tracked some instrumentally. On three occasions lights were seen visually and tracked on radar at the same time, casting a reflection on the radar screen so strong that a Norwegian defense expert later said, "If this isn't a reflection of a solid object, but only gas in the air, the gas has to be locally and strongly ionized" (Strand, 1988). He was referring to one hypothesis advanced to explain the Hessdalen phenomena, that they were free-floating plasma. One of the lights was tracked moving at 8500 meters a second. On one occasion a light under constant visual observation showed up on radar only on every second sweep of the radar dish. But in most instances—33 in all—when radar showed something, the eye could see nothing, nor could the camera. Most sightings were unaccompanied by radar confirmation, possibly because, Strand would suggest, "We had the radar adjusted to show only 5.5 km. Those three times we did get anything on radar together with [a] light happened when the screen was adjusted on a longer distance. The reason might be that the lights were out of distance when the radar was adjusted to 5.5 km."

On two occasions the observers directed a laser beam on passing lights. Out of a total of nine times, the lights responded all but once in a curious way. One of these incidents took place on February 12 at 7:35 p.m. A slow-moving, regularly-flashing light passing overhead. "As soon as the laser was aimed at the light," Strand reports, "it changed its flashing sequence from a regular flashing light to a regular double flashing light, i.e., flash-flash . . . flash-flash . . . flash-flash. After about ten seconds we stopped the laser and the light immediately changed back to its previous flashing sequence. After about another ten seconds we repeated the exercise and again the light responded by changing to a double-flash sequence. In all we repeated this exercise four times and every time we got the same reaction from the light."

The single most unusual incident took place in the early evening of February 20. Two local men who were aiding the investigation, Age Moe and Edvin Kvaernes, had come to pick up Leif Havik; the three planned to go to Oyungneset, a mountain from which they hoped to view the lights. Just as Havik emerged from the trailer, a small red light zipped around his feet for a few seconds and disappeared. The three men were perplexed. Moe suggested it was a "reflection," but Havik had already noted that the light looked very much like the light from the laser they had been using—only the device was now back in Oslo.

On the 25th, when the laser was brought to the site of the incident at around the same time of early evening, Strand shone it on the snow in front of the trailer and Moe, who had never seen a laser light before, exclaimed, "That's exactly what I saw! But it was a little bit weaker." Strand then shone it on the trailer floor and Moe said, "It was a little bit stronger than that."

The investigators could find no explanation for the odd light the three had seen. "All the lights in the caravan [trailer] had been switched off before this happened," Strand reports. "There were no lights outside. It could not have been a light from the houses. The nearest house is about 500m away and it is below a hill. The nearest house you can see is 2km away, in the south. The light showed up on the northern side of the caravan. All the houses you can see [are] on the southern side."

Havik and the others were struck by curious "coincidences" which kept occurring in the course of their work. "On four separate occasions,"

Havik recalls, "it happened that we came to the top of Varuskjolen, stopped the car, went outside, and there 'it' came immediately and passed by us. The same thing happened once on Aspaskjolen. All these instances happened at different times of the day and most of the time it was an impulse which made us take an evening trip to Hessdalen by car. . . . On some occasions other observers had been looking for hours without success. . . . 'Coincidences' also happened to the video equipment which recorded the radar screen. One evening the pen of the magnetograph failed to work. At the same time the video tape had come to an end, and the phenomenon appeared less than one minute later. The next evening we made certain that the pen had sufficient ink and turned on the video recorder ten minutes later than the night before. We thought that now everything was ready for the usual 10:47 'message.' [One light regularly appeared at 10:47.] The video tape ran out at 10:57 p.m. and we thought that tonight 'it' had failed us. But at 10:58 the usual phenomenon appeared" (Havik, 1988).

In the month of observation, project personnel made 188 sightings, some of which they attributed to passing aircraft. Only four of the photographs taken through the special lens gratings came out well enough to show light spectra, and only two of these were strong enough to be useful for analysis. According to researcher Paul Devereux, who served on the project's advisory committee, "One spectrum of one 'high strangeness' object was analyzed and showed a wavelength range from 560nm (nanometers) to the maximum the film could respond to—630nm. . . . The spectrum analyzer did not register anything unusual while lights were being seen, but odd readings were obtained at times. . . . These showed up as 'spikes' at approximately 80mHz (megaHerz)" (Devereux, 1989). Changes in the magnetic field were recorded during 40 percent of the sightings, but the Geiger counter and the infrared viewer proved unhelpful, possibly, the investigators thought, because the phenomena were too far away. The seismograph registered no earthquake activity.

The next winter Project Hessdalen II was launched, with Hynek's participation. Unfortunately, the venture proved disappointing and little light activity was noted. In 1986 the phenomena ceased altogether.

Investigators disagreed on what the Hessdalen lights were. Roed, though conceding that the lights "seemed intelligent in their movements," holds that they probably had some "complex" natural cause. Strand says, "If the lights were natural, it's strange that they existed for a five-year period and that they were recorded in Hessdalen and nowhere else. If this was a natural phenomenon, it was in the sense that everything is ultimately a natural phenomenon. It is definitely an unknown phenomenon, perhaps even the basis of a new science" (Clark, 1989). Devereux is convinced that they were earthquake lights resulting from seismic activity which the investigators failed to recognize because of their naivete about geophysics. But one of the scientists involved in the project, University of Oslo physicist Elvand Thrane, says the lights remain a mystery. Of the many witnesses he interviewed, he remarks, "These were experienced outdoor people, many of them hunters used to observing things. I'm sure the lights were real. It's a pity we cannot explain them" (Clark, 1989).

Sources:

Clark, Jerome. "UFO Update." *Omni* 11, 10 (July 1989): 73.

Devereux, Paul. *Earth Lights Revelation: UFOs and Mystery Lightform Phenomena: The Earth's Secret Energy Force.* London: Blandford Press, 1989.

Havik, Leif. "Project Hessdalen." *MUFON UFO Journal* 237 (January 1988): 4-7.

Stacy, Dennis. "Hessdalen: An Introduction." *MUFON UFO Journal* 237 (January 1988): 3.

Strand, Erling. *Project Hessdalen 1984: Final Technical Report, Part One.* Duken, Norway: Project Hessdalen, 1985.

HESSDALEN LIGHTS (*continued*)

Strand, Erling. "Site Instrumentation." *MUFON UFO Journal* 237 (January 1988): 7-10.

HOPKINS, BUDD (1931-)

Budd Hopkins, a specialist in the UFO **abduction phenomenon** and one of current ufology's most visible figures, is the author of such important books as *Missing Time* (1981) and *Intruders* (1987).

Hopkins was born on June 15, 1931, in Wheeling, West Virginia. After graduating from Oberlin College in 1953, he moved to New York City, where he has lived ever since. A painter and sculptor whose works are in the permanent collections of the Whitney, Guggenheim and Hirshhorn Museums, as well as the Museum of Modern Art, the Carnegie-Mellon, the Brooklyn Museum and many others, he has been awarded fellowships by both the Guggenheim Foundation and the National Endowment for the Arts. His articles on painting and sculpture have appeared in most major American art magazines and he has lectured frequently at universities, colleges and art museums. He is married to art historian April Kingsley. The couple has one daughter, Grace, born in 1973.

Hopkins' interest in the UFO phenomenon was sparked by a 1964 sighting, with two other witnesses, of a daylight disc which remained in view for two or three minutes. Intrigued, he joined the National Investigations Committee on Aerial Phenomena (NICAP) and began reading the UFO literature. In 1975 he investigated a multiply-witnessed landing in a park in New Jersey directly across the Hudson River from 88th Street in Manhattan. His article on the case was published in *The Village Voice* and from it he found himself at the receiving end of other, similar reports, some involving periods of unexplained missing time. Working with ufologist Ted Bloecher, psychiatrist Robert Naiman and psychologist Aphrodite Clamar, he investigated a

number of cases in which previously-unrecalled UFO abductions came to light. He wrote two books based on these investigations and is currently at work on a third.

Through his public work he hopes to bring the abduction phenomenon to the attention of an ever-wider audience of physicians, scientists and mental-health professionals as well as the lay public. In 1989 he founded IF—the Intruders Foundation—as a means of intensifying and supporting these educational efforts. To help possible abductees deal with their disturbing experiences, IF has established a network of cooperating therapists and hypnotist/investigators in many cities across North America. IF also publishes a quarterly bulletin dedicated to abduction research and emotional support of those reporting such experiences. Since 1976 he has worked personally with nearly 300 abductees, investigating their cases and often conducting hypnotic-regression sessions. The IF databank contains a huge amount of pertinent information and functions as a resource for other investigators in the field.

Hopkins' letters and articles have appeared in a number of publications such as *The New York Review of Books*, *Omni*, *Discover* and *Cosmopolitan* as well as the *International UFO Reporter*, *MUFON UFO Journal* and *UFO*. One of the early investigators of the **Gulf Breeze sightings**, he wrote the introduction to a book on the episode, Ed and Frances Walters' *The Gulf Breeze Sightings*, published in 1990. Hopkins' latest book, written with Penelope Franklin, will be titled *A Crack in the Universe: The Psychological Impact of UFO Encounters*.

He says, "From the beginning I've held few preconceptions about the UFO phenomenon, and as any scientifically-inclined investigator would do, I've gone simply where the data led. I was originally suspicious of UFO-abduction accounts, but the sheer preponderance of credible people reporting these events and the accompanying physical evidence persuaded me that these accounts were generally truthful. The data unavoidably make clear that UFO abductions—

like UFO sightings of any sort—have a physical dimension as well as a paranormal dimension.

"The specific patterns I have discovered in my years of investigation of abduction cases are central to my overall view of the phenomenon. It might be helpful to list them here:

"(1) Unlike the classic Betty and Barney Hill, Travis Walton, or Hickson and Parker cases, an abduction can easily occur with little or no conscious recall on the part of the abductee, who may not even remember having seen a UFO. The evidence shows that the phenomenon is vastly more widespread than had been thought in the first 3½ decades of UFO investigations and involves hundreds of thousands of persons across the globe. The sheer scale of the phenomenon is staggering and the number of abductees literally unknowable.

"(2) The phenomenon almost invariably entails decades-long abductions of the same individuals at irregular intervals. The abductee becomes, in effect, a 'tagged animal' whose earliest experiences begin in childhood, even as early as the first year of life, and continue afterwards with special frequency in the first ten years or so of adulthood.

"(3) A 'cell-sampling' operation is often inflicted upon the abductee, leaving scars of two types: a round, shallow depression or 'scoop mark' or a long, thin, scalpel-like cut. (These discoveries were detailed in my first book, *Missing Time*. The following were stated for the first time and expanded upon in *Intruders*.)

"(4) The central focus of the entire UFO phenomenon is the 'study and laboratory use' of human beings with special attention to our physical, genetic and reproductive properties.

"(5) If individuals are 'tracked' very nearly across their entire lifetimes, these individuals' bloodlines are apparently of equal interest to the UFO occupants. Members of the same family are often abducted in what seems to be a longitudinal genetic study or experiment.

"(6) Apparently at the center of this ongoing genetic experiment is a systematic attempt to create a hybrid species, a mix of human and alien characteristics.

"(7) A widespread use of advanced artificial insemination techniques results in human pregnancies. During subsequent abductions these pregnant women are abducted again so that the developing embryos can be removed and grown in laboratories or nurseries within the UFOs themselves. As a corollary, many men are abducted and sperm samples are taken from them, presumably to be added to alien ova in the converse of the artificial-insemination procedures.

"(8) The final event involves the reabduction of the ostensible human 'mother'—and sometimes the 'father'—so that the human being can hold the infant or child in a kind of bonding procedure.

"(9) The alien personality, if that is the word for it, seems to lack emotions of the most basic human sort, such as maternal or paternal feelings, human sexual needs, humor, nuanced emotional variety and richness, and so forth. Abductee accounts suggest that the aliens are interested in acquiring, or at least understanding, the basic human emotional spectrum and that this interest is behind some of the incidents that occur during abductions.

"In the years since I first published these nine characteristics of the abduction phenomenon, they have been encountered again and again—replicated—by many other investigators in this and other countries. As to what all this portends, I can only guess. If I have not seen any signs of malevolence or acts of deliberate harm on the part of the UFO occupants, neither have I seen any signs of consistent, believable good will. I see no evidence that different groups of aliens are working at cross purposes or from different moral standpoints. All seem to be doing the same thing. I see vast psychological damage and an inexcusable level of physical harm resulting from these alien 'experiments' upon innocent human beings, and for those acts they deserve our heartfelt anger and condemnation. We are given no opportunity to

135

HOPKINS, BUDD (*continued*)

refuse these often frightening procedures, or any explanation as to why they are being inflicted upon us. I have dealt with too many terrified little children ever to condone the UFO occupants' blithe disregard for human rights and feelings, however desperate their needs may be.

"Though they are not cannibals or body snatchers bent on invasion and war, as certain imaginative and paranoid writers would have us believe, they are most certainly not benign 'visitors' or Space Brothers either. They seem to be coldly following their own private agenda, though with a routine attempt to lessen the pain and psychological suffering they inevitably inflict. One gets the idea that they are desperate, that they do need to revivify their own species from our ostensibly more primitive and more vital genetic pool, but that explanation is only a guess. I also sense an escalation of their abduction activities, a widening of scale, and a lessening of the attempt to operate covertly. I do not know where all this is leading, but I am not encouraged.

"Speaking optimistically, I can suggest that what the future may bring is a heightened sense of the richness of our own species and the value of the love we human beings share with one another. Other men and women in other times of crisis have been brought together this way by these same shared feelings. But this time I fear the crisis may be deeper and more profoundly wrenching than human history has ever known."

Sources:

Clark, Jerome. "A Conversation with Budd Hopkins." *International UFO Reporter* 13, 6 (November/December 1988): 4-12.

Hopkins, Budd. *Intruders: The Incredible Visitations at Copley Woods.* New York: Random House, 1987.

Hopkins, Budd. *Missing Time: A Documented Study of UFO Abductions.* New York: Richard Marek Publishers, 1981.

Hopkins, Budd. "What They're Doing to Us." *International UFO Reporter* 12, 5 (September/October 1987): 4-8, 24.

HYNEK, JOSEF ALLEN (1910-1986)

For 20 years, from the mid-1960s until his death in 1986, astronomer and former Project Blue Book scientific consultant J. Allen Hynek was the world's most famous and influential proponent of UFO research.

Hynek had been involved in the subject practically from the beginning, since 1948, when representatives of Project Grudge, the Air Force's UFO project, asked Hynek, director of the MacMillan Observatory at Ohio State University, to examine the reports they had received and to alert them to those that resulted from misidentifications of stars, planets and other astronomical phenomena. Hynek later would write that, where UFOs were concerned, he was the "innocent bystander who got shot" (Hynek, 1972). By the time he and the Air Force parted company, in 1969, they were expressing very different views about the significance of the UFO phenomenon.

Born on May 1, 1910, in Chicago, the son of Josef and Bertha Hynek, Josef Allen Hynek graduated from the University of Chicago with a B.S. degree. In 1935, having achieved a Ph.D. in astrophysics at the university, he left Chicago to join the Ohio State University faculty. There his work on stellar spectroscopy won him the respect of his scientific colleagues. From 1950 to 1953 he served as assistant dean of the OSU graduate school. Hynek's fame spread outside scientific circles, however, when in 1956 the Smithsonian Astrophysical Observatory at Harvard was given the task of training observers to track the manned satellites the U.S. government planned to launch in the near future. Director Fred L. Whipple appointed Hynek associate director, with the responsibility of putting the proper instrumentation into place and disseminating information. Hynek organized an international group of amateur astronomers, under the name Project Moonwatch, to assist in the tracking of the satellites. Project Moonwatch was a great success, both scientifically and popularly, and Hynek became something of a celebrity.

In 1960, as Hynek was working with the Air Force on Project Stargazer, in which balloons bearing telescopes were placed in the upper atmosphere, he became professor of astronomy and department chairman at Northwestern University in Evanston, Illinois. As he rebuilt and strengthened the department, which had been moribund, he became director both of the university's Dearborn Observatory and later, in 1964, of the Lindheimer Astronomical Research Center. He was a popular teacher and lecturer and besides writing for astronomical journals, he also contributed articles to popular magazines on astronomical subjects.

But it was Hynek's association with the UFO phenomenon that made him the most famous and even controversial. Intellectual curiosity, though no certain anticipation of a major scientific breakthrough, made him take up the Air Force's invitation to look at UFO reports. Hynek was initially skeptical and remained skeptical for a long time; nonetheless he soon noticed that not all of the reports seemed easily reducible to conventional explanations. In his first (albeit cautious) statement to this effect, he wrote in a 1953 issue of a scientific journal these destined-to-be-much-quoted words:

"Ridicule is not a part of the scientific method, and the public should not be taught that it is. The steady flow of reports, often made in concert by *reliable* observers, raises questions of scientific obligation and responsiblity. Is there, when the welter of varied reports are shorn of, in the words of Pooh Bah, all 'corroborative detail to lend artistic verisimilitude to an otherwise bald and unconvincing narrative,' any residue that is worthy of scientific attention? Or, if there isn't, does not an obligation still exist to say so to the public—not in words of open ridicule but seriously, to keep faith with the trust the public places in science and scientists?" (Hynek, 1953).

Hynek's reference to "ridicule" came in part from a poll he had conducted quietly among his professional colleagues in astronomy in 1952. Five percent of the 44 astronomers he contacted said they had seen UFOs themselves, but they were deeply fearful of publicity, feeling that such admissions, if publicized, could harm their careers.

Yet Hynek, too, kept his thoughts mostly to himself, even as he noted with growing dismay the Air Force's inept handling of UFO reports and its desire to explain them at any cost, even when those doing the explaining were technically unqualified to propose the "scientific" solutions they were concocting and popular media were all too happy to accept. Still, by the late 1950s Hynek was stating privately and publicly that the UFO question had come to nothing and it was time to go on to something else.

Nonetheless some of the puzzling reports he had seen continued to haunt him. In the early 1960s a graduate student who had come over from France, **Jacques Vallee**, as well as a small number of other trusted friends and colleagues, encouraged Hynek to think more boldly about what might be happening. In 1965 Hynek made his most positive public statement ever in a blurb published on the back cover of Vallee's *Anatomy of a Phenomenon*, a book arguing that UFOs might be extraterrestrial vehicles. Calling the book "provocative," Hynek endorsed Vallee's "suggestion that the persistence of such reports on an international scale be given increased scientific attention" (Vallee, 1965). The following year Hynek wrote the introduction to Vallee's next book (written with his wife Janine), *Challenge to Science; The UFO Enigma* (1966). By this time Hynek's apparent turnaround on the UFO question was an open secret.

Ironically, Hynek's decision to become an outspoken UFO proponent—one, in other words, who did not qualify his words—came as a result of an episode in which he acted as a debunker. In March 1966 a flurry of sightings erupted in Michigan. Two sightings in particular attracted national press attention: an incident on the evening of the 20th, when a farmer and his son

HYNEK, JOSEF ALLEN (*continued*)

near Dexter reported seeing a craftlike object descend into a swamp a quarter of a mile away. Summoned to the scene, police found no object but observed a glow in the woods. The next evening young women at Hillsdale College 60 miles away saw faint lights in nearby trees.

As the press clamored for an explanation, Hynek and an aid from Selfridge Field near Detroit went to the farm. "The scene that greeted us," Hynek was to recall, "was one of utter confusion, much like the crowd that gathers around the scene of a catastrophe, or perhaps it might better be likened to a circus, with many rings in full action" (Hynek, 1976). When Hynek went to Hillsdale the next day, he found similar excitation. At one point the police took him on a ride in pursuit of a flying saucer which turned out to be the star Arcturus. Pressed for answers by the Air Force, newspaper reporters, and several members of Congress, Hynek consulted with a University of Michigan chemistry professor and afterwards declared, at a packed press conference, that the Dexter and Hillsdale lights were probably of "swamp gas."

In the resulting uproar Hynek was ridiculed in newspapers and cartoons all over the country. In a sense he became the butt of a long-simmering frustration with what many citizens were taking to be Air Force incompetence or dishonesty regarding UFOs. On April 5, 1966, the House Armed Services Committee held a one-day hearing on UFOs. Hynek was one of those who testified, stating that "it is my opinion that the body of data accumulated since 1948 through the Air Force investigations deserves close scrutiny by a civilian panel of physical and social scientists, and that this panel should be asked to examine the UFO problem critically for the express purpose of determining whether a major problem really exists" (Hynek, 1976).

Eventually such a panel was formed, via an Air Force contract with the University of Colorado, under the direction of physicist Edward U. Condon. The Condon Committee, as it was called, early became mired in controversy, amid charges that its leader and major personnel were hostile to the subject (those who held other views, such as psychologist David Saunders, were fired), and in 1969 the committee report declared that the study of UFOs had no scientific value and the Air Force should get out of the business, which it did a few months later.

Another prominent scientist who had become interested in the UFO phenomenon, University of Arizona atmospheric physicist James McDonald, criticized Hynek for his slowness in alerting the scientific community to the importance of UFO sightings. McDonald, whose fiery, aggressive personality could not have contrasted more with Hynek's, launched his own campaign to spread the word but encountered personal misfortune unrelated to his UFO interests. In 1971 he committed suicide, leaving Hynek the one major American scientist willing to express his conviction that UFOs are a real and important issue.

In 1972 Hynek wrote *The UFO Experience*, in which he charged the Air Force with indifference and incompetence in its UFO investigations. He also critiqued the Condon report and detailed puzzling, well-documented reports of six types; nocturnal lights, daylight discs, radar/visual observations, close encounters of the first kind (in which UFOs appear at less than 500 feet from the witness); second kind (in which UFOs leave "physical effects"), and third kind (in which occupants are reported). In his concluding words Hynek wrote, "When the long awaited solution to the UFO problem comes, I believe that it will prove to be not merely the next small step in the march of science but a mighty and totally unexpected quantum leap."

The book was generally well received by Hynek's colleagues. A major review appeared in the British journal *Nature*, where D.G. King-Hele remarked that "Hynek's catalogue is cumulatively impressive. . . . [T]he best argument in favor of UFOs is . . . that all striking new advances in science are at first treated with derision by scientists" (King-Hele, 1972). In *Science* Bruce C. Murray wrote, "Hynek has won a reprieve for UFOs with his many pages of provocative unexplained reports and his articulate challenge to his colleagues to tolerate the study of something they cannot understand" (Murray, 1972). Joachim P. Kuettner, reviewing the book in *Astronautics and Aeronautics*, called *The UFO Experience* "courageous" (Kuettner, 1973). Yet hostility to the subject remained. *Science* at first refused to publish a letter Hynek wrote on the subject in August 1966, but eventually relented, running an abridged version. It would publish nothing else favorable to UFOs, though several would-be contributors were to try over the years.

In 1973, with Sherman J. Larsen, who headed a small UFO-study group in suburban Chicago, Hynek founded the Center for UFO Studies (which would be renamed the **J. Allen Hynek Center for UFO Studies** after his death). In 1976 CUFOS started issuing a magazine, *International UFO Reporter*, and later a refereed *Journal of UFO Studies*. It held conferences in 1976 and 1981 and published long monographs on well-documented cases, from the Kelly-Hopkinsville, Kentucky, CE3 of 1955 to the UFO/helicopter encounter over Mansfield, Ohio, in 1973. For a time it could even afford a full-time investigator, Allan Hendry, owing in part to publicity Hynek and CUFOS received in the wake of the response to Steven Spielberg's 1977 UFO epic, its title taken directly from Hynek, *Close Encounters of the Third Kind*, in which Hynek had a cameo role.

Hynek freely interacted with the UFO community from which at one time he had made a point of distancing himself. He became a regular speaker at conferences and conventions, where he was hailed by most as a hero of ufology. With the passing of time he started espousing ideas that made the more conservative ufologists, including some of his associates in CUFOS, uncomfortable and of which his critics among professional debunkers were to make much. By now his friend Vallee had rejected extraterrestrial UFOs in favor of more exotic phenomena of a psychic nature. Hynek, always fascinated by Vallee's adventurous speculation, agreed and the two discussed the subject frankly in *The Edge of Reality* (1975), a book consisting of transcripts of conversations between the two. The book had

few admirers and was seen as a disappointing follow-up to the much-praised *UFO Experience*. A third and final book, *The Hynek UFO Report* (1977), a review of and commentary on the Project Blue Book records, was largely ghostwritten by Elaine M. Hendry, at the time the wife of CUFOS' chief investigator and a graduate student in Northwestern's astronomy department. (A fourth book bearing Hynek's name, *Night Siege* [1987], was written by the two other listed authors, Philip J. Imbrogno and Bob Pratt; by the time the contract was signed, Hynek was far too ill to contribute more than a by-line.)

From the founding of CUFOS onward, Hynek sought major funding for UFO research, but the money proved elusive. Finally in 1984 Hynek believed he had secured a promise of significant financial support from a wealthy European benefactor. He resigned as president of CUFOS (putting designated successor **Mark Rodeghier** in his place) and in the spring of 1985 moved with his wife Mimi to Scottsdale, Arizona, to establish the International Center for UFO Research (ICUFOR). But he soon grew disenchanted with his new associates, whose concerns he found to be metaphysical and commercial rather than scientific. He disassociated himself from the new operation not long after medical diagnosis revealed that he was suffering from the brain tumor that eventually would kill him. He died on the evening of April 27, 1986, in the Scottsdale Memorial Hospital.

To some of his scientific colleagues, those who had never sympathized with his UFO interests, Hynek was an example of a good scientist gone bad. Others, however, were willing to let history decide. In an obituary in *Sky & Telescope*, his onetime colleague, astronomer and astronaut Karl G. Henize, wrote that "it remains for future generations to decide the validity of his basic concept and whether his attempts to treat such investigations with scientific rigor were fruitful" (Henize, 1986). On the other hand, historian **David M. Jacobs**, author of *The UFO Controversy in America* (1975), saw Hynek as a heroic and pioneering figure. Jacobs wrote, "This kindly, unprepossessing man will be remembered in history as a giant. Hynek set the tone for UFO

HYNEK, JOSEF ALLEN (*continued*)

research for a generation, launched scores of research projects, symbolized UFO research to the press and public, led the campaign to establish credibility for UFO research and above all was the epitome of what a scientist should be—fearless of the evidence and honest about its meaning. His influence and inspiration are incalculable. Others will come forward to fill the void left by him, but there will be only one J. Allen Hynek. He will be missed but he will not be forgotten. His place in history is assured" (Jacobs, 1986).

Sources:

Cook, Joan. "J. Allen Hynek, Astronomer and U.F.O. Consultant, Dies." *New York Times* (May 1, 1986).

Henize, Karl G. "J. Allen Hynek: 1910-86." *Sky & Telescope* 72, 2 (August 1986): 117.

Hynek, J. Allen. *The Hynek UFO Report*. New York: Dell, 1977.

Hynek, J. Allen. "Swamp Gas Plus Ten . . . and Counting." In N. Joseph Gurney, and Walter H. Andrus, Jr., eds. *1976 MUFON Symposium Proceedings*, 76-83. Seguin, TX: Mutual UFO Network, Inc., 1976.

Hynek, J. Allen. *The UFO Experience: A Scientific Inquiry*. Chicago: Henry Regnery Company, 1972.

Hynek, J. Allen. "UFOs Merit Scientific Study." *Science 21* (October 1966): 329.

Hynek, J. Allen. "Unusual Aerial Phenomena." *Journal of the Optical Society of America 43* (April 1953): 311-314.

Hynek, J. Allen, and Philip J. Imbrogno, with Bob Pratt. *Night Siege: The Hudson Valley UFO Sightings*. New York: Ballantine Books, 1987.

Hynek, J. Allen, and Jacques Vallee. *The Edge of Reality: A Progress Report on Unidentified Flying Objects*. Chicago: Henry Regnery Company, 1975.

Jacobs, David M. "J. Allen Hynek and the UFO Phenomenon." *International UFO Reporter* 11, 3 (May/June 1986): 4-8, 23.

Jacobs, David M. *The UFO Controversy in America*. Bloomington: Indiana University Press, 1975.

King-Hele, D. G. "UFOs Analyzed." *Nature* 239 (October 27, 1972): 529.

Kuettner, Joachim P. "A New Start on the Whole UFO Problem?" *Astronautics and Aeronautics* (November 1973): 8-10.

Murray, Bruce C. "Reopening the Question." *Science* 177 (August 25, 1972): 688-689.

Vallee, Jacques. *Anatomy of a Phenomenon: Unidentified Objects in Space–A Scientific Appraisal*. Chicago: Henry Regnery Company, 1965.

Vallee, Jacques, and Janine Vallee. *Challenge to Science: The UFO Enigma.*, Chicago: Henry Regnery Company, 1966.

I

INTERNATIONAL UFO REPORTER
2457 West Peterson Avenue
Chicago, Illinois 60659

International UFO Reporter, referred to as *IUR*, is the magazine of the **J. Allen Hynek Center for UFO Studies**. Edited by Jerome Clark, the 24-page bimonthly reports on case investigations, recent and historical case investigations, and hypotheses, serving as a forum for the most serious research in the field. It takes no editorial position beyond the view that the UFO phenomenon deserves scientific attention. It is often critical of the excesses of both believers and debunkers. *IUR* began in November 1976 as an eight-page newsletter, edited by Allan Hendry, dealing almost entirely with cases under CUFOS investigation, but as the number of sightings declined in the early 1980s, *IUR* adopted a longer-range approach and under Clark's editorship has taken to publishing longer, more analytical pieces rather than short synopses of reports. On occasion, if the case warrants it, *IUR* has devoted an entire issue to one incident, as it did with a November 1986 radar/visual encounter over Alaska ("The Fantastic Flight of JAL1628," by **Bruce Maccabee**, March/April 1987).

INVISIBLE COLLEGE

In his 1972 classic report on *The UFO Experience: A Scientific Inquiry*, astronomer **J. Allen Hynek** bemoaned the lack of scientific work on UFOs, a result, in part, of the public image of the phenomenon. In a tactful statement, he noted that the subject had been sullied by its association with an unnamed "lunatic fringe" and its sponsorship of individuals who were not equipped to bring to it the necessary proper critical judgment. However, he had learned that a number of individual scientists, usually operating without awareness of or connection with each other, were quietly studying the problem presented by UFO reports. These scientists, who had begun to correspond with him as he became known as a person interested in UFO phenomena, were dubbed an "invisible college." Hynek borrowed the designation for a label applied to a group of outlaw scientists who had to work *sub rosa* in the seventeenth century when they were suspected of cavorting with the devil.

In 1973 Hynek sought to give some organizational focus to the college through the Center for UFO Studies (now the **J. Allen Hynek Center for UFO Studies**, [CUFOS]). CUFOS hoped to give the research some legitimacy and hence pave the way for members of the college to become visible. As CUFOS established that legitimacy, the need for and idea of an invisible college dropped from the literature, but not before it was given a slightly new connotation by Hynek's colleague **Jacques Vallee**.

In 1975 Vallee published his fourth major UFO book, *The Invisible College*, borrowing Hynek's concept. He argued that because of the disdain of UFOs in the scientific community, as the invisible

141

INVISIBLE COLLEGE (*continued*)

college attained some coherency and focus in its research program it would be lacking an adequate theoretical framework. He went on to propose such a framework.

Vallee then emerged as a major exponent of an alternative to the hypothesis of the extraterrestrial origin of UFOs. He suggested that UFOs are a physical phenomenon, with measurable physical properties such as mass, but, more importantly, they are a "window into another reality." In making his case, he argued cogently that the psychic element in UFO reports could no longer be ignored and thus there was a need to integrate the experience of **contactees** (he championed psychic Uri Geller) and a wide variety of other religious phenomena, such as apparitions and visions, into his approach.

In the end, Vallee proposed the idea of UFOs as manifestations of a control system of human consciousness. This idea was further explored in his 1979 book *Messengers of Deception*, in which the idea of a control system took a decidedly negative, even paranoid turn. Before he could interest the UFO community in his approach, however, a basic problem had to be confronted. Vallee had to restate his idea of a control system, basically a metaphysical assertion, in such a way as to make it amenable to scientific inquiry. To date he has not accomplished that task. *Messengers of Deception* did not receive a warm welcome from ufologists and for the next nine years Vallee remained essentially silent about his perspective. Then in 1988, he picked up on the notion of the invisible college, actually reprinting verbatim the introduction from his 1975 book, and made a new assertion of his control system hypothesis which he hoped to have reconsidered in the light of the ufological interest in the **abduction phenomenon.**

In general, American ufologists have limited their attention to investigating the possibility that abduction reports involve extraterrestrial contact and refuting attempts to reduce the reports to simple psychological explanations. They have paid little heed to Vallee's call for a more religious-metaphysical approach.

J. Gordon Melton

Sources:

Hynek, J. Allen. *The UFO Experience: A Scientific Inquiry.* Chicago: Henry Regnery Company, 1972.

Hynek, J. Allen. "The UFO Mystery." *FBI Bulletin* 44, 2 (February 1975): 16-20.

Hynek, J. Allen, and Jacques Vallee. *The Edge of Reality: A Progress Report on Unidentified Flying Objects.* Chicago: Henry Regnery Company, 1975.

Vallee, Jacques. *Dimensions: A Casebook of Alien Contact.* Chicago: Contemporary Books, 1988.

Vallee, Jacques. *The Invisible College: What a Group of Scientists Has Discovered About UFO Influences on the Human Race.* New York: E. P. Dutton & Co., 1975.

Vallee, Jacques. *Messengers of Deception: UFO Contacts and Cults.* Berkeley, CA: And/Or Press, 1979.

J

J. ALLEN HYNEK CENTER FOR UFO STUDIES
2457 West Peterson Avenue
Chicago, Illinois 60659

The J. Allen Hynek Center for UFO Studies grew out of an association between Sherman J. Larsen, an insurance salesman active in ufology through the National Investigations Committee on Aerial Phenomena (NICAP) since the 1950s, and Northwestern University astronomer **J. Allen Hynek**, who between 1948 and 1969 was the chief scientific consultant for the Air Force's Project Blue Book. In the 1960s Hynek had begun expressing open disenchantment with the Air Force's handling of UFO investigations, and his 1972 book *The UFO Experience* chronicled the shortcomings of Project Blue Book's approach. Hynek had quietly gathered a handful of scientists and engineers, an **"invisible college"** as he called it, to reconsider the UFO problem and devise a scientific approach to it.

Larsen, who like Hynek lived in the Chicago area, met Hynek for the first time in 1960. Over the next few years they met hundreds of times. According to Larsen's account, "During one of those meetings he showed me five drawers of government documents, correspondence and sighting reports he had collected during his early years as the consultant to Wright-Patterson Air Force Base, Foreign Technology Division, Dayton, Ohio, where Project Blue Book was located. I told him I would be happy to straighten out the files and create an index over the next few years. This relationship went on through the years until

one evening in October 1973 when again we were in his office at Lindheimer Observatory. He was expressing his regrets that after all of his years devoted to UFO study he had failed to stimulate significant scientific interest.

"I replied that perhaps, if he had a structured UFO organization into which he could draw his 'Invisible College' of scientists and make them visibly active, things would change. I added that as a tax-exempt organization rather than as an individual he could provide a publication as a source of raising funds to support his efforts.

"He brushed this idea aside, saying he did not want to get bogged down trying to organize a group.

"'Then join a group that's already set up and functioning,' I said. I pointed out that I had operated the nonprofit, tax-exempt NICAP-Chicago Affiliate for a number of years and when new NICAP officers in Washington, D.C., closed all local offices, I had set up a not-for-profit, federal-tax-exempt organization called PEG, Public Education Group.

"'I don't like the name!' he quickly responded. When I asked him what name he would like, he replied without hesitation, 'Center for UFO Studies'" (Larsen, 1986).

CUFOS was headquartered in Evanston, Illinois, for a time at a downtown office, then in Hynek's home. Its first periodical was an irregularly pub-

J. ALLEN HYNEK CENTER FOR UFO STUDIES
(*continued*)

lished *CUFOS News Bulletin*. The first issue of a more formal newsletter, *International UFO Reporter* (*IUR*), edited by Hynek and CUFOS' one full-time investigator, Allan Hendry, appeared in November 1976. Three issues of the *Journal of UFO Studies*, a refereed publication whose contributors were mostly scientists, appeared in the late 1970s and early 1980s. CUFOS also held invitation-only scientific conferences in 1976 and 1981. CUFOS produced a series of monographs on such subjects as electromagnetic effects associated with UFO sightings, the October 1973 Mansfield, Ohio, UFO/helicopter case, close encounters of the third kind, and other subjects. In 1979 Hendry wrote a iconoclastic assessment of ufology, *The UFO Handbook*, which concluded that UFO investigators did not have the tools needed to deal in a meaningful way with the issues raised by the UFO problem.

In the late 1970s, as CUFOS' fortunes declined along with UFO reports and public interest, CUFOS was unable to pay Hendry's salary and was forced to let him go. Hendry retired from ufology, convinced that no further progress in UFO research could be made, and CUFOS staggered along, sustained largely by Hynek's good name, though hampered by his casual approach to organizational matters. In early 1985 Hynek asked Jerome Clark to take over editorship of *IUR*, a duty Hynek had handled since Hendry's departure. As the new editor, Clark has changed *IUR* from a UFO-reporting newsletter to a magazine focusing on broader theoretical issues involved in UFO investigation and analysis, and featuring articles of debate and criticism. With a renewal of popular fascination with UFOs in the latter 1980s, *IUR*, CUFOS' principal source of income, attracted new subscribers and came to rival the *MUFON UFO Journal*, published by the **Mutual UFO Network** (MUFON), as the major voice of American ufology.

In 1985, following Hynek's move to Arizona, CUFOS was relocated to an office in Glenview, Illinois, where daily activity was overseen by

Larsen. When Hynek died on April 27, 1986, Hynek's hand-picked successor, **Mark Rodeghier**, assumed the post of president and scientific director, with Clark as vice president. The organization was renamed the J. Allen Hynek Center for UFO Studies but retained the acronym CUFOS. With its already-considerable collection of UFO materials augmented by the addition of the NICAP files, CUFOS moved to larger headquarters in Chicago. Under Rodeghier's skilled leadership CUFOS has prospered both financially and intellectually. In 1989 the *Journal of UFO Studies* was revived, with Western Michigan University professor **Michael D. Swords** assuming the editorial post once held by Elaine M. Hendry and, later, Mimi Hynek. CUFOS mounted major new inquiries into the **abduction phenomenon** and the Roswell, New Mexico, UFO crash of 1947.

Sources:

Davis, Isabel, and Ted Bloecher. *Close Encounter at Kelly and Others of 1955*. Evanston, IL: Center for UFO Studies, 1978.

Hendry, Allan. *The UFO Handbook: A Guide to Investigating, Evaluating and Reporting UFO Sightings*. Garden City, NY: Doubleday & Company, Inc., 1979.

Hynek, J. Allen. "Estimate of the Situation." *International UFO Reporter* 1, 1 (November 1976): 3-4.

Hynek, J. Allen, ed. *Proceedings of the 1976 CUFOS Conference*. Evanston, IL: Center for UFO Studies, 1976.

Hynek, Mimi, ed. *The Spectrum of UFO Research: The Proceedings of the Second CUFOS Conference, Held September 25-27, 1981, in Chicago, Illinois*. Chicago: J. Allen Hynek Center for UFO Studies, 1988.

Larsen, Sherman J. "Reflections on J. Allen Hynek: The Founding of CUFOS." *International UFO Reporter* 11, 3 (May/June 1986): 13-14.

Quade, Vicki. "UFO Hunters." *Reader* 17, 1 (September 25, 1987): 1, 18, 20, 22, 24-27, 30-32.

Zeidman, Jennie. *A Helicopter-UFO Encounter Over Ohio*. Evanston, IL: Center for UFO Studies, 1979.

JACOBS, DAVID MICHAEL (1942-)

David Michael Jacobs is an American historian who has written extensively on UFO-related matters. His Ph.D. dissertation in history, *The Controversy Over Unidentified Flying Objects, 1946-1972*, was the second ever written on the subject. It formed the basis of Jacobs' 1975 book *The UFO Controversy in America*, considered a classic work in the literature. He has spent the last several years investigating the **abduction phenomenon** and has completed a book-length manuscript, *Secret Life: The Structure and Meaning of UFO Abductions*, on his findings.

Born in Los Angeles in 1942, Jacobs got his B.A. in history from UCLA in 1966. His graduate degrees in history (M.A., 1968; Ph.D., 1973) were from the University of Wisconsin at Madison. He is married and is the father of two young boys. He is an associate professor at Temple University, where he teaches the only regularly-scheduled undergraduate course in America on the UFO phenomenon. He is the first person to give a paper on the abduction phenomenon to a scientific organization, the **Society for Scientific Exploration** (SSE), when it met at Cornell University in 1988. His articles on ufological issues appear frequently in the *MUFON UFO Journal* and *International UFO Reporter*.

He says, "The UFO phenomenon is the abduction phenomenon. Sightings of the outside shells of objects were early indications of the objects' validity. The meaning of what was happening inside the UFOs eluded researchers until the importance of abductions became evident. Abductions have cracked open the UFO mystery like a cosmic egg. Inside we see alien life, the creation of bizarre life, and the exploitation of human life. We did not expect to discover this. The majority of societal theorizing about contact with extraterrestrials foresaw initially tentative but friendly meetings of aliens and humans for an interchange of ideas. Some darker-thinking science-fiction authors imagined evil aliens using humans as food or bent on death and destruction. The abduction scenario does not reveal either of these scenarios. But it is unfortunately closer to the latter than to the former.

"The content of abductions make this evident. Victims are rendered without will or physical control. They are subjected to a series of mental, physical, and reproductive procedures calculated to satisfy an alien agenda. They are then made to forget immediately what has happened to them. This occurs again and again over the course of their lives from childhood through adulthood, as if the aliens were using their bodies as a physiological mine from which they can remove the ore at will.

"Abductees described activity not far removed from human treatment of animals needed for medical and scientific purposes. It is the animal basis of our lives, rather than the rich tapestry of our society and culture, that is the subject of fascination and exploitation.

"The effect on the abductees can be severe. They desperately wish that it had not happened and that it will cease. Their lives are diminished, disrupted, and sometimes ruined. They find no metaphysical or tangible benevolence in their predicament.

"The entire abduction phenomenon is depressing. It was not this way before. There was intellectual sport in studying sightings and speculating about the purposes for their appearance. There was even a degree of comfort in not knowing what it was all about; our ignorance precluded our fear. But research into UFO sightings advanced as far as was possible. All reports that did not involve occupants simply heaped on monotonous confirmation. The occupant reports had an amazing, yet ingenuous, quality about them—aliens

JACOBS, DAVID MICHAEL (*continued*)

seemingly avoiding human beings and going about their business. Without knowledge of the occupants' motivations and purposes, theorizing about them was a mind game innocently played.

"Now we have knowledge. Now the UFO phenomenon has assumed the realistic dimensions that early and incomplete abduction material only hinted at. Now I am frightened."

Sources:

Jacobs, David M. "Post-Abduction Syndrome." In Walter H. Andrus, Jr., and Richard H. Hall, eds. *MUFON 1988 International UFO Symposium Proceedings*, 86-102. Seguin, TX: Mutual UFO Network, Inc., 1988.

Jacobs, David M. *The UFO Controversy in America*. Bloomington, IN: Indiana University Press, 1975.

Jacobs, David M. "UFOs and the Search for Legitimacy." In Howard Kerr, and Charles L. Crow, eds. *The Occult in America,* 218-31. Urbana, IL: University of Illinois Press, 1983.

JAL SIGHTING

One of the most publicized UFO encounters of the 1980s occurred on November 17, 1986, over Alaska. The witnesses were the captain, first officer and flight engineer of a Japanese Airlines Boeing 747 cargo plane on a flight from Paris to Tokyo.

At 5:10 p.m. local time, as the aircraft, at 35,000 feet, was passing over northeastern Alaska, Capt. Kenju Terauchi, a veteran pilot, noticed some unusual lights to his left and about 2000 feet below him. He decided that they were probably from military aircraft on a special mission. But a few minutes later, when the position of the lights had not changed, suggesting they were

keeping pace with the 747, Terauchi and his crew began to suspect that they might be something out of the ordinary.

As Terauchi completed a left turn, the lights abruptly were directly in front of the aircraft, and much closer. Now they resembled two pairs of rectangular-to-square arrays of "amber and whitish" lights, with "jets" pulsating in the direction of a dark vertical panel at the center of each object. After several seconds the jets ceased shooting fire and became "small circles of lights" like "numerous exhaust pipes." The two UFOs, between 500 and 1000 feet in front of the 747, were "about the same size as the body of a DC-8 jet" (Maccabee, 1987). After about five minutes the objects positioned themselves side by side.

At 5:19 Terauchi contacted Anchorage flight control to ask if it was tracking anything above the aircraft. It wasn't. A conversation ensued in which efforts were made to identify the lights. The transmission, however, was sometimes garbled. As the captain reported later, "The VHF communications, both in transmitting and receiving, were extremely difficult for 10 to 15 minutes while the little ships came close to us and often interfered with communication from Anchorage."

The Anchorage controller notified the Air Force at Elmendorf Regional Operational Control Center (ROCC) and asked it to try to see what its radar was picking up.

Meanwhile the two lights moved off to the left. Terauchi saw an object, apparently a third UFO, some seven or eight miles away. The two other, smaller lights were flying toward it. He was able to pick up the distant object on the aircraft's radar. Although it was barely visible to the eyes of the crew, the radar indicated it was quite large. It remained on the screen for several minutes.

On the ground the ROCC radar controller reported to Anchorage that he was getting some "surge primary return," meaning a radar signal unaccompanied by a transponder signal. (A transponder is an airplane transmitter that sends out a coded signal in response to a signal from a ground station.) When the ROCC controller speculated that the track could be erroneous, Anchorage, which was also picking it up, assured him that "it's not erroneous." Anchorage wanted to know if the base was certain it did not have military aircraft in the area. ROCC said it did not.

Now ROCC was tracking a "primary return" in the approximate location the pilot was describing. But by 5:28 the return was gone. In the air the JAL crew were watching the lights off to the left and below them, near the horizon. The objects were too far to the left now to be tracked on the aircraft radar. To the crew's left the sky was dark; stars and planets had now become visible and the two smaller UFOs were becoming indistinguishable from the other lights.

As the plane approached within 20 miles of Eielson Air Force Base to the northeast and within 30 miles of Fairbanks to the east-northeast, they looked behind them at a pale white light, the one they had tracked earlier. This time they saw, according to Terauchi, the "silhouette of a giant spaceship," apparently visible because it was reflecting the lights from the ground. It looked like an enormous Saturn-shaped object. Terauchi would refer to it as the "mothership," speculating that the two relatively smaller objects had come from and gone back to it. He estimated that it was the size of "two aircraft carriers."

Badly frightened for the first time, the captain frantically radioed Anchorage and asked for permission to take evasive measures. Approval was granted quickly, but the huge UFO stayed behind them in the same position even when they turned and descended. At 5:39 it disappeared, but not before ROCC had tracked an anomalous target in the vicinity of the plane. At 5:40 Anchorage asked the captain if he would like a jet to be scrambled, but Terauchi declined. (He later explained that he feared for the safety of the interceptor pilot.)

ROCC was briefly tracking the target again and the JAL crew were seeing the "mothership" behind them once more. The 747 was running low on fuel and Terauchi knew he had to land at Anchorage no matter what.

At 5:40 a United Airlines passenger jet had left Anchorage heading north for Fairbanks. Soon it was at 29,000 feet. Since it was at the same approximate elevation as the JAL 747 (which was at 31,000 feet), Anchorage, which had an unidentified target on its radar, asked the UA pilot if he could see anything behind the JAL flight. But by the time the UA aircraft got close enough to see, the "mothership" had disappeared and, as Terauchi put it, "there was nothing left but the light of the moon."

The Federal Aviation Administration (FAA) launched an investigation. FAA official Jack Wright interviewed the crew shortly after the plane had landed. Another interview was conducted that same evening by FAA special agents James Derry and Ronald Mickle. An FAA investigation continued into January. On March 5 the FAA announced it "was unable to confirm the event" because "a second radar target near the JAL flight at the time of the reported sighting was not another aircraft but rather a split radar return from the JAL Boeing 747." (Nonetheless Hank Elias, in charge of the FAA's air traffic division in Alaska, said the FAA was less than "absolutely positive" about this explanation [Del Giudice, 1987].)

Physicist/ufologist **Bruce Maccabee**, who conducted his own investigation, noted, "The [FAA] press release did not mention that the 'split return effect' was contradicted by the fact that the extra echo did not come back with every sweep of the radar and by a statement by an air traffic controller who said that they don't usually get a split image in the area that the JAL jet flew. The press release offered no explanation for the sighting, nor did it dispute the crew's claim that something unusual was seen" (Maccabee, 1987).

A month and a half before the FAA announcement, the **Committee for the Scientific Investigation of Claims of the Paranormal** (CSICOP), a debunking group, declared it had

JAL SIGHTING (*continued*)

"solved" the JAL sighting. In a January 22 press release it said, "An investigation of the incident in which an Unidentified Flying Object reportedly paced a Japanese Air Lines 747 enroute to Anchorage, Alaska, for nearly 40 minutes on Nov. 18, 1986, reveals that at least one extraterrestrial object was involved—the planet Jupiter, and possibly another—Mars" (*Extraterrestrial*, 1987). The solution was credited to the chairman of CSICOP's UFO Subcommittee, **Philip J. Klass.**

Unfortunately, the "solution" was offered before all the facts were in, Maccabee said, remarking that Klass "made a major error in not waiting for the release of the complete package of information compiled by the FAA. Had he waited he would have found that the publicized versions of the sighting were actually quite accurate in their descriptions of the lights, although they were far from complete, and the descriptions certainly rule out Jupiter and Mars as explanations. . . . For example, because the analyst did not have the information package he did not know that the widely publicized drawings of the arrays of lights were more detailed versions of the sketches made by the captain only hours after the event. Nor did he know that the other crew members, in separate interviews, supported the captain's report of seeing a multiplicity of lights appear in front of the plane and pace the aircraft for 10 minutes or more. Nor did he know that the arrays of lights rearranged themselves from one above the other to side by side, a reorientation that Jupiter and Mars would have found difficult to do.

"Without the information package it was impossible to reconstruct from radar data the flight path of the aircraft. Without the flight path it was impossible to determine the exact heading of the aircraft, and therefore the directions that the pilot and crew were looking at various times, since they gave sighting directions with respect to the heading of the aircraft. Therefore the analyst might not have realized that just before the end of the sighting, when Jupiter was ahead of the plane and to the left (about at the 10 o'clock position), the UFO 'mothership' was behind and to the left (at the seven-to-eight o'clock position)" (Maccabee, 1987).

Since then no one has suggested a credible mundane explanation for the JAL sighting, regarded as one of the most spectacular and best-documented UFO encounters of the 1980s.

Sources:

Andrus, Walter. "Strange Alaskan Encounter." *MUFON UFO Journal* 226 (February 1987): 3-8.

Del Giudice, Marguerite. "The UFO That Can't Be Explained." *Philadelphia Inquirer* (May 24, 1987).

Extraterrestrial Object Involved in Japan Air Lines Pilot's UFO Sighting, According to Leading UFO Investigator. Buffalo: CSICOP, January 22, 1987.

Maccabee, Bruce. "The Fantastic Flight of JAL1628." *International UFO Reporter* 12, 2 (March/April 1987): 4-23.

K

KEEL, JOHN ALVA (1930-)

John A. Keel is a radical theorist who believes that UFOs are "ultraterrestrial" rather than extraterrestrial. By that he means they are shape-changing phenomena from another order of existence. These ultraterrestrials are basically hostile to, or at least contemptuous of, human beings and manipulate them in various ways, for example by staging "miracles" which inspire unfounded religious beliefs. Ultraterrestrials and their minions may also manifest as monsters, space people, ghosts and other paranormal entities.

Born Alva John Kiehle in upstate New York in 1930, Keel has been a professional writer since his teens. He has been a radio and television scriptwriter, a syndicated columnist, and frequent contributor to a wide range of magazines. Long a devotee of the writings of anomalist/satirist Charles Fort (1874-1932), Keel surfaced in ufology in the mid-1960s with a series of articles in England's *Flying Saucer Review* in which he attacked mainstream ufologists for their obsessions with extraterrestrials and scientific respectability and contended that UFO phenomena are far more bizarre and frightening than ufologists were willing to acknowledge. Keel managed to outrage many prominent ufologists, even some who thought he might have a point, but no one denied that he had interesting stories, most coming from his field trips to the Ohio River Valley, where people were reporting a strange creature called "Mothman," men in black, hairy apelike bipeds, and UFOs.

His two major books are *UFOs: Operation Trojan* (1970) and *The Mothman Prophecies* (1975). After some years of relative inactivity, Keel reemerged in the late 1980s to found the New York Fortean Society and to publish a collection of his articles as *Disneyland of the Gods* (1988).

He says, "We are like ants, trying to view reality with very limited perceptive equipment and then basing our theologies and philosophies on what are essentially misperceptions. The real problem is that there is a much larger reality around us that we cannot see but can only sense. While we grovel on our way to the 21st Century, someone or some thing is watching with amusement. Like Columbus, we don't know where we've been, where we're going or even where we are. . . . We are biochemical robots helplessly controlled by forces that can scramble our brains, destroy our memories and use us in any way they see fit. They have been doing it to us forever."

Sources:

Boyd, Robert D. *International Who's Who in Ufology Directory*. Mobile, AL: The Author, 1988.

Keel, John A. *Disneyland of the Gods*. New York: Amok Press, 1988.

Keel, John A. *The Eighth Tower*. New York: Saturday Review Press/E. P. Dutton & Co., Inc., 1975.

KEEL, JOHN ALVA (*continued*)

Keel, John A. *The Mothman Prophecies*. New York: Saturday Review Press/E. P. Dutton & Co., Inc., 1975.

Keel, John A. *Our Haunted Planet*. Greenwich, CT: Fawcett, 1971.

Keel, John A. *Strange Creatures from Time and Space*. Greenwich, CT: Fawcett, 1970.

Keel, John A. *UFOs: Operation Trojan Horse*. New York: G. P. Putnam's Sons, 1970.

KLASS, PHILIP JULIAN (1919-)

Philip Julian Klass is the world's leading UFO debunker. The author of three books (and a number of articles and white papers) which seek to explain UFO reports as the products of hoaxes or misinterpretations of conventional stimuli, he heads the UFO Subcommittee of the **Committee for the Scientific Investigation of Claims of the Paranormal** (CSICOP) and is the anti-UFO spokesman most often quoted in media reports on UFO controversies.

Born in 1919 in Iowa, Klass graduated from Iowa State University in 1941, where he majored in electrical engineering. Over the next decade he worked for the avionics division of General Electric. But it was as an editor of *Aviation Week & Space Technology*, for which he began working in 1952 (when it was called *Aviation Week*), that he made his name as an award-winning aviation journalist. He retired from his position as senior avionics editor in 1986 but continues to serve as a contributing editor and to report on relevant issues. On January 18, 1990, he was given the Lauren D. Lyman Award for "distinguished achievement in the field of aviation and aerospace journalism."

To ufologists, however, Klass is known as a relentless, uncompromising foe of the UFO phenomenon. But his first book on the subject, *UFOs–Identified* (1968), held that UFOs are genuinely anomalous, though not alien, in nature. He theorized that UFOs are caused by ball lightning and free-floating plasmas, a theory rejected as scientifically unsustainable by a panel of scientists assembled by the Air Force-sponsored University of Colorado project (usually called the Condon Committee, after its director, physicist Edward U. Condon). Klass quietly abandoned the idea (though he has never publicly disassociated himself from it) in favor of a more conventionally-skeptical view, that UFO witnesses are untrustworthy and sometimes of questionable character.

In widely-distributed "white papers" Klass has attacked ufologists on a personal level, sometimes labeling them "UFO promoters," and characterizing their work as credulous, careless or even crooked. These notions are explored at length in three books: *UFOs Explained* (1974), *UFOs: The Public Deceived* (1983), and *UFO-Abductions: A Dangerous Game* (1988). Klass' allegations and theories have been vigorously challenged by UFO proponents, who have written lengthy rejoinders to his explanations of major cases.

In 1977 Klass helped found CSICOP, an organization devoted to the debunking of all unorthodox claims not only about UFOs but about psychic and anomalous phenomena as well. He is a regular contributor to its quarterly magazine *Skeptical Inquirer*.

He says, "Those who engage in the legitimate scientific search for extraterrestrial intelligence recognize that if it exists, it very probably will be much too distant to ever visit earth. . . . The credulity of UFOlogists and some segments of the news media," he adds, recalls "Francis Bacon's sage warning: '*A credulous man is a deceiver.*' If UFOlogists and some journalists only deceived themselves, it would be simply their personal problem. But for much too long, they have deceived the public as well."

150

Sources:

Boyd, Robert D. *International Who's Who in Ufology Directory*. Mobile, AL: The Author, 1988.

Bullard, Thomas E. "Klass Takes on Abductions; Abductions Win." *International UFO Reporter* 12, 6 (November/December 1987): 9-13, 20.

Clark, Jerome. "Phil Klass vs. the 'UFO Promoters.'" *Fate* 34, 2 (February 1981): 56-67.

Klass, Philip J. *UFO-Abductions: A Dangerous Game*. Buffalo, NY: Prometheus Books, 1988.

Klass, Philip J. "UFOs." In George O. Abell and Barry Singer, eds. *Science and the Paranormal: Probing the Existence of the Supernatural*, 310-328. New York: Charles Scribner's Sons, 1981.

Klass, Philip J. *UFOs Explained*. New York: Random House, 1974.

Klass, Philip J. *UFOs–Identified*. New York: Random House, 1968.

Klass, Philip J. *UFOs: The Public Deceived*. Buffalo, NY: Prometheus Books, 1983.

Zeidman, Jennie. "The Mansfield Helicopter Case: Anatomy of an Investigation." In Walter H. Andrus, Jr., ed. *MUFON 1989 International UFO Symposium Proceedings, 2-30*. Seguin, TX: Mutual UFO Network, Inc., 1989. [A critical commentary on Klass' explanation of a famous Ohio helicopter/UFO encounter on October 18, 1973.]

L

LORENZEN, CORAL E. LIGHTNER (1925-1988) AND LESLIE JAMES LORENZEN (1922-1986)

Two of ufology's pioneering figures, Coral and Jim Lorenzen, died little more than a year and a half apart from each other. The organization they founded, the Aerial Phenomena Research Organization (APRO), the longest-lived serious UFO-research group in the United States, died with them.

Leslie James Lorenzen, born on January 2, 1922, in Grand Meadow, Minnesota, worked professionally as an electronics technician. Among his employers were Holloman Air Force Base (1954-1960) and Kitt Peak National Observatory (1960-1967). When he died of cancer on August 28, 1986, in Tucson, he had been serving as head of his own music company for nearly 20 years. Coral E. Lightner was born on April 2, 1925, in Hillsdale, Wisconsin, and held various jobs as writer, editor, and proofreader for technical publications. She died on April 12, 1988, of respiratory failure.

The Lorenzens' great achievement was APRO, which at its peak had some 3000 members. The organization was the outgrowth of Coral's long interest in the UFO phenomenon, beginning with a 1934 sighting of a white hemisphere-shaped object crossing the western sky from south to north in an undulating trajectory. Three years later, after she related her experience to the family doctor, he loaned her the books of Charles Fort, the great collector of reports of aerial and other anomalies, and she learned that other persons had seen similarly unusual phenomena.

On September 29, 1943, she and Jim Lorenzen were married. Four years later, in Douglas, Arizona, on June 10, 1947, Coral saw her second UFO: a tiny luminous sphere which rose from the ground and vanished into the night sky. Kenneth Arnold's classic sighting, the one that started the "flying-saucer" era, was exactly two weeks away.

Fascinated by the flood of reports from 1947 onward, she entered into correspondence with other individuals who were monitoring the emerging UFO phenomenon. In January 1952, while living in Sturgeon Bay, Wisconsin, she formed APRO and soon was publishing the *APRO Bulletin*, which for the next two decades would be essential reading for anyone looking for a comprehensive, intelligent guide to worldwide UFO activity. Eventually the Lorenzens moved to the Southwest and in due course settled in Tucson. In 1964 Jim became director and Coral assumed the position of secretary-treasurer.

APRO was shaped by Coral's strong personality, with the gentle-natured Jim serving as a calming influence on his wife's occasional volatility. She and her organization were early champions of reports involving occupants, 20 years before **J. Allen Hynek** coined the term "close encounters of the third kind," which they insisted were not to be confused with the tales told by the **contactees** who claimed to be intimate with Venusians and other Space Brothers. Other early ufologists were reluctant to embrace humanoid reports—which to them seemed excessively exotic—but in time

LORENZEN (*continued*)

APRO's claims were vindicated. Persons who made these reports, as even Project Blue Book spokesmen would acknowledge on occasion, proved to be no different from other UFO witnesses; they were normal, sane, puzzled and sincere.

APRO collected these and other reports not only from the United States but from South America, where the organization was ably represented by such notable investigators as Olavo T. Fontes in Brazil and Horacio Gonzales Gauteaume in Venezuela. Through Fontes' and Gonzales' reports in the *APRO Bulletin*, North American ufologists learned of such seminal cases as the Venezuelan humanoid encounters of December 1954, the Trindade Island photographs, the Itaipu Fort "attack" and others.

Unlike Maj. Donald Keyhoe, who headed the other major organization of the 1950s, the National Investigations Committee on Aerial Phenomena (NICAP), Mrs. Lorenzen discounted theories of an official cover-up and criticized NICAP's attempts to force Congressional hearings on alleged UFO secrecy. She thought ufology was better served by concentrating on investigation and documentation of cases and making the subject palatable to scientists. The Lorenzens were articulate, outspoken advocates of the extraterrestrial hypothesis (ETH) and had little time for the psychological and parapsychological theories that came to prominence in the 1960s and gained great popularity in some circles.

In 1969 **Walter H. Andrus, Jr.,** an APRO regional officer from downstate Illinois, left the organization with a coterie of followers to form the Midwest UFO Network, subsequently renamed the **Mutual UFO Network** (MUFON), which in the 1970s would become the dominant force in organized ufology in America, eclipsing APRO. The split was far from amicable and for the rest of their lives the Lorenzens remained outspokenly bitter about the episode, resulting in an organizational and personal rivalry which ended only when APRO ended.

To the larger public the Lorenzens were best known for the popular paperbacks they wrote in the 1960s, such as the luridly-titled (by its publisher) *Flying Saucers: The Startling Evidence of the Invasion from Outer Space* (1966; an updated version of Coral's earlier hardcover *The Great Flying Saucer Hoax* [1962]). Four other titles soon appeared: *Flying Saucer Occupants* (1967); *UFOs Over the Americas* (1968); *UFOs: The Whole Story* (1969); and *The Shadow of the Unknown* (1970), which included UFOs in a discussion of psychic phenomena.

As the health of both the Lorenzens deteriorated in the early 1980s, the *Bulletin* was published infrequently and the few issues that did appear lacked the focus, clarity and editorial care that had characterized the periodical in happier days. Rumors circulated about APRO's imminent demise, especially following Jim's death, but the organization survived, if only in name, until shortly after Coral's death.

Sources:

Boyd, Robert D. *International Who's Who in Ufology Directory*. Mobile, AL: The Author, 1988.

Clark, Jerome. "Coral E. Lorenzen (1925-1988); APRO (1952-1988)." *International UFO Reporter* 13, 3 (March/April 1989): 6, 11, 20.

Lorenzen, Coral E. *The Great Flying Saucer Hoax: The UFO Facts and Their Interpretation*. New York: The William-Frederick Press, 1962. Revised edition as: *Flying Saucers: The Startling Evidence of Invasion from Outer Space*. New York: New American Library, 1966.

Lorenzen, Coral E. *The Shadow of the Unknown*. New York: New American Library, 1970.

Lorenzen, Coral, and Jim Lorenzen. *Abducted!: Confrontations With Beings From Outer Space*. New York: Berkley, 1977.

Lorenzen, Coral, and Jim Lorenzen. *Encounters With UFO Occupants*. New York: Berkley, 1976.

Lorenzen, Coral, and Jim Lorenzen. *UFOs Over the Americas*. New York: New American Library, 1968.

Lorenzen, Coral, and Jim Lorenzen. *UFOs: The Whole Story*. New York: New American Library, 1969.

Story, Ronald D. *The Encyclopedia of UFOs*. Garden City, NY: Doubleday & Company, 1980.

M

MACCABEE, BRUCE SARGENT (1942-)

Since the death of **J. Allen Hynek**, Bruce Maccabee, a physicist, has been the American scientist most actively and visibly involved in ufology, both as a researcher and as head of a major organization. Maccabee, chairman of the **Fund for UFO Research**, specializes in technical analysis (primarily of alleged UFO photographs) and in study of government involvement in UFO matters.

Born in 1942, Bruce Sargent Maccabee attended Worcester Polytechnic Institute, from which he received a B.S. in physics in 1964. An M.S. (1957) and Ph.D. (1970) from American University followed. Since 1972 he has been employed as a research physicist at the U.S. Naval Surface Weapons Center.

In his private life he has pursued UFO studies since 1969. He has investigated numerous UFO sightings, including such cases as the New Zealand film (1978), the McMinnville photo (1950), and the Japanese airliner sighting (1986), and published three dozen articles and papers on ufological subjects. He was the first person to receive documents from the FBI file on "Flying Saucers" as a result of his pioneering Freedom of Information Act request. In 1980, he participated in the **Smithsonian UFO debate**.

He says, "My studies have led me to conclude that 'they' are here. (I wish they weren't!) What we can do about their presence, if anything, I don't know. Nor do I know what the impact on society will be when the realization of the reality of 'visitations' sets in. However, I expect that the impact will be immense."

Sources:

Boyd, Robert D. *International Who's Who in Ufology Directory*. Mobile, AL: The Author, 1988.

Maccabee, Bruce. "The Fantastic Flight of JAL1628." *International UFO Reporter* 12, 2 (March/April 1987): 4-23.

Maccabee, Bruce. "The McMinnville Photos." In Mimi Hynek, ed. *The Spectrum of UFO Research: The Proceedings of the Second CUFOS Conference, Held September 25-27, 1981, in Chicago, Illinois*, 13-34. Chicago: J. Allen Hynek Center for UFO Studies, 1988.

Maccabee, Bruce S. "Photometric Properties of an Unidentified Bright Object Seen off the Coast of New Zealand." *Applied Optics* 18 (1979): 2527-28.

Maccabee, Bruce. *Revised UFO History*. Silver Spring, MD: The Author, 1983.

Maccabee, Bruce. "Scientific Investigation of Unidentified Flying Objects." *Journal of UFO Studies* Part I: 1 (old series, 1979): 70-92; Part II: 3 (old series, 1983): 24-52.

MACCABEE, BRUCE SARGENT (*continued*)

Maccabee, Bruce S. "Still in Default." In Andrus, Walter H., Jr., and Richard H. Hall, eds. *MUFON 1986 UFO Symposium Proceedings: UFOs: Beyond the Mainstream of Science*, 130-160. Mutual UFO Network, Inc.: Seguin, TX, 1986.

Maccabee, Bruce. "What the Admiral Knew: UFOs, MJ-12 and Roscoe Hillenkoetter." *International UFO Reporter* 11, 6 (November/December 1986): 15-21.

Maccabee, Bruce. "The Wrath of Philip J. Klass." *Fate* 36, 11 (November 1983): 68-74.

Story, Ronald D. *The Encyclopedia of UFOs.* Garden City, NY: Doubleday & Company, 1980.

MAGONIA
John Rimmer
John Dee Cottage
5 James Terrace, Mortlake Churchyard
London SW14 8HB, England

Magonia, one of ufology's liveliest, best-edited and most controversial magazines, is a prominent voice within **British ufology** for the **psychosocial hypothesis**, which seeks to explain UFO beliefs and experiences as a result of mundane social and psychological processes, rather than the operation of alien intelligence.

The publication began in Liverpool, England, in 1965 as *Merseyside UFO Research Group Bulletin*, under the editorship of John Harney. In 1968 it became *Merseyside UFO Bulletin*, an independent publication unconnected with the Merseyside group. Harney remained editor, with John Rimmer assuming the post of associate editor. In 1975, when Rimmer became editor and moved the magazine's base to New Malden, Surrey, its title changed to the acronym *MUFOB*, the "M" now standing, it was said, for "Metempirical."

The last name change occurred in 1979, when the magazine was rechristened *Magonia*, after the

supernatural realm referred to in the title of **Jacques Vallee's** 1969 book *Passport to Magonia*. Rimmer remained as editor, with an editorial panel consisting of such regular contributors as Harney, Peter Rogerson and Roger Sandell. *Magonia*, a 16-to-20-page quarterly, is now published out of London.

Rimmer says, "Coverage includes all aspects of ufology and a wide range of related topics. Primarily we are a magazine which examines people's *beliefs* about UFOs and suchlike. Although open to well-written arguments propounding almost any theory of UFO origin, the magazine, its editors, and the bulk of its contributors tend towards an attitude which sees the UFO broadly as a psychological, sociological and behavioral phenomenon. It attempts to promote a skeptical yet sympathetic approach to the UFO problem. However, *Magonia* also has a great fear of being taken too seriously, and feels that much earnest ufological debate can be usefully leavened with a little humor."

MENZEL, DONALD HOWARD (1901-1976)

To Donald H. Menzel, American scientist and professor of astronomy at Harvard University, UFOs were a "modern myth," something that "scientists of the 21st century will look back on as the greatest nonsense of the 20th century" (Menzel, 1972). Menzel was so obsessed with this "modern myth" that he wrote three books debunking it: *Flying Saucers* (1953); *The World of Flying Saucers*, with Lyle G. Boyd (1963); and the posthumously-published *The UFO Enigma*, with Ernest H. Taves (1977). Until the emergence of aviation journalist **Philip J. Klass** as the world's premier foe of the UFO phenomenon, Menzel was ufology's leading critic, the one most cited in skeptical articles in magazines and newspapers.

To the author of the MJ-12 briefing document, however, Menzel was someone else entirely: a member of an above-top-secret project involved in the study of the remains of crashed spacecraft and their humanoid occupants. This surprising claim revived ufologists' fading memory of Menzel and made him a prime figure in the UFO controversies of the 1980s, even though he had died on December 14, 1976. If the document was to be believed, Menzel's apparent loathing of the very concept of alien visitation was a pose, intended to send a signal to the public and, perhaps more important, to his scientific colleagues that UFOs were a subject to be avoided.

Donald Howard Menzel, born in Florence, Colorado, on April 11, 1901, was a boy genius who learned the Morse code and was devouring books before entering first grade. An early interest in chemistry led him to enroll, at age 16, in the University of Colorado, but an observation of a total eclipse of the sun on June 8, 1918, persuaded him to switch to astronomy—as did a 1919 chemical-plant accident which damaged his lungs and kept him out of chemical laboratories. He received a graduate assistantship in astronomy at Princeton University and studied under Raymond S. Dugan, with whom he made photometric observations of eclipsing binary stars with a 23-inch refracting telescope. He also came into contact with physics and mathematics and became enthralled with the emerging discipline of astrophysics.

During the summers Menzel worked as a research assistant to Harlow Shapley at Harvard Observatory. His doctoral thesis was written in 1923 and 1924, and for a time he and Princeton astronomer Henry Norris Russell were the only two practicing theoretical astrophysicists in America. Already an accomplished scientist known for wide-ranging interests and unflagging intellectual energy, he taught briefly at the University of Iowa and at Ohio State University. In 1926 he became assistant astronomer at Lick Observatory on Mount Hamilton in California, where he conducted pioneering astrophysical research. He met the celebrated physicist J. Robert Oppenheimer and from him learned how to apply atomic theory to astrophysics. Menzel joined the Harvard faculty on September 1, 1932, and achieved full professorship in 1938. He was appointed acting director of Harvard Observatory in 1952 and served as full director from 1954 to

1966. During this period the observatory became a major center for radio astronomy and other space research. From 1954 to 1956 he was elected president of the American Astronomical Society, and was its director-at-large between 1959 and 1961. Besides making significant contributions to other, nonastronomical areas of science—atmospheric geophysics, radio propagation and communication, and cryptanalysis, among others—from 1964 until his death, he was a State Department consultant in Latin American affairs. He retired from Harvard in 1971.

Although Menzel was active in numerous scientific, business, and government organizations, the standard biographies do not list him as a member of a group called Operation MJ-12. The one document linking him to this mysterious group arrived in December 1984 on a roll of 35mm film in an envelope addressed to the North Hollywood, California, residence of producer Jaime Shandera. There was no return address. When the film was developed, it revealed seven pages of a briefing supposedly given on November 18, 1952, to President-elect Dwight Eisenhower by Adm. Roscoe H. Hillenkoetter, first head of the CIA. The briefing paper reported that the U.S. government had recovered two crashed UFOs and the bodies of four extraterrestrial humanoids. On September 24, 1947, Operation Majestic-12 was established by executive order to oversee policy and research relating to such matters. Its members were 12 prominent figures in military, intelligence and science—all but one, Donald Menzel, known to have had high security clearances.

Following the release of the MJ-12 document to the public in the spring of 1987, **Stanton T. Friedman**, a ufologist and nuclear scientist, embarked on an investigation of Menzel's background and made some interesting discoveries. Friedman found that Menzel led a double life: one as a scientist, the other as the keeper of some of America's most important national-security secrets. This fact was not known even to his biographers, though his World War II chairmanship of the Radio Propagation Committee of the Joint and Combined Chiefs of

MENZEL, DONALD HOWARD (*continued*)

Staff (dealing with radar and communications matters) and of the Section of Mathematical and Physical Research of U.S. Naval Communications was in Menzel's public biographies.

Friedman's discoveries did not come easily. They required an enormous amount of research on his part, including probes into private archives and interviews with persons who never before had been approached on the subject. From them Friedman learned that Menzel had a long association with the highly-classified National Security Agency. He also possessed a Navy TOP SECRET ULTRA security clearance, did consulting for 30 industrial companies on classified projects, and worked for the CIA.

Friedman found that Vannevar Bush, President Harry Truman's chief science adviser and supposed MJ-12 member, had been a close professional associate and personal friend of Menzel's. In fact, they had known each other since 1934. During the McCarthy period, when through trumped-up charges Menzel was briefly deemed a security risk by the Air Force, his staunchest defender at the resulting secret hearings was Bush. Menzel also had known associations with other identified MJ-12 members such as Detlev Bronk and Lloyd Berkner. He was also known as a man who kept his mouth shut on national-security matters. Furthermore, as a communications specialist during the war, he knew well the effectiveness of disinformation as a technique of concealing secrets. In other words, contrary to what was known outside the intelligence community prior to the surfacing of the MJ-12 document, Menzel had the proper credentials to be picked to serve on a super-secret UFO project. But did this in fact happen?

According to Friedman, Menzel pretended to be a UFO debunker because he sought to keep "almost a whole generation of scientists in both the U.S.S.R. and the U.S.A. from even nibbling at the UFO phenomenon" (Friedman, 1988). His double role explains, he says, "how such an important astrophysicist could be such a lousy

ufologist." During his life Menzel was often criticized for his facile explanations of puzzling UFO reports, rejected even by Project Blue Book personnel.

Persons close to Menzel scoff at the suggestion that he secretly believed UFOs to be real. Psychiatrist and science-fiction writer Ernest Taves says he knew Menzel as well as anybody and saw no hint of a favorable view of possible extraterrestrial visitation in any private utterance. (Taves concedes, however, that if there had been a crashed UFO, Menzel would have been among those likely to be informed of its existence.) Menzel's widow, Florence, dismisses Friedman's suggestion as silly (Moseley, 1989).

Friedman counters that "denial is the standard response of close family and friends to surprises about people one has known very well for a long time. . . ." He writes, "For examples of people who have managed to lead double lives, one need not go far. Take the three Soviet spies who were well-established in the British Intelligence Service (MI-6), Burgess, MacLean and Philby. They fooled their associates, family, friends, for more than 15 years, in a very much more difficult situation. Klaus Fuchs was the brilliant scientist who turned over an enormous amount of information about the atomic bomb project to the Soviets. His traitorous efforts came as a complete shock to his associates." In Friedman's view Menzel led a similar double life, though as a patriot, not as a traitor.

"It is certainly true that I have not been able to provide a smoking gun about Donald Howard Menzel's involvement in Operation Majestic-12," Friedman acknowledges, but argues that Menzel "could very well have been a part of such a high-level group" and that he could have hidden that even from friends and family. Friedman speculates that Menzel's frequent trips in the 1947-49 period to Washington, D.C., and New Mexico (where the 1947 Roswell crash took place) were on MJ-12 business, despite a "cover story" that he was working on the "establishment of the Air Force-sponsored Sacramento Peak Observatory."

A critic would argue that the evidence for Menzel's role in a secret UFO project is thinly circumstantial at best. It is certainly interesting, possibly significant, that Menzel's heretofore-hidden life as an intelligence figure was found out, and only with difficulty, after the MJ-12 document appeared. This could be interpreted to mean that the document was written inside the intelligence community—other such officially-sponsored "disinformation" documents circulated throughout the 1980s—using information not then known to the unofficial public. The problem is not so much the idea that Menzel could have served as a disinformation agent as the particularly obsessive, even embarrassing way he went about it.

It would be wise to remember that Menzel was not only a patriot but a scientist as well, and a proud one at that. His UFO debunking was so incompetent as to be a stain on his scientific reputation. (Blue Book investigators noted, for example, that he could not even correctly explain sightings whose cause was known.) Would he have been willing to go that far even to protect national security—especially when he didn't have to? Menzel could have used his influence far less visibly to keep colleagues and others without security clearances away from UFO study. He could have quietly told fellow scientists that his research had convinced him UFOs are unworthy of their time; he could even have spoken on the subject at an occasional scientific conference. He was respected and his views would have been heeded. Perhaps he could have written an article or two for widely-read popular magazines to deliver the same message to a general office. These modest efforts would have sufficed.

It is rather less likely that Menzel would have acted, as he did, like a man obsessed. He would not have needed to write three books on the subject, putting himself farther and farther out on a limb which one day he would have known would surely be cut off. He would not have maintained a vast personal correspondence with witnesses, ufologists and other relative nonentities whose pro-UFO views could not possibly have threatened

government secrecy on the subject. In fact, the only people who had the resources to put the lie to official anti-UFO pronouncements were his scientific colleagues, and putting them off a scent they were not inclined to pursue anyway did not require these kinds of strenuous (and potentially humiliating) endeavors.

Until direct evidence of involvement with a secret UFO project comes to light, Menzel's career in ufology is better seen as a case history in pathological science than as a chapter in the cover-up saga.

Sources:

Friedman, Stanton T. "The Secret Life of Donald H. Menzel." *International UFO Reporter* 13, 1 (January/February 1988): 20-24.

Menzel, Donald H. *Flying Saucers.* Cambridge, MA: Harvard University Press, 1953.

Menzel, Donald H. *UFO: Fact or Fiction?* Cambridge, MA: The Author, 1967.

Menzel, Donald H. "UFO's—The Modern Myth." In Carl Sagan, and Thornton Page, eds. *UFO's–A Scientific Debate,* 123-182. New York: W. W. Norton & Company, 1972.

Menzel, Donald H., and Lyle G. Boyd. *The World of Flying Saucers: A Scientific Examination of a Major Myth of the Space Age.* Garden City, NY: Doubleday, 1963.

Menzel, Donald H., and Ernest H. Taves. *The UFO Enigma: The Definitive Explanation of the UFO Phenomenon.* Garden City, NY: Doubleday, 1977.

Moseley, James W. "Misc. Ravings." *Saucer Smear* 35, 1 (January 25, 1988): 1-2.

Sparks, Brad. *Refuting the Skeptics: A Close Look at Donald Menzel.* Berkeley, CA: The Author, 1977.

MENZEL, DONALD HOWARD (*continued*)

Story, Ronald D. *The Encyclopedia of UFOs.* Garden City, NY: Doubleday & Company, 1980.

MOORE, WILLIAM LEONARD (1943-)

William L. Moore was one of the most controversial figures in the ufology of the 1980s. He made his reputation initially as an investigator, with **Stanton T. Friedman,** of the Roswell incident, a long-neglected 1947 report of a UFO crash in New Mexico. In the late 1970s Moore and Friedman, suspecting the full story of the event (explained away as a misunderstanding resulting from the plummeting to earth of a radar-calibration device attached to a balloon) had not been told, interviewed dozens of first-, second- and third-hand participants and from their mutually-confirmatory accounts concluded that an alien spacecraft, possibly with humanoid bodies, had been recovered at the site. In 1980 Moore began a long association with military-intelligence personnel and even, by his own admission, informed them of the activities of some ufologist-colleagues. Moore's informants claimed that the U.S. government is in contact with extraterrestrial intelligences.

On May 28, 1987, Moore released a slightly-censored copy of a document his associate Jaime Shandera had received on a roll of 35mm film in the mail in December 1984. The document purports to be a briefing paper prepared for President-elect Dwight Eisenhower on December 18, 1952, informing him of the recovery of two UFOs, one near Roswell in 1947, the other along the Texas-Mexico border in 1950, and of the existence of a supersecret Operation Majestic-12, created by executive order of President Harry S Truman to oversee the study of extraterrestrial artifacts. The document, never verified yet never conclusively disproven, caused an uproar and was written about in the *New York Times* and discussed on ABC-TV's *Nightline.* Critics charged that Moore had forged the document, though clear evidence to that effect has never emerged. Other critics held that Moore was the victim of a disinformation scheme.

Born in Pittsburgh on October 31, 1943, William Leonard Moore received his B.A. from Thiel College in 1965 and did graduate work at Duquesne University and Moorhead State University. He taught English, French and humanities at several junior and senior high schools until he retired in 1979 to devote full time to writing and investigating. Moore is co-author, with Charles Berlitz, of *The Philadelphia Experiment* (1979) and *The Roswell Incident* (1980). From 1981 to 1985 he served on the board of directors of the Aerial Phenomena Research Organization (APRO). In the summer of 1984 he oversaw the incorporation of the Fair-Witness Project, intended "to investigate certain specific 'unusual events' which are known for their irregular parameters, and to publish the results of these inquiries." The project publishes a quarterly newsletter, *Focus,* which is co-edited by Moore and Jimmy Ward, and sells UFO literature. (The project's address is 4219 West Olive Avenue #247, Burbank, California 91505.)

Moore says, "A highly active extraterrestrial civilization is visiting planet Earth and is actively manipulating our awareness of their presence here. At least two of the U.S. government's intelligence agencies are aware of this, and both are presently conducting highly classified, on-going, UFO-related projects. . . . [A]t least one of these efforts (and probably both) has access to electromagnetic, optical and infrared signature data which, if released to the public, would provide proof positive that some UFOs represent someone else's highly advanced technology." Commenting on the government's role, Moore adds, "U.S. government counterintelligence people have conducted an on-again, off-again campaign of deception and disinformation against the American public about the UFO phenomenon for more than 40 years. . . . We have been able to establish that there is in fact a group known as MJ-12 which operates at the White House/National Security Council level. . . . The level of security around this group is such that we have not yet succeeded in establishing whether or not its functions are UFO-related or precisely how long it has been in existence . . . " (Moore, 1989).

Concerning the **abduction phenomenon**, Moore says, "The matter of alien abductions of humans is regarded as serious by those within the government who are aware of the extraterrestrial nature of UFOs. This is evidenced by the fact that the government has gone so far as to disinform its own counter-intelligence people on this subject. . . . The 'secret' behind the government UFO cover-up is essentially an awareness of what UFOs are by a few people in high places who have connections with the National Security Council and the White House. . . . Within the 'in group' there are strong differences of opinion as to whether information should be released to the public and how fast. There also seems to be some consternation about exactly who is in control of the situation" (Moore, 1989).

Sources:

"The MJ-12 UFO Documents: Major Breakthrough or Clever Hoax?" *Focus* 2, 8 (September 1, 1987): 1, 3-4.

Moore, William L. "Crashed Saucers: Evidence in Search of Proof." In Walter H. Andrus, Jr., and Richard H. Hall, eds. *MUFON 1985 UFO Symposium Proceedings*, 130-179. Seguin, TX: Mutual UFO Network, Inc., 1985.

Moore, William L. *An Excursion into the Unusual.* [Prescott, AZ: The Author, [1981?].

Moore, William L. *UFOs and the U.S. Government: Part I.* Burbank, CA: The Author, July 1, 1989.

Moore, William L., ed. *Nazi Flying Saucers.* Prescott, AZ: The Author, 1984. Rev. ed.: *Project V-7: Hitler's Flying Discs.* Burbank, CA: The Author, 1984.

Moore, William L., and Charles Berlitz. *The Roswell Incident.* New York: Grosset & Dunlap, 1980.

MUTUAL UFO NETWORK, INC.
103 Oldtowne Road
Seguin, Texas 78155

The Mutual UFO Network (MUFON) was founded in Quincy, Illinois, on May 31, 1969, under the direction of **Walter H. Andrus, Jr.,** who left the Tucson-based Aerial Phenomena Research Organization (APRO) to create the Midwest UFO Network, later renamed the Mutual UFO Network to reflect its expanded base. From the beginning it was conceived as a grass-roots organization, with state and local leadership overseeing activities and investigations in their area. One of the two major American membership groups (the other is the **J. Allen Hynek Center for UFO Studies,** head-quartered in Chicago), since 1975 it has operated out of Seguin, Texas, under Andrus' continued direction. MUFON, with many members in foreign countries (total membership is well over 1000), publishes the monthly magazine *MUFON UFO Journal* (called *Skylook* until its June 1976 issue), edited by Dennis Stacy. (Former editors include Norma E. Short, Dwight Connelly, Dennis William Hauck, Bob Pratt and **Richard Hall.**)

MUFON conducts a symposium each summer in a different North American city, where ufology's leading lights present current findings and theories. The lectures are published in an annual *MUFON UFO Symposium Proceedings.* A *MUFON Field Investigator's Manual* provides guidance to members who wish to look into reports in their area, and Dan Wright serves as the coordinator of investigations for the organization.

MUFON is governed by a board of directors consisting of 17 persons and administered by an executive committee. MUFON's board of consultants is made up of scientific, medical and other professionals. The organization holds no corporate views on the nature of the UFO phenomenon, though many of its officers and representatives have publicly expressed support for the extraterrestrial hypothesis (ETH). MUFON's statement of objectives makes its orientation clear:

"(1) Are UFOs some form of spacecraft

MUTUAL UFO NETWORK, INC. (*continued*)

controlled by advanced intelligence conducting a surveillance of Earth, or do they constitute some unknown physical or psychological manifestation that is not understood by 20th-Century science?

"(2) If UFOs are found to be extraterrestrial craft controlled by intelligent beings, what is their method of propulsion, or if they have the technique to operate in another dimension, how is this accomplished?

"(3) Postulating that they may be controlled by an extraterrestrial intelligence, where do they originate—in our universe or in another dimension?

"(4) Assuming that some of the craft are piloted by beings, what can we learn from their apparently advanced science and civilization that will benefit mankind on the planet Earth?"

Nonetheless, under Stacy's editorship the *MUFON UFO Journal* has taken to publishing pieces by proponents of the **psychosocial hypothesis**, which argues that UFO phenomena are the product of cultural processes and unusual mental states, as well as those by partisans of more traditional ufological views. After some readers protested, Andrus defended his editor, stating, "If we are to solve the UFO phenomenon in our lifetime . . . we must maintain an open mind as true scientists to various theories and hypotheses" (Andrus, 1989).

Sources:

Andrus, Walt. "Director's Message." *MUFON UFO Journal* 259 (November 1989): 30, 29.

Andrus, Walter H., Jr., ed. *MUFON 1989 International UFO Symposium Proceedings*. Seguin, TX: Mutual UFO Network, Inc., 1989.

Fowler, Raymond E., ed. *MUFON Field Investigator's Manual*. Seguin, TX: Mutual UFO Network, Inc., third edition, 1983.

Story, Ronald D. *The Encyclopedia of UFOs*. Garden City, NY: Doubleday & Company, 1980.

N

NEVADA AERIAL RESEARCH GROUP
Box 81407
Las Vegas, Nevada 89180

The Nevada Aerial Research Group, under the direction of "Val Valarian," the pseudonym of John Grace, declares it is committed to "investigate negative factors in the social structure" and "all processes that impede evolution of the species." It publishes an occasional *Newsletter* in which UFOs are treated as one element of a massive conspiracy against the human race. Another agent of the conspiracy is the drug-trafficking U.S. government, which in cooperation with aliens is engaged in a program to reprogram human genetics so that the human race can be enslaved without resistance. There is also a "secret space program" in which the evil American government, aliens, and genetically-created android agents are seeking dominion beyond the earth.

The conspirators, who seek "planetary control," have taken over UFO groups, **contactee** organizations, occultism, major religions, peace groups, all major media and press-wire services, financial institutions, the television networks, police and intelligence agencies, the American Medical Association, all significant Western political parties, Communism, the World Health Organization, all aerospace corporations, colleges and universities, the Rotarians, the Better Business Bureau, the Club of Rome, fraternities, political science and economic organizations, most European royal families, and *Playboy* and the *National Enquirer*. "This is only a partial list," the

September 1989 issue of the *Newsletter* cautions. The group's political beliefs are grounded in the conspiracy theories of the far right.

In the same issue, the group offers an account of who the UFO visitors—who are given various names such as the Greys, the Draconians, the Sirians, and so on—are and what their motives are:

"The Greys are an extremely old species. The older the species of the race the darker the skin. The Greys use the Flying Serpent Emblem. The Big-nosed Greys are featured in the Herbert Schirmer case. The Greys in generaloriginal [sic] from Ursa Major. They are members of the 4th Invader force.

"The Draconians are also part of the Markab Confederacy. Draconis is an operational center for the Confederacy. Both the Greys and the Draconians are members of what used to be called the Confederation of Espinol, but now they are know [sic] amongst themselves as the Imperial Alliance of Righteous Worlds. They use Pluto in our solar system for a way station and use bases on the Dark Side of the Moon for Earth access.

"The Sirians are a negative force that use the Eye of Horus (Eye in a Triangle) as one of their symbols. They also use lightning bolts. The MIB [men in black] are associated with the Sirians. The Sirians and the Essessani view the Earth as theirs. The Sirians being the first to colonize the Earth. The Sirians are humanoid. There are Sirian Blonds [sic] that enter and exit the North

NEVADA AERIAL RESEARCH GROUP
(*continued*)

Pole and frequent Canadian territories. Alpha Centari [sic] system is involved. . . ."

The group believes that the Ashtar Command, a early name used to designate extraterrestrial visitors by some UFO contactee organizations, especially those with a Spiritualist background, is a bogus group that originally started in Germany under the Thule Group. The Nazis had contact with negative Grey groups working out of the South Pole entrance to the hollow earth.

"The original two groups were the Federation of Planets, having the Sirians and the Essessani as members, and the Markab Confederacy, having the Greys and the Draconians as members. The Federation is made of groups in the 4th, 5th and 6th density, while the Markabs are primarily a negative 4th density, with some members acquired from Earth (third density). They also have a very small number of 5th density beings. The Markab Confederacy has about 25% of the entities that the Federation has.

"The Arcturans, often referred to as the Greys with the white skin, also feature bright glowing eyes. They are a younger race than the Greys, who are billions of years down the evolutionary scale in a devolving direction. . . .

"In 1908, the two groups agreed to an uneasy truce after a conflict which involved the Tungiska [sic] explosion."

Sources:

"Trap Groups Created or Infiltrated by Planetary Control." *Nevada Aerial Research Group Newsletter* (September 1989): 24-26.

NEW BEING PROJECT
Box 11542
Berkeley, California 97401

The New Being Project was created by David Pursglove, a New Age-oriented psychologist, who seeks "to develop and support ongoing groups composed of individuals with creative and respectful intent to invoke constructive, high quality communication with intelligences different from ourselves" (New Being Project, 1989). Pursglove calls these intelligences Other Consciousnesses (OCs). "The idea," he says, "is to avoid some of the narrow implications of the more common terms like 'visitors' (*We* may be the visitors, after all)."

Pursglove had moved Gestalt therapy to transpersonal psychology and from there to the study of altered states of consciousness. In 1988 he heard a speech by Esalen Institute director Michael Murphy, who suggested that human beings are on the verge of an evolutionary leap. One indication of this, he said, is the burgeoning of paranormal abilities, "budding limbs of new evolutionary growth" (Pursglove, 1989). Inspired to do what he could to facilitate this growth, Pursglove reflected on the importance of communications with nonhuman intelligences. Pursglove hopes to create "calling circles," with a maximum of eight members, in which individuals will gather at an isolated location for the purpose of contacting OCs through group telepathy, meditation or other means. Pursglove says he hopes to film any UFOs or beings who answer the calling circles.

The New Being Project has neither publication nor formal membership. It seeks to work with rather than direct persons who share its goals. "'E.T.' doesn't mean what you think it does," Pursglove writes. "It means *Evolutionary Transformation*."

Sources:

Calling Circles. Berkeley: The New Being Project, September 21, 1989.

Pursglove, David. Personal communication (October 12, 1989).

NORTHERN UFO NEWS
37 Heathbank Road
Cheadle Heath
Stockport, Cheshire SK3 0UP
England

Northern UFO News, edited by **Jenny Randles,** one of the giants of **British ufology,** for the Northern UFO Network (NUFON), was first issued in 1974. Its 16 pages of tiny print report on investigations, publications, theories and controversies in England but also, to some extent, in America and France. The regular "Media Matters" column takes note of how the British press, radio and television are treating UFOs and ufologists—usually abominably, Randles says. *Northern UFO News* is issued monthly.

O

ORBITER

c/o Jim Melesciuc
43 Harrison Street
Reading, Massachusetts 01867

Orbiter is a bimonthly newsletter, usually eight to 12 pages in length, of reporting and commentary on events current on the UFO scene. Editor Jim Melesciuc is a conservative, sometimes acerbic observer of the enthusiasms and excesses of his colleagues. For example, he has remained unimpressed by the photographs produced in support of the alleged **Gulf Breeze sightings**, a prominent incident in which an observer took pictures of what he claims are spacecraft, and he is highly suspicious of the MJ-12 document (which purported to detail a government coverup of crashed flying saucers). On the other hand he has not shown any enthusiastic acceptance of the work of professional debunkers.

OVNI-PRESENCE

L'Association d'Etude sur les Soucoupes Volantes
B.P. 324
F-13611 Aix-en-Provence
Cedex 1, France.

OVNI-Présence, published quarterly under the editorship of Yves Bosson, is a handsome-looking, four-color magazine at the forefront of **French ufology**. During the 1980s it emerged as one of the more important UFO journals in continental Europe with a wide range of coverage of the field, including news, investigative reports, reviews and theoretical essays.

OZ FACTOR

In *UFO Reality* (1983) **Jenny Randles** refers to the "sensation of being isolated, or transported from the real world into a different environmental framework," and suggests this feeling, occasionally reported by UFO witnesses, "is one of great importance to our understanding of UFOs. It is almost suggestive of the witness['] being transported temporarily from our world into another, where reality is but slightly different. . . . I call it 'the Oz Factor,' after the fairytale land of Oz." In *Sixth Sense* (1987), her study of psychic phenomena, Randles equates the Oz factor with what parapsychologists call "altered states of consciousness."

In the UFO context, one Oz Factor report took place on July 21, 1978, at 10:15 on a warm summer's evening in Davyhulme, Manchester, England, to a couple Randles calls Mr. and Mrs. W. The two observed a dark disc hovering in the twilight sky. It was surrounded by an aura, from which 30 to 40 beautiful purple "rays" shot out at various angles like spokes from a wheel, extending to about 12 times the diameter of the central disc. After 1½ minutes, Randles writes, "the 'rays' collapsed inwards in sequence, and the object slowly extinguished itself. It was massive, compared with the size of the rooftop opposite." During the sighting the Ws noted with puzzlement that the normally busy street was strangely quiet and devoid of vehicular or pedestrian traffic. Mrs. W said later that she felt "singled out" and "alone" as she and her husband watched the object.

OZ FACTOR (*continued*)

Another such incident was reported by Jean Findlay of Poole, Dorset. At 9:01 on the morning of December 6, 1980, as she was waiting for a bus, she felt an urge to "look up . . . almost as if a voice in my head told me to do so." She saw a disc-shaped UFO with a dome on top hovering above nearby trees. Feeling "spellbound" and experiencing a sensation of "peace, calm and warmth," she watched the object emit a beam of light, rotate once and fly away at a great rate of speed. When she looked at her watch, she found "time had flown by"—four minutes when it seemed as if the sighting had lasted only a few moments. Although the sighting had occurred at rush hour in a busy city, she said everything became "quiet" during the sighting and she saw no one else around.

A possible Oz Factor episode figures in a sighting reported in Novato, California, on April 15, 1989. At 5:30 that afternoon a father and son saw, from their front lawn and at about 75 degrees on the horizon, a slowly-descending object shaped like "two spheres connected together by a stem"—a dumbbell, in other words. The two spheres were golden with a white halo around them.

According to psychologist-UFO investigator **Richard F. Haines**, who interviewed the witnesses five weeks later, "the apparent angular size of the dumbbell was just less than the apparent width of [the father's] thumbnail (at arm's length) or about 1.5 degrees." By naked eye and through binoculars, four smaller objects, golden discs, maneuvered near the original object. Haines writes that the father "also noted the strange absence of kids and dogs at the time they watched the object. There are usually many present at this time of day." The witness remarked, "It was strange—there was no one else who saw it" (Haines, 1989). No report of the objects appeared in the newspapers.

In Randles' view, "The existence of the Oz factor certainly points towards the consciousness of the witness as the focal point of the UFO encounter. . . . [S]ubjective data that over-ride objective reality . . . could be internal (from a deeper level of ourselves) or external (for example, from some other intelligence). It may even be both."

Sources:

Haines, Richard F. "Daylight Dumbbell." *International UFO Reporter* 14, 5 (September/October 1989): 12-13, 23.

Randles, Jenny. *Sixth Sense*. Topsfield, MA: Salem House Publishers, 1987.

Randles, Jenny. *UFO Reality: A Critical Look at the Physical Evidence*. London: Robert Hale, 1983.

P

PARANET
Box 928
Wheatridge, Colorado 80034

ParaNet, founded in 1986, is an electronic international computer network owned and directed by Michael Corbin. It also has an investigation branch headed by Robert B. Klinn.

In 1989 ParaNet expanded its network operations into the worldwide Unix environment. It now publishes an electronic news digest containing its daily echomail traffic. The digest and other information are available to over 61,000 users. ParaNet has a large electronic library containing news clippings and articles submitted by subscribers and it has started a bimonthly print publication called *Odyssey*, which offers a capsulized version of what appears on ParaNet. The organization maintains relationships with the **Mutual UFO Network** (MUFON), the **J. Allen Hynek Center for UFO Studies** (CUFOS), and the Australian UFO Research Society (AUFORS). It also has bureau chiefs in Australia (Bob Fletcher) and the United Kingdom (Archie Clark).

"It's an electronic revolution," Corbin says. "Through our international reporting center we can take a report, assign investigators and place a report on the network. Thousands of our subscribers can know what is going on virtually instantly."

PENNSYLVANIA ASSOCIATION FOR THE STUDY OF THE UNEXPLAINED
6 Oakhill Avenue
Greensburg, Pennsylvania 15601

The Pennsylvania Association for the Study of the Unexplained (PASU) was formed in 1981 by Stan Gordon to supersede the earlier Pennsylvania Center for UFO Research (formed in 1975), which in turn replaced the Westmoreland County UFO Study Group (1970). Gordon also headed these two latter groups.

PASU is a volunteer group, headquartered in Greensburg, consisting of about 120 active members, described as "selected individuals with training or experience in the fields of science, engineering, technology, or medicine, who act as field investigators." Assisting these investigators are technical consultants who, when the occasion warrants, test samples in their laboratories. PASU combines a primary interest in UFO sightings with a broader concern for creature reports (such as accounts of Bigfoot/Sasquatch) and anomalous animal killings/mutilations. Gordon, whose files on Pennsylvania anomalies go back to the 1940s, believes UFOs and Bigfoot-like creatures (which have been reported in his area) are related.

In Gordon's personal view UFOs may have various origins: extraterrestrial, extradimensional or even underwater, but PASU takes no official position, holding only that while a high percentage of UFO reports] can be logically explained, many well-documented incidents remain essentially

PENNSYLVANIA ASSOCIATION FOR THE STUDY OF THE UNEXPLAINED (*continued*)

unexplained." PASU works closely with the Mutual UFO Network (MUFON).

The organization publishes an irregular newsletter, *PASU Data Exchange*, which reports on recent claims, sightings and investigations.

Sources:

Gordon, Stan. Personal communication (October 10, 1989).

Nilson, Todd. "UFO Group: Is Something Out There?" *Greensboro* [Pennsylvania] *Tribune Review* (August 14, 1989).

PSYCHOSOCIAL HYPOTHESIS

The roots of what would become known as the psychosocial hypothesis, which holds that UFO experiences are largely psychological in nature and which by the 1980s would be widely popular in ufology, are to be found in a book by Carl Gustav Jung (1875-1961), the eminent Swiss psychotherapist and philosopher. First published in Switzerland in 1958 as *Ein Moderner Mythus von Dingen, die am Himmel gesehen werden*, it appeared the following year in English as *Flying Saucers: A Modern Myth of Things Seen in the Skies*. An interesting though minor work (at least relative to Jung's earlier writings, in which he laid the groundwork for analytical psychology and to which this book is no more than a long footnote), it represents Jung's reflections less on UFOs as such, though they do flit in and out of the text, as on dreams, paintings, visions and science-fiction novels in which more-or-less UFO-like images are depicted.

In his introduction Jung wrote that his "conscience as a psychiatrist . . . bids me fulfil my duty and prepare those few who will hear me for coming events which are in accord with the end of an era." There were "symptoms of psychic change" in the air (in the most literal sense). "We are now nearing," he said, "that great change which may be expected when the spring point enters Aquarius," a time of transition comparable to the emergence of the Piscean age, "whose beginning coincides with the rise of Christianity." One symptom of this is reports of flying saucers, an "ostensibly physical phenomenon" which "provokes . . . conscious and unconscious fantasies." Jung believed that the uncertainties of the age, caused by a dominance of rational (conscious) thought over intuitive (unconscious) feeling, were bringing images from deep within the collective unconscious to the surface. The flying saucer, frequently reported as circular in shape, represents an archetype of psychic wholeness, in which both sides of the mind are in balance, and so becomes a focus for fantasies and hopes of a mystical religious nature.

"If the round shining objects that appear in the sky be regarded as visions," he wrote, "we can hardly avoid interpreting them as archetypal images. They would then be involuntary, automatic projections based on instinct, and as little as any other psychic manifestations and symbols can they be dismissed as meaningless and merely fortuitous. . . . [C]ircular symbols have played an important role in every age. . . . There is an old saying that 'God is a circle whose center is everywhere and the circumference nowhere.' God in his omniscience, omnipotence, and omnipresence is a totality symbol *par excellence*, something round, complete, and perfect. Epiphanies of this sort are, in the tradition, often associated with fire and light. They are impressive manifestations of totality whose simple, round form portrays the archetype of the self, which . . . plays the chief role in uniting apparently irreconcilable opposites and is therefore best suited to compensate the split-mindedness of our age."

UFOs fulfill humanity's expectations of a redeeming supernatural event, Jung speculated. He cautions, however, that this does not explain what UFOs are, only how some people see them. The book mentions actual UFO sightings only briefly. In a short closing chapter, "UFOs

Considered in a Non-Psychological Light," Jung indicates that psychology cannot explain the UFO phenomenon as such and that the world's then-most prominent UFO debunker, Prof. **Donald H. Menzel,** "has not succeeded, despite all his efforts, in offering a satisfying scientific explanation of even one authentic UFO report. It boils down to nothing less than this: that either psychic projections throw back a radar echo, or else the appearance of real objects affords an opportunity for mythological projections."

Reflecting on the implications of his statement, Jung remarked that the "notion of a materialized psychism [a psychic phenomenon with physical properties] opens a bottomless void under our feet. . . . [T]his surpasses our comprehension." (As we shall see, however, it would not surpass the comprehension of later theorists.) Moreover, he notes, the evidence gathered by psychical research gives us no reason to believe such dramatic mind-over-matter manifestations are possible. He suggests another possibility: that UFOs are spacecraft that have quietly visited the earth for a long time but just now are being noticed because people's "earthly existence feels threatened [and] unconscious contents have projected themselves on these inexplicable heavenly phenomena and given them a significance they in no way deserve." Their presences here at a crucial moment in human history "coincide in a meaningful manner," though they "bear no causal relationship to one another." Jung here alludes to his famous concept of synchronicity.

In retrospect Jung's book seems a sensible and modest statement which unlike much psychological speculation to follow does not stray beyond the boundaries of evidence and logic (if, of course, one accepts Jung's premise that archetypes of the collective unconscious exist in nature and not just as intellectual constructs). *Flying Saucers: A Modern Myth* was mostly ignored by ufologists, who saw it as largely irrelevant to their interests, and misread by journalists, who reported that Jung had dismissed flying saucers as fantasy. Jung made no further pronouncements on the subject and died unaware of what a later generation would do with his ideas.

Magonians and Ultraterrestrials: **Jacques Vallee,** although not a Jungian (ufologists would not rediscover Jung until a few years later), would be the first individual within ufology to lay out the basic elements of what would become known as the psychosocial hypothesis. In 1965 and 1966 Vallee had written two books, *Anatomy of a Phenomenon* and *Challenge to Science: The UFO Enigma* (the latter with his wife, Janine Vallee), in which he argued impressively, as a trained astrophysicist, that extraterrestrial visitation is the most reasonable reading of the UFO evidence. But in 1969 he produced an entirely different kind of book, one in which, he acknowledged in the preface, had nothing to do with science. He said, "I frankly confess it: I entirely forgot that I was a scientist by profession when I began the manuscript of *Passport to Magonia.* My only guide has been the persistent feeling that science had offered no answer to some basic needs in our hearts, and that perhaps the present loneliness of man, echoed in the great miseries of times past, had provided most of the emotional power, most of the intellectual quality, mobilized in that unreachable goal: Magonia—a place where gentle folks and graceful fairies dance, and lament the coarse world below."

The term "Magonia" comes from a Latin manuscript, *Liber contra insulam vulgi opinionem* (A.D. 840), written by the Archbishop of Lyons as an expression of outrage against what he viewed as popular superstitions. The archbishop raged, "We have . . . heard so much foolishness, so much stupidity and enmity, that [people in the Lyons area] believe and say there is a certain region called Magonia from whence come ships in the clouds. . . ." In the nineteenth century, puzzling over ninth and tenth century traditions of cloud ships and their occupants, the folklorist Jacob Grimm suggested that "'Magonia' takes us to some region where Latin was spoken, if we may rely on it referring to Magus, i.e., a magic land."

Although the Magonia reference was brought into ufology (in "Spacemen in Norman Times," *Flying Saucer Review*, March/April 1966) by the late W. R. Drake, a pre-Erich von Däniken enthusiast of ancient astronauts and a **contactee**

PSYCHOSOCIAL HYPOTHESIS (*continued*)

follower, the term would come to represent an approach which eschewed extraterrestrial UFOs. A decade after Vallee's *Passport to Magonia*, a British UFO magazine would rename itself *Magonia* and become the principal outlet, in the English language at least, for psychosocial speculators.

Passport did not spring out of nowhere. Although it was the first major book by a ufologist to question the extraterrestrial hypothesis, England's *Flying Saucer Review* (generally referred to as *FSR*), which under Charles Bowen's editorship had become the leading UFO magazine in the world, was seeking alternative interpretations of UFO reports as early as 1965. The impetus was the first serious research into the 1896-97 "airship" wave. Reports of dirigible-shaped objects from that era had been noted as early as 1919, in Charles Fort's *The Book of the Damned*, arguably the first UFO book; Fort took note of a few of the more dramatic fly-over reports and suggested these were vehicles from another world. In 1950 Donald E. Keyhoe, who would become head of the National Investigations Committee on Aerial Phenomena (NICAP), devoted a few sentences to the airship sightings but added little to what Fort had written, and other, subsequent books would cite the 1896-97 sightings as evidence that UFOs were appearing five decades before the Kenneth Arnold sighting of June 24, 1947, brought in the UFO age. But little effort was made to learn more until the early 1960s when Jerome Clark, Lucius Farish and Charles Flood went back to original newspaper accounts and resurrected hundreds of reports.

These reports seemed incompatible with the extraterrestrial hypothesis. It turned out that the reports were not, for the most part anyway, of cigar-shaped "spaceships" but of craft that were clearly airships, though of types of airships then unknown in America. (Charles H. Gibbs-Smith would declare, "Speaking as an aeronautical historian who specializes in the periods before 1910, I can say with certainty that the only airborne vehicles, carrying passengers, which could

possibly have been seen anywhere in North America in 1897 were free flying spherical balloons, and it is highly unlikely for these to be mistaken for anything else. No form of dirigible [i.e., a gasbag propelled by an airscrew] or heavier-than-air flying machine was flying—or indeed *could* fly—at this time in America" [Clark, 1966].) Moreover, in most of the landing/close-encounter stories reported in the newspapers, the occupants identified themselves as ordinary Americans who had invented marvelous flying machines and who soon would be announcing as much to the world. It was clear that the earlier, abbreviated accounts of the airship in the literature were misleading.

In a series of articles in *FSR* Clark gave the UFO community its first clear look at what the airship phenomenon really was about. In an article in the July/August 1966 issue, Clark, noting the "Magonia" story, suggested a reflective quality to UFO appearances, with the objects and their occupants conforming to cultural expectations and "supporting the technology and temperament of the times." If this is so, he speculates, perhaps modern "extraterrestrial" UFOs are not what they appear to be either. Clark did not reject the idea that an other-intelligence might be behind these manifestations, but expressed agnosticism about the nature of that presumed intelligence.

Not long afterwards **John A. Keel**, a New York-based writer and admirer of Charles Fort, set out to write what was intended to be the definitive book on UFOs. A generous advance from his publisher allowed him to spend some months in the Ohio River Valley, where unidentified flying objects were being reported along with an unidentified flapping object, a monstrous flying creature dubbed "Mothman" after a character in the *Batman* television series. Keel talked with persons who claimed bizarre contactee experiences (some of which other investigators would later determine to be hoaxes), encounters with menacing and not-quite-human "men in black," monsters, poltergeists and other extraordinary manifestations. Keel even claimed some strange experiences of his own. From all this he concluded (in articles that appeared in a variety of periodicals from *FSR* to men's magazines such as *Saga* and *Male*) that "ultraterrestrials," rather than extraterrestrials, were responsible for these manifestations. The ultraterrestrials, an incomprehensible intelligence from another reality, are able to create and manipulate matter, and they don various guises (as spacemen, demons, angels, nineteenth-century aeronauts, fairies, creatures) as they go about their sinister business, which often results in psychological or even physical harm to human beings, whom they hold in contempt. In his writings, including his *magnum opus, UFOs: Operation Trojan Horse* (1970), Keel launched emotional attacks on "UFO buffs" too ignorant, foolish or frightened to face the truth about ultraterrestrial intrusion.

Within ufology he would be both hated and loved. Even his admirers acknowledged, however, that his conclusions outdistanced his evidence by some considerable margin, that his historical, psychological and social analysis was amateurish, that many of the reports he cited were questionable, that the extreme kinds of experiential claims on which he was fixated were hardly characteristic of the UFO phenomenon as a whole, and that his speculations were laced with paranoia. Yet no one denied that as a teller of scary stories he could be wonderfully entertaining. More important, by the sheer volume and intensity of his assault on conventional ufological wisdom, he drew the attention of many from the traditional evidence (daylight discs, radar/visual cases, the more credible close encounters) to the phenomenon's wild and woolly fringes. Soon even a few of ufology's less excitable thinkers would begin at least to entertain the idea that Keel might be right after all, that the truth lay out there on the fringes, where, just as Keel had claimed, all sorts of outrageous occurrences were being reported. Those who came after Keel would come to conclusions very different from his, but Keel would help them to get there.

Keel, of course, was not ready, as the psychosocial theorists of the next generation would be, to write aliens, however defined, out of the UFO equation. Neither was Vallee, despite a certain coyness (which he would come to regret)

on the issue. But between them the two proposed a model of the UFO phenomenon which within a few years would lead others to conclude other-intelligences are unnecessary.

It is important to emphasize that what was happening as Keel and Vallee sought to reshape and redefine the UFO phenomenon had nothing to do with science. Openly anti-intellectual, Keel expressed nearly as much contempt for scientists and other eggheads as he did for the despised "UFO buffs." (In his disdain for science Keel stood in the Fortean tradition, though more as defined by Tiffany Thayer, the angry, crankish social critic who founded the Fortean Society [to study the scientific anomalies first described in the books of Charles Fort (1874-1932)], than by the gentle, good-natured Fort himself.) Vallee, something of an intellectual himself, did not hold his educated colleagues in disdain; he felt merely that the UFO phenomenon could be understood only as a transcendental experience, something science could not comprehend; thus according to Vallee, to be able to write on the subject, he "forgot" his scientific training.

In *Passport to Magonia* the groundwork for the psychosocial hypothesis is laid. It would be one of the most influential books ever written on UFOs, but its influence would not be on the larger public, which took little notice of it. Its effect was entirely on ufologists, especially on a younger generation who were not technically trained, who had no desire to believe in a technological UFO phenomenon and who themselves were being moved by the currents of the 1960s counterculture. More than any other ufological writer, Vallee spoke in a 1960s voice, expressing, with sentimental melancholy, a vision of a preindustrial, pastoral world in which it was possible to believe in graceful fairies dwelling amid rocks and in green meadows.

Vallee, like Jung and all the psychosocial speculators to come, assumes implicitly that UFO phenomena fulfill some human "need." Vallee does not further define that need, except to note the obvious: that human beings, at least some of them, enjoy dreaming and fantasizing. As he

PSYCHOSOCIAL HYPOTHESIS (*continued*)

outlines his case, he cites anecdotes selected from the pioneering folklore studies of W. Y. Evans-Wentz (*The Fairy-Faith in Celtic Countries* [1911]) and Thomas Keightley (*The Fairy Mythology* [1878]), who had recorded beliefs about fairies and other supernatural denizens of the earth, and argues that such tales are comparable to modern UFO experiences. But these earlier experiences, because they occurred in a different cultural context, took on a different surface form. Yet underneath these and other otherworldly encounters, such as those reported in religious texts of medieval Europe and in the technological contexts of 1897 airships (which Vallee believes "especially relevant in this connection") and late-twentieth-century UFO/spacecraft, is the same hidden hand. Vallee believes that the mechanisms that have generated these various beliefs are the same and that the phenomenon has some stable, invariant features. But, he adds, it also has a "chameleonlike character: the shapes of the objects, the appearances of their occupants, their reported statements, vary as a function of the cultural environment into which they are projected."

According to Vallee, "the UFO phenomenon does appear to have a real effect" on human culture, and this can be no coincidence. It says something, in his view, about the nature and purpose of the phenomenon, which may occasion a "new mythological movement and . . . give our technological age its Olympus, its fairyland, or its Walhalla. . . . Because many observations of UFO phenomena appear self-consistent and at the same time irreconcilable with scientific knowledge, a logical vacuum has been created that human imagination tries to fill with its own fantasies." Here Vallee echoes Jung, as he does in the assertion that follows: "Such situations have been frequently observed in the past, and they have given us both the highest and the basest forms of religious, poetic, and political activity." On this last point he subsequently elaborates, offering a foreshadowing of the conspiracy themes that would figure in later (and forgettable) books such as *The Invisible College* (1975) and *Messengers of*

Deception (1979): "The entire myth we are discussing contains all the elements of a myth that could be utilized [sic] to serve political or sociological purposes, a fact illustrated by the curious link between the contents of the reports themselves and the progress of human technology, from aerial ships to dirigibles to ghost rockets to flying saucers—a link that has never received a satisfactory interpretation in a sociological framework."

Vallee remarks that a 1950 novel by Bernard Newman, *The Flying Saucer*, contained the "first reference to UFO effects on car ignition." (Actually, the first known such case occurred in the spring of 1944 near Auberry, California.) He remarks that the "fact remains that the coincidences between these works of imagination [the Newman novel and a 1933 play by Arthur Koestler about extraterrestrials who warn humanity, as in later contactee claims, to mend its ways] and the actual details of the reports that came from the public is a remarkable one, and it opens the way to unlimited speculation." Indeed it would; later, as we shall see, a French ufologist, a champion of the psychosocial hypothesis, would explore it at book's length.

It is possible, though only with the closest possible reading, to conclude that Vallee thinks a nonhuman intelligence is behind these varying phenomena. A more casual reading leads to the opposite conclusion, that the phenomena are illusory, the products of cultural and folkloric processes. He offers several conjectures to "explain" the occurrences: "a natural phenomenon whose manifestations border on both the physical and the mental"; "mental entities"; "a superior intelligence . . . projecting various artificial objects whose creation is a pure form of art." But then he says he "must apologize. . . . I only wanted to show how quickly one could be carried into pure fantasy. . . ." Later he writes that the "search may be futile; the solution may lie forever beyond our grasp. . . . Perhaps what we search for is no more than a dream. . . . We cannot be sure that we study something real. . . ."

Although elegantly written, *Passport to Magonia*

is a flawed book, more successful as a literary exercise than as a serious analysis of the UFO phenomenon. Vallee's reading of folklore is simplistic; the parallels between traditional fairy beliefs and modern UFO encounters are, as folklorist **Thomas E. Bullard** has written, "oblique and speculative" (Bullard, 1987). Vallee picks and chooses his material carefully and in the process fails to do justice to the richness and complexity of fairylore which, when seen in its entirety (as documented by Evans-Wentz and Keightley as well as such modern scholars as the late Katharine Briggs), intersects with UFO lore rarely and fleetingly. The most obvious intersection is in the belief that fairies, like UFO occupants, are mostly small in size, though there are no ufological equivalents to brownies, banshees, mine goblins, fairy animals, mermaids, selkies, or any number of the varied entities (and behaviors associated with them) catalogued in, for example, Briggs' *An Encyclopedia of Fairies* (1976). Vallee notes the belief that time is different in fairyland and tries to link this idea with missing-time episodes in the UFO **abduction phenomenon**. The latter, however, have to do with amnesia (i.e., a memory anomaly), not with time supernaturally expanded or compressed. Moreover, Vallee's citation of claims later proven to be hoaxes (an 1897 airship calf-napping; a 1915 mass disappearance of a British regiment; a 1963 Wiltshire, England, "UFO landing") as "real-life" equivalents to fairy and folk traditions hardly inspires confidence. (Further, owing to Vallee's vagueness concerning key elements of his argument, it is never entirely clear whether Vallee believes encounters with fairies were in some sense real-life experiences [or even how that determination could be made when one is relying on literary texts quoting long-dead informants from remote places]. At some points he seems to be arguing one way, then another, and then at times intimating that it makes no difference. But of course it does, if one seeks to make a coherent argument, or draw a distinction between scientific inquiry and literary criticism.)

Most damning of all, perhaps, was Vallee's reliance on turn-of-the-century airship accounts, which subsequent investigators, notably Clark,

Bullard and Robert Neeley, would find to be almost wholly without substance. If the most distinguishing feature of modern UFO reports is that the most puzzling of them usually withstand the most rigorous investigation, the airship stories were notable for the rapidity of their collapse under scrutiny. Every close-encounter claim about which sufficient information existed to make investigation possible proved a hoax, usually a journalistic invention or a tall tale spun by a practical joker. Most of the fly-over reports turned out to be of astronomical bodies or of balloons launched by pranksters. The "airship phenomenon," in short, was nothing more than a combination joke/mild-mass-hysteria episode—so transparent, in fact, that this determination could be made decades after the fact, without personal access (in all but a handful of instances) to witnesses and informants. This constituted a fundamental departure from the modern UFO phenomenon which, whatever its cause, resists such accounting even under far more favorable conditions for investigators.

Emergence of the Psychosocial Model: The first explicit statement of the psychosocial hypothesis was Jerome Clark and Loren Coleman's *The Unidentified* (1975), which rejected the notion of alien involvement in UFO experiences and employed Jungian analysis to unlock the alleged symbolic meaning of the same sorts of claims on which Vallee drew: religious visions, fairylore, nineteenth-century aeronauts, and modern contactee tales. Clark and Coleman wrote that the "UFO mystery is primarily subjective and its content primarily symbolic," and experiences of it are largely the product of unusual mental states. Its ideas, with elaborations and variations, would form the basis of a large body of UFO literature in the next 15 years.

"No one knows just how it is that an individual comes to enter the otherworld," they write, referring to the imaginary realm of Magonia. "The 'X Factor,' however, seems to have to do with the lowering of the threshold of consciousness, when one's psychic barriers are relaxed and the ego is vulnerable. This can occur when one conscientiously seeks out the experience

PSYCHOSOCIAL HYPOTHESIS (*continued*)

through the ritual use of psychedelic drugs, ecstasy, sleep, and other self-induced methods. Sometimes it can occur when one is engaged in some monotonous pursuit requiring minimal mental activity: driving a car along a deserted road at night, working at an undemanding job . . . fishing . . . and so on. Sometimes the sudden appearance of an 'objective' manifestation [such as an airplane or a star misinterpreted as a UFO] may provoke an agitated state in which one's hold on ordinary reality is so shaken that the ego is temporarily overwhelmed by the contents of the collective unconscious."

Following in the tradition first enunciated by Jung, Clark and Coleman maintain that UFO visions are the psyche's attempt to escape the stranglehold that strict rationalism has on twentieth-century humanity. The purpose is to restore what is seen as the natural balance between the mind's thinking and feeling aspects. From this perspective, they argue, "If this balance is not soon restored, the UFO myth tells us, nature will have its way. The collective unconscious, too long repressed, will burst free, overwhelm the world, and usher in an era of madness, superstition, and terror—with all their sociopolitical accoutrements: war, anarchy, fascism. . . . When the unconscious can no longer be contained, its liberated contents will destroy all that the conscious mind has produced: the fruits of science and technology, civilized order, and the very process of reason itself. . . . In the way the UFO phenomenon symbolizes, often naively, the resolution of the great dualities which trouble our time—in it, as John Rimmer has demonstrated, magic and machine are one—it sounds a warning and yet it offers us hope."

Perhaps the kindest thing that can be said about this sort of speculation is that it is "romantic." It would be attacked by no less than one of its authors, Clark, who came to feel its conclusions were as unverifiable and ill-conceived as they were grandiose. Moreover, they did not address in any coherent way the evidence associated with some of the most puzzling UFO cases: ground traces,

radar/visual trackings, photographs and other phenomena traditionally central to any consideration of the UFO question. In later years Clark would characterize *The Unidentified*, in print, as "naive" and "phenomenally silly" (Clark, 1989).

Yet, although it was hardly a popular success, the book, like *Passport*, made an impact on ufology. Already the *Merseyside UFO Bulletin*, subsequently renamed *Magonia*, was exploring what its major contributors, such as John Rimmer, Peter Rogerson and Roger Sandell, saw as the psychological, social and folkloric dimensions of the UFO phenomenon, and suggesting that UFO experiences had more to do with altered states of consciousness than with alien visitors from elsewhere.

Although English-speaking psychosocial theoreticians would be criticized for their consistent preference for the armchair over the field, this was less true of some of the leading voices in **French ufology** such as Michel Monnerie, who wrote two skeptical books (*Et si les OVNIs N'existaient pas?* [1977] and *Le Naufrage des Extraterrestres* [1979]). These books would have been seen as standard debunking exercises—with the usual arguments: witnesses are deluded or deceitful; ufologists are gullible, and so on—had the author not come from within the UFO community and, just as important, had he not argued that visions experienced in altered states of consciousness (rather than hoaxes, the traditional debunking explanation) are the principal cause of close-encounter claims. Monnerie would later claim, without justification, to be the inventor of the psychosocial hypothesis and the "first ufologist to suggest that we should consider man as the center of the problem" (Monnerie, 1987).

In 1979 a more important book, Gérard Barthel and Jacques Brucker's *La Grande Peur Martienne*, appeared. Its authors declared they had reinvestigated the great autumn 1954 French UFO wave, the subject of Aimé Michel's *Flying Saucers and the Straight-Line Mystery* (1958), and determined that many of the most celebrated cases were dubious. Michel had relied primarily on newspaper accounts, which Barthel and Brucker learned were unreliable. They concluded from their investigation that *no* UFOs exist, although a more modest conclusion would have been more supportable, if less sweeping: one should not place too much faith in newspaper accounts of UFO sightings. Yet because the 1954 wave had loomed so large in French UFO history—it is probably the one episode in French UFO history that every ufologist everywhere has heard of—Barthel and Brucker's work had an extraordinary effect on ufology in France, causing the psychosocial hypothesis to become the French UFO theory of choice and to some considerable extent relegating the extraterrestrial hypothesis (ETH), ironically, to the few French scientists actively involved in field investigation. In France, as elsewhere, the psychosocial hypothesis, which would appeal almost exclusively to nonscientists, is itself a psychosocial response to the UFO phenomenon, a nontechnical model of the phenomenon suitable to the liberal-arts majors, librarians, social scientists, Jungians and counterculturists who are its major proponents.

Another significant French psychosocial work—one directly traceable to a brief remark of Vallee's in *Passport* (see above)—is Bertrand Méheust's *Science Fiction et Soucopes Volantes* (1978), which compared old (pre-1947) science-fiction stories with modern UFO accounts that contain some of the same elements. Méheust does not claim that witnesses read these obscure yarns and patterned hoaxes after them, as one perhaps might expect, but asserts boldly that both science-fiction writers and UFO percipients are drawing on the same well of images in the human imagination. A more likely explanation is coincidence. There is a vast body of pre-1947 fantastic literature dealing with imagined aliens, and very little of it anticipates modern UFO phenomena. But when one considers the quantity of this literature, it would be surprising indeed if on occasion a writer did not conjure up an idea that later would have a "real-life" parallel in a UFO experience—just as spectacular real-life crimes are sometimes anticipated in crime fiction. Metheust would have done well to argue a more modest but plausible

case, which could have been accomplished with the more pragmatic approach taken by psychical researchers, who have been able to trace some reincarnation and spirit-return stories to printed or other sources *with which the investigators were able to establish the claimants were familiar.* In other words, the investigators were not content simply to observe that such sources existed and to speculate loosely that in some unfathomable way images are held in psychic space and released, in precisely identical form, to individuals widely separated in time and space. Jung, whose own speculations are daring enough, held that archetypal images from the collective unconscious are alike only in the *broadest* sense.

One of England's leading psychosocial theoreticians, Peter Rogerson, writes that he got interested in UFOs as a schoolboy, read the major books and joined a local group, composed largely of ignorant and gullible individuals. Then the "Appollo [sic] moonshot . . . destroyed my naive faith in the ETH [extraterrestrial hypothesis]. The idea of electromagnetic spaceships visiting the Earth seemed somehow absurd. . . . I [took] a serious interest in parapsychology, and I soon realized that serious psychic researchers thought along very different lines from the occult gibberish which circulated in UFO groups. The final synthesis was easy. Ufologists had argued that the UFOs had always been with us, and deeply involved with human culture, and acted like apparitions. The answer seemed simple: UFOs were created by people, they were products of the human imagination, and were hallucinatory, like apparitions. I still thought along fairly radical lines, involving collective hallucinations, psi, idea patterns and a collective unconscious possibly able to alter the physical environment. Over the intervening years I have been forced to de-escalate hypotheses as it became clear that a far wider range of cases can be explained in 'normal' terms than was once thought possible" (Rogerson, 1984). Rogerson goes on to declare that UFO encounters can be easily explained as simple, or complex, dreams and hallucinations.

This sounds more like a statement of faith—perhaps it was intended to be—than a logical

PSYCHOSOCIAL HYPOTHESIS (*continued*)

argument. What American moon-landings have to say, positive or negative, about extraterrestrial UFOs will probably be unclear to everyone but Rogerson, and the attraction of the crankish and the credulous to flying-saucer clubs is an undeniable social fact but does not help us to explain well-documented, high-strangeness UFO cases, such as landing-trace and radar/visual incidents, which have puzzled the noncrankish and the nongullible—and which by the early 1980s (when Rogerson was writing) had become notably absent from the writings of the psychosocial pundits. The UFO phenomenon of the psychosociologists' universe consisted almost entirely of bizarre and extreme claims: "entity encounters," as one would call them, involving men in black, monsters, angelic Space Brothers and other nonevidential fringe claims.

Evans' Entities: The limitations of the psychosocial hypothesis are nowhere more apparent than in the writings of its leading English-language proponent, **Hilary Evans**, whose books *Visions, Apparitions, Alien Visitors* (1984) and *Gods, Spirits, Cosmic Guardians* (1987) recount a wide range of "entity" experiences, pronounce them related, and then explain them as psychological events which occur because the percipient "needs" them to happen; the stimulus may even be a need, Evans says, that the individual doesn't know he has—but which Evans is able to detect. Evans' speculations about "needs" are based, it appears, on a sort of instant analysis of persons he "knows" only because he has read a few sentences or paragraphs about them and their experiences in a book on psychical research, religious visions, or ufology. (Near the conclusion of *Visions*, after reporting on a psychological study of a victim of multiple-personality disorder, Evans laments the lack of "detailed studies of other percipients" so that we could "establish their motivation more clearly," but adds that the "majority of entities . . . *plainly* [emphasis added] reveal in broad terms the role they are playing in a percipient's life." Such speculations, founded as they are on Evans' subjective impressions from very little evidence, have no empirical basis.) Evans' speculations

often seem based on a tautology which might be expressed this way: Why did X have an entity experience? Because he had certain psychological needs. How do we know he had these needs? Because he had an entity experience.

Evans is convinced both that "belief systems" underlie people's anomalous experiences and that because he himself is part of no "belief system" he can render objective judgments on these matters. (At one point Evans implicitly includes himself among those persons [such as psychologists and parapsychologists] who work outside a belief system—as if the various forms of psychology are not themselves "belief systems"—and who can therefore reject the idea that anomalous encounters need an underlying external agent—as if that too, in the absence of conclusive evidence either way, were not itself an expression of a belief system.) He cites the work of iconoclastic behavioral scientist/folklorist David J. Hufford but with little understanding of one of Hufford's major arguments—that psychological deconstructions of anomalous experiences often are at their core as much based in culturally-determined, unexamined assumptions (sometimes called faith) as are "believers'" arguments. And at least believers, Hufford notes, often have the benefit of direct experience with the anomaly in question.

In a penetrating essay in a folklore journal Hufford remarks on the "standard skeptical view of supernatural belief—a view that has existed for centuries, probably millennia—namely, that supernatural beliefs arise from and are supported by various kinds of obvious error. . . . The research design begins with the question 'Why and how do some people manage to believe things which are so patently false? . . .' Such a perspective has its usefulness but . . . it is necessarily ethnocentric in the most fundamental sense. It takes a body of knowledge and considers it to be simply 'the way things are' rather than a product of culture. It says over and over again: 'What *I* know I *know*, what you know you only *believe*'. . . ." (Hufford, 1982b).

Evans declares early in his *Visions* book that it is a "fact" that "we do not have a scrap of evidence for the extraterrestrial origin of UFOs." If this were true, of course, there would be no controversy about UFO reports. Belief in UFOs as possible spacecraft would be confined in its entirety to crackpots. This is demonstrably not the case; prominent and informed skeptics such as Marcello Truzzi and Daniel Cohen, who do not believe in extraterrestrial UFOs, acknowledge that evidence to support such an interpretation of UFO sightings exists and that a rational person may hold such a view. A 1977 poll of members of the American Astronomical Association revealed that most astronomers are at least open-minded on the subject. After a thorough review of the scientific literature on the possibility of life on other worlds, **Michael D. Swords** of Western Michigan University has shown that the extraterrestrial hypothesis of ufology, whether ultimately correct or not, is an eminently defensible theory from a scientific point of view and, moreover, can reasonably be argued from the body of UFO evidence, including the "entity encounters" that Evans is so certain are imaginary. The real debate is not over whether *any* evidence for extraterrestrial visitation exists, but over whether the evidence that does exist is sufficient to prove the claim.

Having taken an absolutist position, Evans fails to consider, in any serious way, the possibility that the UFO experiences he reviews are what they appear to be, encounters with a genuine alien intelligence, or to defend meaningfully the principal thesis of his book: that *all* alleged "entity experiences" (as he calls them), whether involving angels, demons, fairies, apparitions, or UFO beings, are subjective in nature. Evans proceeds from the implicit assumption that since such things cannot be, they must be delusions. No doubt some, or perhaps even most, and conceivably all, are; but in his careless lumping together of what may be entirely different questions and separate problems, Evans reminds one of Hufford's description of a "man who is told that the camels at the zoo have humps; he then goes to the zoo and states, 'I shall define camels, or elephants as they are sometimes called, as any animal found at the zoo, some of which are said to have humps'" (Hufford, 1982a).

In contrast to other ufologist-writers who aspire to intellectual seriousness, Evans is remarkably indifferent to the truth status of the claims he examines. He writes in *Visions*, "I present these unsupported anecdotes for what they are worth, which is next to nothing as scientific evidence"— a remarkable admission from someone who is using "these unsupported anecdotes" as evidence for a hypothesis he clearly believes to be scientific. In *Gods* he acknowledges, with disarming candor (and italics), that *"every case cited here is dubious."* Thus charlatans such as the late contactee George Adamski, whose tales of interplanetary contacts were long ago exposed as fraudulent, and the late Buck Nelson, remembered chiefly for his marketing of hair from a Venusian dog, are treated as seriously as UFO abductees Barney and Betty Hill, whose sincerity (however one interprets their experience) has never been questioned. Evans remarks that (his italics) *"the concept of 'genuine' is meaningless. . . ."*

Even most disbelievers in entity experiences would assume dreams and lies, hallucinations and hoaxes to be different categories of psychological and social phenomena. It is not enough simply to declare, as Evans does, that they are alike because all are products of the human mind and let it go at that. But even if we do let it go at that, granting the proposition that all "subjective" mental experiences are basically alike, what *empirical* evidence is there that imaginary and "real" encounters with UFO entities are basically alike? Evans claims to have that empirical evidence—and it is worth noting, in light of what the next paragraphs tell us about the strength of that "evidence," that it is the *only* empirical evidence Evans brings to bear on the question.

In 1977 an ingenious experiment on the UFO abduction question was conceived and conducted by two California ufologists, Alvin H. Lawson and John DeHerrera, and a physician interested in UFOs, William C. McCall. They wanted to find out if "real" and "imaginary" abduction stories told under hypnosis bore any resemblance to each other. If they did, they thought, this would suggest that the "real" stories are probably fantasy, too.

PSYCHOSOCIAL HYPOTHESIS (*continued*)

They brought together a small group of student volunteers, quizzed them about their prior UFO knowledge and selected those who said they knew little about the subject. These students were then put under hypnosis and asked to imagine seeing a UFO, boarding it, observing its interior, encountering its occupants, undergoing a physiological examination, communicating with the beings, exiting the UFO, and experiencing subsequent life changes.

After the completion of the experiment Lawson would claim that the imaginary accounts were all but identical to the real ones, thus indicating that abductions are internally, not externally, generated. Reporting on these developments, Evans writes (his italics again), "[T]*hese experiments establish, beyond question, the ability of hypnotized subjects to replicate, not simply in broad but in intricate detail, scenarios to which they have not had access by any conventional means.*" To Evans this means such a feat is possible in any unusual state of consciousness and proves that "*anyone who subconsciously wishes* [to have an entity encounter] *is able to find within himself the necessary resources.*"

Lawson's experiment established no such thing, as a number of critics have made clear since then. The first of them, Willy Smith, observed that in over 70 percent of "real" cases abductees describe humanoids; such beings figure in only 20 percent (other critics say 10 percent) of the imaginary cases, where entities never reported in "real" cases are featured prominently. D. Scott Rogo found that the experiment had a "crucially flawed methodology" and that Lawson's "evaluations are contaminated by several sources of bias and experimental error," beginning with the use of leading questions (considered a major blunder in investigations of "real" cases) and the employment of McCall, a UFO investigator knowledgeable about the intricacies of the abduction phenomenon, as hypnotist when by "any proper experimental criterion, Lawson should have used a clinician unfamiliar with the UFO literature." Worst of all, Rogo wrote of Lawson (Rogo's

italics), "*Convinced that the content of his imaginary abduction scenarios matched the content of real-life cases . . . he chose four accounts post-hoc from the literature and pointed out the considerable coincidences between them and imaginary reports. . . .* His process of selection was . . . about as scientific as asking subjects to describe an imaginary cat, collecting reports of real cats, extracting whatever common descriptions there might be, and then concluding that all cats are imaginary" (Rogo, 1985).

In 1989, as part of a large-scale comparative analysis of all known abduction narratives, Thomas E. Bullard found a "sharp distinction between real and imaginary cases." The real ones have a "consistency in context and narrowness of variation [in] contrast with the much greater looseness and diversity of imaginary abductions. Such contrast denies any impression of coherency to the imaginary cases. Real hypnotic and non-hypnotic abduction stories share more in common with each other than with imaginary abduction stories, strengthening the sense that not hypnosis or the hypnotist, not cultural or personal elements can explain the unity behind real reports" (Bullard, 1989).

In short, Evans' one claim to experimental confirmation of the psychosocial hypothesis is almost certainly unfounded. Yet while Lawson's hypothesis appears to have been falsified, at least it *is* falsifiable—unlike Evans' own hypotheses. For example, he proposes that entity-generating psychological states include relaxation, excitation, boredom, ecstasy, isolation, participation in a group, concentration, distraction, a crisis of faith, an unquestioning faith, anxiety and peace of mind. When none of these conditions obtains—if that is conceivable—the weather, the phase of the moon, or the individual's diet, may trigger the imaginary encounter. Evans may as well have argued that the psychological state in which one is most likely to have an entity encounter is being alive.

If nothing else, Evans can be counted on to cover all his bases. In another instance of base-stretching—one of a number that could be cited—he informs us that CE3 accounts could not involve true extraterrestrials because the alleged ETs' behavior is "illogical, no matter how much allowance we make for the possibility ET logic may be different from ours." Scarcely 50 pages of *Gods* later, Evans remarks that such reports cannot be interpreted as alien encounters because the supposed ETs' patterns of behavior are "humanlike in so many . . . ways."

In 1988 Keith Basterfield, an Australian, and Robert E. Bartholomew, an American pursuing graduate studies at an Australian university, proposed a falsifiable version of the psychosocial hypothesis. They suggested that close-encounter claimants are **"fantasy-prone personalities"** (as defined in a 1983 study by T. X. Barber and Sheryl C. Wilson) and that psychological testing designed to probe that possibility would confirm as much. Two years earlier, in 1986, Peter Rogerson, the first ufologist to take note of the Barber-Wilson hypothesis, predicted, *"All* contactees and abductees will be [found to be] fantasy-prone personalities (FPPs). The vast majority of CE3 percipients will be FPPs" (Rogerson, 1986).

The first experimental test of the FPP hypothesis, conducted in 1989 by University of Connecticut psychologist Kenneth Ring, found no discernible difference between close-encounter percipients and a control group of non-UFO witnesses. A second independent study, conducted elsewhere in the United States and not yet published, came to the same conclusion.

Despite the absence so far of any empirical support for his ideas, by 1989 Evans was sufficiently confident of the cogency of his analysis to launch a rhetorical inquiry into the psychology of those (he calls them "believers") who remain unmoved by his interpretation of UFO experiences. Referring to one such individual, Evans remarks on the "paradox" of one who, "sober and undrugged, with all his wits about him, uninfluenced by divine revelation, is willing to commit himself to belief" in "improbable" notions "for which there is insufficient evidence" (Stillings, 1989).

Failure and Triumph: The problem with the psychosocial hypothesis is not that the quite real psychological and sociological aspects of the UFO problem are unworthy of attention; it is that the psychosocial hypothesis simply fails to deal plausibly with ufology's most interesting questions, the ones that brought it into being in the first place: namely, those related to physical evidence, instrumented observations, and multiply- and independently-witnessed events. Even Vallee has begun to complain that *Passport to Magonia* was misread, that the psychosocial theorists whom that book inspired are ignoring the "actual material facts." His book *Confrontations* (1990) insists on the primacy of the physical evidence and cites many striking examples of it. It will be interesting to see how his erstwhile followers respond.

In place of falsifiable hypotheses, psychosocial speculations substitute a closed system from which it would be all but impossible for a genuinely new and novel phenomenon to emerge. All claims suggestive of other-than-human intelligences—however credible or noncredible, whoever the claimant, whatever the circumstances, whatever the particular details of the story, whatever evidence may or may not exist—become the same thing. Similarities, however slight, matter more than differences, however substantial. In science one must note similarities, of course, but one must also isolate differences. Psychosocial speculators seem to regard differences as irrelevant. They maintain, for example, that contactees and abductees are essentially indistinguishable, when in fact both the experiences the two groups report and the kinds of people they are could hardly be less alike. If one is to argue that ostensibly profound dissimilarities are in fact trivial, one has to do a far better job of demonstrating that than anyone has done to date.

In the 1980s psychosocial approaches came to dominate European ufology, as American ufology focused increasingly on UFO-crash claims (especially the Roswell incident), cover-ups and the extraterrestrial hypothesis. Reflecting on this growing schism in the international UFO community, Italian ufologists Edoardo Russo and Gian Paolo Grassino wrote, "In fact the basic

PSYCHOSOCIAL HYPOTHESIS (*continued*)

attitudes of American and European ufologists toward each other do not differ much from the average man's attitudes. Americans tend to think Europeans are much too complicated in their abstract reasoning, with their noses up to the sky instead of being pragmatic in their approach to reality. And Europeans tend to think of Americans as gullible, naive, superficial people, unable to see behind appearances. Of course such stereotyped images are crude and inadequate, but they nonetheless gain a grain of truth. . . . Will the day come when no common assumptions link the two sides of the Atlantic?" (Russo and Grassino, 1989).

In late 1989 the first book-length treatment of the psychosocial hypothesis to appear in America since Clark and Coleman's *The Unidentified* was published, an anthology edited by Dennis Stillings, *Cyberbiological Studies of the Imaginal Component in the UFO Contact Experience.* Stillings, a supporter of spoon-bending "psychic" Uri Geller, revives the traditional occult notion of "materialized psychisms" (sometimes called "thought forms"). "It is becoming more apparent," he writes in the preface, "that mind-directed self-regulatory effects—whether one refers to conscious or unconscious mind as the agent—are not 'skin-bounded,' but can be exteriorized into other systems. Neither do these effects have to arise from a single mind: they may be the product of a 'group psyche.'" In other words, psychological "needs" can create *physical* (not just hallucinatory) effects and phenomena in the world, including flying saucers and entities.

This idea, as Jung wrote three decades ago, has no support from parapsychology, much less from mainstream science. Most European psychosocial speculators are as skeptical of psychic phenomena (even the less dramatic forms described by academic parapsychologists) as of extraterrestrial visitors. One of Stillings' contributors, in the course of what is otherwise a pure psychosocial analysis of the UFO phenomenon, states almost in passing that psychokinetic constructs are able to leave burn marks on the ground and traces on

radar. What Stillings and his colleagues are proposing seems as much supernatural as psychosocial, a kind of New Age radical-Jungian metaphysics in which the mind assumes the powers of God.

Stillings' book is noteworthy mostly for the reappearance of the long-silent Alvin Lawson. Before repeating his original claims Lawson says of his critics only that their response to his imaginary-abduction findings consists in its entirety of "derisive hoots and snorts." In fact, his critics have been rather more articulate and pointed than that, and Lawson has yet to address meaningfully their objections to his claims.

In common with other works of psychosocial speculation, *Cyberbiological Studies* suffers from an affection for grand pronouncement and a concomitant inattention to empirical evidence. But if the psychosocial hypothesis has yet to become a scientific theory, it has become by now a belief system all its own. Whether in the 1990s it will evolve into something more than that remains to be seen.

Sources:

Briggs, Katharine. *An Encyclopedia of Fairies: Hobgoblins, Brownies, Bogies, and Other Supernatural Creatures.* New York: Pantheon Books, 1976.

Bullard, Thomas E. "Hypnosis and UFO Abductions: A Troubled Relationship." *Journal of UFO Studies* 1 (new series, 1989): 3-40.

Bullard, Thomas E. *UFO Abductions: The Measure of a Mystery. Vol. 1: Comparative Study of Abduction Reports. Vol. 2: Catalogue of Cases.* Mount Rainier, MD: Fund for UFO Research, 1987.

Clark, Jerome. "The Fall and Rise of the Extraterrestrial Hypothesis." In Walter H. Andrus, Jr., and Richard H. Hall, eds. *MUFON 1988 International UFO Symposium Proceedings.* Seguin, TX: Mutual UFO Network, Inc., 1988. Pp. 58-72.

Clark, Jerome. "The Strange Case of the 1897 Airship." *Flying Saucer Review* 12, 4 (July/August 1966): 10-17.

Clark, Jerome. "Two Cheers for American Ufology." *International UFO Reporter* 14, 2 (March/April 1989): 8-12.

Clark, Jerome, and Loren Coleman. *The Unidentified: Notes Toward Solving the UFO Mystery.* New York: Warner Books, 1975.

Evans, Hilary. *Gods, Spirits, Cosmic Guardians: A Comparative Study of the Encounter Experience.* Wellingborough, Northamptonshire, England: The Aquarian Press, 1987.

Evans, Hilary. *Visions, Apparitions, Alien Visitors.* Wellingborough, Northamptonshire, England: The Aquarian Press, 1984.

Evans-Wentz, W. Y. *The Fairy-Faith in Celtic Countries.* New York: University Books, Inc., 1966.

Hufford, David J. *The Terror That Comes in the Night: An Experience-Centered Study of Supernatural Assault Traditions.* Philadelphia: University of Pennsylvania Press, 1982a.

Hufford, David J. "Traditions of Disbelief." *New York Folklore Quarterly* 8, 3-4 (Winter 1982b): 47-55.

Jung, C. G. *Flying Saucers: A Modern Myth of Things Seen in the Skies.* New York: Harcourt, Brace and Company, 1959.

Keightley, Thomas. *The Fairy Mythology.* London: G. Bell, 1878.

Lawson, Alvin H. "Hypnosis of Imaginary UFO 'Abductees.'" In Curtis G. Fuller, ed. *Proceedings of the First International UFO Congress*, 195-238. New York: Warner Books, 1980.

Monnerie, Michel. "The Case for Skepticism." In Hilary Evans, and John Spencer, eds. *UFOs 1947-1987: The 40-Year Search for an Explanation*, 367-370. London: Fortean Tomes, 1987.

Rogerson, Peter. "It's All in the Mind." *Magonia* 15 (April 1984): 10-13.

Rogerson, Peter. "Northern Echos." *Magonia* 23 (July 1986): 13-14.

Rogo, D. Scott. "Imaginary Facts: The Case of the Imaginary Abductions." *International UFO Reporter* 10, 2 (March/April 1985): 3-5.

Russo, Edoardo, and Gian Paolo Grassino. "Ufology in Europe; or, What Is America Coming to?" *International UFO Reporter* 14, 2 (March/April 1989): 4-7.

Smith, Willy. "A Second Look." *Magonia* 6 (December 1981): 3-5.

Stillings, Dennis, ed. *Cyberbiological Studies of the Imaginal Component in the UFO Contact Experience.* St. Paul: Archaeus Project, 1989.

Vallee, Jacques. *Passport to Magonia: From Folklore to Flying Saucers.* Chicago: Henry Regnery Company, 1969.

R

RANDLES, JENNY (1951-)

Jenny Randles, the most well-known researcher in **British ufology**, is national director of field investigations for the British UFO Research Association (BUFORA) and the author of a number of serious books on UFO matters.

Born in Lancashire in 1951, she was trained as a science teacher for children between eight and 12 and later worked on educational video projects at an adult college. After reading books by **John A. Keel** and **Jacques Vallee** and subscribing to *Flying Saucer Review*, she joined BUFORA in 1970 and three years later helped form the Northern UFO Network (NUFON), an informal alliance of regional groups combining to produce a common database and share resources. She has edited *Northern UFO News* since 1974 and in 1975 became a member of BUFORA's board of directors. Between 1977 and 1983 she was a columnist for *Flying Saucer Review*. She is also a contributing editor to *International UFO Reporter*, the magazine of the **J. Allen Hynek Center for UFO Studies**.

She was the first ufologist to be published in such prestigious magazines as *New Scientist*, *London Guardian* and *Police Review*. In October 1975 she scripted and co-presented a 15-minute television program for the BBC showing how serious investigators tackle a case. Since then she has written and helped put together radio and television programs dealing with UFOs and other anomalies. In 1978 she became a full-time writer.

Her first book, written with Peter Warrington, was *UFOs: A British Viewpoint*. Her most recent is *Crop Circles: The Mystery Solved?* (1990, with Paul Fuller).

She says, "The single most important fact that we have uncovered about UFOs since 1947 is that there is no such thing as *the* phenomenon. UFO is a collective term which covers a range of quite different phenomena.

"Considerable experience as a field investigator confirms that up to 95 percent of all reported UFO sightings have conventional explanations and are not truly anomalous, although often IFO [identified flying object] reports have interesting insights to offer on visual perception or sociology.

"The remaining five percent are small only in relative terms; they comprise a substantial number of puzzling cases reported globally in any one year. Many (probably most and perhaps even all) of these cases are the result of natural physical energy forces generated by at least one, and likely several, processes which are not fully understood by science and may represent new knowledge in fields such as atmospheric physics and geophysics.

"There is also a small residue (perhaps one percent of the data) of what ufologists call close encounters of the third and fourth kinds. These relate to apparent contact with alien intelligences and cover such material as abduction stories. I am not convinced these are related in any way to the rest of the UFO evidence. It may be that the

RANDLES, JENNY (*continued*)

abduction, in particular, is an entirely separate problem which is being linked with the physical UFOs through social and cultural factors. For this reason I prefer to call the physical UFO data 'unidentified atmospheric phenomena' (UAP).

"On the other hand, I recognize as a potentially productive area for research the possibility that close encounters may be essentially subjective experiences triggered in the minds of sensitive witnesses who come in close proximity to novel radiative energy fields from one or more of the physical-UFO types.

"Whether there is *any* alien intelligence behind any close encounter remains, to me, an unanswered question. I see no overwhelming reason to believe there must be, on present evidence, while recognizing that some data may support that contention. But the close encounter is a surprisingly consistent experience which I believe is subjective in nature, involving visually creative witnesses who enter an altered state of consciousness demarked by symptoms I term the **'Oz Factor'**" (personal communication, 1989).

The Oz Factor serves as a bridge concept between Randles' broad interest in psychic phenomena, an interest equaling her concern for UFOs, and the numerous instances she has researched the psychic aspects she believes are integral to many UFO reports. Her more psychically-oriented writings include *Beyond Explanation* (1985), which details a number of accounts of UFOs involving celebrities, and *Sixth Sense* (1987), a discussion of psychic awareness as an extension of the five senses. Besides directing the work of BUFORA, Randles is the coordinator for the Association for the Scientific Study of Anomalous Phenomena (ASSAP) (30 South Row, London SE3 0RY, England), an organization founded in 1981 to study and disseminate information on psychic and anomalous phenomena.

Sources:

Randles, Jenny. *Abduction: Over 200 Documented*

UFO Kidnappings Investigated. London: Robert Hale, 1988.

Randles, Jenny. *Beyond Explanation?* Topsfield, MA: Salem House Publishers, 1985. Rept.: New York: Bantam Books, 1987.

Randles, Jenny. *Sixth Sense*. Topsfield, MA: Salem House Publishers, 1987.

Randles, Jenny. *The UFO Conspiracy: The First Forty Years*. Poole, England: Blandford Press, 1987.

Randles, Jenny. *UFO Reality: A Critical Look at the Physical Evidence*. London: Robert Hale, 1983.

Randles, Jenny, Brenda Butler, and Dot Street. *Sky Crash: A Cosmic Conspiracy*. Suffolk, England: Neville Spearman, 1984.

Randles, Jenny, and Peter Warrington. *Science and the UFOs*. Oxford, England: Basil Blackwell, 1985.

Randles, Jenny, and Paul Whetnall. *Alien Contact: Window on Another World*. London: Coronet, 1983.

RODEGHIER, MARK (1953-)

Mark Rodeghier is president and scientific director of the **J. Allen Hynek Center for UFO Studies**, a post he has held since 1986. A close professional and personal associate of the late **J. Allen Hynek**, he joined the CUFOS board of directors in 1981 and that same year published an important monograph on UFO-related electromagnetic effects. He is consulting editor to CUFOS' *Journal of UFO Studies* and contributing editor to its *International UFO Reporter*.

Born in Hammond, Indiana, on April 20, 1953, he has a B.S. in astrophysics from Indiana University (1975). In 1975 and 1976 he pursued graduate study at the University of Sussex in

England. He received an M.A. in sociology from the University of Illinois at Chicago in 1984. He is currently a doctoral candidate in sociology at the same university. His professional interests encompass the sociology of science, collective behavior, and statistics and methodology.

His most recent concerns in ufology have been the construction of a sociological and psychological profile of persons who report UFO abductions; investigation of the Roswell UFO crash of 1947; and the study of patterns and trends in the worldwide fluctuation in UFO reports over the past four decades.

Rodeghier says, "UFO reports remain, in many respects, as puzzling today as they did when such events were first reported in large numbers after World War II. Several factors have contributed to this ostensible lack of progress in our understanding. First, the scientific community has, for the most part, disdained the subject and found it unworthy of serious consideration. Moreover, two projects sponsored by the U.S. government, the Robertson Panel and the Condon Committee, concluded that nothing of *scientific* importance was likely to result from a study of UFO sightings. Second, the UFO phenomenon, like other large-scale, nonperiodic, uncontrollable phenomena (ball lightning, for example), is simply difficult to study effectively. If one cannot predict where and when a sighting will occur, and as a consequence one must rely upon the vagaries of human testimony for data collection, the problems of analysis are clearly evident.

"Third, the public fascination with alien life and the concomitant willingness to believe in the extraterrestrial explanation for UFO reports has actually hindered, rather than assisted, serious study. It is one thing to measure the evidence and judge the most likely explanation for some UFO reports to be alien activity; it is another matter entirely to make a blind leap in logic and move to that position *without* an intimate knowledge of the phenomenon. The latter course is what a large number of Americans seem to have taken, as shown by Gallup poll data from the late 1960s onward. It is difficult to study UFO

reports seriously and garner support from the public when it is convinced that the answer to the puzzle is already available.

"I take a rather eclectic approach to the UFO subject, for I expect that several rather disparate bodies of new knowledge will be required before we can fully understand UFO reports. For example, I am convinced by both personal research and the work of others that some UFO reports are caused by unknown natural phenomena, generated by diverse mechanisms. Witnesses to these objects report seeing, for the most part, luminous balls of light which move in irregular trajectories.

"I am similarly convinced that such phenomena are not the causes of *all* unexplained sightings. First, some aspects of the **abduction phenomenon** point to little-understood psychological mechanisms of disassociation which may generate some abduction reports or, at the least, contribute to the reported characteristics of these experiences. These mechanisms may have influenced the reports of **contactees**, some of whom appear to be honestly reporting unusual experiences.

"Second, several UFO reports have been explained, sometimes years later, as observations of secret military and government projects. Though this category may explain only a small percentage of sightings, it is critical that we do not forget that all governments keep certain matters hidden from public view and that it is possible to use the UFO phenomenon as a means to that end.

"Finally, I believe that certain UFO reports seem to resist any easy explanations based upon either peculiarities of human consciousness, natural agencies, or man-made technology. I refer here to such events as the McMinnville, Oregon, photos, the many daylight sightings of structured objects by commercial and civilian pilots, the best physical-trace cases (such as the **Trans-en-Provence CE2** in France), and the boomerang-shaped UFO seen by thousands near New York City. I have no explanation for these reports and

RODEGHIER, MARK (*continued*)

we certainly have no conclusive evidence that they were caused by the actions of some nonhuman intelligence. But I find reports like these the most puzzling aspect of the UFO phenomenon and, taking the long view, the ones that most deserve our attention" (personal communication, 1989).

Sources:

Rodeghier, Mark. "Boomerang." *International UFO Reporter* 12, 6 (November/December 1987): 14-16.

Rodeghier, Mark. "Editorial." *International UFO Reporter* 9, 5 (September/October 1984): 2-3.

Rodeghier, Mark. "Editorial: Whither American Ufology?" *International UFO Reporter* 14, 2 (March/April 1989): 3, 18, 24.

Rodeghier, Mark. "Roswell, 1989." *International UFO Reporter* 14, 5 (September/October 1989): 4-8, 23.

Rodeghier, Mark. *UFO Reports Involving Vehicle Interference: A Catalogue and Data Analysis.* Evanston, IL: Center for UFO Studies, 1981.

S

SARBACHER, ROBERT IRVING (1907-1986)

Robert Irving Sarbacher was born on September 6, 1907, in Baltimore, Maryland. He received a bachelor of science degree from the University of Florida in 1933. Three years later Harvard University granted him a master of science degree and in 1939 a doctoral degree. Between 1936 and 1940 he taught physics and communications engineering and was a professor of electrical engineering at the Illinois Institute of Technology between 1940 and 1942. He served as a science consultant to the U.S. Navy between 1942 and 1945 and was dean of the graduate school at the Georgia Institute of Technology from 1945 to 1949. In 1950 Sarbacher left the academic world to enter the corporate arena, working for or directing businesses involved in science and technology as well as joining the boards of several major insurance companies. His books included *Hyper and Ultra-High Frequency Engineering* (1944) and the *Encyclopedic Dictionary for Electronics and Nuclear Engineering* (1955).

Sarbacher was to enter UFO lore because of one special position he held: a guided missile consultant to the U.S. Defense Department's Research and Development Board, headed by Vannevar Bush. His name was first spoken among ufologists in a lecture delivered to the 1982 conference of the **Mutual UFO Network** (MUFON), held in Toronto in early July. Arthur Bray stated that "Wilbert B. Smith, the late great Canadian ufologist, was informed by a top American scientist who was deeply involved in UFO research for the U.S. government, that 'the facts reported in the book [Frank Scully's *Behind the Flying Saucers*, 1950] are substantially correct.' The notes made by Smith recording this interview are in my possession. *No one* has contacted me for further information on this gem in order to pursue it. . . . If anyone out there has sufficient interest to pursue this matter, the scientist who made that startling statement was Dr. Robert I. Sarbacker [sic], Dean of the Graduate School at Georgia University and Director of Research, National Science Laboratories Inc., Washington, D.C." Smith was a radio engineer employed by the Canadian government.

The document in question was dated September 15, 1950, and was written, Smith noted, "from memory following the interview. I have tried to keep it as nearly verbattum [sic] as possible" (Maccabee, 1987). The interview was conducted in Robert Sarbacher's office in Washington, with Sarbacher speaking in his capacity as a consultant to the Research and Development Board. It is not clear if Smith himself participated in the interview. His handwritten account is headed, "Notes on interview through Lt./C. Bremner with Dr. Robert I. Sarbacher," implying that he wrote questions which were asked by a Canadian Naval officer; yet the questioner is identified only as "WBS."

The interview began, according to Smith's rendition of it, with "WBS'" stating, "I am doing some work on the collapse of the earth's magnetic field as a source of energy and I think our work

SARBACHER, ROBERT IRVING (*continued*)

may have a bearing on the flying saucers. . . . I have read Scully's book [about crashed UFOs in the Southwest] and would like to know how much of it is true." According to Smith, Sarbacher replied, "The facts reported in the book are substantially correct." "Then the saucers do exist?" Smith asked. "Yes," Sarbacher said. "They exist. . . . We have not been able to duplicate their performance. . . . All we know is, we didn't make them, and it's pretty certain they didn't originate on the earth."

Smith said, "I understand the whole subject of saucers is classified."

"Yes," Sarbacher replied, "it is classified two points higher even than the H-bomb. In fact it is the most highly classified subject in the U.S. Government at the present time." "May I ask the reason for the classification?" Smith said, and Sarbacher responded, "You may ask, but I can't tell you." When Smith asked how he could learn more, Sarbacher said, "I suppose you could be cleared through your own Defense Department and I am pretty sure arrangements could be made to exchange information. If you have anything to contribute, we would be glad to talk it over, but I can't give you any more at the present time."

Upon his return to Ottawa, Smith attempted without success to learn more through Canadian government channels. On December 2, 1950, Smith was appointed engineer-in-charge of a small UFO-research effort, Project Magnet, under the Department of Transport. Magnet was closed down in 1954 and Smith went on to pursue his UFO interest privately. Eventually he became convinced he had established psychic contact with extraterrestrials. He died in 1961.

In due course Smith's personal papers came into Bray's possession and the memo was discovered. Bray's mention of the memo in his lecture for the MUFON brought the matter to the attention of researcher **Stanton T. Friedman**, who immediately set out to determine if Sarbacher was still alive. Friedman found Sarbacher's name and

address in *Who's Who in America*, and proceeded to contact him.

When he spoke with him over the phone, Friedman learned immediately that Sarbacher had *not* been, Bray to the contrary, "deeply involved in UFO research for the U.S. government." He did confirm the essentials of the Smith account but said his knowledge of the UFO project was based only on what he had heard from other scientists who were involved. At one point, he said, he had been invited to Wright-Patterson Air Force Base to hear a presentation by scientists and military men who were studying UFO remains, but other pressing business had kept him from attending. Sarbacher said his colleagues had told of wreckage and bodies, but with the passage of years his memory had grown hazy about the specifics. He said he did not know why the matter had been covered up all these years.

Eventually, in early 1983, Friedman met personally with Sarbacher, then living in semiretirement on a yacht, but learned little if anything he had not already been told over the phone. Sarbacher, as he would with other, subsequent inquirers, apologized for not knowing more and never elaborated on his interesting but sketchy account. Friedman, in common with all others who would speak with him, was impressed with Sarbacher's modesty and evident sincerity, but he concluded that the scientist's testimony was long short of sufficient to prove an official cover-up. Although Friedman did not publicize the story, he passed it on to his colleague **William L. Moore**, with whom he had investigated the Roswell incident. Moore then mentioned it to a California UFO enthusiast named William S. Steinman, who became persuaded that Sarbacher knew a lot more than he was telling.

Subsequently Steinman wrote Friedman and asked him to help "put pressure" on Sarbacher to tell the whole truth. Since Friedman believed Sarbacher already had, he refused. Steinman then wrote Sarbacher himself and received a response, dated November 29, 1983. Steinman kept the letter to himself, claiming that its author, the mysterious "Dr S," feared for his life and insisted his identity be kept secret. Soon Steinman wrote the late Gray Barker, a **contactee**-oriented publisher, and gave him this account of what "Dr S'" letter contained:

"I recently received a letter from a currently prominent and very active scientist, who presides over a major American university. This scientist acknowledges that the United States Government DID RECOVER THREE FLYING SAUCERS between 1947-50.

"He named names, gave descriptions, told dates and places of meetings (which he attended) pertaining to those recovered Flying Saucers." Steinman declared that the meetings that Sarbacher had attended had four purposes: to determine (1) exactly what had been recovered; (2) who might have manufactured the craft; (3) where they could have come from; and (4) how much the American public should be told about the saucers. At the end of the discussions, those who participated decided that (1) they did not know what they had; or (2) who manufactured them; or (3) where they came from. Finally, they determined that the subject matter was to remain the most highly classified subject matter in the United States."

Steinman continues, "Hence certain diversionary measures were set up to draw public attention away from the truth pertaining to Flying Saucers.

"1. Sign, Grudge, Bluebook [sic].

"2. Robertson Panel, Condon Study.

"3. Civilian study groups, etc.

"Now, because of what this scientist says, 'The cat is out of the bag.' In a few short months the 35-year-old security lid will be lifted, the public will know the truth, and perhaps a new 'Pandora's Box' will be opened. But this is what we all have been anxiously waiting for these past 35 years. Now, we must determine where we go from here.

"Please publish this in your next NEWSLETTER" (Steinman, 1984)."

Eventually a copy of Sarbacher's original letter to Steinman began to circulate within the ufological community. It bore a passing resemblance, if little more, to Steinman's characterization of it:

"I am sorry I have taken so long in answering your letters. However, I have moved my office and have had to make a number of extended trips.

"To answer your last question in your letter of October 14, 1983, there is no particular reason I feel I shouldn't or couldn't answer any or all of your questions. I am delighted to answer all of them to the best of my ability.

"You listed some of your questions in your letter of September 12th. I will attempt to answer them as you had listed them.

"1. Relating to my own experience regarding recovered flying saucers, I had no association with any of the people involved in the recovery and have no knowledge regarding the dates of the recoveries. If I had I would send it to you.

"2. Regarding verification that persons you list were involved, I can only say this:

"John von Neuman was definitely involved. Dr. Vannevar Bush was definitely involved, and I think Dr. Robert Oppenheimer also.

"My association with the Research and Development Board under Doctor Compton during the Eisenhower administration was rather limited so that although I had been invited to participate in several discussions associated with the reported recoveries, I could not personally attend the meetings. I am sure that they would have asked Dr. [Wernher] von Braun, and the others that you listed were probably asked and may or may not have attended. This is all I know for sure.

"3. I did receive some official reports when I was in my office at the Pentagon but all of these were left there as at the time we were never supposed to take them out of the office.

193

SARBACHER, ROBERT IRVING (*continued*)

"4. I have to make the same reply as on No. 4.

"I recall the interview with Dr. Brenner [sic] of the Canadian Embassy. I think the answers I gave him were the ones you listed. Naturally, I was more familiar with the subject matter under discussion, at that time. Actually, I would have been able to give more specific answers had I attended the meetings concerning the subject. You must understand that I took this assignment as a private contribution. We were called 'dollar-a-year men.' My first responsibility was the maintenance of my own business activity so that my participation was limited.

"About the only thing I remember at this time is that certain materials reported to have come from flying saucer crashes were extremely light and very tough. I am sure our laboratories analyzed them very carefully.

"There were reports that instruments or people operating these machines were also of very light weight, sufficient to withstand the tremendous deceleration and acceleration associated with their machinery. I remember in talking with some of the people at the office that I got the impression these 'aliens' were constructed like certain insects we have observed on earth, wherein because of the low mass the inertial forces involved in operation of these instruments would be quite low.

"I still do not know why the high order of classification has been given and why the denial of the existence of these devices.

"I am sorry it has taken me so long to reply but I suggest you get in touch with the others who may be directly involved in this program." (Steinman, 1984)

Unfortunately, as Sarbacher himself would note ruefully in later interviews, all of those persons were dead. Sarbacher himself died on July 26, 1986.

Those who talked with Sarbacher, including Jerome Clark, who interviewed him for *Omni*, and **Bruce Maccabee**, of the **Fund for UFO Research**, were struck not only by his apparent sincerity but also by his ignorance of UFO history. When asked if the Vannevar Bush project was related to Project Blue Book, Sarbacher did not know what the latter was; nor did he recall the name of the Bush project, which inevitably ufologists' speculation tied to the rumored "Majestic-12." Sarbacher seemed not to be endorsing the story told by Frank Scully, about an alleged crash in Aztec, New Mexico, in 1948, an almost certain hoax—just the general idea that crashes (he could not recall where) had occurred. His reference to the quality of the recovered materials echoes the testimony of Roswell witnesses.

Apologizing for his faulty memory, Sarbacher said that his old colleagues, the ones who could confirm his story, "are all dead," not from sinister causes but simply from the passing of years.

However sincere Sarbacher appeared to be, his testimony is—unless and until confirming evidence comes to light—at worst little more than a curiosity and at best a small part of a broader tapestry of related (but also unverified) claims about secret government UFO projects and top scientists engaged in the study of wreckage and bodies.

Sources:

Bray, Arthur. "Professionalism in Ufology." In Walter H. Andrus, Jr., and Dennis W. Stacy, eds. *UFO's . . . Canada: A Global Perspective: Thirteenth Annual MUFON UFO Symposium Proceedings*, 13-24. Seguin, TX: Mutual UFO Network, Inc., 1982.

Clark, Jerome. "UFO Update." *Omni* 7, 11 (August 1985): 85.

Maccabee, Bruce, ed. *Documents and Supporting Information Related to Crashed Flying Saucers and Operation Majestic Twelve*. Mount Rainier, MD: Fund for UFO Research, 1987.

Steinman, William S. "Leading Scientist Tells All." *Gray Barker's Newsletter* 21 (April 1984): 4.

SAUCER SMEAR
James W. Moseley
Box 1709
Key West, Florida 33041

Saucer Smear, long ago and in a different format (magazine as opposed to bulletin) known as *Saucer News* (originally *Nexus*), is an eight-page insiders' newsletter of gossip, commentary (often caustic), innuendo, feuds and personality conflict. The first issue of *Smear* appeared in July 1981. It is not an organ of "serious ufology" but it is undeniably the funniest—or at least *intentionally* funniest—UFO periodical ever. There probably was a time when James W. Moseley, the editor, was interested in actual UFO reports and theories, but that was not recently. Like the old *Saucer News*, *Smear*—"dedicated," its logo cheerfully informs us, "to the highest principles of ufological journalism"—is far more interested in the personal foibles of UFO buffs and debunkers, sparing nobody. Although hardly anyone will admit it, *Smear* is just about the only UFO bulletin everybody reads from cover to cover.

Sources:

Moseley, James W. "What I Really Believe." *Caveat Emptor* 3 (Spring 1972): 9-12; 6 (Winter 1972-73): 5-6, 21-22.

SMITHSONIAN UFO DEBATE

On September 6, 1980, at the Smithsonian Institution in Washington, D.C., UFO proponents and debunkers squared off for a day-long debate on the merits of the case for UFOs—a debate that debunkers had long lobbied for, convinced that it would show up the weakness of the ufologists' case. Proponents were **Bruce Maccabee**, an optical physicist employed by the U.S. Navy; **J. Allen**

Hynek, Northwestern University astronomer and former Project Blue Book scientific consultant; and Allan Hendry, chief investigator for the Center for UFO Studies (now the **J. Allen Hynek Center for UFO Studies**). The debunkers were **Philip J. Klass**, aviation journalist and head of the UFO subcommittee of the **Committee for the Scientific Investigation of Claims of the Paranormal** (CSICOP); James E. Oberg, aerospace engineer and science writer; and Robert Sheaffer, writer. The debate was moderated by Fred Durant.

During morning and afternoon sessions proponents and debunkers repeated arguments familiar to those who had kept more than a passing interest in the subject. The former cited the persistence of the UFO phenomenon and the puzzling nature of the best reports. The latter charged that there is "no scientifically credible evidence" (Klass) and that UFOs "seem to behave like fairies and ghosts" (Sheaffer). Some of the debate concerned the relevance of polygraph tests to UFO investigation, with Hendry citing studies indicating their unreliability and Klass asserting, "I'm prepared to take a polygraph test on everything." Hynek said, "Reading a good UFO report is like reading Agatha Christie—except there is no last page to turn to." Oberg, citing tabloid tales of aliens on the Moon, declared ufology a "failed science" (Rohrer, 1980).

The most heated exchanges occurred between Klass and Hendry. Klass accused Hendry of "withholding data" which would have led to a prosaic explanation for a case Hendry had investigated the year before, an incident in which Deputy Sheriff Val Johnson of Marshall County, Minnesota, reportedly saw a UFO shooting down a deserted country highway toward his patrol car. Johnson suddenly passed out. When he awoke, he discovered his vehicle had been damaged and his eyes injured.

"I would agree there are only two possible explanations to this case," Klass said. "It could not have been Venus. It could not have been a weather balloon. It could not have been an hallucination." Either it was a spaceship "*or* Deputy Val Johnson did it himself because he

SMITHSONIAN UFO DEBATE (*continued*)

likes to play practical jokes, especially in the late evening when he gets a little bored, as *I* learned—Hendry did not—by talking to some of the people who have worked with him and know him very well.

"I also discovered that he once talked about setting up a UFO patrol to go out looking for UFOs. Yet, according to Hendry, this was a deputy who . . . prior to his sighting 'was rather indifferent to the UFO subject. . . .'

"I would wish that Allan Hendry . . . had taken the final step and said, 'Val Johnson, will you take a polygraph—a lie-detector test—given by a very experienced examiner? Let's see what the results are.'"

Hendry responded, "We've already heard from Philip Klass today a perfectly excellent illustration of why it would be difficult to ever convince the skeptics based on the facts." Hendry said that Klass' penchant for digging out irrelevant episodes in UFO witnesses' past and using them as evidence that their testimony should be rejected amounted to "character assassination." Hendry cited another case, the alleged abduction of Travis Walton, in which polygraph tests had come to conflicting conclusions, as had two polygraph experts who later reviewed the charts. "Thus," he said, "you begin to understand why I do not feel that the final step in an examination of Deputy Val Johnson necessarily rests on a polygraph examination." He added sarcastically, "Actually I'm inclined to agree with Klass. I think that Val Johnson is such a practical joker that he deliberately injured his eyes—as judged by two doctors—and he deliberately entered a phony state of shock for the benefit of the ambulance driver who removed him from the scene of the accident" (Clark, 1981).

As an effort to settle the UFO controversy, the Smithsonian debate was a good public spectacle, settling nothing and changing nobody's mind. No one has suggested a sequel.

Sources:

Clark, Jerome. "Phil Klass vs. the 'UFO Promoters.'" *Fate* 34, 2 (February 1981): 56-67.

Rohrer, Stuart. "Tempest in a Saucer." *The Washington Post* (September 8, 1981).

SOCIETY FOR SCIENTIFIC EXPLORATION
Laurence W. Frederick, Secretary
Department of Astronomy
University of Virginia
Box 3818
Charlottesville, Virginia 22903

In 1982 the "Society for Scientific Exploration, formed for the Study of Anomalous Phenomena," was founded but is seldom referred to by anything but the first half of its name, and more often as the SSE. The SSE states, "The term 'anomalous' is here used to characterize those phenomena that appear to contradict existing scientific knowledge and which, for these or other reasons, are generally regarded by the scientific community as being outside their established fields of inquiry. The Society seeks to provide for discussion of these topics in a form modeled on that of mainstream science. For this reason, its membership is drawn from practitioners of science who have acquired a first-hand knowledge and understanding of the scientific process. Most Full Members are associated with major research institutions, and have an established reputation in a traditional branch of science."

The organization is headed by Peter A. Sturrock, professor of space science and astrophysics at Stanford University and (since 1983) deputy director of Stanford's Center for Space Science and Astrophysics. It is open to Corresponding Members (who must belong to "designated organizations"), Student Members, Emeritus Members (qualified retirees) and Associate Members.

The SSE, which holds a conference every year, publishes a refereed semiannual *Journal of*

Scientific Exploration and a newsletter, *The Explorer*, also released twice a year. These periodicals contain articles, news, reviews and commentary on ufology, parapsychology, cryptozoology and other controversies on the borders of science. "Progress towards an agreed understanding of such topics (beginning with the basic question of their reality) is likely to be achieved only if they are subject to the normal processes of open publication, debate, and criticism which constitute the lifeblood of science and scholarship," the SSE says in a position statement. "The Society has no intention of endorsing the reality or significance of any particular topic. Neither does the Society regard current scientific knowledge as immutable, and no subject will be prohibited from discussion or publication simply because it is not now an accepted part of scientific or scholarly knowledge."

Sources:

Goldman, Bruce. "Something Strange: An Interview with Peter Sturrock." *New Realities* 9, 5 (May/June 1989): 36-41.

Sturrock, Peter A. *Evaluation of the Colorado UFO Project.* Palo Alto, CA: Stanford Institute for Plasma Research, 1974.

Sturrock, Peter A. *Report on a Survey of the Membership of the American Astronomical Society Concerning the UFO Problem.* Palo Alto, CA: Institute for Plasma Research, Stanford, University, 1977.

SOLAR LIGHT CENTER
7700 Avenue of the Sun
Central Point, Oregon 97501

The Solar Light Center was established in the mid-1960s by "Telethought Channeler" Marianne Francis, who claims to receive psychic messages from a highly-evolved Space Brother named Sut-Ko. Francis, an active channeler since the 1950s, was associated with one of the early **contactee**

groups, the Solar Cross Fellowship, headed by Rudolph H. Pestalozzi, a channel for Baloran, an extraterrestrial. Eventually Francis' Solar Light group absorbed the Solar Cross. Francis, also known as Aleuti Francesca, is a popular speaker on the New Age occult circuit. Her organization publishes the quarterly *Starcraft*.

Sources:

Francis, Marianne [Aleuti Francesca]. *The Call of the Phoenix.* Central Point, OR: Solar Light Center, n.d.

Francis, Marianne. *New Dimensions and the New Age.* Central Point, OR: Solar Light Center, n.d.

Francis, Marianne. *Starcraft Contact.* Central Point, OR: Solar Light Center, n.d.

Pestalozzi, Rudolph H. *Letters to You from Baloran: A Space Being's Observation of Earth.* Auburn, CA: Solar Cross Fellowship, 1965.

SPACE TECHNOLOGY AND RESEARCH FOUNDATION
448 Rabbit Skin Road
Waynesville, North Carolina 28786

The Space Technology and Research (S.T.A.R.) Foundation is run by Dick and Greta Smolowe, a well-to-do corporate couple who moved to western North Carolina from Westport, Connecticut, at the direction of the Ogatta group, extraterrestrial beings with whom Greta believes herself in psychic communication. As Greta Woodrew she has written two books, *On a Slide of Light* (1981) and *Memories of Tomorrow* (1988), recounting her experiences and relating the Ogattans' role in ushering in a New Age, which will arrive only after massive earth changes in the near future destroy much of the world's population. The Smolowes publish a bimonthly newsletter, *Woodrew Update*, which reports on the Ogattan messages and ecological and other events which point in the editors' view to imminent upheaval.

SPACE TECHNOLOGY AND RESEARCH FOUNDATION (*continued*)

Sources:

Woodrew, Greta. *Memories of Tomorrow*. New York: Dolphin/Doubleday, 1988.

Woodrew, Greta. *On a Slide of Light*. Black Mountain, NC: New Age Press, Inc., 1981.

SPRINKLE, RONALD LEO (1930-)

R. Leo Sprinkle was one of the first psychologists to study the UFO phenomenon from a sympathetic perspective. His openness to the subject stemmed from his own sighting of a daylight disc in 1951, when he was a student at the University of Colorado, and another sighting, this one five years later, which he experienced with his wife. In 1962 Sprinkle, who uses hypnosis in his practice, became a consultant to the Aerial Phenomena Research Organization (APRO). A few years later he served as a psychological consultant to the Condon Committee, the University of Colorado's UFO project sponsored by the U.S. Air Force and directed by Edward U. Condon. In this capacity he authored his first important work in ufology, a survey of attitudes held by people who were interested in UFOs. It was also in this capacity that Sprinkle was called in to the investigation of the case of Nebraska police officer Herbert Schirmer who had reported a puzzling loss of time during what otherwise seemed to be a fairly routine UFO experience. Under hypnosis Schirmer, whose case became one of the most celebrated in ufological annals, recounted a classic abduction experience.

Sprinkle later became involved in the investigation of the **abduction phenomenon** through such prominent abduction cases as those of Carl Higdon (Rawlins, Wyoming) and Sandy Larson (Fargo, North Dakota). In 1980, after years of corresponding with people who believed

themselves to be in psychic and other contact with friendly space people, he hosted the Rocky Mountain Conference on UFO Investigation, which brought contactees to the University of Wyoming campus in Laramie to discuss their beliefs and experiences. The conference has been held every summer since then, with published proceedings. Sprinkle, a genial New Ager with a strong interest in reincarnation, has identified himself as a contactee, but he also has encouraged his colleagues in the mental health field to study the psychological make-up of contactees. One result was his colleague June Parnell's research into Rocky Mountain Conference attendees, the subject of her 1986 Ph.D. thesis for the University of Wyoming's Department of Counselor Education.

Born on August 31, 1930, Ronald Leo Sprinkle graduated with a B.A. from the University of Colorado in 1952, earned his master's degree in personnel services from the same institution four years later, and got his Ph.D. at the University of Missouri in 1961. He taught at the University of North Dakota for three years (1961-64) and during his final year there assumed the directorship of the school's counseling center. In 1964 he joined the faculty of the University of Wyoming and in time became director of counseling and testing. He left the university in the summer of 1989 to take up private practice in Laramie.

Sprinkle, in outlining his own position, notes, "I take the position that there are physical craft, there are biological beings, that these beings are advanced to the point where they can use psychic events and manipulate time and space in such a way that we would regard them as 'angels' or 'demons.' Both physical and psychological processes are variable in the universe and these persons or these beings are in some way moving back and forth through what we think of as the limitations of space and time. . . . There is the possibility that UFO observers are being taught by this very significant event in their lives, perhaps down deep on a level removed from verbal communication" (Clark, 1976).

Sources:

Boyd, Robert D. *International Who's Who of Ufology Directory.* Mobile, AL: The Author, 1988.

Clark, Jerome. "Psychologist-Researcher Dr. R. Leo Sprinkle: Exclusive *UFO Report* Interview." *UFO Report* 3, 2 (June 1976): 30-32, 72-76, 78.

Sprinkle, R. Leo. "Hypnotic and Psychic Aspects of UFO Research." In J. Allen Hynek, ed. *Proceedings of the 1976 CUFOS Conference,* 251-258. Evanston, IL: Center for UFO Studies, 1976.

Sprinkle, R. Leo. "Investigation of the Alleged UFO Experience of Carl Higdon." In Richard F. Haines, ed. *UFO Phenomena and the Behavioral Scientist,* 225-357. Metuchen, NJ: The Scarecrow Press, Inc., 1979.

Sprinkle, R. Leo. *Personal and Scientific Attitudes: A Survey of Persons Interested in UFO Reports.* Laramie, WY: The Author, 1968.

Sprinkle, R. Leo. "Psychological Implications in the Investigation of UFO Reports." In Coral and Jim Lorenzen. *Flying Saucer Occupants.* New York: Signet, 1967. Pp. 160-186.

Story, Ronald D. *The Encyclopedia of UFOs.* Garden City, NY: Doubleday & Company, 1980.

STAR BEACON
Earth Star Publications
Box 174
Delta, Colorado 81416

Star Beacon is an eight-page monthly newsletter for New Age-oriented flying-saucer enthusiasts who are also interested in spiritual awareness, healing, psychic phenomena, crystals and channeling. It is as likely to report on its readers' dreams of UFO contacts as on their fully-conscious UFO sightings. Its editor, Ann Ulrich, is the author of what may be the only romance novel about the UFO **abduction phenomenon.**

Intimate Abduction is described as the saga of "beautiful, sensitive Johanna" who "suddenly finds her life turned upside down by a conspiracy in the form of a bizarre abduction. Her struggle with her own sanity strengthens her for what is to come . . . a journey aboard a mother ship to a planet colony where advanced beings breed with humans in order to acquire their talent and artistic abilities. Amidst the stir of rebellion, Johanna has fallen in love with her abductor, Serassan, and must choose between her allegiance to Earth of [sic] spending the rest of her life with a man whose true appearance frightens her."

Sources:

Ulrich, Ann. *Intimate Abduction.* Delta, CO: Earth Star Publications, 1988.

STEIGER, BRAD (1936-)

Brad Steiger, a prominent figure in the New Age movement, emerged as the major chronicler of the extraterrestrial **contactee** movement in the 1970s and then in the 1980s as a significant advocate of it. In a series of books, he developed the concept of "Star People," a category of contactee embraced by many who felt that they, too, were descendants of extraterrestrials and agents of an interstellar plan to bring a New Age upon the earth.

Born Eugene Olson on February 19, 1936, Steiger grew up on an Iowa farm, where at the age of five he was to encounter a humanoid being which in later books he would describe variously as a smiling elf and as an emotionless, hairless figure with "vertical, reptilian pupils." A near-death experience when he was 11 contributed to a youthful interest in the paranormal. In the early 1960s he began selling stories and articles to various magazines and in 1965 produced his first book, *Ghosts, Ghouls and Other Peculiar People.* A number of paperbacks followed, all in the style virtually invented by the late Frank Edwards, author of such best-sellers as *Stranger Than Science* (1961) and *Strange World* (1964), in which

STEIGER, BRAD (*continued*)

short chapters based on newspaper clippings, articles in paranormal magazines, and other books uncritically recount "true mysteries." Steiger's books were immensely popular and by 1967 the income he was receiving from them allowed him to leave his teaching job at Luther College in Decorah, Iowa, and to embark on a full-time career as author and lecturer. By interesting a large Middle American audience in psychic phenomena and other anomalies, such as UFOs (about which he wrote several books, beginning with *Strangers from the Skies* [1966]), he helped spawn the psychic boom of the early 1970s in which the concept of the "New Age" came into prominence.

Possibly more significantly, for the UFO community, his early UFO books, such as *Strangers from the Skies* (1966) and *Flying Saucers Are Hostile*, written with Joan Whritenour (1967), have played an important role in shaping popular conceptions of the UFO phenomenon while building popular support for belief in the existence of UFOs, their extraterrestrial character, and their possible hostile intent. There is probably no one who has written so many books on the subject of UFOs or has been so widely read as Steiger.

Their popular appeal notwithstanding, Steiger's early books were dismissed by critics as potboilers. His first undeniably important book was the hardcover *Revelation: The Divine Fire* (1973). A cover blurb describes it as "An Investigation of Men and Women Who Claim to be in Spiritual Communication with a Higher Intelligence." In the book Steiger interviewed dozens of persons who believed they had encountered extraterrestrials and through psychic and visionary means believed themselves to be recipients (via what has traditionally been termed mediumship but which they renamed "channeling") of regular philosophical and theological messages from benevolent beings from other planets and dimensions. *Revelation*, along with its earlier companion volume, *Aquarian Revelations* (1971), is an invaluable survey of an emerging movement which introduced the concept of channeling as a major element to the New Age Movement in the 1980s.

A sequel, *Gods of Aquarius: UFOs and the Transformation of Man* (1976), would narrow its focus to flying-saucer contactees. Steiger introduces the concept of "Star People," human beings tied by physiology, past lives or both to extraterrestrials who long ago came to earth. These persons have had encounters all their lives with otherworldly companions who are preparing them for the "approaching time of transition, the great cleansing, which the entire species must endure and survive in order to attain a higher state of consciousness and to effect personal and societal transformation."

Steiger left his first wife to marry one of the Star People, Francie Paschal of Schenectady, New York, and the two moved to Scottsdale, Arizona, to begin an active metaphysical and business partnership. Steiger wrote that the two were karmically tied (they had been copassengers on a starship that crashed on earth thousands of years ago) and had a mission to "activate" the Star People. An article about them in the *National Enquirer* brought hundreds of letters and phone calls from persons claiming to be Star People. Between 1981 and 1983 Berkley published five paperbacks in the "Star People" series, two of them reprints of *Revelation* and *Gods* and three of them originals by Brad and Francie writing alone or in collaboration with one another.

In the mid-1980s the couple, by this time superstars of the New Age, broke up, and Brad married Sherry Hansen, a Phoenix-based contactee. In 1988 he wrote *The Fellowship*, something of a follow-up to *Gods*.

Steiger says, "I have come to the conclusion that, throughout history, some external intelligence has interacted with *Homo sapiens* in an effort to learn more about us—or in an effort to communicate to our species certain basic truths. I am also convinced that some kind of subtle symbiotic relationship exists between mankind and the UFO intelligences."

Sources:

Steiger, Brad. *Alien Meetings*. New York: Ace, 1978.

Steiger, Brad. *The Aquarian Revelations*. New York: Dell, 1971.

Steiger, Brad. "Eighteen Theories on UFOs." *California UFO* 1, 1 (September/October 1986): 16-17.

Steiger, Brad. *Encounters of the Angelic Kind*. Cottonwood, AZ: Esoteric, 1979.

Steiger, Brad. *The Fellowship*. New York: Dolphin/Doubleday, 1988.

Steiger, Brad. *The Flying Saucer Menace: The Untold Story of the UFO Threat*. New York: Award, 1967.

Steiger, Brad. *Gods of Aquarius: UFOs and the Transformation of Man*. New York: Harcourt Brace Jovanovich, 1976.

Steiger, Brad. *Revelation: The Divine Fire*. Englewood Cliffs, NJ: Prentice-Hall, Inc., 1973.

Steiger, Brad. *The Seed*. New York: Berkley Books, 1983.

Steiger, Brad. *Strangers from the Skies*. New York: Award, 1966.

Steiger, Brad. *You Too May Be from Krypton*. [Scottsdale, AZ]: The Author, n.d.

Steiger, Brad, ed. *Project Blue Book*. New York: Ballantine Books, 1976.

Steiger, Brad, and Francie Steiger. *The Star People*. New York: Berkley Books, 1981.

Steiger, Brad, and Joan Whritenour. *Flying Saucer Invasion: Target-Earth*. New York: Award, 1969.

Steiger, Brad, and Joan Whritenour. *Flying Saucers Are Hostile*. New York: Award, 1967.

Steiger, Brad, and Joan Whritenour. *New UFO Breakthrough*. New York: Award, 1974.

Steiger, Brad, and John White, eds. *Other Worlds, Other Universes: Playing the Reality Game*. Garden City, NY: Doubleday & Company, 1975.

Steiger, Brad, and Joan Whritenour, eds. *The Allende Letters: A Challenging New Theory on the Origin of Flying Saucers*. New York: Universal, 1968.

Story, Ronald D. *The Encyclopedia of UFOs*. Garden City, NY: Doubleday & Company, 1980.

STRIEBER, WHITLEY (1945-)

Whitley Strieber was the most popular writer of UFO books in the 1980s—he wrote three of them—and all landed on the best-seller lists for varying periods of time. By far the most successful was the first, *Communion: A True Story* which stayed on the *New York Times* list for most of 1987. *Communion* and its sequel, *Transformation: The Breakthrough* (1988), were deeply personal, autobiographical works which recounted the author's abduction experiences with beings he called "the visitors." *Majestic* (1989) is a science-fiction novel based on the Roswell incident and on Strieber's theories about the meaning of UFO visitation.

Before 1986 Strieber was unknown to the UFO community, though to the larger world he was known as the author of horror and futuristic novels. He was born on June 13, 1945, in San Antonio, the son of Karl and Mary Strieber. Strieber's father was a prominent lawyer who had amassed wealth through investments in oil and gas. His mother was the daughter of a local construction magnate. He attended the University of Texas. After a semester of work at the law school there, he set off for Europe, then moved to New York City to take up what proved to be a financially-rewarding writing career. His life

STRIEBER, WHITLEY (*continued*)

changed dramatically after a bizarre event on the evening of December 26, 1985, when a series of strange encounters of which he did not have full conscious memory took place. Later, under hypnosis, he related an encounter with humanoids who inserted a needle into his brain.

Strieber subsequently learned of **Budd Hopkins**, a famous abduction investigator who lived not far from Strieber's Manhattan apartment, and through Hopkins met psychiatrist Donald F. Klein, who gave him a series of tests and concluded he was psychologically normal. Through hypnosis Strieber began to explore other puzzling events in his earlier life and concluded he had been interacting with "visitors" since he was a child. Soon he was writing *Communion*, which was published in January 1987, to generally favorable (and often bemused) reviews. (By far the most hostile was written by fellow science-fiction writer Thomas M. Disch in *The Nation* on March 14, 1987. Disch accused Strieber of making up the story. But most other reviewers, including those not prepared to accept the literal reality of "the visitors," echoed *People*'s sentiments: "Strieber is hardly the sort to risk his reputation in the service of mere sensationalism; there are easier ways for him to make money than chronicling his bizarre encounters with what he suggests are intelligent nonhuman beings" [Green, 1987].) Two other UFO books came out not long afterwards, Hopkins' *Intruders* and Gary Kinder's *Light Years* (the latter dealing with the controversial claims of Swiss contactee Billy Meier), and they and the Strieber book were often reviewed together and treated as evidence of renewed popular interest in UFOs.

Strieber and Hopkins fell out, partly for personal reasons and partly because of their differing interpretations of the **abduction phenomenon**. Despite the terror and trauma he chronicles in his books, Strieber sees the visitors as essentially benevolent beings who are aiding in our spiritual education—essentially a **contactee** interpretation, though without the blond-haired Space Brothers of traditional contactee lore.

Hopkins, on the other hand, rejected this view, saying that it was not true to the almost wholly negative experiences reported by other abductees, who felt the UFO beings were coldly indifferent to their welfare. Strieber gave an emotional address to the 1987 conference of the **Mutual UFO Network** (MUFON) in Washington, D.C., but after that he and the UFO community mostly went their separate ways, though not particularly amicably. He gave some financial support to the **Fund for UFO Research** and maintained friendships with Fund president **Bruce Maccabee** and California ufologist **William L. Moore**, but in his lectures and writings he tended to disparage ufologists for their generally suspicious view of "the visitors" and warned abductees and contactees to stay away from them. In 1989 he set up the **Communion Foundation**, a New Age-oriented group, one of whose major purposes is to establish a productive relationship with the UFO intelligences.

In November 1989 William Morrow, the publisher of *Communion* and *Transformation*, released a thick book by San Antonio writer Ed Conroy, *Report on "Communion,"* dealing with Conroy's extensive investigation of Strieber's claims and also with his controversial interactions with the UFO community. Conroy concluded that Strieber was telling the truth; he also said he had had bizarre abductionlike experiences while working on his book. Conroy was not alone in alleging such things. Guests at Strieber's cabin in upstate New York, where many of his encounters are said to have occurred, also claim to have witnessed out-of-the-ordinary phenomena.

Undoubtedly the wildest story told in association with *Communion* and Strieber was first chronicled in *New York* magazine. A man identified only as a "senior editor at William Morrow" said he had seen the aliens in Womrath's bookstore on Lexington Avenue. "A man and a woman, bundled in mufflers, hats, and long overcoats, rushed over to the rack and picked up *Communion*," he was quoted as saying. "I heard them say, 'He's got it all wrong—look at that.' They spoke rapidly in what sounded like educated Upper East Side Jewish accents." The editor said they were wearing large tinted glasses through which huge "dark, almond-shaped eyes" could be seen (Cochran, 1987).

In his book Conroy identifies the editor as Bruce Lee, a former *Newsweek* Washington correspondent who underwent and passed a polygraph test about the encounter. Lee told Conroy that he approached the "very short" couple, introduced himself as an employee of the publisher, and asked what it was they didn't like about the book. The man ignored him but the woman somehow communicated "complete loathing, hatred." Badly shaken, Lee quickly retreated, grabbed his wife and left the bookstore.

Sources:

Cochran, Tracy. "Invasion of the Strieber Snatchers." *New York* (March 30, 1987): 26.

Conroy, Ed. *Report on "Communion": An Independent Investigation of and Commentary on Whitley Strieber's "Communion."* New York: William Morrow and Company, Inc., 1989.

Green, Michelle. "Making Communion with Another World." *People* (May 11, 1989): 34-39.

Strieber, Whitley. *Communion: A True Story.* New York: Beach Tree/William Morrow, 1987.

Strieber, Whitley. *Majestic.* New York: G. P. Putnam's Sons, 1989.

Strieber, Whitley. *Transformation: The Breakthrough.* New York: William Morrow and Company, Inc., 1988.

SWORDS, MICHAEL D. (1940-)

Michael D. Swords, professor of natural sciences at Western Michigan University, is an active figure in scientific UFO study. He edits the *Journal of UFO Studies*, published by the **J. Allen Hynek Center for UFO Studies**, the only refereed scientific journal in the field. Swords' articles on the extraterrestrial hypothesis (ETH), the sociology of science as it relates to controversies about anomalous phenomena, and other subjects have appeared in the *MUFON UFO Journal*, *International UFO Reporter* and *Pursuit*.

Born in East St. Louis, Illinois, on November 11, 1940, Swords has degrees in chemistry (B.S., University of Notre Dame), biochemistry (M.S., Iowa State University), and history of science and technology (Ph.D., Case Western Reserve University). During the past two decades he has taught human biology, environmental planning, history and philosophy of science, and cosmic evolution. He has also received his university's teaching excellence award. In 1974 he devised and taught a class on scientific methodology, using anomalies (UFOs, parapsychological occurrences, and cryptozoological animals) as the subject matter. He is a board member of CUFOS and an active member of the **Society for Scientific Exploration** (SSE), an organization of scientists and academics studying controversial claims and unexplained phenomena.

Swords says, "I believe that there are, *at a minimum*, very interesting and scientifically important de novo discoveries to be uncovered in the range of UFO phenomena. Some of these almost surely include geological and meteorological anomalies, perceptual and brain-response anomalies, and unclassified psychological conditions or states. I believe that the whole thrust of science indicates the commonness of extraterrestrial life, and therefore the feasibility of the ETI/UFO hypothesis. Rare ETI-based UFO phenomena could be the solution to the Fermi Paradox, though I believe that no individual case comes even close to proving this at this time. I believe that the vast majority of UFO reports have nothing to do with ETI and that the vast majority of humans feeling (albeit honestly) that they've had contact with ETI have *not* had such contact. I believe that the majority of **contactee**-abductees are really looking for religion and deep spiritual answers and that the majority of traumatic-abductees (a different subset) are, rather, creating shield fantasies based in

SWORDS, MICHAEL D. (*continued*)

information in pop culture and the UFO cult-culture. These fantasies are to mask earlier very human traumatic experiences (rape, incest, abuse, deaths, et al) and may be intensely believed by the shield-makers.

"Whether anything within the scope of UFO phenomena turns out to be scientifically productive or not, those phenomena, and the serious researchers who investigate them, and the wonder-filled public who report them, must be dealt with in objective and (until indicated otherwise) respectful ways. The current atmosphere has made what should be wonderful opportunities to engage the public's (and students') interest in research methods, relevant related science knowledge, and the thrill of discovery rather a distasteful negative interaction in which few observers or researchers wanted to openly participate. . . . Perhaps soon some sociologist-writer will chronicle these aspects of the sociology of science in our times and marvel at the spectacle of a community of scholars effectively and counterproductively programmed to react toward many subjects of great public fascination in ways which continually distance themselves from that public and . . . markedly hinder what research is possible in those difficult fields. We scientists need to have more faith *in* science and its method. Let the data, not the opinions, talk" (personal communication, 1989).

Sources:

Swords, Michael D. "Are There Parallel Universes?" *International UFO Reporter* 12, 6 (November/December 1987): 17-20.

Swords, Michael D. "Close Encounters: Mind or Matter?" *International UFO Reporter* 10, 5 (September/October 1985): 13-14.

Swords, Michael D. "Science and the Extraterrestrial Hypothesis in Ufology." *Journal of UFO Studies* 1 (new series, 1989): 67-102.

Swords, Michael D. "UFO Research: Status Quo." In *Using Concepts from UFO Studies to Teach Science and Critical Thinking*, 43-48. Phoenix, AZ: prepared for National Science Teachers Association Conference, privately published, 1989.

T

TRANS-EN-PROVENCE CE2

In ufology, a close encounter of the second kind (CE2) occurs when a UFO leaves physical traces at the place where a UFO was reported to have appeared. While numerous CE2 cases have been investigated and accounts compiled (Phillips, 1974; Merritt, 1977), few compare with one that occurred in France early in the 1980s.

At 5 p.m. on January 8, 1981, an old man named Renato Nicolai was working in his garden in the village of Trans-en-Provence. When he heard an odd whistling sound, he looked up to see what he would describe as a "ship" just above two pine trees at the far edge of his property. The object was moving toward the garden as if intending to land. When it did so, Nicolai fled to a small cabin on a hill above his house. From this perspective he looked down and saw the object resting on the ground. He was about 250 feet from it. As he would later describe it to investigators, "The ship was in the form of two saucers upside down, one against the other. It must have been just about 1.5 meters high. It was the color of lead. The ship had a border or type of brace around its circumference."

Suddenly the whistling sound resumed, only this time more loudly and constantly. Then the object rose up from the ground to about treetop height before shooting off toward the northeast. Nicolai said, "Underneath the brace I saw, as it took off, two kinds of round pieces which could have been landing gear or feet. There were also two circles

which looked kind of like trap doors. The two feet or landing gear extended about 20 centimeters beneath the body of the whole ship."

As the object lifted from the ground, it kicked up a small amount of dust. Gathering speed, it passed between the two trees through which it had arrived.

Nicolai went inside to tell his wife what he had seen. She thought he was joking, but the next day, when the two of them went outside to inspect the landing site, they found traces on the soil—traces that suggested some kind of large vehicle had settled on the soil and left impressions of its presence. Nicolai, a near-illiterate who knew nothing of UFOs (investigators would later have to explain to him what the concept means), thought he had seen a secret aerial device developed by the French military.

The Gendarmerie were notified and were at the site the day after the sighting, noting in their official report, "We observed the presence of two concentric circles, one 2.2 meters in diameter and the other 2.4 meters in diameter. The two circles form a sort of corona 10 centimeters thick on this corona, one within the other. There are two parts clearly visible, and they also show black striations." The officers took soil samples, both from within the circles and from outside them, the latter intended to serve as a control.

On the 12th **Groupe d'Etude des Phénomènes Aérospatiaux Non-Identifiés** (GEPAN), France's

TRANS-EN-PROVENCE CE2 (*continued*)

official UFO-investigation agency, learned of the incident and the following month conducted its own on-site inquiries. The traces were still intact. After extensive interviews, the GEPAN investigators concluded Nicolai was telling the truth and suffered from no psychological problems. Initial study of the traces suggested interesting effects on the plant life. The samples were taken to a leading specialist in plant traumatology, botanist Michael Bounias of the Institut National de la Recherche Agronomique. Bounias conducted an extensive investigation over the next two years. The results, published in 66 pages of small print in GEPAN's *Technical Note 16* (1983), can be summarized as follows:

(1) The chlorophyll pigment in the leaf samples was weakened from 30 to 50 percent.

(2) The young leaves "withstood the most serious losses, evolving toward the content and composition more characteristic of old leaves." In other words, the leaves had aged in some way that neither natural processes nor laboratory experiments could duplicate.

(3) There was evidence, GEPAN reported, of the "occurrence of an important event which brought with it deformations of the terrain caused by mass, mechanics, a heating effect and perhaps certain transformations and deposits of trace minerals [phosphate and zinc]. . . . We cannot give a precise and unique interpretation to this remarkable combination of results. . . . We can state that there is, nonetheless, confirmation of a very significant event which happened on this spot."

In 1987 GEPAN head Jean-Jacques Velasco would say of the case, "The effects on plants in the area can be compared with that produced on the leaves of other plant species after exposing the seeds to gamma radiation. Data show that a considerable amount of gamma radiation (10 to the sixth power rads) must be applied to produce a disturbance equivalent to that observed at the site. Should we consider the presence of ionizing

(nuclear) radiation? Almost certainly not, since no measurable residual radioactivity is present in plants. However, could the trauma be caused by an electromagnetic field? Probably?" (Velasco, 1987).

GEPAN considered the Trans-en-Provence CE2 the "most significant" and evidential case it had investigated. As Alain Esterle, the group's director at the time of the incident, would remark, "For the first time we have found a combination of factors which conduce us to accept that something similar to what the eyewitness has described actually did take place there."

GEPAN's conclusions about this extraordinary event have never been seriously challenged, but GEPAN did not escape criticism for incompetence in related areas. Physicist Jean-Pierre Petit has complained, "We know that other landings occurred in France, but Bounias, in spite of his excellent work about the Trans-en-Provence affair, was kept away. Just one year later a UFO stood 20 minutes in the garden of a researcher, in northern France. But the grass and flower samples were ruined. The policemen sent samples to a biology laboratory in Toulouse, but they cut the stalks too short and packed the samples in plastic bags. When the grass samples arrived at the laboratory, they were completely rotten" (Petit, 1988).

To ufologists the Trans-en-Provence case was, as **Mark Rodeghier** of the **J. Allen Hynek Center for UFO Studies** would remark, "perhaps the most significant investigation ever undertaken of a single UFO report." Rodeghier noted the taunt of UFO debunker Robert Sheaffer, who had written that UFOs are a "jealous phenomenon," never producing real evidence of their reality, meaning, to Sheaffer, that they do not exist. Rodeghier countered Sheaffer in an editorial in *International UFO Reporter*:

"What is the significance of the GEPAN investigation? Fundamentally, it is evidence that the UFO phenomenon is *not* jealous, but rather that its careful investigation is very costly. Doing significant physical science is quite expensive today—the cost of a new particle accelerator is measured in the tens of millions of dollars. It is very likely that the key explanation of why there does not exist substantial and reliable evidence for the existence of UFOs, such as spectra, instrumented photos, and well-analyzed soil samples, has to do with the lack of money and facilities for UFO research and investigation. What progress could be made today in studying earthquakes without instrumented recording stations? Very little, to be sure, and supplying the appropriate instrumentation to geophysicists is costly. The same principle applies to the UFO phenomenon.

"If UFOs have appeared to be a jealous phenomenon—and they have—that is because the means were not available by which a systematic study of their properties might be undertaken. GEPAN has proven this to be true. Given the means by the French government, it was able to produce a thorough and revealing report about *one* UFO event. Imagine what we would know today if there had been sufficient funds to investigate 100 physical trace cases to the depth attained by GEPAN in their work."

Sources:

Enquête 81/01: Analyse d'un Trace. Toulouse, France: GEPAN, March 1, 1983. A partial translation appears as "GEPAN's Most Significant Case." *MUFON UFO Journal* 193 (March 1984): 3-16.

Merritt, Fred. *Physical Traces of UFO Sightings: A Computer Printout.* Evanston, IL: Center for UFO Studies, 1977.

Petit, Jean-Pierre. "The UFO Impact." *Pursuit* 21, 1 (First Quarter 1988): 10-13.

Phillips, Ted, Jr. *Physical Traces Associated with UFO Sightings.* [Evanston, IL]: Center for UFO Studies, 1975.

Rodeghier, Mark. "Editorial." *International UFO Reporter* 9, 5 (September/October 1984): 2-3.

Velasco, Jean-Jacques. "Scientific Approach and Results of Studies Into Unidentified Aerospace Phenomena in France." In Walter H. Andrus, Jr., and Richard H. Hall, eds. *MUFON 1987 UFO Symposium Proceedings*, 51-67. Seguin, TX: Mutual UFO Network, Inc., 1987.

TREATMENT AND RESEARCH ON EXPERIENCED ANOMALOUS TRAUMA
13 Summit Terrace
Dobbs Ferry, New York 10522

Treatment and Research on Experienced Anomalous Trauma (TREAT) is the brainchild of Rima E. Laibow, M.D., a Westchester County, New York, psychiatrist who seeks to bring the mental-health community into the investigation of the **abduction phenomenon**, which she prefers to call (as the organization's name suggests) "experienced anomalous trauma." Laibow, who does not regard herself as a ufologist, sees the abduction experience not as a symptom of pathology but as an unknown, an event that may be outside the realm of conventional psychological explanation. If its cause remains mysterious, therapists can at least treat its effects, which Laibow contends are indicative of post-traumatic stress disorder. As a psychiatrist, Laibow became involved with a family of abductees who reported that they were victims of child abuse.

The first TREAT conference was held between May 12 and 14, 1989, at Fairfield University in Connecticut, bringing together about 50 invited specialists from the sciences and ufology under conditions of anonymity and confidentiality for private discussions of how appropriate methodologies could be developed to study the abduction phenomenon. Discussion about the nature of the phenomenon was proscribed, held to be outside the conference's purpose. The meeting, with financial support from the **Mutual UFO Network** (MUFON), the **Fund for UFO Research** and the **J. Allen Hynek Center for UFO Studies** (CUFOS) as well as by a member of a European royal family, was regarded as a success. TREAT established a broadly-based program

TREATMENT AND RESEARCH ON EXPERIENCED ANOMALOUS TRAUMA (*continued*)

which was delegated to committees on ethics, research protocols, data collection, interdisciplinary relations, professional training, clinical issues, funding, and public relations.

In the weeks and months following the conference, a schism developed between TREAT members over a variety of issues, including Laibow's leadership (especially in her decision to throw two leading ufologists and abduction experts, **Budd Hopkins** and **David M. Jacobs**, out of TREAT), her assertion that mental-health professionals should have the primary role over, not just a cooperative association with, ufologists in abduction investigation, and her controversial interactions with several individual abductees. There was also serious disagreement over the structure and purpose of the next TREAT meeting, set for February 1990 at the Virginia Polytechnic Institute. As the dispute grew more bitter and more personal, most ufologists and many mental-health professionals left TREAT, taking much of the organization's original funding with them. Laibow was able, however, to secure other funding and made plans for the next meeting, with a largely new group of invited participants.

Meantime disaffected TREAT members were securing financial support for a new organization to deal with many of the issues TREAT was intended to address. At the same time Toronto psychotherapist David A. Gotlib, M.D., onetime member of TREAT's ethics committee, created a newsletter, *Ratchet Patrol: A Monthly Networking Newsletter About Experienced Anomalous Trauma for Interested Scientists*, as a forum for psychiatrists, psychologists and other professionals interested in "experienced anomalous trauma."

Sources:

Laibow, Rima E. "Dual Victims: The Abused and the Abducted." *International UFO Reporter* 14, 3 (May/June 1989): 4-9.

Laibow, Rima E. "Therapist and Investigator: A Definition of Roles." *MUFON UFO Journal* 261 (January 1990): 10-14.

Laibow, Rima E., ed. *Abduction Conference. May 12-14, 1989.* Fairfield, CT: TREAT, 1989.

U

UFO CONTACT CENTER INTERNATIONAL
30001 South 288th Street #304
Federal Way, Washington 98003
and
Box 337
Bagdad, Arizona 86321

UFO Contact Center International (UFOCCI) came into being in Washington state in 1978, under the direction of Aileen Edwards, now Aileen Bringle, following her September 2, 1989, marriage to Gerald Bringle, director of UFOCCI's newly-formed Southwest Headquarters in Arizona.

Aileen Bringle says, "At the time we were having meetings every week for abductees in our home and one monthly meeting for the public in a public place. On June 4, 1981, we officially incorporated. . . ."

UFOCCI holds private monthly meetings for abductees in which, Bringle says, they "discuss their cases and find that others experience the same type of phenomena. Through this group therapy they work out what has been subconsciously bothering them. I am a hypnotist so I am able to work with them to find out what all happened. I do not charge for that service. Some of the centers do. . . . Each of our centers throughout the U.S. and Canada are [sic] headed up by abductees or **contactees**. Each center is autonomous." As of 1989, 36 such centers existed across the United States.

"Once a year we hold the annual 'Jorpah.' That word came from Dr. Greta Woodrew's book, *On a Slide of Light*. It means universal or cosmic gathering. . . . The Jorpah is always on Labor Day weekend. The next one [1990] will be held in Seattle and after that they will be held in Arizona."

UFOCCI publishes a monthly newsletter, *The Missing Link*, consisting largely of reprints of newspaper and magazine articles on UFO and New Age subjects. A letters section relates readers' views and experiences.

The focus of the bulletin and the organization is largely uncritical, taking even the most extreme claims on their face, from contactee stories to speculations about cannibalistic aliens. UFOCCI is committed to what might be described as a broad pluralistic interpretation of the extraterrestrial hypothesis (ETH), noting, "Along with human extraterrestrials, we have discovered 'animal-beings,' 'insect-beings,' and other forms of life which we alternately find interesting or repulsive. All of these are currently visiting, staying, have been here, and/or coming periodically. They have interests in earth people, [and] the planet, or need our resources. These life forms exhibit all the traits of earth people, examples: kindness, warmth, evil, trickery, etc. So it would seem we must acquaint ourselves with them in order to understand what, and who, we are dealing with."

Among the principal extraterrestrial visitors, according to UFOCCI, are benevolent, attractive-

UFO CONTACT CENTER INTERNATIONAL (*continued*)

looking Pleiadians who have "bases here on earth . . . generally in the mountainous regions. They live an average of 900 years or more, and long ago solved the problems which plague us." There are also the "Greys" who hail from Zeta Reticuli I and II and who "are from a civilization dedicated completely to interstellar research and life analysis. Their skin is grey, they are small and short, with large heads and large black 'wraparound' eyes, which may or may not be part of their space suits. They are human like, or either robots or humanoids. They . . . abduct, at will, many humans for genetic purposes. . . ."

In 1991 UFOCCI's Northwest Headquarters will close down and all operations will be run out of Southwest Headquarters.

UFO MAGAZINE
1800 South Robertson Boulevard #355
Los Angeles, California 90035

UFO magazine, "a forum on extraordinary theories and phenomena," was founded under the title *California UFO* in 1986. Edited by Vicki Cooper and Sherie Stark, it is published bimonthly, has over 1000 subscribers and claims a circulation of 10,000. Each issue is 48 pages long. *UFO* covers all aspects of ufology, with a strong emphasis on current news. The magazine takes no single position and publishes articles, interviews and reviews on all sides of the UFO controversy, with contributions by many of ufology's leading figures.

UFO NEWSCLIPPING SERVICE
Route 1, Box 220, Plumerville, Arkansas 72127

UFO Newsclipping Service, co-edited by Lucius Farish and Rod B. Dyke, is a monthly whose 20 legal-sized pages contain offprints of newspaper clippings about recent American and foreign UFO sightings, personalities and speculations. The last several pages are devoted to "Forteana News": clippings dealing with monster reports, falls from the sky, and other physical anomalies of the kind originally defined by curiosity-collector/satirist Charles Fort.

UNICAT PROJECT

UNICAT is a database for high-quality UFO events developed by Willy Smith, in association with the late **J. Allen Hynek**, in the early 1980s. Smith, who had taught physics at a small college in Pennsylvania, retired in 1980 to devote full-time to UFO study, a subject that had interested him since the 1950s but with which he became more fully engaged following a 1973 European trip, when he met with leading Spanish and French ufologists.

According to Smith, for a case to be entered into UNICAT it must have multiple witnesses ("although high quality single-witness incidents could also be considered under special circumstances"), be investigated by "well-known ufologists" and include at least ten "characteristic parameters" (out of a possible 225) as defined by Hynek (Smith, 1985). Preferably there ought to be a "lengthy written report" which would allow the "developers" (Smith and Hynek) to break down a case into "bits of information." By 1987, Smith claimed (Hynek died in 1986), some 600 cases had passed all the necessary tests and qualified as solid data unlikely to be refuted.

In a two-part article published in *International UFO Reporter* Paul Fuller, a professional statistician associated with the British UFO Research Association (BUFORA), and Wim van Utrecht, a prominent Belgian ufologist, criticized UNICAT for methodological flaws and for bias in the selection of cases and variables. "We are concerned," they wrote, "that the project's director seems to believe that—if the unexplained cases represent anything at all—they must represent a technological phenomenon . . . when the whole point of applying statistical methodology to the analysis of the UFO data is to avoid any possible charge of bias by ufologists." They also pointed out that a "written report" prepared by a "known researcher" is no guarantee of quality of investigation.

They conclude that "unless UNICAT adopts a more representative sampling procedure, the existing method of selecting cases introduces all kinds of bias which distorts or masks real quantitative variations between explained and unexplained events. Even if UNICAT was adopting a random sampling procedure, the method by which UFO reports come to the attention of ufologists still introduces statistical bias into the UNICAT database which at present we are unable to evaluate. For this reason alone any current database of UFO reports cannot be used to infer characteristics of UFO reports in general, let alone one that introduces all manner of additional bias into the sampling procedure" (Fuller and van Utrecht, 1989).

Sources:

Fuller, Paul, and Wim van Utrecht. "The Trouble with UNICAT." *International UFO Reporter* Pt. I. 14, 4 (July/August 1989): 7-10; Pt II. 14, 5 (September/October 1989): 14-16.

Hynek, J. Allen. "Profile—Dr. Willy Smith." *International UFO Reporter* 9, 5 (September/October 1984): 3.

Smith, Willy. "The Case Against Skepticism." In Hilary Evans, and John Spencer, eds. *UFOs 1947-1987: The 40-Year Search for an Explanation.* London: Fortean Tomes, 1987. Pp. 371-376.

Smith, Willy. "On the Nature of UFO Reports." *MUFON UFO Journal* 237 (January 1988): 17-18, 22.

Smith, Willy. "The Uniqueness of UNICAT." *International UFO Reporter* 10, 5 (September/October 1985): 19.

UNIVERSE SOCIETY CHURCH
Box 38132
Los Angeles, California 90038

The Universe Society Church (UNISOC) was founded in 1951 under the name Institute of Parapsychology. Later it was known as the Universe Society before assuming its present name in the early 1980s. Its past and present head is Hal Wilcox, who began as a Spiritualist medium. Then in the early 1950s he began channeling psychic communications from the Ancient Brother-hood of Fahsz (TABOF). Fahsz, a resident of the planet Narvon in the Altair system, relates that the earth lives in a sector (comprising seven galaxies) of the universe under the guidance of Master Brsgv and that flying saucers are spacecraft used in the colonization of habitable planets. TABOF teaches that God—"The Father, The Ultimate One, The Force behind All Force, the Ultimate Cause Behind All Cause"—created the universe.

The UNISOC conducts regular short services at its one existing center in Hollywood. During these services a mantrum is chanted and a 30-minute channeled message delivered through one of UNISOC's 12 oracles. During the service the pineal gland is activated and linked to a galactic computer bank operated by one of the Space Brothers under Fahsz's command.

In 1963 Wilcox had his first physical contact with a Space Brother, Zemkla, governor of the planet Selo in the Barnard's Star system.

Through its Galaxy Press UNISOC publishes the teachings of TABOF and accounts of Wilcox's interactions with extraterrestrials.

Sources:

Melton, J. Gordon. *Encyclopedia of American Religions.* Detroit: Gale Research Company, 1989.

Rochette, Ed. "Use of Money Universal." *Numismatic News* (November 14, 1989).

UNIVERSE SOCIETY CHURCH (*continued*)

Wilcox, Hal. *Gateway to Superconsciousness*. Los Angeles: Galaxy, [1965?].

Wilcox, Hal. *Going Up! Practical Methods of Astral Projection*. Hollywood, CA: The Author, 1964.

Wilcox, Hal. *UFO Flight: Visit to Planet Selo*. Azusa, CA: Galaxy, 1968.

Wilcox, Hal. *Zemkla: Interplanetary Avatar*. Los Angeles: Galaxy, 1966.

V

VALLEE, JACQUES FRANCIS (1939-)

Jacques Francis Vallee is one of ufology's most influential theorists, the author of several widely-read books, and possibly the only UFO investigator to serve as the model for a character in a blockbuster movie (the French scientist played by François Truffaut in Steven Spielberg's *Close Encounters of the Third Kind*).

Vallee came into prominence as the author of *Anatomy of a Phenomenon* (1965), regarded as one of the classic works in the UFO literature, a scientist's brief for the extraterrestrial hypothesis (ETH) of UFO origin. A more technical work, *Challenge to Science: The UFO Enigma* (written with Janine Vallee), followed in 1966; *Challenge* is best remembered for its falsification of the theory of orthoteny proposed by French ufologist Aimé Michel in *Flying Saucers and the Straight-Line Mystery* (1958). But in *Passport to Magonia* (1969), Vallee proposed a radical reinterpretation of the UFO phenomenon, arguing that UFO phenomena are better understood when related to folk traditions about supernatural creatures than to astronomers' speculations about life on other planets. Although Vallee was later to insist that he was not dismissing UFOs as imaginary, many readers took him to mean just that and *Passport* helped bring into being the **psychosocial hypothesis** which would come to dominate European ufology in the 1980s. The psychosocial theorists hold that UFO phenomena and beings exist only in subjective visionary experience.

In the 1970s Vallee added political-conspiracy theories to the mix in two books, *The Invisible College* (1975) and *Messengers of Deception* (1979), which even many of his admirers found unconvincing. Vallee suggested that a shadowy group is manipulating UFO beliefs for its own purposes. He also speculated that the UFO phenomenon operates as a "control system"—manifested in "intense [UFO] activity followed by quiet periods"—intended to lead human consciousness to new concepts of reality.

After a long period out of the limelight, in 1988 Vallee returned with *Dimensions*, a one-volume compilation of his three previous, out-of-print works. In 1990 his most important book since *Passport*—and arguably his best since his first two—appeared. *Confrontations* is an account of Vallee's investigations of UFO-related deaths and physical-evidence cases in California, South America and elsewhere.

Born in France in 1939, Vallee got his bachelor's degree in mathematics from the University of Paris in 1959. Two years later he received a master's degree in astrophysics from Lille University. In 1962 he moved to the United States and to Northwestern University in Evanston, Illinois. There he met **J. Allen Hynek**, then head of the Northwestern astronomy department. Vallee's interest in UFOs had been sparked by a 1961 incident which occurred when he was tracking satellites at the Paris Observatory. After a UFO was tracked, the project director

VALLEE, JACQUES FRANCIS (*continued*)

erased the data tape almost immediately. Vallee was stunned both by the UFO tracking and by the director's actions, and he decided that the UFO question was well worth pursuing. He and Hynek became personally and professionally close and Vallee was instrumental in the creation of Hynek's "**invisible college**" of scientists quietly monitoring and researching UFO data. In 1967 Vallee got his Ph.D. in computer science. He moved to the San Francisco area, where he has lived ever since, writing and working in the computer field.

He says, "For many years, UFO phenomena have served as a support for human imagination, a framework for human tragedy, a fabric of human dreams. We react to them in our movies, our poetry, our music, our science fiction. And they react to us. . . . The phenomena function like an operational system of symbolic communication at a global level. There is something about the human race with which they interact, and we do not yet know what it is. They are part of the environment, part of the control system for human evolution."

Sources:

Clark, Jerome. "Vallee Discusses UFO Control System." *Fate* 31, 2 (February 1978): 60-68.

Story, Ronald D. *The Encyclopedia of UFOs.* Garden City, NY: Doubleday & Company, 1980.

Vallee, Jacques. *Anatomy of a Phenomenon: Unidentified Objects in Space–A Scientific Appraisal.* Chicago: Henry Regnery Company, 1965.

Vallee, Jacques. *A Century of UFO Landings.* N. p.: The Author, [1969?].

Vallee, Jacques. *Contact Survey: Based on Sighting Documentation and Case Investigation in UFO Phenomena.* Belmont, CA: The Author, [1974].

Vallee, Jacques. *Dimensions: A Casebook of Alien Contact.* Chicago: Contemporary Books, 1988.

Vallee, Jacques. *The Invisible College: What a Group of Scientists Has Discovered About UFO Influences on the Human Race.* New York: E. P. Dutton & Co., Inc., 1975.

Vallee, Jacques. *Messengers of Deception: UFO Contacts and Cults.* Berkeley: And/Or Press, 1979.

Vallee, Jacques. *Passport to Magonia: From Folklore to Flying Saucers.* Chicago: Henry Regnery Company, 1969.

Vallee, Jacques, and Janine Vallee. *Challenge to Science: The UFO Enigma.* Chicago: Henry Regnery Company, 1966.

VORONEZH (U.S.S.R.) CE3

In a dispatch dated October 9, 1989, the Soviet news agency Tass reported, "Scientists have confirmed that an unidentified flying object recently landed in a park in the Russian city of Voronezh. They have also identified the landing site and found traces of aliens who made a short promenade about the park." The following day Western news wires picked up the story and for the next few days it was an international sensation, less because of what it said about UFOs than because of what it said, in Western commentators' views, about the new press freedom in the Soviet Union.

The incident allegedly occurred at 6:30 p.m. on September 27 in a city park in Voronezh, 300 miles southeast of Moscow. Three boys, Vasya Surin, Zhenya Blinov and Yuliya Sholokova, were playing soccer when a glowing red ball-shaped object 30 feet in diameter landed nearby. A hatch opened in the lower part of the UFO and three beings, one apparently a robot, emerged. The two other entities stood three to four meters tall and wore silvery overalls and bronze boots. They had no real heads, just a "bump" between the shoulders. On this "bump" were three eyes: one in front and one on each side of the bump where ears would be. At one point, according to witnesses, the first alien "said something" and a shining triangle briefly appeared on the ground. When a boy began screaming in fear, one of the aliens stared at him with "shining" eyes and paralyzed him. Either it or its partner reentered the ship and emerged with a long tubular "gun." It pointed the device at the boy, who promptly vanished. When the beings returned to the UFO and flew away in it, the boy reappeared.

Western reporters poked fun at the story, seeing it as evidence that *National Enquirer* types of obsessions were now manifesting in the glasnost-era Soviet media. In fact, Soviets, including Soviet scientists, have long been interested in UFO reports and in 1979 the U.S.S.R. Academy of Sciences even published a 74-page report titled *Observations of Anomalous Phenomena in the U.S.S.R.: Statistical Analysis*. In 1984 the Soviet Union established a Commission on Anomalous Atmospheric Phenomena, headed by Vsevolod Troitsky, of the Soviet Academy of Sciences; the vice chairman, Pavel Popovich, was both a military general and a cosmonaut. Four years later 300 scientists attended a UFO conference, sponsored by the Academy of Sciences, in Tomsk, Siberia. Reports of UFO sightings, including UFO waves, have filtered out of the Soviet Union for years.

Despite ridicule Tass stood by its report of the incident. At the International UFO Congress in Frankfurt, Germany, in late October, Sergei Bulantsev, chief of the Tass Foreign Bureau, claimed a colonel in the local militia had found an inexplicably high level of radiation at the Voronezh landing site.

Ufologists outside the Soviet Union were largely skeptical, however. The "investigators" seemed less than credible. Press accounts quoted one of them, Genrikh Silanov, as saying he had led a team to the area and found the landing site using a dowsing technique. He also claimed to have found rocks composed of an unearthly substance. Later analysis showed that the rocks were hematite, hardly unknown either to the planet or to the U.S.S.R. Ufologists also had reservations

about the aliens, whose descriptions matched none in other reports.

The Western media displayed no inclination to investigate the story further, although they did see to it that a picture of young Vasya Surin was reproduced in newspapers around the world. In the absence of reliable information, there seemed no way of knowing what, if any, truth may lie behind the alleged encounter.

One account claims to represent what really happened. Ufologist Bill Knell, citing "two friends and UFO news sources in the eastern bloc," says the episode has its origins in a late-September incident, when a disc-shaped object appeared over a sensitive Soviet air base outside Voronezh. As the UFO hovered overhead, electronic jamming of radar and other instruments kept MIG interceptors on the ground. MIGs from two other bases were called to the scene but they saw nothing. Soon afterwards the object appeared in Voronezh, landing in a park and leaving a circle of burned ground. It flew over the base again and disappeared in the northern sky.

Knell writes, "Two journalists from Sweden were in Voronezh at the time of the incident and heard about it from three adult witnesses. Soviet officials, after learning about the three witnesses and the fact that the story had been given to the journalists, detained all involved for several days. The journalists assured the officials that the story *would* be reported, despite threats and warnings. But later, through agreement with the Swedish government, the journalists were returned to Sweden and this actual account of the Voronezh UFO was suppressed." After threatening the real witnesses into silence, officials found several children and directed them to tell a UFO story based on an old American science-fiction movie about aliens with big bodies and tiny heads. They reasoned that a UFO tale of some sort was bound to get out; therefore, Knell writes, "Tass reported the version that we've all come to know and laugh at" (Knell, 1989).

If this story is true, it would not be the first time Soviet officials have used disinformation in

VORONEZH (U.S.S.R.) CE3 (*continued*)

a UFO context. For years, as authorities on the Soviet military have noted, the Kremlin covered up secret rocket launchings by treating civilian reports of the missiles and their flaming exhausts as "UFO" sightings. In the case of Voronezh, however, an absurd UFO story allegedly is concocted to cover up a real UFO sighting. There is no way of knowing whether this story is true. Paul Stonehill, a Los Angeles man who grew up in the Soviet Union and who closely monitors the UFO scene in his native country, says, "I think that the Voronezh incident was a pre-planned farce, to discredit further UFO-related stories in the Soviet press from ever being taken seriously and to dissuade the populace from becoming serious about the whole issue of UFO phenomena" (Stonehill, 1990).

Another explanation of the story's origin comes from professional practical joker Alan Abel, who claims to have engineered the stunt by sending detailed plans for it to a "couple of Russians he had listed in his hoax-lovers Rolodex," according to *The New Yorker*. It is possible, of course, that this claim is itself a practical joke.

Whatever the case, unless documentation and reliable information attesting to the incident's authenticity become available, most Western ufologists will view the Voronezh "landing" as a likely hoax.

Sources:

Chorvinsky, Mark, and Douglas Chapman. "Incident at Voronezh." *UFO* 5, 1 (January/February 1990): 20-22.

Knell, Bill. "Russian Ufology: Greater Light or Deeper Darkness?" *The N.Y. UFO Report* 8 (November 1989): 1-3.

Stonehill, Paul. Personal communication (January 4, 1990).

"The Talk of the Town: The Last Frontier." *The New Yorker* 65, 51 (February 5, 1990): 34-35.

W

WESTCHESTER SIGHTINGS

Near midnight on December 31, 1982, Edwin Hansen, a 55-year-old warehouse foreman, was driving home on an interstate highway near Kent, New York, when he saw lights hovering above the road just ahead of him. At first he took them to be from a helicopter shining a searchlight on the ground, but when he drew closer, he could hear no sounds. The lights began making slow, tight circles, moving together as if they were part of one object, and Hansen strained to see what shape, if any, was behind them. He wished the lights would come closer. No sooner had the thought crossed his mind than they did. The searchlight was suddenly shut off and the lights descended toward Hansen's car.

"It was shaped like a boomerang with lights running up and down its wings," Hansen told investigators. "Part of what seemed to be a long, triangular tail section loomed behind the boomerang pattern of lights. It was so huge it filled up the entire sky" (Hynek, Imbrogno, Pratt, 1987).

By now the light was so intense that Hansen was forced to shield his eyes with his hands. Once again the searchlight beam flashed down on the road, moving closer and closer. Thoroughly panicked, Hansen honked the car horn and pleaded for the object to go away. Then "thoughts that weren't my own" came into his head and "a kind of voice" told him to be calm. The object turned away and Hansen sped past the cars of onlookers who had pulled over to the side of the road to observe the spectacle.

Just moments later a Kent police officer standing outside his home observed what apparently was the same object. The lights, he said, "seemed to be connected by some type of structure." V- or boomerang-shaped, the object emitted a "faint, deep, hum." The lights vividly lit up the ground all around the witness. "I never saw anything like this before," he said, "but I can tell you this was not any type of aircraft that I know of" (Hynek, Imbrogno, Pratt, 1987).

These are the first known sightings to figure in one of the most extraordinary UFO events in history: the repeated appearance of large (and at times enormous) structured objects over seven densely-populated counties in New York and Connecticut. (To ufologists the episode would be referred to as the "Westchester sightings," because that New York county claimed a plurality of the reports.) The sightings would occur most intensely in the early spring of 1983 and the summer of 1984 but would take place sporadically at other times, ending in 1986. The witnesses numbered in the many thousands. The great majority of witnesses would relate some or all of the features described above. In that sense, at least, the sightings were somewhat monotonous; yet their very consistency suggested the presence of a genuinely out-of-the-ordinary phenomenon.

The principal investigator was Philip J. Imbrogno, a science teacher at a school in White

WESTCHESTER SIGHTINGS (*continued*)

Plains, New York. Imbrogno interviewed numerous witnesses and even saw a UFO himself on two occasions. The first sighting was at 1 a.m. on October 5, 1984, as he and another investigator, Fred Dennis, were returning from an interview with witnesses to spectacular sightings at a nuclear-power plant, to be described shortly. Imbrogno and Dennis saw a large half-circle of six bluish-yellow lights, connected to a partially-illuminated structure. Suddenly it flipped on its side and turned like a ferris wheel—just as innumerable observers had described its doing. Imbrogno saw and chased a boomerang-shaped object in a car on March 21, 1985.

One of the most dramatic events associated with the affair was a 2½-hour localized sighting flap on the evening of March 24, 1983. The first known sighting was at 7:30 p.m. when a corporate executive in Bedford, New York, saw a half-circle of lights hovering behind some trees near a commuter-bus station. There was no sound. After watching for five minutes, the man went inside his house to alert his family, but when they came outside, the lights were gone. Half an hour later, in Carmel, 10 miles to the north, four persons saw a half-circle of red and white lights and the vague outline of a larger object to which the lights were attached. The lights were hovering over trees several hundred yards away. The lights drifted to the east and were lost to view, but almost immediately a family living a quarter-mile away saw them drift into view. They saw, in one's words, a "*huge* object" which stopped over some trees. Through binoculars the observers saw a dull-green metallic structure connecting the lights. When the UFO turned slightly, they could see it had a V shape. At that moment a brilliant beam of white light shot down from the center of the object and in it a small reddish object descended, then shot off "very, very fast toward the north" (Hynek, Imbrogno, Pratt, 1987). The beam was shut off and the object turned and headed slowly east.

Half an hour later sightings erupted in two locations 15 miles apart. In Millwood and Yorktown in Westchester County over a thousand persons, by conservative estimate, saw a huge array of V-shaped lights flying slowly, at altitudes varying between 2000 feet and treetop level, and sometimes hovering over cars and individuals. Most witnesses heard no sound and all were astounded at the object's size. One compared it to a "flying city." Another said it was the size of an aircraft carrier.

The object seen to the north, in several Putnam County communities, was somewhat smaller, but it was also boomerang-shaped, silent and capable of hovering. As one witness, Ruth Holtsman, who was in a car with her family at the time, put it, "The strange thing about it was that the object made no sound. It just hung there motionless in the sky. It was like seeing a ghost" (Hynek, Imbrogno, Pratt, 1987). While it was in view, a driver pulled up and stopped almost directly underneath it. The lights started to flash in a wild sequence up and down the "wings." That driver jumped into his car and fled in the direction from which he had come. Then the UFO approached the Holtsmans' car, which was bathed in a blinding white light as it sped under the boomerang.

Around the same time John Miller, in a car on his way home, saw the object hovering just above a pond near his Brewster home. The UFO was scanning two "very bright" searchlight beams over the surface of the water as if, Miller thought, it were looking for something. He could hear a "faint whooshing sound." At 8:45 several dozen diners at a ski-resort restaurant near Stormville saw white lights in a boomerang shape hovering over a utility pole 200 yards away. Three other persons were much closer to it: they were driving by the utility pole and stopped. The driver, a Putnam County correctional officer, got out and studied the object, about 200 feet above him, carefully. It was silent and the structure that held the lights was dark and nonreflective—a detail all those who saw the object behind the lights were to remark on. After watching it for 20 minutes, the officer headed back to his jeep, at which time the UFO moved down the road.

"I followed it to Interstate 84," he told Imbrogno. "As it started to move, all the lights went out and I could see the outline of it against the sky. I could see the dark V moving." Ten seconds later the lights came back on, relatively dim red and white ones; then the bright white lights came on again and the others disappeared. He and his companions followed the object for over an hour, clocking its speed at 20 mph.

Sightings continued in the two counties until about ten o'clock. Among the witnesses was a veteran aircraft mechanic who was certain what he saw could not have been caused by an aircraft. The last sighting occurred over nearby Danbury, Connecticut, when an IBM executive saw a lighted object "larger than a 747" hovering over pine trees near his home.

Of all the sightings, perhaps the most important from a number of points of view, not the least of them national-security concerns, took place at the Indian Point nuclear reactor complex on the Hudson River at Buchanan, New York. This sighting, unlike many of the others, was not reported in the newspapers at the time it occurred. Imbrogno learned of it only because one of the witnesses called a radio show on which Imbrogno was discussing the UFO wave. The caller, a New York State Power Authority police officer, said he and 11 other officers had seen a giant UFO hovering 300 feet over one of the reactors for ten minutes on the night of July 24, 1984.

Imbrogno asked for a personal interview, but the guard (whom Imbrogno identifies only as "Carl") said he would have to get clearance from his supervisor. At first permission was granted but then withdrawn, and the guards were ordered not to discuss the incident. When Imbrogno threatened to take the story to ABC News, the manager relented, explaining that the authorities were reluctant to admit that guards were seeing "flying saucers" because they feared critics of the plant would use this as evidence that the already-controversial reactor was in the hands of unstable persons. Imbrogno was able to meet with Carl and a number of the other guards twice in a restaurant. From them he got this story:

There had been, it turned out, two sightings. The first was on June 14, when Carl and other security personnel saw "10 or more lights arranged in a boomerang pattern" hovering for about 15 minutes a quarter of a mile away. The lights were "incredibly bright" and behind them was a "dark mass" which blocked out the lights of a plane that flew behind it. Carl estimated it was 300 feet long.

On the night of the 24th the object appeared from the same direction as before. The lights, in a semicircle, first flashed yellow, then white, then blue. Far to the rear was a blinking red light. The dark mass behind the lights blocked out the stars as it approached, slowly and steadily, even as winds gusted at 30 knots an hour. By the time it got to within 500 feet, the witnesses could see an ice-cream-cone shape and a solid body the length of three football fields. As it passed overhead, it was moving so slowly that the witnesses could keep up with it simply by walking, suggesting to them its speed was something like 5 to 10 mph. It took all of five minutes to pass over them. Only one of the three reactors was operating at the time and it was the one over which the UFO flew, at one point getting as close as 30 feet to it. An officer inside the plant was instructed to film the object on a security camera atop a 95-foot pole. The object was so enormous that the officer had to pan the camera almost 180 degrees in order to cover all of it. Another officer told Imbrogno, "There was this series of lights in the shape of a boomerang, and behind it was this dark structure, and there were these two things on the bottom that looked like hollow spheres of some sort. They looked like portals that could open up and rockets or something could fly out of there. They were very dark. It was very low. It was so close I actually got scared looking at it" (Hynek, Imbrogno, Pratt, 1987).

During the object's approach toward the east gate of Reactor Number Three, the plant's movement-detecting sensors and the alarm system failed, as did the computer in charge of security and communications. When a National Guard base 10 miles away was notified and asked to provide an armed helicopter to shoot down the UFO, the object flew away.

WESTCHESTER SIGHTINGS (*continued*)

The next day the commander of the security guards instructed his charges to forget what had happened. The video and audio records of the event were removed, and in the next days representatives of the U.S. Nuclear Regulatory Commission oversaw a shakeup of the security operation at the plant. The efforts of Imbrogno and radio reporter Gerry Culliton to gather more information from plant officials and, through the Freedom of Information Act, from relevant government agencies came to naught. They did learn, however, of civilian sightings, one recorded on videotape, near the plant on the nights in question.

In the midst of the Westchester flap, *Discover*, a popular-science magazine edited by Leon Jaroff, a hostile critic of UFOs and other unorthodox phenomena, declared it had solved the mystery. The "UFO," *Discover* announced, was an illusion fostered by a group of Stormville pilots who flew ultralight aircraft in tight formation and used their lights in such a way as to create boomerang or circle patterns. As to the silence or very slight sounds witnesses reported, *Discover* noted that single-engine planes, even when directly overhead, are hardly audible at ground level when the craft fly "above 3000 or 4000 feet." *Discover* failed to note that many witnesses were considerably closer to the object than that—anywhere from a dozen to a few hundred feet—nor did the magazine inform its readers of one of the phenomenon's most consistently remarked-on features: its ability to hover, and to do so, moreover, for extended periods of time. Also, some witnesses reported that the object accelerated from a very slight speed to an extremely rapid one in less than five seconds—a remarkable feat for so small and unstable a craft as an ultralight.

Witnesses who were experts on aircraft, including an ultralight pilot, continued to insist that the "object" could not have been a formation of planes or even a single airplane. An analysis of one of the videotapes made of the lights was conducted at the Jet Propulsion Laboratory in Pasadena, California, where it was concluded that

the object was an unknown. Some witnesses saw *both* the Stormville aircraft and the boomerang and concluded they were in no way similar. One even took videotapes of both to make his point.

In *Night Siege* (1987) Imbrogno lists 12 reasons for rejecting the Stormville-pilots explanation, remarking among other points that on those occasions when witnesses saw both a plane and the UFO in the sky, they could hear the former even when it was farther away than the latter, which was silent. Furthermore, the UFO appeared on nights when "it was definitely established that the Stormville pilots were not in the air." The UFO's maneuvers—great speed at times, at other times speed so slow as to be below the stall speed of an aircraft, and of course, hovering—simply are beyond the capacity of most aircraft, including those alleged to be responsible for the sightings. Also, Imbrogno wrote, "The number and intensity of the UFO lights was far beyond the power capacity of small planes."

Another problem with the Stormville-pilots hypothesis is that sightings of boomerang-shaped objects were not confined strictly to a small area of New York and Connecticut. Reports of identical objects have been made all across the United States beginning as early as 1951 with a series of sightings in west Texas. More recently, in 1987, this sighting took place in southern Ohio:

One autumn evening Rich and Kathy Dicenzo, their four children and a family friend were sitting before a bonfire on the south side of the Dicenzos' cabin. The sky was clear and full of stars. Suddenly a dark shape appeared overhead, blocking out the stars in a boomerang shape. Along its perimeter the boomerang carried 12 to 20 lights. Rich Dicenzo would later tell investigator **Jennie Zeidman**, "Just east of the zenith I first saw the stars winking out and soft, slightly yellowish lights moving due south over the house's edge. The dark gray shape and two or more rows of lights began to dominate more and more of the sky [and became] an ever-widening wing-arc of lights. I stood up for a better view . . . [and said] 'What is this, *Close Encounters*, or what?' The scale was so grandiose" (Zeidman, 1989).

220

The object was moving very slowly, taking six or seven seconds to come fully into view, and making no sound. It was long enough to extend beyond the house's 72-foot length. After a minute the lights "wobbled" and changed color to amber and then red. "It came over the house extremely slowly," Dicenzo said, "but when it decided to go, it was just gone." The object, or at least the lights on it, split into three sections and spread out and "dissipated" in the distance. Except for this last, somewhat ambiguous detail, this sighting could be of the Westchester phenomenon.

Yet the presence of the Stormville pilots is a genuinely complicating factor in the Westchester affair, even if it fails to account for much of what was reported. Dick Ruhl and Richie Petracca, investigators for the Aerial Phenomena Research Organization (APRO), were on Interstate I-84 at 9:30 one evening during the flap when they saw, Ruhl would write, "a brilliant white wedge-shaped object floating and turning in the sky." The lights on it turned red and then other colors. Another object appeared to the left. "We watched in utter amazement," Ruhl would later recall, "as the two objects glided extremely slowly and maneuvered about themselves, constantly changing from white as they approached us, to red as they turned away[,] and then from the side, the red, green-blue and white lights appeared. They finally formed up into a huge boomerang-shape and it was then that I saw some light [through binoculars] reflected on the bodies of six aircraft. We knew we had the evidence on the 'Stormville pilots'" (Ruhl, 1984).

Ruhl and Petracca went to the Stormville airport and saw the "UFO" from there. The planes then broke formation and landed, but when Ruhl tried to photograph the lead pilot as he stepped out of his Cessna Skyhawk, he was threatened. The two investigators left the airport soon after.

Ruhl subsequently talked with an area airport owner who told him he, his family and others had seen the pilots flying in a wedge formation. Once, while flying, he approached them and heard the lead pilot order the others to turn out their lights.

This itself was illegal, but they were also flying at a lower altitude than the law permitted. Ruhl speculated that the pilots were using mufflers on their engines to cut down on the sound their planes made.

Although Ruhl's account is more persuasive than *Discover*'s, it should be said that Ruhl and Petracca's sighting differs from most of the Westchester reports, both before and after their discovery of the true nature of the lights. Ruhl says the lights "seemed to hover," an optical illusion sustained for seconds at best, while a number of other witnesses stood beneath the hovering object for 15 to 20 minutes or longer. This means, since here optical illusion is out of the question, that either they are lying or the object *was* hovering. Other witnesses, moreover, saw the lights through binoculars at considerably closer range than Ruhl and Petracca did, and invariably they reported a dark, nonreflecting metallic structure consistent with the lights' boomerang configuration. They did not spot aircraft. Conceivably some may have been mistaken, but this description occurs so often—and some of it comes from witnesses who work professionally with aircraft—that it is difficult to believe all the observers were in error.

Nonetheless the Stormville pilots are undeniably a part of the Westchester story, and the exact nature of their role will likely remain the subject of continued discussion, dispute and controversy.

Sources:

Garelik, Glenn. "The Great Hudson Valley UFO Mystery." *Discover* 5, 11 (November 1984): 18-20, 22-24.

Hynek, J. Allen, Philip J. Imbrogno, and Bob Pratt. *Night Siege: The Hudson Valley UFO Sightings.* New York: Ballantine Books, 1987.

Rodeghier, Mark. "Boomerang." *International UFO Reporter* 12, 6 (November/December 1987): 14-16.

WESTCHESTER SIGHTINGS (*continued*)

Ruhl, Dick. "The Westchester Sightings." *The APRO Bulletin* 32, 6 (1984): 1, 3-7.

Zeidman, Jennie. "Boomerang UFOs." *Fate* 41, 10 (October 1988): 68-75.

Zeidman, Jennie. "Strangeness in the Night." *International UFO Reporter* 14, 1 (January/February 1989): 4-5, 22.

Z

ZEIDMAN, JENNIE (1932-)

Jennie Zeidman has been an active figure in ufology since the early 1950s, when she served as a technical assistant to **J. Allen Hynek**. Her field study of an October 1973 incident involving a UFO and a helicopter over Mansfield, Ohio, is considered a classic episode in UFO research.

Born in 1932, Zeidman received a B.A. in English from Ohio State University in 1953. She also worked as a teaching assistant and technical assistant to the university's department of physics and astronomy. Between 1953 and 1956 she worked with Hynek and the Battelle Memorial Institute, a Columbus, Ohio-based think tank which does consulting work for the U.S. government.

She serves as a board member of both the **J. Allen Hynek Center for UFO Studies** (CUFOS) and the **Mutual UFO Network** (MUFON). A frequent contributor to UFO publications, she is the author of two important case studies, *The Lumberton Report* (1976) and *A Helicopter-UFO Encounter Over Ohio* (1979).

She says, "I remained associated with Dr. Hynek until his death, thereby having continual access to the hard data and to the evolution of his thoughts on the subject. Over the years my position has changed from one of almost complete skepticism to the absolute conviction that something of major scientific importance is going on. What UFOs are I cannot say, but I certainly feel that the extraterrestrial hypothesis must be considered seriously" (personal communication, 1989).

Sources:

Boyd, Robert D. *International Who's Who of Ufology Directory*. Mobile, AL: The Author, 1988.

Story, Ronald D. *The Encyclopedia of UFOs*. Garden City, NY: Doubleday & Company, 1980.

Zeidman, Jennie. *A Helicopter-UFO Encounter Over Ohio*. Evanston, IL: Center for UFO Studies, 1979.

Zeidman, Jennie. *The Lumberton Report: UFO Activity in Southern North Carolina, April 3-9, 1975*. Evanston, IL: Center for UFO Studies, 1976.

Zeidman, Jennie. "The Mansfield Helicopter Case: Anatomy of an Investigation." In Walter H. Andrus, Jr., ed. *MUFON 1989 International UFO Symposium Proceedings*, 12-30. Seguin, TX: Mutual UFO Network, Inc., 1989.

Zeidman, Jennie. "Reflections on J. Allen Hynek: The Comet and the Circle." *International UFO Reporter* 11, 3 (May/June 1986), 20.

ZETETIC SCHOLAR
Department of Sociology
Eastern Michigan University
Ypsilanti, Michigan 48197

Zetetic Scholar, the journal of the Center for Scientific Anomalies Research (CSAR), is one of the handful of serious academic periodicals dealing with controversies on the borderlands of science, but it is different from the rest in providing a regular forum for both proponents and critics. The editor, sociologist of science Marcello Truzzi, was co-founder (with Paul Kurtz) of the **Committee for the Scientific Investigation of Claims of the Paranormal** (CSICOP) but left the organization because he thought its hard-line debunking posture exceeded the bounds of reasonable skepticism about disputed but not disproven phenomena such as UFOs, ESP and cryptozoological animals. "Regretfully," Truzzi would write, "the term 'skeptic' today is being used by many who adopt that label for themselves in a misleading way. To many, it is falsely equated with the term 'rationalist.' The dictionary meaning of the term indicates that a skeptic is one who raises doubts. Thus the word is meant to reflect *nonbelief* rather than *disbelief*. But when we look at those who trumpet that they are skeptics towards claims of anomalies, we find disbelievers and debunkers rather than those who express uncertainty or doubt. The public 'skeptics' of today present us with answers rather than questions" (Truzzi, 1987).

Truzzi, a skeptic (a "doubter" rather than a "denier" [debunker]), views ufology (along with parapsychology and cryptozoology) as a "protoscience," not (as CSICOP would have it) a "pseudoscience," since serious UFO investigators "aspire to a truly scientific approach to UFOs. They make statements that are amenable to investigation just like any scientific statement" (Clark and Melton, 1979). *Zetetic Scholar* debates UFO issues on an intellectual level not often encountered elsewhere in the literature.

Zetetic Scholar had its first incarnation in April 1972 as *Explorations*, a privately-published newsletter under Truzzi's editorship. It became *The Zetetic* with volume three. In 1976 it was taken over by the CSICOP and became the organization's official publication. When Truzzi and CSOCOP parted ways, the essence of the old *Zetetic* was then reborn in the *Zetetic Scholar*, the first issue of which appeared in May 1978. CSICOP's periodical changed its name to *The Skeptical Inquirer*, its current title. Although irregularly published (the last issue appeared in 1987), *Zetetic Scholar* still exists, and a new issue is scheduled to appear in 1990.

Sources:

Clark, Jerome, and J. Gordon Melton. "The Crusade Against the Paranormal." *Fate* 33, 9 (September 1979): 70-76.

Truzzi, Marcello. "Zetetic Ruminations on Skepticism and Anomalies in Science." *Zetetic Scholar* 12/13 (1987): 7-20.

224

Index

A

Abduction phenomenon, 1-14, 17-18, 25, 31-32, 34, 42, 50-51, 75, 84, 88-91, 99, 101, 107, 111-12, 114-15, 117, 122, 129, 134-36, 142, 144-46, 163, 177, 181-84, 187-88, 189, 198, 199, 201-02, 203, 207-08, 209-10
Abel, Alan, 216
Abounader, Jean, 97
Adamski, George, 29, 51-52, 55-56, 104, 181
Aerial Anomalies International (AAI), 14-15
Aerial Phenomena Research Organization (APRO), 2, 41, 43, 47, 53, 57, 88, 90-91, 93, 106, 116, 153-54, 162, 163, 198, 221
Aetherius Society, 29, 53
Airships, 34, 174, 176-77
Alien Life Forms (ALFs), 100
Allan, Christopher D., 68
Allingham, Cedric (pseud. of Patrick Moore), 29
Ancient Astronaut Society, 15-16
Ancient astronauts, 15-16, 30, 173
Ancient Brotherhood of Fahsz, 211
Androids, 91, 99
Andrus, Walter H., Jr., 16-17, 103-04, 154, 163-64
Anstee, Ronald W. J., 42
Anti-Christ, 102
Appel, Jean-Paul, 115
Archbishop of Lyons, 173
Arcturans, 166
Arcturus Book Service, 17
Armchair ufology, 28, 178
Arnold, Kenneth, 57, 153, 174
Ashtar Command, 166
Association d'Etude Sur les Soucoupes Volantes (AESV), 114
Association for the Scientific Study of Anomalous Phenomena (ASSAP), 188
Australian Centre for UFO Studies (ACUFOS), 17-19
Australian Coordination Section (ACOS), 17-18, 20
Australian Entity Study Group, 19
Australian Flying Saucer Bureau (AFSB), 18
Australian Flying Saucer Research Society (AFSRS), 18
Australian International UFO Research (AIUFOR), 18
Australian UFO Research Society (AUFORS), 171
Australian ufology, 17-25

B

Bailey, Martin, 67
Ball lightning, 79, 84, 150, 189
Baloran, 197
Barber, T. X., 111, 183
Barker, Edward, 41
Barker, Gray, 193
Barthel, Gérard, 113, 178-79
Bartholomew, Robert E., 111-12, 183
Basterfield, Keith, 5-6, 18-19, 24-25, 111-12, 183
Bauer, Roy, 41
Believer Bill, 126
Bender, Albert K., 29
Bennett, Rob, 41
Bennewitz, Paul, 88-95, 98, 100, 103-07
Bentsen, Lloyd, 45
Berkner, Lloyd V., 65, 160
Berliner, Don, 117
Berlitz, Charles, 60, 69, 89, 162
Bermuda Triangle, 49
Bigfoot, 171
Bilderbergers, 101
Billon-Duplan, Iris, 47
Birth-trauma hypothesis, 6-7
Blanchard, William H., 60-61
Blavatsky, Helena P., 51
Blinov, Zhenya, 214
Bloecher, Ted, 3-5, 134
Blue Room, 58
Bolender, C. H., 63
Borderland Sciences Research Associates, 27
Borderland Sciences Research Foundation, 27-28
Bosson, Yves, 114, 169
Bounias, Michael, 206
Bourret, Jean-Claude, 112
Bowen, Charles, 29, 174
Boyd, Lyle G., 158
Boyd, Robert D., 14, 126
Brandon, Jim, 43

225

Findlay, Jean, 170
First European Conference on Anomalous
    Aerial Phenomena: Physical & Psychosocial
    Aspects, 114
Fjellander, Jan, 131
Flannigan, Charles, 126
Fletcher, Bob, 171
Flood, Charles, 174
Folklore Society, 85
Fontaine, Franck, 46-48
Fontes, Olavo T., 1-2, 154
Ford, Gerald R., 101
Forrestal, James, 65-67, 101
Fort, Charles, 149, 153, 174-75, 210
Fortean Society, 175
Foster, Scott. *See* X, Mr.
Fouéré, René, 114
Fowler, Raymond E., 2
Francesca, Aleuti. *See* Francis, Marianne
Francis, Marianne (Aleuti Francesca), 197
Franklin, Girard, 3
Franklin, Penelope, 134
Frederick, Laurence W., 196
French ufology, 112-15, 119, 169, 178-79, 206
Freud, Sigmund, 6
Friedman, Florence, 115
Friedman, Louis, 115
Friedman, Stanton T., 42, 59-60, 62, 64, 68-69,
    71, 105-06, 115-17, 159-60, 162, 192
Friend, Robert, 116
Fuhr, Edwin, 38
Fuller, John G., 1, 4
Fuller, Paul, 187, 210
Fund for UFO Research, 4, 8, 34, 45, 63, 68,
    117-18, 130, 157, 194, 202, 207
Furnell, Jim, 23
Futura, 115

G

Galacteus, 115
Galactic Federation, 51
Galley, Robert, 112-13
Gallup poll, 189
Gasparovic, Stephane, 115
Geller, Uri, 49, 142, 184
Gersten, Peter, 45, 48, 94-95, 106
Gibbs-Smith, Charles H., 174
Girard, Robert, 17

Giraud, Jean, 115
Gironda, Bobbi Ann, 59
Giscard d'Estaing, Valéry, 120
God, 30, 54-55, 172, 184
Godic, Pony, 25
Godic, Vladimir, 18, 25
Goldfeather, Lorne, 41
Goldwater, Barry, 58
Gonzales Gauteaume, Horacio, 154
Good, Timothy, 31, 67, 98
Gordon, Stan, 171
Gotlib, David A., 41-42, 208
Grace, John (Val Valarian), 103, 165
Graham, Lee, 67, 105
Grassino, Gian Paolo, 183-84
Gray, Gordon, 65
Greenwell, J. Richard, 15
Greenwood, Barry, 49, 67-68, 92, 106-07
Greys, 100-01, 165-66, 210
Grimm, Jacob, 173
Grof, Stanislav, 6
Groupe d'Etude des Phénomènes Aérospatiaux
    Non-Identifiés (GEPAN), 113-15, 119-21, 205-
    07
Grousset, Pascal, 114
Guérin, Pierre, 114
Guieu, Jimmy, 48, 114
Gulf Breeze sightings, 121-28, 134, 169

H

Hagen, Geneva, 46
Haines, Richard F., 24, 118, 129, 170
Haisell, David, 2
Hall, Richard, 27, 104, 118, 127, 130-31, 163
Hall, Robert, 118
Hansen, Edwin, 217
Hansen, Sherry, 200
Harney, John, 158
Hauck, Dennis William, 163
Hastings, Robert, 68, 104-05
Haut, Walter, 61
Havik, Leif, 131-33
Heard, Gerald, 28
Hendry, Allan, 3, 45, 82, 139, 141, 144, 195-96
Hendry, Elaine M., 139, 144
Henize, Karl G., 139
Henley, Graham, 23
Henry, Richard C., 118